RECRUITING YOUNG LOVE

RECRUITING YOUNG LOVE

HOW CHRISTIANS TALK
ABOUT HOMOSEXUALITY

MARK D. JORDAN

THE UNIVERSITY OF CHICAGO PRESS
Chicago and London

MARK D. JORDAN is the Richard Reinhold Niebuhr Professor of Divinity at the Harvard Divinity School. He is the author of several books, including *The Invention of Sodomy in Christian Theology*, *The Silence of Sodom*, and *Blessing Same-Sex Unions*, also published by the University of Chicago Press.

The University of Chicago Press, Chicago 60637
The University of Chicago Press, Ltd., London
© 2011 by Mark D. Jordan
All rights reserved. Published 2011.
Printed in the United States of America.

20 19 18 17 16 15 14 13 12 11   1 2 3 4 5

ISBN-13: 978-0-226-41044-9 (cloth)
ISBN-10: 0-226-41044-7 (cloth)

Library of Congress Cataloging-in-Publication Data

Jordan, Mark D.
    Recruiting young love : how Christians talk about homosexuality / Mark D. Jordan.
        p. cm.
    Includes bibliographical references and index.
    ISBN-13: 978-0-226-41044-9 (cloth : alk. paper)
    ISBN-10: 0-226-41044-7 (cloth : alk. paper)
    1. Homosexuality—Religious aspects—Christianity.
2. Teenagers—Sexual behavior. 3. Sex—Religious aspects—Christianity. I. Title.
    BR115 .H6J67 2011
    277.3'08208664—dc22

                            2010035386

FOR KENT, FOR LYNNE

EVER MORNING AT QUÉ TAL

CONTENTS

INTRODUCTION
Sexual Characters

In 2005—it could have been any of our recent years—the blog entries of a gay teenager in Tennessee, circulated urgently by his friends, attracted a news swarm. Zach was then a sixteen-year-old high school student who had recently come out as gay to his Christian parents. "They tell me that there is something psychologically wrong with me, and they 'raised me wrong.' I'm a big screw up to them, who isn't on the path God wants me to be on." In response, so Zach's blog reported, they were forcing him to enroll in a religious treatment program called Refuge. It would address his homosexual desires and prevent destructive behaviors by affirming his correct gender identity. Facing this news, Zach worried about responding melodramatically before typing out thoughts of suicide and thwarted rage.[1]

Refuge was then a program aimed by Memphis-based Love in Action International at thirteen- to seventeen-year-olds. It advertised itself as "the most developed . . . intensive program in America for youth struggling with homosexuality." According to published reports, participants spent their days at Refuge studying the Bible, undergoing counseling, and confessing their temptations. They were forbidden to watch television or read anything unapproved. Throughout the day, they monitored each other for campy actions or "gay/lesbian behavior and talk." Because these adolescent "clients" spent nights at home, Refuge reportedly searched them each morning for smuggled "False Images"—signs of gender-bending or a taste for queer culture.

While Zach was still in the program, his father defended the decision to enroll him by denouncing the homosexual "lifestyle" on Christian television and appealing to parental authority. He told Pat Robertson's CBN, "Until he turns eighteen and he's an adult in the state of Tennessee, I'm responsible for him. And I'm going to see to it that he has all options available to him." The state of Tennessee had other worries: media complaints led it to investigate Love in Action for operating an unlicensed medical facility.

The ministry retracted some of its claims about therapy, then countersued the state. Articles and op-ed pieces about the case rehearsed the collision of abstractions: freedom of religion or of youthful choice, state regulation of schooling and churches, parental control or the "best interests of the child." Policy abstractions could not explain the ready passions that the story aroused—or why its rhetoric was at once so vehement and so practiced.

I have not met Zach or interviewed those who knew him then. I repeat his story as it appeared in media reports and other public sources because I am after its rhetorical representations of sexual characters. However sharp my sympathy for Zach's circumstances as I imagine them, my reason for writing is to understand how churchly names and narratives tried to shape him—and how they do shape us.

By chance, the archives preserve the voice of another sixteen-year-old from forty years earlier. His voice is not captured in news clippings. He writes for a private survey by an organization never fully public. In April 1964, one of the earliest advocacy groups for same-sex desire, the Mattachine Society, distributed the survey through its mailing list and at some of its meetings. It hoped to gather information about "the problems and conflicts that the homosexual finds in regards to the Church."[2] The archives don't tell how the sixteen-year-old Catholic on the East Coast got the survey. Once he got it, he responded at length, covering four pages of lined notebook paper in a neat hand, stopping to refill his fountain pen. He begins by describing pastoral reactions to his confessions of same-sex passion:

one priest tells me "go see a doctor," another tells me, "forget the whole matter and don't think about it," another tells me that "your inclinations are abnormal because carnal love should only result in offspring" and another tells me that "you can desire latently but it is a sin to follow through overtly!" This makes me come to the conclusion that church is only for the majority and THAT CHURCH is ALWAYS MEASURING UP TO *CONFORMITY*

Faced with these reactions, he can't imagine himself changing—and yet he can't feel confidence in his own conviction.

I don't have visions. I don't see and converse with Christ every night before I go to bed. How am I supposed to know what my Creator thinks of me? The Church says that God thinks I am a "monster." Throughout my whole life I've received the sacraments, done good and bad things, sinned and confessed. Now—since a couple of months ago, I am "against nature, which is the law of God, and unless you [referring to me] don't change you are doomed."

The response ends with pleas for understanding and even mercy.

How is the church to know how an invert feels? . . . In other words, a person or group should experience the feelings of a "monster," and an "abnormal, diverse degenerate" before judging it. . . . I don't want to be condemned. Please don't make me feel I'll go straight to Hell—at least send me to Purgatory, then I'll have a slight chance to progress.

The angry pain speaks to us, for itself. The language of the self-description may not. The sixteen-year-old identifies himself several times as an "invert." He bears a name that we no longer use.

There are many instructive comparisons between the survey response and Zach's blog. The anonymity of the archived survey contrasts, of course, with the national and international circulation of stories about Zach. So do the private pastoral reactions reported from 1964 and the ex-gay program of 2005. There were no programs to which his confessors could have referred the unnamed teenager. There was little enough preaching or teaching in churches about homosexuality. Everything is different for Zach. His father can send him to a program, then appear on national news to vindicate his decision fluently, invoking whole bodies of argument and evidence already familiar to his primary audience. Zach has an assigned role in a new set of Christian institutions, but he also fits neatly under topics set for public debate, both inside and outside churches.

The remarkable shifts in the surrounding debate shouldn't distract from the change of names. While the young man answering the survey knows the contrast between homosexual and heterosexual, he identifies himself rather as an *invert*. Zach is described as a homosexual by some, but he comes out as *gay*. In the decades that separate them, churchly discourse about their desire has altered remarkably—in its range and volume, in its varieties of evidence and manners of argument, but above all in its stock of identities or, as I prefer to say, of characters. Two American sixteen-year-olds, separated by forty years, find around them different sets of characters to inhabit. Both young men learn the names that they apply to themselves, but the names have changed.

During the long half-century of American church debate from the first Kinsey Report (1948) to ex-gay programs for newly out teens, Christian rhetoric deployed a startling succession of characters for same-sex desire. Neither the characters nor their order of appearance was determined by sustained theological reflection. On the contrary, church debates over this desire have been conducted almost entirely in hastily borrowed language.

Christian writers have appropriated clinical terminology from modern sexology or psychiatry, the political coinage of social reformers, and slang devised for urban enclaves. They have appropriated them without much justification—and without commenting on the rapid shift from one to another. The debates go on, but the names keep changing.

You can hear the borrowed terms in Zach's report of his parents' reproaches: they do not accuse him of demonic possession, the nameless sin, unnatural vice, or consorting with exiled descendants of Sodom. They say instead that something is "psychologically wrong" with him. You can notice the borrowed terms as well in the rhetorical self-contradiction of a program like Refuge. It claims to strip away "False Images" of gender variation or queer affiliation, but most of all it wants to cut off contact with queer speeches—with email and chatrooms, of course, but also with whatever speech might justify queer love. A young man can repent of carnal copulations, he can bewail them (year after year) as so many falls, but once he begins to describe them in the enemy's language, perhaps even to defend them, he is lost. What he feels or does is not half as dangerous as what he says. So someone like Zach has to be cut off from queer words in order to fill his ears and eyes with words that claim to be exclusively Christian—through Bible reading, group therapy (that biblical practice!), and mutual policing of small talk. Yet the program's effort to isolate him in a sphere of pure Christian speech contradicts itself. The characters that it presupposes—that motivate its exegesis, its therapy, its policing—are all variations on characters borrowed from the fearful world outside.

In this book, I follow church debates over same-sex desire, but I keep turning to that wider world of speech. American churches had to learn a bewildering series of new characters, but also how to talk publicly and persistently about a range of topics they had tried hard to keep silent—or at least pastorally private. Across the half century of debates, churches learned how to speak about same-sex desire, but only by negotiating and renegotiating their relation to new rhetorics of sex and gender that they did not launch. In order to understand the differences between Zach's rhetorical circumstances and those around that other teenager forty years earlier, I read and listen widely, outside churches as much as inside them, from well before Kinsey into our present.

Following these differences is moving through a series of languages. If they are to register on my pages, no one language can be imposed across the rest. Each local idiom has to be preserved intact. I cannot then standardize my language. I have to release it to register the shifts of metaphors and forms of argument, but also of names. Here at the beginning, and again at the end, I speak more or less in my own voice—using "queer" as a weak umbrella term for those who do not identify as heterosexual, perhaps because they do not identify at all. For the great span of the book, I do my best to mimic whatever I am hearing. I quote it often, so that the reader can learn to speak it too.

The rhetorical spectacle around Zach offers another lesson for understanding our debates: many of them have centered on the adolescent, conceived as both threatened and threatening. The most effective American rhetoric for condemning civil or religious toleration of homosexuality has repeatedly warned of dangers to the young. But admitting the vulnerability of adolescents implies that happily heterosexual adults are made, not born. Every adolescent must be recruited, for one sexual side or the other, for God's procreative plan or the devil's murmured perversions. Every adolescent promises a productive future of sexual conformity while threatening a rebellious future of sterile dissent.

The *figure* of the adolescent in the debates is not any real teenager or social cohort of teenagers. Indeed, the voices of actual teenagers have rarely sounded in our long-running quarrels. Zach's story is a reminder in this way too: he falls silent before the debate begins to roar. Actual teenagers are often talked about, fretted over, but rarely questioned, much less allowed to speak freely. Indeed, they are typically presumed to be incompetent to speak for themselves until they are ready to profess submission to the norms of adulthood. Before that moment, they are judged unable to know themselves, precisely because they cannot give the settled account of themselves as sexual subjects. They are liable to corruption, and so liable to corrupt. It is safer then for churches to speak about them and, indeed, for them.

In our debates, the figure of the adolescent embodies an adult preoccupation—an uncomfortable recollection that sexual desire has at least once in a life *to be* settled. The adolescent figures the need for sexual persuasion—for a sexual resolution. Adolescence is a scene in which an unformed character must be instructed to fix sexual choice reliably on the right gender. It is the episode for mastering the story of desire, for practicing and then putting on a sexual character. Adolescence as the occasion for narrating desire is only loosely connected to adolescence as a particular chronological period. Indeed, adolescence has such elastic chronological boundaries because it is a rhetorical task more than a measured time. Whenever the task of making sexual characters arises, it can be painted with the lurid colors of adolescence. The famous "delayed adolescence" of gay coming out is more than anecdote. It shows that the figure of adolescence represents the possibility and the peril of sexual indeterminacy.

In this book, I trace adolescence as a rhetorical figure, not as countable span of years—and certainly not as an empirically verifiable cohort of teenagers. Sometimes the teenager will appear as I follow the adolescent, sometimes not. At certain moments in our debates, the young do seem to stand at the center—say, in tales of juvenile delinquents and hustlers, in Anita Bryant's campaign, in street activism at and after Stonewall, or in legal struggles over adoption and same-sex marriage. At other moments, the young disappear from view, while the figure of the adolescent persists in the assumption that having a sexuality requires a narration about how you grew up. Even when this book turns away from things said by or about teenagers, it is still considering adolescence as the scene for forming sexual characters. Whenever same-sex desire is defined as a delayed development or a deviation in puberty, whenever it is conceived as requiring a story for coming out or repenting, it is conceived in relation to adolescence. Adolescence is the possibility that desire could be different.

Where can we overhear connections between church debates over same-sex desire and the larger speeches around them? They are not as readily available as you might think. For reasons that will be explored, official histories of gay and lesbian liberation have typically excluded religion. They denigrate the religious interests of their "homophile" predecessors; they forget the role of religious organizations in launching liberation; they condescend toward gays and lesbians who still need the crutch or opiate of religious membership. Only recently have there been efforts to gather and retell this history as a whole—to write religion back into it.[3] For other and more obvious reasons, some churches have not wanted to emphasize their earlier involvement with same-sex politics. The denominational websites of LGBT groups offer slices of the history, and there is now a national project to gather a virtual archive.[4] But websites can be fickle sources; they change with politics or PR plans or the flow of donations. They sometimes privilege the memories of organizational survivors.

One obvious way to remedy these gaps in history writing or institutional self-presentation is to conduct and collate interviews. I have done that—but not as narrative history, much less as empirical research. I have tried to catch the rhetorical energies of characters as they are remembered or re-performed when people tell their religious and erotic lives together. I didn't want countable "facts" about people's opinions or even statistics about their words. I didn't assume that people could fluently report what I wanted to know. People are unable to say when or where they learned the deepest patterns in their speech about sex. They may remember emblematic episodes from adolescence—the discovery of an erotic book or a

dictionary entry, the humiliation felt during a fiery sermon or medical examination, the rebuff of an awkward proposition to a special friend. These
episodes are only tokens of deeper habits in language. The task is to take
in enough speech, to swallow it, so that its characters have space in which
to speak and act.

They do speak—and often more fluently when they are not suffering the
peculiar constraints of the interview. So I supplemented my interview notes
with a much larger store of first-person speech—transcripts of oral histories conducted by others, long and short memoirs, collected testimonies
and printed declarations, letters and diaries. There are many more kinds
of speech than answers to questionnaires or standard interviews allow. But
listening to them, through them, is even harder than listening to interviews.
When people talk about sex and religion, they speak a series of references,
known and unknown, to other speeches they have been taught. It is not
enough to list quotations, citations, allusions in the hopes that recognizing
fragments of speech will allow you to construct a sort of rhetorical genealogy. The footnotes of even a single page in an oral history or a journal entry
tend to multiply. There can be some verses of scriptures or a childhood
hymn or the lessons of a Sunday school teacher, but also parental scolding
or bits of family lore, something from a movie or a television series, the lyric
of a popular dance tune, a favorite "affirmation," and then, under or over it
all, these urgent generalizations, these passionate professions of some cliché
that is meant to hold it all together—but actually to stop uncomfortable
requests for more justification. "I believe that God doesn't make garbage."
"I know I was put here for a reason." "I have a personal relationship with
Jesus." The influence of rhetoric is located not in particular remembered
sources, but in the characters that shape speech. So I listened through the
fragmentary quotations, most of them unconscious or involuntary, for the
persistence of clustered categories, images, metaphors that pointed in turn
to characters who enacted purposes or plots.

Once I began to follow the characters, I found myself at large in the
archives for American speech about religion and sex. Archives are always
both too small and too big. They never have all that you want; they always have more than you can use. As I followed rhetorical characters for
sex, I had to choose among the uncountable links that led from one box
to another. At times I had the sort of experience that Michel Foucault
describes—the startling vibrations of a folder that contains an infamous
life.[5] (I felt them when I discovered the handwritten response to the 1964
survey that you have just been reading.) But most often I had to hazard
choices among possible connections. Since I was mainly interested in the
succession of characters that Christians and those around them put on as

sexual characters, I concentrated on church debates over the "essence" of homosexuality and its moral implications. But those debates cross a number of others—say, the role of women in churches, the permissibility of abortion, the codification of sexual ethics, and the moral character of nonwhite races. These ongoing arguments deploy characters that are kin to the ones for adolescents with troubling sexuality. Making my impossible choices among the archival boxes, I couldn't pretend to anything like completeness. I don't imagine that I captured every character: the archives contain any number of unactualized possibilities, of empty forms. Nor do I think that I traced or counted all significant patterns of circulation. I only wanted vivid instances of forms that were filled in by living, on the supposition that studying the effects of rhetoric means studying its circulation into lives.

I keep speaking of archives. I mean the term both literally and metaphorically (as Foucault does).[6] Literally, archives are instruments both of memory and of control. They include forgotten scrapbooks in the local library and the active files of the police. So too, metaphorically, archives are both a record and a law. I must keep all these doubled meanings in play to show the relation of any rhetorical archive to performance. The records I cite are often found in boxes of files or shelves of books. Still they are records of characters that shape lives only when they speak, when they perform. Some of my archival records are almost like scripts, but others are no more than scraps of notes on performances partly observed. At best, my records register the lived transmission of an ensemble of gestures, expressions, acts, styles—the elements in a character. I use them to revivify what was originally not passed down only or mainly on paper. When you read the word "archive," keep in mind the doubled meanings, but conceive also the badly incomplete record of a repertoire.[7]

Reading an archive as a repertoire for characters around sex requires shifts of attention. Here are three of them.

1. Characters are prescribed by church rhetoric to those who listen, but they are also modeled in the voice that speaks. Characters surround acts of persuasion—in the audience and the performer as much as in the figures that are presented for admiration or insult. A preacher warning a congregation that same-sex desire is abominable projects a character for a sexual sinner, but also for an authoritative preacher and a pious congregant. Figures of unholy condemnation are surrounded by figures of godly authority and submission.

2. Every sexual character condenses a story. The stories vary considerably in complexity and interest, but even reduced religious characters or

polemical political identities condense plots. These characters are allotted their lines, their slogans, but more importantly their schemes of promised reward and punishment. They have their turns of phrase, but they feast on offers of love and recoil from angry threats. They act—and act on those who watch them. In my archive, I listened for how these characters and identities desired, grieved, reasoned, repented, or despaired before me, but also over me. They act—and they falter. I listened perhaps most of all for their incoherencies, fumbled segues, awkward transitions, or abrupt silences.

3. Sexual characters disregard boundaries between the documentary or empirical and the literary or theoretical. In rhetoric, the most empirical is often the most literary or fantastical, since it is in those genres that the characters are fully elaborated, most articulately performed and studied. But characters are not confined by genres. They appear wherever speech carries them, in answers to questionnaires or in dreams, in sermons or pulp novels. They migrate across all the tidy boundaries of speech, as mobile and insistent as our languages. They even cross time. Some characters are more prominent in one decade than another, but they have remarkable capacities for reappearing—for anticipation and return. So I follow them wherever they lead, from Sunday school lesson plans to pulp novels.

Even as they circulate common characters and plots, samples of rhetoric can be stubbornly particular. Persuasion often aims for a single audience at one time and place, relying on local references and exploiting familiar sentiments. Religious traditions, including those that claim universality, are notoriously liable to local variation, much of it inaudible except to insider ears. There is no universal translator for rhetoric around sex, no omnidirectional microphone to assure equal hearing in all directions. Listening responsibly means knowing the limits of one's ears.

I have made decisions about my own limits before my limited archive. Let me mention two of the most obvious. Over the last years, I interviewed both women and men, and I read as widely in the rhetoric of lesbianism as in speeches around gay men. After long hesitation, I have decided to concentrate on gay (male) adolescence. I do this because of my limits, my confinement by specific characters, but also because of how our American speech has been organized and preserved. The archives or repertoires often treat the sexuality of men and women separately, oppositely. The languages for them are notoriously asymmetrical. Lesbian and gay characters are not matching subspecies of the homosexual, except in the fantasy of clinical legislators and their latter-day adherents. The recorded experience of men and women within Christian churches (or in opposition to them) is also markedly different, even for churches claiming that men and women ought to be equal. At the same time, our most familiar constructs of male-male desire make no sense except in relation to misogyny, and the peculiarities of the verbal violence directed at effeminate boys must be compared with the insults aimed at butch girls. So I offer the book as a study of rhetoric around *gay* characters, but I add immediately that gayness cannot be studied without having both lesbianism and the "feminine" always in view. Some prominent church voices define homosexuality as a sinful failure of gender, rather than of sex, and they respond to it by restoring what they regard as the right relation between male and female. In the archives of church debate, the *figure* of the feminine is used both to humiliate and to cure gay men.

Here is my second limitation: the historical evidence and my own interviews are overwhelmingly (though not exclusively) white. I acknowledge the defect, and I admit how badly placed I am to overcome it. I feel the limits of my skin and of my sources. I worry about the possibilities for discovering the missing records of African American or Latino/a or Asian American queers in churches during the 1940s, 1950s, and 1960s, but I also see that the brightest hopes for discovery lie within those communities. None of this implies that I can ignore race. Predominantly white archives must be marked as what they are. More importantly, race itself must be kept in view as one of the recurring analogies for homosexuality. In the archives of church debate, the *figure* of the racial minority is used both to justify and to rebuke any claim for a homosexual minority.

Recently, much work on sexuality has reminded readers to pay attention to the "intersection" of various kinds of social identity—to points at which race, nationality, gender, class, and sexuality meet. The reminder is imperative, but the metaphor is misleading. To speak of "intersectionality" implies that persons are constituted—like points on a Cartesian grid—by the meeting of preexisting lines.[8] In the same way, when we speak of "hybridity" we imply the preexistence of species that crossbreed. I conceive things the other way around. My race, nationality, gender, class, and sexuality aren't added together in order to produce me. I am continually producing—displaying and enacting—features that are isolated in order to conceive those identities. It is especially important to mark this reversal with respect to gender and sexuality, since one of my main preoccupations is to undo their alleged separation and their reductive fixation into identities.

While the confession of my limits is sincere, I ask you *not* to read it as a contrite declaration of my "subject position." If we could know already the positions that subjects occupy, if we could predict how subjects are constructed out of certain specified components, there would be no need to write this book—or to read it. My assumption is that we do not know the true, significant, or determinative positions of sexual and religious subjects—indeed, that we hardly know what we mean by "sexual" and "religious." The book traces some episodes in the struggles of American churches, their allies, and their critics over producing subjects with rightly settled sex. Its point is that these struggles are unresolved and that the making of subjects remains urgent and contentious. So if I had to declare my subject position, I wouldn't know whether to say that I am an unevenly educated white man in deteriorating middle age with a relatively secure income. Or that one of my earliest religious memories is of almost naked male penitents in a lakeshore village in central Mexico. Or that the nearest I come to speaking "true" desire is histrionic irony. I am a fierce fan of Justin Bond as the ageless lounge chanteuse Kiki. "Total Eclipse of the Heart," that's my subject position. This season.

The book may look like history. It is, and it isn't. It recounts changes that led to the rhetoric of present church debates over religion and sexuality. It is, in that sense, a history of our present speech. But the book does not conform to any standard pattern for history writing, and so it might be better conceived as rhetorical criticism—or, more exactly, as a sequence of rhetorical retrievals, of historically alert re-performances. Captions over the stage will say something about authorship, dating, and performance history, but the captions are secondary to the effect of the rhetorical pieces on display. This is *not* an institutional or social history of queer lives in Christian churches. It is *not* an intellectual history of theological ideas, their sources, and influences. I offer only a sequence of rhetorical tableaux, in which the protagonists are characters projected by a large library of texts and images.[9]

I arrange the tableaux into chapters that study certain interlocking speeches—speeches in which characters, plots, and rhetorical devices play off of each other. The chapters also correspond more or less to periods in which certain characters or genres stand out. But the periodization is artificial and deceptively linear. In rhetoric, a "period" is a complex balancing of clauses or sentences that rounds off a satisfying earful. I dreamed of presenting what follows as a polyphony of periodic orations—the salience of one group of voices following another, propelled by deep rhythm, like the flights of sampled solos over the dance beat of house music. But that would suppose that we still had sophisticated genres for representing religious rhetoric or developed tastes for assessing it. We do not.

Some years ago, I wrote a monograph on the invention of the category "sodomy" in medieval Christian theology. I traced the condensation of an abstract moral category out of the misreading of scriptural texts, the spasms of social fears, and the legislation of Christian moral characters. This book is a sort of sequel. In it, I tell the other end of the story, the end we are now living: *The Oblivion of Sodomy in Christian Theology*. The present story is about the emergence of a series of figures—inverts, homophiles, homosexuals, gays—who try to find a place in Christian churches or to make a better religion outside of them. If medieval authors imagined the "Christian sodomite" as an obscene contradiction or a concealed threat to church and city, the "gay Christian" wants to be a figure of zealous reform and new holiness. But this figure can only speak in the space of the sodomite's retreat.

Writing the sequel has taken much more time than writing the original. Contemporary bodies of evidence are so much larger and more varied than those for the Middle Ages. Then again, the story changes week to week. I have spent about a decade wandering in the archives, rehearsing pieces of the repertoire, and reading the daily news. I decided in the end that it was better to concentrate on a few characters, on a few eminent examples of church rhetoric, and to display the larger patterns so far as possible through them. Other examples will need other books—though not by me.

If my little book, *Invention of Sodomy*, began with an angry indictment of one Christian church and ended with a call to reform in many, this book is both less angry and less hopeful about general reform. Or perhaps I have recognized that church "reform" has never yet been general, and has at its most successful made for new divisions. I have spent much of the last decade at work and at prayer in churches with many queer members. I count those years as some of the most edifying of my life. I'm not sure I could have continued as a Christian except for the witness I saw in so many places. At the same time, I expect that larger church structures will continue to war over sex and gender—increasingly because they have little else to say. Churches will use issues like the ordination of women or honest queer people, like same-sex marriage and adoption, as pretexts for exercising the uglier forms of aggression and domination that always threaten churches. They will split and realign. They will fight over who gets to keep the name or, more importantly, the property. Despite those fights, underneath them, some church communities will continue to care for those who come to them seeking salvation for their whole selves. For me, games of schism matter much less for Christianity than the invention or improvisation of new characters by those still willing to entrust themselves to Eucharist.

I

DEGENERATING YOUTH

American churches did not begin to debate same-sex desire at length or in the public's hearing until around 1950. But to begin in the archives just there would conceal some decisive rhetorical invention that been done fifty years earlier. When churches began to debate the desire, they reached back half a century to a cluster of texts that brought an emphatically scientific roster of new sexual characters into English. They retrieved across exactly the same span a new science of adolescence. By a remarkable coincidence, which is no coincidence at all, the homosexual and the adolescent entered English-speaking science in the same years. Understanding their original connection and disconnection is required for explaining what comes later. So I begin, as do so many historical stories, by stepping back before my announced beginning.

In the decade straddling 1900, the character of the American adolescent was refashioned under the virile supervision of a new science. The science promised to safeguard the normal young through training in what to believe and whom to love. The promises are made famously by the scientific founder G. Stanley Hall in his inaugural compendium, *Adolescence*. The book's wandering subtitle, an omen of digressions to come, declares that it will treat adolescence psychologically in relation to physiology, anthropology, sociology, sex, crime, religion, and education. The list reveals the abiding anxiety: a science covering all of these aspects is needed to fix the American adolescent—who is unfixed in so many ways, with cascading consequences. The breadth of the science must cover all of the adolescent's pliant vulnerability. But the listed terms are not, in the end, equal. Religion and sex will turn out to be the salient elements in the new psychology of adolescence. Their handling by Hall plots out many of the later debates in American churches.

Hall's professional biography is so intertwined with the founding of American academic psychology that it is only too easy to make him an emblem of the new scientific management of developing desire. Hall mentions the claim that he was "the father of child study" in order to demur from it; he confesses that he was extraordinarily pleased to be introduced once as "the Darwin of the mind," though he also disowns that compliment.[1] But his last memoir, written when he was nearly eighty, does present him as the pioneering psychologist of human development. There are ample grounds. Harvard awarded him its first doctorate in psychology (still under the parental roof of philosophy) after an examination by William James and others. Harvard's president had earlier challenged Hall to show that there was anything worthwhile in the study of pedagogy. He did, in a series of crowded and fully reported lectures. Hall launched the first English-language journal of psychology and served as founding president of the American Psychological Association. Having spent two separate periods studying in Germany, he imported its practices of laboratory psychology, but he was also an early (if qualified) promoter of psychoanalysis—indeed, he served as principal host to Freud and Jung on their fatefully divisive visit to America in 1909. But Hall's passion was to apply scientific psychology to rearing the young. He was first head of the child study department of the National Education Association, and he published *Adolescence* in a period when he still hoped to establish a comprehensive Children's Institute at Clark University. The book's thick volumes mean "to epitomize comprehensively and to draw inferences from what had been done for this period of life."[2] "Epitomize" is a charmed word for Hall; it names his lifelong discipline of writing summaries of particular studies before combining them into a single, usable science.

Hall's cultivated identification with scientific psychology might lead to the conclusion that he repudiated religion. Certainly he tells his own life as a slow and secretive withdrawal from Puritan orthodoxy. If, as a child, he suffered terrors about hell and, as an adolescent, feared the judgment that awaited him when the world ended or he died in his sleep, he was all along backing away from his mother's traditional doctrine. Aged three, he made up a conversation with God—but mainly to confess his disobedience of a divine command. Hall the boy read the Bible through—in order to get a pair of skates. At sixteen, he wrote an allegory in which virtues and vices personified as pagan deities deplored sectarian quarrels among local Christians.[3]

Having graduated from Williams College, Hall did go on for ministerial training at Union Theological Seminary, but mainly to buy time for himself. In long retrospect, he remembers spending his seminary career learning what he could from the city of New York, especially the gritty lessons that had to be hidden from his teachers and fellow students. He was saved from an unhappy fate as a Protestant minister when an unexpected loan enabled him to leave immediately for study in Europe—without finishing a congregational assignment in Pennsylvania or going home to consult with his parents. Hall flirted with Unitarianism, but could never bring himself to make the public break with orthodoxy that would pain his mother. So it is not surprising to read in his memoirs that *all* religions and their divinities are human creations. The construction of a "Temple of Science" is the "sublimest achievement of man."[4]

That is the irreligious story Hall tells of himself. But religion remains a key element in his science of childhood and adolescence. He insists on having made the crucial discovery of the adolescent's "religious impressionability." Hall announced it as early as the Harvard-sponsored public lectures on pedagogy. He so emphasizes the discovery because of the importance he assigns to religion in managing the American adolescent. I follow Hall's science for recruiting adolescents into proper sex and resolute religion through several of his books, including his autobiography, but also into the books that he cites or echoes. His writing is an axis around which to measure a whole set of decisive discourses about sex, adolescence, and religion.

THE "EPHEBIC DECADE," ITS PASSIONS AND DANGERS

For Hall, religion is a defining characteristic of his protagonist, the (male) adolescent: "adolescence [is] the age of religious impressionability in general, and of conversions in particular."[5] Conversions are an instrument of recruitment. The "ephebic decade" is barely long enough to cooperate with biology in changing the religious child into the religious adult, turning selfishness to service and crude pictures into sublime conceptions. Yet this crowded period offers "the religious teacher's great opportunity."[6] It appears with the physical maturation of puberty and disappears, roughly a decade later, into the full adulthood of married life. The time between must be monitored scientifically to exploit religious malleability.

Religious experience is a decisive feature of adolescence, but adolescence itself is also described religiously. Hall constructs the character of the adolescent on Christian terms. Childhood recapitulates the history of the whole race. "The child comes from and harks back to a remoter past." Adolescence, by contrast, is "a new birth, for the higher and more completely human traits are now born."[7] This is the imagery of Christian conversion and baptism. The "old man," the human soul born into mire, is trapped by inherited sin. Baptism brings new birth—and a new orientation to the future in heaven. Hall depicts adolescence as a period for individual conversions because it is the grand period of conversion for the species—to the species' ends.

This "best decade of life" merits "reverence" perhaps more than "anything else in the world."[8] In adolescence, the divine energies for change are most active. They align the individual with divine purposes through sex. The "rich and varied orchestration" of sexual life "brings the individual into the closest *rapport* with the larger life of the great Biologos [God]."[9] Adolescent desire can alight anywhere and then become fixed through habit. Only religion can assure safe fixation on appropriate objects. "Between religion and love God and nature have wrought an indissoluble bond so that neither can attain normality without that of the other."[10] Hence the enormous opportunity for religious education during adolescence—and the great peril: both religion and sex can go irremediably astray. They usually stray together.

Hall presumes that the normal or unmarked adolescent is male, and he describes deviations from normalcy in gendered terms. If the "great biotic law" of adolescent susceptibility is made "a psychic fetish, a neurosis, a ritual of initiation instead of a norm of life," efforts at religious formation produce *effeminate* results. "They often tend to cultivate a gushy, religious sentimentalism of a unique type that evirates character, [to] favor flightiness, unctuousness, mobile and superficial sentiments, [to] incline to ultra-femininity and patheticism, and to love of climaxes that react to apathy."[11] Hall likes the word "patheticism." He uses it often, though he never quite defines it. For him, it names an always morbid exaggeration of self-pity, a dangerous attitude of helplessness. He associates it with women or, more exactly, with representations or affectations of the suffering feminine.[12] Indeed, consciously or unconsciously "patheticism" begins to call up its almost homonym, "pathicism," the stigmatized desire of pathics for the "effeminate," penetrated role in male-male relations. An allusion to sexual penetration would reinforce Hall's warning that a certain sort of religion can "evirate" or emasculate character. Earlier he had mentioned a more extreme form of religious effeminacy, the "functional castration" of the Pueblo "mugenados."[13] On Hall's account, these young men are abused into permanent impotence for liturgical and sexual purposes. In these "women-men," "the organs atrophy, the beard falls out, the voice grows feminine, and the breasts give milk."

The danger posed by effeminate Christianity to Hall's readers is described less luridly. Hall offers a few cautionary tales of religious scrupulosity, but they tell only of diverted sentiment, not of sexual acts or atrophied organs. After a conversion, for example, adolescent scruples may be expressed as impossible desires for perfection or urges to reform the world, starting with the churches. Hall mentions the case (from Coe) of "one who in choir would stop singing if there was a sentiment in the hymn he was not sure he believed." Even normal conversions alienate from ordinary life: "The young convert feels estranged to both himself and others, because he is different from what he had so long been before. Hence he is prone to deem himself peculiar and not like others, because unlike his former self."[14] Sentiments of peculiarity are less obviously threatening to Hall than "functional castration," but they carry risks of further deviation.

Hall is more candid about sexual risks when treating them apart from religion, though even then certain details are passed over with the masking language of shame. During adolescence, "sex asserts its mastery in field after field, and works its havoc in the form of secret vice, debauch, disease, and enfeebled heredity." The new psychology arrives on the scene in the nick of time—unless it is perhaps already too late. "There is not only arrest, but perversion, at every stage, and hoodlumism, juvenile crime, and secret vice seem not only increasing, but develop in earlier years in every civilized land."[15] The increase of criminal sexuality (of a sexuality that identifies one with criminals, as criminal) is attributable to the conditions of modernity, compounded in America by the absence of mature national culture. Still much of the sexual harm to adolescents is to be blamed on the local ignorance of those who are supposed to care for them—parents, always, but also teachers, ministers, and physicians. Their ignorance leads them to seek quack cures for normal developments while coddling incipient perversions.

Pleas for scientific enlightenment of adolescent sex recur across the last century in America, but at different points, attaching to different acts or identities. For Hall in *Adolescence*, the perfectly natural sexual activity that science exonerates is nocturnal emission or involuntary ejaculation. (This discussion of sexual development is confined to boys; the corresponding chapter on girls is entitled "periodicity" and worries about the relation of menstruation to criminal madness.) Hall devotes pages to salving the consciences of young men who experience emissions, then further pages to attacking religious authorities who condemn emissions and cruel charlatans who pretend to forestall them. Yet enlightened tolerance is limited: Hall is as vehemently loquacious in denouncing the "secret vice" of masturbation (for which he often retains the mock-biblical name, "onanism," though he knows others). He professes himself pained at having to consider this "very saddest of all the aspects of human weakness," but more appalled at reports of its prevalence.[16] No sympathy for the weak-willed or the degenerate will deter him from frank condemnations. "Because [masturbation] is so dangerous, and liable to occur in individuals who lack stamina, it has its octopus-grasp [an extraordinary metaphor given the context] in nearly all institutions for the defective classes."[17] Masturbation is a symptom of degeneracy and a cause of its propagation in the next generation. It is, to be precise, at the origin of most perversions and it slides imperceptibly into crime. Many young murderers, for example, are "victims of the vicious sexual precocity characteristic of young criminals in large cities."[18] These rhetorical devices and associations will recur in Hall's successors: science proves that unregulated adolescent desire leads by irresistible increments from private pleasures to public crime. Down the familiar slippery slope— another unfortunate metaphor.

Among the effects of masturbation are phenomena curiously like effeminate adolescent religiosity. "Perhaps the most common psychic result [of onanism] is a sense of unworthiness, sin, pollution, . . . occasionally hidden by almost morbid scrupulousness and convictions of foreboding disaster or penalty. In what theologians have described as the conviction of sin, this plays an enormous and hitherto unappreciated rôle."[19] For once, Hall allies himself with the theologians. He does not mean to liberate youth from this oppressive conviction of sin. On the contrary, he joins in condemning masturbation as "the most perfect type of individual vice and sin. Where practised . . . by the young, it is perhaps the purest illustration of mere sense pleasure bought at the cost of the higher life."[20] No Puritan divine could have said it better. Only what Hall means by the "the higher life" is not the promise of heaven, but of heredity. Masturbation imperils heredity by bringing about degeneration. "God and nature" have joined voluntary pleasure to the choice for parenthood.[21] Let no filthy boy put them asunder.

For Hall, the adolescent sexual expression to be excused as natural is involuntary ejaculation. The excuse calls forth triumphant rhetoric of scientific enlightenment. It authorizes rational contempt for superstitions and frauds. But such progressive rhetoric must then justify itself, must reestablish its moral seriousness, by emphatically denouncing a contrasting act, disposition, or character. The new psychology can escape the charge of laxity for excusing nocturnal emissions only if it remains quite stern about something else: masturbation. The scientific authority that excused involuntary ejaculations reestablishes its social responsibility by condemning voluntary ones. It condemns them with rhetorical devices that still motivate our judgments on adolescent sex. For Hall, masturbation frustrates individual physiology, undoes masculinity, produces perversions, links one to criminal classes, and thwarts the progress of one's racial stock. In sum, its consequences embrace, with another "octopus-grasp," everything from metabolism through gender and sexual desire to social standing and family destiny. Excusing one aspect of sexual activity (for Hall, involuntary ejaculation) requires condemning a series of others in terms that invest them with extraordinary moral significance and comprehensive causality. Pleas for enlightenment are purchased at a rhetorical price. The price is paid not only by masturbation, but by the whole of human sexuality, which is now seen as full of hidden risks that require constant, expert surveillance.

The price is paid especially by those uncatalogued "perversions" that Hall passes over in a silence from which the reader is distracted by loud moralizing. For a compendium of sexualized adolescence, Hall's book is remarkably reticent about that one perversion recently christened "homosexuality." The closest he comes to mentioning even his own reticence is the claim that extreme sexual pathologies are best left to the new specialists, such as Krafft-Ebing, Havelock Ellis, and the still young Sigmund Freud, all of whom Hall cites approvingly.[22] One of the very few mentions in *Adolescence* of the new term "homosexuality" occurs in a reference to Ellis. The careful silence only carries over the force of prior condemnation. If masturbation is so terrible, imagine the deformities that lie further down the bleak slope! Imagine the horrors of homosexuality! The reader must do exactly that: imagine them, fearfully and yet murkily. Their explicit discussion is relegated—is exiled—into a separate and expertly guarded discourse.

Hall's rhetorical scheme for judging adolescent sex is not a simple rhetorical dichotomy between a good term and a bad term. It needs three terms, of which the last, the most dangerous, is left deliberately in a fearful silence. This three-term scheme will become characteristic in Hall's rhetorical successors—in our own speech. There is always a newly justified good sex, a common but destructive bad sex, and a supposedly rare extreme of worst sex. The comparison shifts over a range of acts and characters in the last hundred years, but homosexuality often ends up in the last place. In some contemporary evangelical discourse, for example, all kinds of married sex play is good, adultery is bad and yet common, while homosexuality remains in worst place—as bad and rare. For much of the century, the last, worst term has been covered in silence in order to make it more terrible—and more usefully vague. A term masked in silence, colored by fearful imaginings, dangerous to all but trained experts is easy to apply where and how one wishes—but always to create fear. We will need to keep asking why it has proved more useful recently to speak the monster-term loudly, graphically, with comic-book exclamation marks. The strategy of silence gives way to the strategy of melodrama. But that happens long after Hall—after his strategy has lost power.

In Hall's *Adolescence*, the silence about the third member of the triplet, the most abject term, is almost complete. Surprisingly so, since Hall's effort to create an American science of adolescence follows only a few years after parallel efforts to manage that other new character, the homosexual. Though the original for "homosexual" was coined in German in the late 1860s, it was introduced into English only with the 1892 translation of Krafft-Ebing's *Psychopathia sexualis*. Its real American popularity began with the publication of the first volume of Havelock Ellis's *Studies in Psychology* (1897)—though Ellis apologizes for using the word, which he regards as "barbarously hybrid."[23] It is worth retrieving Ellis and his predecessors from Hall's footnotes to get a clearer sense of what Hall refuses to say plainly—and to begin understanding why churches now shout into his silence.

NAMING PERVERSIONS

"Homosexual" is now our standard word, if not our common one. It is the official word, the allegedly scientific word, the word to which we return despite so many efforts to dislodge it. But the "barbarously hybrid" term "homosexual," soldered together out of Greek and Latin pieces, did not gain its prominence at once or without controversy. There were other terms, and some of them remain important for understanding the rhetorical configurations of church speech. "Homosexual" must always be heard against its rivals.

On the presently available evidence, the German *Homosexualität* (homosexuality), *Homosexualist* (homosexual), and their cousins were coined by Károly Mária (or Karl Maria) Kertbeny, a Hungarian writer, translator, journalist, and state-pensioned bibliographer. *Homosexualität* appears in a letter Kertbeny drafted as a sort of summary or valediction to a correspondence he had tried to maintain with Karl Heinrich Ulrichs from 1865 on.[24] In May of 1868, Kertbeny wanted to summarize for Ulrichs his alternate theory, his countervocabulary. Since about 1862, Ulrichs had been championing in public another set of terms with their theories or mythologies—and their allusions to Plato's *Symposium*. Among these was the term *Urning* for the type of individual whose experience could best be described as that of a female soul trapped in a male body. "Urning" crossed over into English in the 1880s and appeared in medical, forensic, and reformist writing for several decades before dying out. Its more apt English version, "Uranian," had a longer history, not least under the pen of Oscar Wilde, but it too has since disappeared. Kertbeny's coinage has not. He proposed *Homosexualist* as a more neutral term that stakes a claim of innate condition useful in securing legal reforms—though also dangerous, as Kertbeny realized, so far as it concedes pathology. Kertbeny first published his "anthropological" plea for male and female homosexualists in a pamphlet seeking reform of the paragraph in the Prussian penal code that criminalized their acts. Over the next decade, he seems to have worked in fits and starts on a magnum opus. In 1879, a summarizing chapter he had drafted for a new edition of a medical reference work was excised at the last minute.[25]

Pointing back to Kertbeny as the originator of the English term "homosexual" makes it seem as if he invented it with our meanings and assumed contrasts. In fact, Kertbeny locates his "homosexuality" and the "homosexual" in various taxonomies that show how differently the terms function for him. In the 1868 letter to Ulrichs, for example, homosexuality is one of four terms or categories: monosexuality (our masturbation), homosexuality, heterosexuality, and heterogeneity (our bestiality). Each term or category embraces activities, dispositions, and individuals. In the pamphlets from 1869, the central division is reduced to a neat trio of three types: the onanist, the normal-sexual, and the homosexual. But the terms slide across various things: Kertbeny writes of "homosexual natures" or "homosexual drive," but also of homosexuality and homosexuals.[26] These terms are accompanied by many others in Kertbeny's writings, including "pygism" or desire for anal intercourse and "Platonism" or same-sex passion that never seeks genital fulfillment.

As Kertbeny's correspondence with Ulrichs makes clear, he was hardly the only inventor of new taxonomies for sexual variations—or the only author trying to use new scientific terms in projects of social reform. Terms multiplied and competed. They traced intersecting, but still distinct paths in the various European languages. Through Hall, we have seen how Havelock Ellis popularized for English-speakers the awkward noun "invert" to describe a person whose "sexual instinct" had been "turned by inborn constitutional abnormality" toward those of the same sex.[27] Ellis did not invent either the metaphor or its implied theory. He borrowed the noun from Italian and French writers of forensic psychiatry—which included diagnostic physiognomy, phrenology, and eugenics.[28] They coined "invert" to capture the notion—proposed by Westphal, applied by Krafft-Ebing—of "contrary sexual feeling."[29] Based on two extended case histories, Westphal had described for science a new "symptom": "an inborn reversal of the sexual feeling with consciousness of the morbidity of this manifestation."[30] Note three things about the symptom: it is inborn, it is a reversal, and it is conscious of its own pathology. The reversal need not determine sexual behavior. On the advice of a classical philologist, Westphal has chosen to call it "contrary sexual feeling" precisely to indicate "that it doesn't always have to do simultaneously with the sexual drive." This is a pathology of affect and sensibility, "of being alienated from one's own sex according to one's whole inner being."[31] According to Westphal the symptom does invariably indicate a "general pathological condition"; it is analogous to other "pathological perversities" in manifesting an underlying disorder, such as melancholy or "moral insanity."[32] These disorders are linked in turn to evidence of criminality, of innate "mental narrowness" or "imbecility," of tainted heredity and failed development.[33]

Much of Westphal's model passes down to Ellis and so into English. "Invert," like so many terms of early sexology, took its meaning within theories of racial superiority and racial degeneration. Ellis was far from wanting to deny these theories or their implications for evaluating individual development. His first book, *The Criminal*, describes with statistical evidence the physical and psychical attributes of criminality, especially when instinctual. The book includes photographs to help the student recognize the physical manifestations. Among these photographs are facial studies of young "sexual perverts": their bodies are immature, boyish or childish, and stereotypically feminine.[34]

In *Sexual Inversion*, Ellis will say much more about inverts—though without the aid of pictures. But before turning to his descriptions, it is important to recognize how far his book presupposes that the invert is a pathological character waiting to be described. The fights over names that Ellis inherits evidently disagree over diagnoses or descriptions of the species, but they increasingly share assumptions about the genus or kind of character they study. This was Foucault's main point in a passage that has provoked misguided controversies over the significance of the origin of the terms "homosexual" or "homosexuality."[35] The central contrast in Foucault is not between acts and identities, but between the sodomite as "juridical subject" of forbidden acts and the homosexual as a medicalized "personage"—with a predictable history, a characteristic morphology, and perhaps even an abnormal physiology. The contrast finds a parallel in Foucault's lectures on abnormals. There he argues that one function of nineteenth-century psychiatric expertise is to *double* the "author of the offense" with a "new personage of the delinquent, previously unknown to the eighteenth century." The old forensic psychiatry was only required to determine whether the "author of the act" was still a responsible "juridical subject," culpable for committing the act.[36] The new forensic psychiatry must discern a special kind of personage behind the act. Foucault's remarks on delinquency explain his passage on the homosexual. The personage of the homosexual doubles the sodomite as "author of the act"—creates an "ethico-moral double," Foucault says in the lectures, an "individual" who is the "bearer" of a "character" with specified traits rather than the merely culpable "juridical subject" of a legally defined offense.[37] The doubling is accomplished by positing a perversion as ground for the sexual acts. Like its nineteenth-century cousins instinct and degeneration, perversion commits its unfortunate bearers to lifelong medical surveillance as members of a new and pathological species.

Whether or not Foucault is right about nineteenth-century forensic psychiatry or the delinquent and the homosexual, he is certainly right to ask how the new terms differ *in kind* from their predecessors and how they function alongside other terms invented with them. The main rhetorical issue is not when and by whom a term was first coined—though those circumstances may be suggestive. Rhetorical analysis wants to know how a term cuts out a new character from human living, to which action and motive, past and future can be persuasively attributed. It makes all the rhetorical difference whether a term is applied to punishable acts or pathological types, how it is distinguished from parallel terms, and how far it can prescribe and predict. It makes a difference too which terms it replaces in authoritative speech. Foucault remembers what many of his readers forget: the homosexual must displace the sodomite. When Ellis begins to describe the invert, the reader should ask not only what the new character does, but how the character ever came to be invented within a set genus, a recognizable troupe, of other characters

SECRETS OF THE INVERTS

Havelock Ellis prefaces the whole series of *Studies in the Psychology of Sex* with an attack on prudish secrecy and a claim for his own sincerity, by which he means both honesty and plain speaking. He then appeals to a combined motive of friendship and respect for the dead. Ellis confesses that he publishes on homosexuality at all—and indeed, first in the series—to repay a debt of gratitude to John Addington Symonds. Symonds was not only a most insistent advocate for the project, he was Ellis's constant collaborator and coauthor until his death. Two of his earlier pamphlets are incorporated into *Sexual Inversion*, along with some of his reflections and a number of his case studies. So the curtain of silence can properly be lifted both in the name of sincere science and to honor the memory of a departed friend. Finally, perhaps most strongly, Ellis justifies his speech as an act of mercy on those in prominent positions who suffer so greatly from this congenital abnormality. For a psychologist to consent to talk about it shows sincerity and friendship, but also clemency—especially toward the prominent, who are arbiters of speech.

Ellis distinguishes homosexuality or "the collective phenomena of sexual attraction within the circle of a single sex" from inversion or "sexual instinct turned by inborn constitutional abnormality towards persons of the same sex."[38] The definition echoes Westphal's description of contrary sexual feeling, and it singles out something other than what Ellis means by "homosexuality." For him, homosexuality is conditioned by particular circumstance or pervasive national custom. It may be a passing phase or a minor manifestation in a larger complex of criminality or insanity, but it is always related to what is "collective," to the "circle" around one. By contrast, inversion is biologically fixed and affects the constitution of individuals rather than the character of their acts. For Ellis, as later for Alfred Kinsey or Gore Vidal, "homosexual" is principally an adjective applicable to acts, feelings, or social arrangements, while an invert is a type of person, a character.

The distinction is easier for Ellis to enunciate than to apply. Evidence of homosexual acts is by definition not enough to diagnose inversion. That diagnosis requires biological knowledge about the individual. Ellis is more comfortable identifying inverts among his contemporary neighbors than in other times and places, but he is willing to venture hypotheses about historical figures when they meet certain criteria. For example, Ellis does not doubt that Michelangelo was an invert. Beyond the sentiments expressed in the master's letters or the themes of his art, there are the reports of his unmarried brothers (hereditary taint), his indifference to women, and his melancholy. Historical figures who have similar profiles but who marry women or father children are diagnosed by Ellis as psychosexual hermaphrodites. Walt Whitman, despite explicit denials in a letter to Symonds, is found by Ellis to have "the homosexual instinct, however latent and unconscious."[39]

Where does the instinct come from? Ellis is as suspicious of dogmatic causal explanations as of elaborate typologies. At several points, he hesitantly endorses the view that inversion is a sort of arrested development. In it, the relatively undifferentiated erotic attractions of (normal) early adolescence are never properly resolved—perhaps because the congenital invert suffers from a "comparative quiescence" of "sexual emotions" or from its opposite, an erotic irritability and genital hypersensitivity.[40] Or perhaps the genetic predisposition to inversion is best conceived of as a sort of neurological cross-wiring that registers erotic attraction where it ought to register friendship. Ellis insists on the difficulty in sorting hereditary from circumstantial factors and ends, if at all, with a mixed view of causes, on which a genetic disposition is triggered by circumstances. "The seed of suggestion can only develop when it falls on a suitable soil" (with curious echoes of the Gospel parable of the sower).[41] On Ellis's reckoning, the three most common triggers are life in sex-segregated schools, seduction by an older invert, or early disappointment in heterosexual love. Without such triggers, a moderate inversion may never reveal itself.

When inversion is triggered, it may or may not act outwardly. If it does, it can become manifest in a wide range of sexual behaviors, determined both by individual taste and by social controls. Ellis offers little hope for curing enacted inversion. Much harm—psychological, moral, social—follows on trying to turn a true (presumptively male) invert into a robust womanizer. It is more sensible to encourage this invert, especially if he is both intelligent and refined, toward the ideals of chaste self-restraint. The ideals are not in Ellis particularly religious, much less Christian. If anything, the mentions of religion in *Sexual Inversion* treat it as one among many social influences or circumstances. Sometimes it appears in the cases as an important force in a particular adolescence—but a force incapable of curing inborn homosexual desire.[42] More frequently, Christianity is rejected or transformed in these reports. Some individuals may be tormented by religious commandments, but others set them aside with the conclusion that homosexual feelings are not sinful *for them*.[43] The view that inversion is some special opposition to God is explained historically as the middle or medieval stage of the social history of the matter. In his conclusion, Ellis recalls the strongest rhetoric for stigmatizing consensual, private homosexual acts only to judge the rhetoric *aesthetic*—and so not sufficient for criminalizing those acts.[44] The harshest words of condemnation—and they are all here—Ellis classifies as expressions of a normal or typical *taste*. These are not sins that cry out to heaven.

With Hall and others, Ellis's notion of inversion is brought into a calculated relation to the new science of adolescence. But the notion also travels along other paths in the archives. I mark them now to make it easier to return later. Ellis's notion of inversion passed rather quickly into English-speaking religious texts. One conduit was Hugh Northcote, an Anglican clergyman in New Zealand, who corresponded with Ellis. Northcote's *Christianity and Sex Problems* was published in America two years after the first edition of *Adolescence*. Northcote is explicitly guided throughout by Ellis's writings, but perhaps especially in the treatment of inversion.[45] Less explicit about its sources, but equally indebted to Ellis's language, is *The Invert and His Social Adjustment* by the anonymous author who styles himself "Anomaly." A forty-year-old Roman Catholic layman, he writes a popular work of practical advice for the clergyman, physician, or teacher who must deal with adolescent inverts.[46] Although he affirms Catholic prohibitions against sex outside marriage, and so offers the inverted young man only a life of chaste friendships and altruistic sublimation, Anomaly is eager to contest both the ignorance about inverts and the prejudices against them, especially among the clergy. He insists that the personal and moral qualities of the invert are exactly like those of the "normally sexed," except for the reversed sexual attraction.[47]

These early appropriations of Ellis by writers for church audiences hint at other ways of dealing with same-sex desire in adolescence than by shifting it into the guarded clinic of expert speech. They also show how impossible it is to guard that speech well enough. Copies of Ellis—or of Krafft-Ebing in English—found their way into research libraries, but also into public collections or parental dens. Many "inverts" found themselves by furtively consulting those books. One man remembers finding Ellis and Krafft-Ebing in his father's medical library in the early 1920s, with all the passages on homosexuality marked. "And I thought, gee, you know, my dad's on to me."[48] Another, twenty years on, learned the word "homosexual" from one of his mother's books on psychology. A few years afterward, he read through all four volumes of Ellis sitting in a library.[49] For a third man, roughly the same age, his brother's copy of the *Psychopathia Sexualis* was "the only, only thing I read about" sex.[50] These books, scattered in various libraries, haphazardly guarded, would begin to teach an alternate speech. Hall's strategy of concealing citation could not hold for long—though we might be surprised that it held as long as it did.

PIOUS EPHEBES AND VIRILE RELIGION

The discreet allusions to Ellis's *Sexual Inversion*—if not to his sources and conclusions—do important rhetorical work in Hall's *Adolescence*. They guarantee both the scientific accuracy and the pedagogical decency of the later book. Hall's refusal to picture homosexuality, to display it, is justified by the exact representations of perversion linked to the foot of his pages, in the notes. The main body of Hall's text can be kept pure in its approach to adolescence—and thus socially authoritative. Hall mentions pathological cases disparagingly and only in remote times or locations. He also quietly reverses Ellis's emphases. Ellis labors over the question of the origin of inversion, but dismisses prospects for genuine cure once it is activated. In *Adolescence*, Hall does not seem interested in anything like congenital inversion—unless as a symptom of degeneracy already far advanced. Congenital weaknesses are precisely the evil to be avoided by aggressively treating those who do not yet suffer them, but are at risk of producing them among their heirs. Within Hall's science of the young, the only perversions worth discussing are those that can be stopped. There is no causal model for congenital inversion, but there is a cure for what might produce it in the next generation.

Hall turns to religion as the antidote for erotic derangements in the young. Religion teaches them the highest form of love and so the most sublime understanding of sexual purposes.[51] It offers the only means for controlling erotic deviations into perversion. Neither ethical formation nor euphemistic preaching is enough to stop masturbation. The stubborn, secret vice requires a truthful appeal to the religious longings of youth, to its capacity for conversion. "The superiority of Christianity is that its cornerstone is love, and that it meets the needs of this most critical period of life as nothing else does." Christianity regulates sex, and sex animates Christianity. "Sex is a great psychic power which should be utilized for religion, which would be an inconceivably different thing without it, and one of the chief functions of the latter in the world is to *normalize* the former."[52]

The connection that Hall claims to have discovered between sexual and religious susceptibility in adolescence now stands forth in full light: it is a connection of mutual dependence and reciprocal causality. The strong, bivalent connection raises another worry: What if religion, instead of normalizing sex, should instead be corrupted by its degeneration? What if the church itself should become a haven for perversion? The question is buried again in Hall's footnotes and the associations they suggest. Ellis's *Sexual Inversion* gives credence to the commonplace that inverts are drawn to religion. "Church" appears first in the list of professions for British inverts known to Symonds.[53] Ellis notes in his own voice the condition's prevalence among religious leaders.[54] The disconcerting association is illustrated by some of the recorded cases. A male invert reports using religious iconography for homoerotic pleasure.[55] A woman identifies her female beloved in religious terms and regrets that the two of them cannot be confirmed together as a sort of sacrament of their affection.[56] A testimony about Albanian same-sex love prescribes veneration for the beloved as for a saint.[57] The figure of sanctity recurs when Ellis urges an idealized chastity as the best outcome for a true invert. "He may not have in him the making of *l'homme moyen sensuel* [the average, red-blooded guy], he may have in him the making of a saint."[58]

Hall's signature claim about adolescent romance and religiosity risks becoming scandalous if the reader passes through his citations to Ellis's compassionate evocation of a class of literary-religious inverts. Beyond Symonds, there is a roster of more notorious authors associated with inverted causes. If Hall won't name them, his first readers would certainly have heard of them. Between Hall's Harvard-sponsored lectures on pedagogy and the publication of his *Adolescence*, the dangerously romantic Christian ephebe—morbidly pious, far too sensitive, suspiciously bookish or musical—was becoming a familiarly scandalous figure in European and

American literatures. In high churches, or polemics against them, he was often connected with the liturgy. Oscar Wilde's Dorian Gray, the eternal adolescent, collects vestments and has a "special passion . . . for everything connected with the service of the Church."[59] In 1894, ten years before the publication of Hall's *Adolescence*, the single issue of *The Chameleon*, an Oxford undergraduate journal linked to Wilde, published anonymously a story entitled "The Priest and the Acolyte."[60] In it, a young priest and a "delicate" fourteen-year-old altar server fall passionately, heedlessly in love. Caught, confronted, the priest recounts his own unhappy and abnormal youth. "I was always different from other boys. I never cared much for games. I took little interest in those things for which boys usually care so much." Given to fits of imprudent affection, the priest too had been a young seeker after beauty. "The whole aesthetic tendency of my soul was intensely attracted by the wonderful mysteries of Christianity, the artistic beauty of our services." Faced with criminal punishment and social opprobrium, the priest and the acolyte commit suicide together at a final Eucharist with a poisoned chalice. Of course, for the critics of effeminate high-churchmanship, every chalice carried poison to impressionable young men.

Such carnal danger was both denounced and counteracted. During the years that Hall lectured on adolescence, schools and youth organizations implemented the policies of a "muscular Christianity." The movement is best known to contemporary Americans not so much through the remnants of the YMCA as in the various "fellowships" of Christian athletes. In the nineteenth century the movement was famous not only for advocating a regime of physical hygiene to improve character, but for organizing a network of moral vigilance around the unmarried young adrift in the dangerous world. Hall praises these organizations for recognizing "the need of amusement, recreation, and athletics to counteract the temptations of city life," and he especially urges their leaders to "profit . . . by every aid that [his] recent ephebic studies can offer" to their leaders.[61] Though he comments at length on the religious practices of these groups, Hall does not here remark that the movement from which they spring expressed an abiding anxiety about the gender of Christianity—not to say, of Christianity's founder. This anxiety would be explicitly articulated in the years around the first publication of Hall's *Adolescence*. Some years later, Hall himself would take up the question explicitly and at length in his psychological study of Jesus, a book that begins by arguing that the founder of Christianity should be represented as large, strong, beautiful, and "magnetic," but then reassures his readers that "Jesus was so absorbed in his own idealistic occupations that he was in a sense above sex."[62] Two books intended for a general audience show more vividly, across theological differences, that Jesus was a real man who passed through a perfectly normal adolescence.

Robert Warren Conant's *The Virility of Christ* was self-published in 1915, but it reworked material originally published the same year as Hall's *Adolescence*. Conant reinterprets Christianity into an allegedly scientific dogma of the survival of the fittest.[63] God created the cosmos as a school to cultivate power through self-help in the face of conflict. It follows that Christ must have been a commanding figure: *"the highest type of a strong, virile man."*[64] He is not feminine, passive, negative, languid, smooth, expressionless, or melancholy. Despite the tastes in some churches, he cannot properly be depicted by adding "a silky, curly beard to a woman's face and hair."[65] He is not, in short, a degenerate pervert. Indeed, "the virile psychology of Christ" is the religious antidote for "weakening tendencies of all kinds."[66] But this emphasis on Jesus as a manly man requires, on the terms of the new psychology, that he be supplied with a normal childhood and adolescence, complete with a regimen of physical development. Absent any scriptural evidence, Conant can let his fancy wander. It takes him in odd directions. Jesus, he tells us, "was a strong, healthy normal boy with a good appetite, and a sound sleeper."[67] He wasn't moody, but he did take to the hilltops around Nazareth to let "emotions and aspirations [fire] his fervid young soul," say, by meditating patriotically on the major battles of Israelite history.[68] He played sports—or their Nazareth equivalent. "Christ was an athlete, the most perfect embodiment of power—physical, mental, and moral—and all-round strong man."[69] If he decided not to marry, for unspecified reasons, his magnetic manliness was still powerfully attractive to women.

A surprisingly similar portrait of the antieffeminate Jesus is painted for different theological purposes by Bruce Barton. Jesus now becomes the "the Young Man of Nazareth," embodiment of the eternal YMCA, leader of the hot-blooded young against the artery-clogging wealth and ornamental religion of those over thirty-five. Barton rhapsodizes about Jesus's perfectly developed muscles. He admires, with the disciples or the surrounding crowds, "the subtle perfection of His manhood," the flawless features of "His splendid manliness."[70] Barton also endows Jesus with a "magnificent normality."[71] "He remains the one all-satisfying ideal of young manhood."[72] So of course he must have had a normal adolescence in which he learned how to manage his father's employees and to detest the brutal impoverishment of his people by the Roman tax collectors and the Temple priests. Barton's Jesus emphasized "the preservation of the family," but had to forego marriage himself because he was too poor.[73] Still there was absolutely nothing effeminate about his celibacy or his faultless life. He remained in the eyes of all a "man of iron"—and a sound sleeper. In sum, the real Jesus was the very opposite of the unreal, negative images of passive suffering presented in most Sunday schools.

Hall shares with Conant, Barton, and the other enemies of a simpering, effeminate Christianity the conviction that religion must produce real men out of dangerously pious boys. Hall finds his surest pedagogy in an appeal to racial continuity. Adolescence is the decade of both religious fervor and passionate first love. To be an adolescent is by definition to be both pious and passionate. Hall is eager to see many connections—genetic, cultural, moral, world-historical—between the stages of love and the stages of religion. He insists on the importance of sexual development for both. What prevents the dangerous eroticization of religion is the logic of reproduction—the logic of evolution at smaller scale. For Hall's adolescent, conversion is not falling in love with Jesus—an ambiguous affect for young men—so much as assuming masculine responsibility for the genetic future. Becoming an adult is taking up one's place in the sequence of generations (though that is precisely what Jesus refused to do). To be an individual is paradoxically to put on the species. Hall says this most succinctly in his memoirs. "The real life of the individual begins when the burgeoning of sex links him up with the race."[74] In those memoirs, he retells his own childhood and adolescence in relation to the overriding imperative.

A NORMAL SCIENTIST GROWS UP

Hall wrote about himself often, but most comprehensively and carefully for his *Life and Confessions of a Psychologist*, published only in the year before his death. Hall there presents himself as a willing subject for detailed psychological examination, the first genetic psychologist to undertake "a frank autobiography."[75] Its frankness should be doubted. The autobiography is professional or didactic. Traumatic personal events are passed over in a few words. The accidental death of his wife and youngest child earns three sentences. Two of them argue that Hall cannot be blamed for taking some months away from his university duties afterward.[76] The life we read is only that of the emblematic psychologist.

The obvious exception to autobiographical frankness is an announced self-censorship. Hall tells us that he resolved recurring doubts about whether to publish by "compromising finally on the elimination of the one most intimate and confessional chapter."[77] Perhaps this was the chapter that recorded the results of a psychoanalysis, but that is only a guess. There are a few other points in the text that mark explicit omissions. When he begins to recall his first adult loves for women in Germany, he pulls back:

"I still have two faded photographs and certain memories which have prompted much thinking along lines too taboo to indicate here."[78] Hall in fact includes only perfectly general remarks about the power of Eros in human life, which "can become in the end all the stronger and deeper for having had its initial fling in the earlier years of nubility when its physical urge is nearest its apex, especially if it is followed by years of chaste sublimation." This is frankness?

Hall lists as one of the causes for a lack of progress in psychology "a prudish reluctance to face the momentous problems of sex life."[79] But he writes later about breaking off a university course in sex education: "it was difficult to exclude those I deemed unfit since too many outsiders got in," then "two or three of my students developed an interest in the subject that I deemed hardly less than morbid."[80] Quitting the course was not all altruism. Though he had deliberately excluded all women from the class, Hall found it "most unexpectedly hard" to speak about perversions "as represented by Tarnowski, Krafft-Ebbing [sic], Havelock Ellis, etc." Even the all-male space of the scientific classroom cannot be cleansed from the dangers of morbid interest or the inhibitions on plain speaking. The "prudish reluctance" he decries is his own, and it remains "unexpectedly hard" to overcome after decades of scientific study. Hall's impulse to censor extended to public life. He served as an officer for the New England Watch and Ward Society, a local successor to the societies for the suppression of vice. Among the works that the society sought to suppress was Whitman's *Leaves of Grass*. Hall remarks of his expert service to the society only that it "greatly deepened" the horror at "the possibilities of precocious evil" first developed at a debauched school he attended during boyhood.[81] We are sent further back into the psychologist's youth.

Earlier in *Life and Confessions*, Hall includes a single, carefully marked passage on his "*vita sexualis*"—he must say it in the clinic's concealing Latin.[82] He accedes to the imagined demand that a "man of science," especially a psychologist, must "write frankly" about sexual development, "painful though it be." The resulting account follows no clear plan. Its surface organization is not evidently chronological or topical. Underneath, familiar themes are arranged according to a slightly expanded three-part scheme of the kind already noticed in *Adolescence*. There is behavior excused by physiology, behavior reproved as common vice, and behavior both condemned and silenced as perversion. So the passage begins by talking about his childhood ignorance and the terrifying parental myths that seemed to reinforce it. This ignorance leads to a long fear about nocturnal erections or emissions. Hall "rigged an apparatus and applied bandages" to himself in order to prevent erections.

The passage slips imperceptibly from nocturnal emissions to some form of self-excitation. "If I yielded to any kind of temptation to experimentation upon myself I suffered intense remorse and fear." The fear sometimes expresses itself as an anxiety that he is abnormal. Hall wastes a valuable dollar on a physician in a neighboring town who laughs and then warns him against the consequences of unchastity. "It was ineffable relief, therefore, to learn, as I did only far too late, that my life in this sphere had, on the whole, been in no sense abnormal or even exceptional." Scientific enlightenment brings freedom from groundless fear.

Then the third term of the rhetorical scheme—still mostly by citation: "homosexuality, exhibitionism, *fellatio*, onanism, relations with animals, and almost every form of perversion described by Tarnowski, Krafft-Ebbing [*sic*] or Havelock Ellis, existed in [my] school." The specialists serve as modest euphemisms for cases that cannot properly be described. "There was every kind of obscene word, tale, and cut, and things utterly indescribable—and I hope and believe incredible—were done." When a much older boy attempts to induce and then to force Hall "to do an indecent thing," he refuses—and his father later beats the soliciting boy. That boy had been corrupted earlier by another, a brilliant older student who "initiated him into every manner of lewdness." The gross suggestions were passed on in turn to the children from two families, "more or less degenerate, as, indeed, the subsequent career of [their] members indicated." If the main corrupter was somehow able in later years to produce satisfactory daughters, most of those who joined in the school's iniquity proved unable to raise families. Their degeneration declared itself in procreative failure.

Hall's "painful" passage on *vita sexualis* is shot through with mentions of religion. His father's myths about disease are confused in childhood with the preacher's insistence on the "unforgivable sin." (That sin is named in Mark 3:29 and Matthew 12:31–32 as blasphemy against the Holy Spirit—another sin of indefinite content. Hall's minister may have meant almost anything by the phrase.) After each illicit "experimentation," Hall resorts to "secret and most fervent prayer." It is ineffective. Guilt over impurity was "the chief factor that brought about my 'conversion' in my sophomore year [of college]." But if the new convert struggles more vigorously to maintain purity, he has no more success. "I fear the good Lord on whom I was told, and tried, to cast my burden did not help me much here. Indeed, perhaps in transferring and committing all to Him I trusted my own power less." Prayer about some sexual acts, far from curtailing them, spurs them on.

At the debauched school, he was too young to be corrupted in act, only in mind. Later on, his fear of spreading or revealing sexual abnormality kept him away from women, though his mind was knotted by fears of his own depravity. It was only in Germany—far from dreary Puritan Sundays, enforced sobriety, his mother's expectations, the sordid schools of his youth—that Hall was able to learn about erotic love. Only after those lessons could he return to consummate a properly American wedding and to father healthy children. Yet Hall seems to have been saved from sexual abnormality not by religion, nor by scientific education, but by the isolation of his sexually mature body from pernicious acts. He was kept from degenerate action until he could reach the more benign space of Germany. "Germany almost remade me, especially the first triennium there [1868–71, when he was twenty-three to twenty-six]."[83] Germany was his (delayed) adolescence. Hall is deliberately vague in his chronology, refusing to assign particular events to one or another of his visits. Even if all of these breakthroughs came early during his first visit, he would have been near or beyond the end of the official "ephebic" decade. Reading the *Life* against the treatise makes adolescence curiously mobile and metaphorical. It is no longer under the sway of fixed "biotic law."

In retrospect, Hall's narrative must also appear uncannily like many homosexual biographies—and not only because it tells of a delayed adolescence. It is a story of a late sexual awakening in a foreign land, after a decade of lonely self-loathing. The pattern of Hall's own life, which he certifies as normal, has since become the pattern for a certain sort of lesbian or gay awakening. Take that as a reminder about the mobility of rhetorical patterns. Take it also as showing a difference between the character shown in the *Life* and the character required by the official theory of *Adolescence*, for all the cross-citations that link the two books. The protagonist of Hall's memoirs is evidently not susceptible during his adolescence to erotic entanglements or religious conversion. He is driven rather by a desire for heterodox knowledge and a fear that it might disclose his own abnormality. The doctrine of adolescent conversion is an attempt to spare others what he himself lived through—to standardize the stages of development and to reduce its hazards. But Hall's life suggests what reserves of distance—what capacities for resistance—the adolescent can command.

GROWING UP OTHERWISE

By the time Hall published *Adolescence*, and even more by the time he wrote his final memoirs, degenerate youth was beginning to speak for itself. Some accounts of adolescence from the early decades of the twentieth century show what it was like to find, under the regime of the new psychology, alternate ways of speaking about youth, religion, and sex.

Among the most interesting is an early novel. I read it as a supplement and rejoinder to Hall's *Adolescence*, but also as a double to his *Life*. The novel shows more fully than my suggestions could how uncannily the shape in which Hall tells his life came to be used to reinforce an opposite lesson—to reach a rather different end. As more inverted adolescences are narrated, the pattern of Hall's own narratives comes to seem more and more mobile. If Hall's own life violates the normative chronology of his science, his life story begins to complicate or evade the morals it is meant to confirm.

Better Angel was originally published in 1934 under the name "Richard Meeker."[84] Its author was Forman Brown, then thirty-three, who was already famous as the founder of a puppet theater in Los Angeles that attracted numerous celebrities. The novel retells an adolescence that overlaps at many points with its pseudonymous author's biography. Indeed, Brown would later identify many of the book's principal characters with figures from his childhood and adolescence. Its protagonist, like Brown, is raised in central Michigan in the first two decades of the century. Kurt Gray (note the punning surname) has a boyhood marked by solitude, bookish seriousness, gender dislocation, and religion. He dislikes sports and delights in staging plays (especially when he can perform a princess). Then Kurt undergoes a perplexing Christian conversion. It turns, by the end of high school, into a faith in music and poetry. Kurt attends the University of Michigan, where he begins a sexual relationship with another young man and perfects his aesthetic philosophy. Then to a scholarship in France and the artsy circles of Manhattan.

The pattern of Gray's life—of Brown's own—will become standard for a certain class of American male homosexual. Indeed, it will become something like the standard myth: escape from the religious and sexual oppression of a small town through (self-)education to an art-filled and sexually gratifying cosmopolitanism. But the novel also represents, on closer inspection, the rhetorical challenge of constructing a homoerotic character from material to hand in an expertly homophobic culture, from within silently condemning churches. Growing up within what Hall describes as corruption and degeneration is an active improvisation, a sustained rhetorical composition. Far from being a genetically fated slide into loosening sterility, it can be the strenuous construction of an alternate genealogy, of another reproduction, with its worries for a genealogical past and even a quasi-racial future. Degenerates, it turns out, also found sciences and write exemplary memoirs.

In *Better Angel*, Kurt Gray's education requires that he match words to his disconcerting sentiments and initially shameful acts. Education is naming and narration. Kurt is set apart from his companions by "the love of beauty and the sensitiveness" received from his mother.[85] He also feels set apart by the early discovery of masturbation. (Here and in the following I translate the novel's euphemisms into more familiar speech—though not without noting that euphemism both conceals and constructs. It is characteristic of this novel and of Kurt's desire that they replace blunt descriptions of acts with evocations of sensation and emotion.) The reaction to this secret discovery is a shame without evident origin. "He felt, though he had never been told, that what he did was wrong."[86] The puzzle of not being fully a boy combines with the secret sexual discoveries to drive Kurt in search of words.

Kurt hears apparently pertinent words from many different sources. Early on his mother sets him to memorizing Bible stories. His father buys him books so that he can learn through them, if not from life, what it is to be a boy. There are the taunts of schoolboys who call him "sissy." A mystery read at age eight makes him afraid of the dark, while stories of the miraculous inspire his theatricals. At a certain point the passive reception of stories becomes an active search for words about his erotic desires. First he tries the encyclopedia. Then he rereads biblical passages "that suggested hidden knowledge: Leviticus, the story of Onan, the affairs of David, of Sodom, of Lot, the Song of Solomon."[87] This scriptural reading excites him: he is drawn to his mother's room, where he masturbates for the first time to the point of ejaculation. Kurt's hunt for words that contain "hidden knowledge"—that will decipher the hidden knowledge that expresses itself in his body—leads to actions that demand more words.

The words around Kurt fall roughly into three classes. There are expert or mock-expert sciences about sex. Kurt sends away for a brochure on a patent medicine that will cure him of the secret vice.[88] He anguishes over nocturnal emissions until a friend reports from a doctor that they are natural. In short, Kurt encounters the new science of adolescent sex more or less as Hall represents it. He is growing up in the shadow of *Adolescence*. But there is a counterdiscourse as well, not so much scientific as historical and literary. Childhood reveries about pirates and princesses are somehow confirmed by Greek myths about Hercules and Hylas. The dire medical warnings meet a sort of response in what the Greeks called *musikê*, in the Muses' arts. Homosexuality revivifies our original cultural contest between pagan and Christian.

Into this contest between scientific and artistic words comes a third rhetoric, a church revival. By contrast to the bland, wandering Methodist services to which Kurt was accustomed, the revival preaching is fiery and quite pointed (if not quite candid) about sex. At a special Sunday afternoon session for fathers and their sons, the revivalist launches into a condemnation of "one of the blackest sins in the world," "a sin some of you boys are guilty of." The preaching tells the horrible medical and spiritual effects of this sin on boys who do not repent. Afterward, Kurt's father ratifies the lesson: "Playing with yourself is bad business. I'm glad you're a clean boy."[89] The effect is powerfully incriminating. It leads to Kurt's public conversion. At the culminating service of the revival, a surge of emotion carries him to the front of the church where he, like Hall before him, stands up for Jesus. The conversion leads to renewed efforts to stop masturbating, though it cannot curb nocturnal emissions. Kurt places all his hopes on the church for salvation—especially from his sexual pollution. As with Hall, again, the confidence in the efficacy of this salvation ebbs quickly enough—and then it changes over into a doubt that any salvation is needed. There will be spasms of religious guilt later on, especially after Kurt begins his male-male relations. But the religion of the revival would quickly enough be surpassed by a new religion, an aesthetic religion.

For Kurt, the decisive stage in the search for words to narrate his bodily experiments comes in and after college at Ann Arbor. Aged nineteen, he discovers the poetry of Swinburne, which comes to him "as a revelation."[90] His new love, enacted erotically, finds its words in archaesthetic verse— though it means nothing to his actual lover. Then, in the summer after graduation, Kurt discovers the "new psychology"—not Hall, but precisely the authors Hall relegated to footnotes in *Adolescence*: "Brill, Jung, Freud, Ellis."[91] He finds, in other words, psychologists who describe the persistence and the prevalence of homosexuality even if they still diagnose it or pity it. To these, Kurt adds the socialist edifications of Edward Carpenter, a successor as public advocate to Ellis's collaborator, Symonds. *Love's Coming of Age* and *The Intermediate Sex* by Carpenter provide cultural-psychological justifications for the religious importance of same-sex love. They offer a historical vindication and literary frame for it. In Carpenter, Kurt could have read not only of the large number of prominent Intermediates or Uranians, but of their altruistic roles in the arts, in education, and as missionaries of love. Some of Carpenter's themes would have been confirmed by the texts and the examples of Wedekind, another of Kurt's discoveries. Kurt most probably was reading Wedekind's *Spring Awakening*. Its New York production closed after one night in 1917 on charges of obscenity. In its melodramatic gallery of adolescent sexuality, the happiest couple looks to be two young men who finally declare their love for each other. Through the new psychology, Kurt is led to discover not only an alternate science or history, but a specifically homoerotic canon of literature. He can read Plato's *Phaedrus* and *Symposium* with open eyes. Soon enough, he is savoring Oscar Wilde. Such reading provides authoritative comforts, but it also reinforces estrangement. All its authors are European. So too is the life it depicts. To become part of the homosexual world means leaving America.

It certainly requires abandoning the assurances of Main Street American Christianity. The discovery, the revelation of these discourses leads Kurt eventually to a revised religion. Back from conservatory for a first Christmas home, Kurt sees that the church of his childhood might be at best a sort of neighborhood club. But he also judges himself of a superior spirituality, the spirituality of art. He remembers his composition teacher remarking of a poet that he was "*un homme spirituel*," that he was "spiritual." Kurt reflects: "That was the thing, '*spirituel*.' The English never had created so exact a word for it; though many of them, he suspected, possessed the quality to a higher degree than the French."[92]

We Americans now do speak routinely of spirituality, but then we are the heirs of readers like Kurt and of the library he read. Some of us might even find both familiar and interesting the novel's vision of a sort of queer cathedral, "dim with incense, trembling with music."[93] In this temple of spirituality, homoerotic desire assumes priestly functions. The book's title suggests another scriptural figure for these intermediaries: they are ministering angels. Against all of society's accusations of debauchery, this angelic choir stands immune, innocent. Of course, the envisioned choir is soon enough contrasted with the "great and terribly secret society" of debauched, cosmopolitan homosexuality.[94] Here again, both the spiritual church and the corrupting secret society are international—are specifically not American. If Hall was proud of having imported a new science and then establishing its laboratories, societies, and organs of communication in America, Kurt Gray feels that America is still mainly hostile territory and that the work of importation has been done here only in secret. So far as he can see, the visionary cathedral is not going to be built on a Michigan Main Street any time soon.

THE ELEMENTS OF OUR RHETORIC

Reading *Better Angel* against Hall's two books, each a mix of fact and fiction, each a register of rhetorical characters, contemporary Americans must be struck by how uncannily they anticipate many of our own speeches about adolescents, religion, and sex. A hundred years ago, the motifs of the ex-gay movement or Focus on the Family were already activated for rhetorical use. We have heard scientific emphasis on normal development, worries about destruction of the race through unchecked effeminacy, and scriptural lessons on Jesus as a man of iron. We have seen Hall deploy a three-fold pattern of praise and blame that uses science to correct some religious teachings on sex while redoubling others—indeed, while offering the services of scientific condemnation to religion in exchange for religion's role in managing adolescence scientifically. We have watched in Hall the rewriting of Jesus to prevailing science, and in Conant or Barton the wholesale invention of a normal biography for Jesus—a biography in which the resurrection is either omitted (Conant) or allegorized (Barton). It is not enough to reinterpret the Christian Bible. It must be rewritten for American men.

The resonances with contemporary debates are indeed uncanny. But it is important to notice that these familiar motifs were then connected differently than they are now. In Hall, for example, there is a strong claim by scientific expertise to describe and superintend adolescent normalcy in sex and religion. But this claim is certainly not tied to evangelical use of scripture. Again, we can hear in Hall, Conant, and Barton familiar remonstrances of "normal" masculinity against effeminacy. We may suspect that they mean more than they say—that the critique of sensitive, languid, melancholy youth is crude code for the critique of onanistic and inverted youth, for perverted youth. But the reticence to speak about it more specifically is significant. So too is the prominence of the allied attack on masturbation.

Continuities in Christian rhetoric of sexual condemnation are not found in the particular acts condemned so much as in the figures of blame or shame being deployed. When contemporary churches claim that certain acts have always been condemned, they fail to mention that they were earlier grouped in condemnation with changing sets of other acts under shifting descriptions that relied for rhetorical effect on silence or vagueness. Many of the rhetorical devices now deployed in religious polemic against homosexuality were used against inversion a hundred years ago—but they were then also applied to masturbation, nocturnal emissions, and a host of other sexual activities now counted innocent. Any study of sexual condemnation must notice not only the constant regrouping of the acts under attack, but the lack of specific connection between the details of the condemnations and the details of sexual performance. The connections among the condemnations are more important than their targets. The history of the rhetoric we are following is a history of alliances among general insults, not a history of evidence-based arguments against specific sexual acts. In this church rhetoric, the nouns move while the approving or disapproving adjectives keep their places.

The most significant difference between Hall's speech and our own has to do with silence. In *Better Angel*, Kurt Gray searches for words even to name his desires. Growing up today, in an American church or high school, he would not have to search far. The words are now spoken directly to him—loudly, insistently, with the authority of newer new science and what pretends to be the old time religion. What has happened?

2

FIRST REPORTS OF HIDDEN WORLDS

No rhetoric functions on an empty stage or with a single character. Rhetorics and the characters they project must always be taken in clusters, in the context of their oppositions and contrasts. I have been tracing some connections among characters in texts on either side of 1900 because those connections underwrite much church rhetoric that emerges a half century later. Some of the continuity is explicit: later church writers reach back to those earlier texts for help in talking about sex. Much of it is implicit—and, indeed, occluded. Later church authors want to use, but also to ignore what was said by their predecessors.

I approach the midcentury emergence of American church debates on same-sex desire through another set of textual oppositions and contrasts. The almost simultaneous publication of two texts, neither of them religious, begins to describe the rhetorical forces within which church rhetoric had to be elaborated around 1950. The first "Kinsey report," on male sexuality, appeared on January 5, 1948. Five days later, there came a novel by a still plausibly adolescent writer, twenty-two years old, already praised for his war fiction. He was Gore Vidal, and the new novel was called *The City and the Pillar*. Within two months, the Kinsey report sold more than two hundred thousand copies in bulky, unattractive hard cover. Vidal's novel was also selling well—where it could be sold. No major American newspaper would review it, and the *New York Times* would not accept advertising for it.[1] In its own way, even the Kinsey report faced various kinds of official silence—from the broadcast networks, but rather more from the pulpit. The rhetorical success of both books proves the eagerness of some reading publics for new speech in place of sexual silence.

SEXUAL OUTLETS

The impact of the first Kinsey report is part of American mythology about a sexual revolution—and for the majority's mythology, a much more significant part than Stonewall or other vindications of same-sex love. I pass over the mythology to concentrate on rhetorical effects that it tends to conceal. I begin by noticing that our cultural memory of the Kinsey report obscures precisely its language about homosexual acts. The report, after all, took pains to make a rhetorical proposal.

Cultural memory of Kinsey and male homosexuality fixes on numbers: the numbers of homosexuals reportedly discovered and the numbers on a scale remembered as a gauge for the degree or intensity of a man's homosexuality. Both memories are mistaken. In Kinsey's 1948 report, there are strictly speaking neither homosexuals nor homosexuality. There are only "overt sexual relations" or erotic "stimuli" that can be described as homosexual. "It would encourage clearer thinking on these matters if persons were not characterized as heterosexual or homosexual, but as individuals who have had certain amounts of heterosexual experience and certain amounts of homosexual experience."[2] The distinction is driven by the discovery—startling to Kinsey and his colleagues—of just how much homosexual experience registered in the interviews. Between adolescence and old age, the report concludes, more than a third of the male population has some homosexual contact to the point of orgasm. "This is more than one male in three of the persons that one may meet as he passes along a city street."[3] One may meet them on the street, but one doesn't greet them—at least, as men with such a sexual history. Elsewhere the report raises the total even higher: "a considerable portion of the population, perhaps the major portion of the male population, has at least some homosexual experience between adolescence and old age."[4] If so many men have homoerotic experiences, then the criterion for stigmatizing some men as "homosexual" must be statistical rather than essential. It can only be a question of how often or how exclusively you had certain experiences, not of what kind of entity you are.

The famous "Kinsey scale" does not then pretend to measure the degree of one's essential homosexuality. It is rather a rating scale "based on both psychologic reactions and overt experiences."[5] The scale would like to describe the balance between heterosexual and homosexual responses or actions over a life, but it focuses in fact on particular periods. Kinsey's refusal of the category of homosexual person not only shifts from essences to acts or responses, thus undoing the model of inward inversion, but from the long duration of an alleged metaphysics to shorter segments of lived time. It makes little sense to speak, favorably or unfavorably, of "real homosexuals." We encounter instead varying percentages of homosexual acts and responses that typically shift over a lifetime in response to social sanctions.

The first Kinsey report spins from its numbers an alternate story of adolescent development—one very different from Hall's. In "primitive" human societies, according to the report, there was "unrestrained pre-adolescent sex play" and the start of "regular sexual intercourse well before the onset of adolescence."[6] Homosexual activity found a place in this Edenic festival. "The homosexual [act or response] has been a significant part of human sexual activity ever since the dawn of history, primarily because it is an expression of capacities that are basic in the human animal."[7] Under conditions of "moral suppression," which the report judges to have been especially severe in America after 1850, the original pattern of human sex has changed, but not disappeared. In Kinsey's surveys, more than half of preadolescent boys engage in homosexual play, and most men who are going to have homosexual contacts have them by the age of eighteen. Later adolescence, far from being the period of remote preparation for adult sex, is the period of highest sexual activity.[8] It is only under the pressure of social disapproval that males in their late teens give up homosexual activity and "try to make the heterosexual adjustments which society demands."[9]

For G. Stanley Hall, the child of flourishing racial stock is an innocent who must be protected from degenerates, from leering school chums and their debauching parents. As the child enters adolescence, the risks increase because of puberty. The new adolescent is vulnerable because both passionate and pliable. A psychologically informed society will do what it can to shape pliability, to habituate passion, through education and religion. For Kinsey, the values in this narrative are reversed. Childhood innocence was once—for some, might still be—freedom *for* sexual exploration. Such happiness is followed by the risks of adolescence—only now the risks are chiefly external repression and false fixation. Social disapproval reinforces the appearance of an essential distinction between heterosexuals and homosexuals by driving certain adolescents into exclusively homosexual behavior. Caught in what may have been his first homosexual act, "the high school boy is likely to be expelled from school and, if it is in a small town, he is almost certain to be driven from the community."[10] Social mechanisms that are supposed to discover and punish the homosexual essence work in fact to create it.

Notice too what Kinsey's new narrative of adolescence omits. It does not associate homosexual behavior with degeneracy and the destruction of the race. On the contrary, it treats the desire for such behavior as naturally occurring and ineradicable. Kinsey's story does not equate homosexual activity with gender disorder or inversion. On the contrary, the report stresses that "there are a great many males who remain as masculine, and a great many females who remain as feminine, in their attitudes and their approaches in homosexual relations, as the males or females who have nothing but heterosexual relations."[11] This refusal raises questions about the model of effeminacy in Hall and the theorists of inversion, but it also undoes many earlier pleas for toleration on the basis of gender reversal. Kinsey's report on men would cast doubt not only on passages in Hall's *Adolescence*, but on the gender scheme of *Better Angel*.

Nor is Kinsey's account of adolescence psychoanalytic. The report criticizes psychoanalytic theories stridently. While he shares with American Freudianism the narrative pattern of polymorphous desires channeled by repression, Kinsey disagrees with the analysts on the time of the repression, its mechanisms, and its social value. For Kinsey, the decisive moment is not the resolution of the oedipal triangle; the main agent is not the nuclear family; and the social value is not justifiable as a tragic necessity. As Hall debunked the quacks who offered to cure nocturnal ejaculations, so Kinsey denies the reigning therapy of the American Freudians (if not quite so derisively). Scientific authority over adolescent permits—or requires—ongoing revisions of authority in the name of new science.

The 1948 report gives little support to the notion of a special role for religion in shaping adolescent sexuality. Adolescents are generally less plastic than supposed, and the role of religion in shaping their attitudes or acts is weak in comparison with other forces. There are correlations between religion and homosexual behavior, but they are unsurprising—and in part definitional. For groups of men of the same religious denomination and the same educational level, Kinsey found only modest statistical differences in rates of homosexual activity between "religiously active" and "religiously inactive groups."[12] A more interesting conclusion from the interviews is mentioned in passing. Silence about homosexuality in preaching or religious education means that many hear less about its sinfulness than about the evils of masturbation or premarital heterosexual intercourse. "It is not unusual to find even devoutly religious persons who become involved in the homosexual without any clear understanding of the church's attitude on the subject."[13] Kinsey here notes an old irony in Christian pastoral practice with regard to same-sex desires. The "nameless sin" of sodomy, so called after a misreading of Ephesians 5:3, could not safely be preached against or inquired after. Homilists, catechists, and confessors were sternly warned not to be candid in describing or investigating the sin. The silence raises ethical objections: how can an allegedly serious sin never be mentioned? But it also opens a certain space for private action in good conscience: how could I be blamed for doing what was never named in my hearing? The silence in preaching invites the silence that is the closet.

CHURCHMEN RESPOND

Reactions to the first Kinsey report were swift and numerous. There were quite justified complaints from the beginning about Kinsey's narrow sample, his statistical method, his biological bias, and his psychological naiveté.[14] Other objections were less justified—and some of the justified objections were insincere, perhaps especially in church circles. Some readers found truly objectionable not Kinsey's numbers, but his audacity in conducting detailed interviews about sexual behavior and then publishing the results. His sin was to bring sex into *public* speech. Seward Hiltner, who reviewed the first report for the national organization of Protestant denominations, divided early church reactions into three groups. One group, by far the largest, consisted of congregants and pastors who reflected general middle-class values in "react[ing] against facts being brought into the open."[15] The second group comprised (Protestant) theologians, many of them typed as liberal. "Most theologians simply put their heads in the sand and said nothing at all." The third group was the small cadre of clergy and their seminary professors actually trained in clinical settings. These "reacted against what they believed to be Kinsey's assumptions . . . and thus paid virtually no attention to the extraordinary data that Kinsey had collected." Three reasons for ignoring an awkward and immensely popular book.

It was not entirely ignored by church leaders. Anthologies including theologians were assembled almost immediately after the book's publication.[16] Responses in religious reviews tried on various answers. Some responded to the first report as if Kinsey had identified a lack of purpose or enthusiasm in Christian sexual education.[17] Others thought the task was simply to absorb Kinsey back into the established guilds of psychiatry and psychology, with their guards on speech.[18] These responses are moderate and precise in comparison with others that come later, especially after publication of the report on female sexuality in 1953. There are to be sure rhetorical differences between the two Kinsey reports. The second is more aggressive in its attacks on the enemies of candor and adult freedom. But these differences cannot explain the ferocity of the attacks unleashed after the second volume. They make sense only in relation to the ideology of female purity, that is, to the double standard of patriarchy. It was one thing for Kinsey to write about boys and men. Their grosser nature has its excuses—its privileges. It was something else entirely for Kinsey to besmirch the honor of the American Wife and Mother. Churches were quick to respond.

Consider the little book *I Accuse Kinsey*, written (or, rather, pasted together) by the Baptist radio evangelist E. J. Daniels. A colleague introduces him as "a Sir Gallahad for the Saviour of men."[19] Daniels certainly shows a zealous gallantry in defense of "the purity of womanhood." But then he fears a domino effect. "If our women go on the rocks morally, the men will surely go with them. We must defend the women to defend the men."[20] Daniels offers a scrapbook of quotations from religious, medical, literary, and patriotic leaders. The result is not elegant, but it is revealing. In Daniels, we glimpse devices that will be perfected in coming decades to discredit scientific research about sex whenever it contradicts church teaching. But we also see the devices that allow useful scientific evidence to be incorporated piecemeal, without having to contend with its contexts or implications. The defects of Daniels's text—its disorganization, its sweep, its shrillness—are a now familiar rhetorical strategy. The booklet is not meant to be read whole. It works better if you don't try to study it. It aims to pepper you in any handful of pages with disconnected facts and authorities that reiterate an urgent message. Sprayed facts cannot be studied, but they can repeat prophecy: I come to warn you of terrible danger to your family and your country. There is no time to reflect. There is only time to react.

Beneath the book's disorganization, there is a discernible persuasive pattern. Daniels begins by winning over readers to his earnest motives: He means no harm to Kinsey the man; he means only to warn of the pernicious doctrine. (Love the sinner, hate the sin.) Daniels assures his readers that he takes no pleasure in talking about the filth that fills Kinsey's book. He must do so, out of courage and divine conviction, because Kinsey is spreading malignant lies. (He started the fight—and the dirty talk.) Daniels promises to prove that they are lies. He does so in many ways: by quoting counterauthorities, by referring to a countersurvey of his own, and by attacking Kinsey's methods and statistical consistency. (We have real science too.) His rehearsal of a scientific corrective is combined with a certain suspicion of public discourse: great scientists have already disproved Kinsey's results, but no one knows this because the media let themselves be duped. (Liberal media conspire against us.) Most of all Daniels opposes to Kinsey the rising crescendo of outraged decency: what Kinsey describes cannot be normal, because no normal woman would talk about her sex life with strangers.[21] The facts are abnormal because the normal do not give evidence. (The moral majority has been bullied into silence.) When they allow Kinsey's calumnies to go unrefuted, Americans risk uncountable social consequences, including a flood of perverted sex, diluted sensibility of sin, enervated law enforcement, wrecked marriages, and a higher tax burden. The consequences Daniels enumerates fit perfectly with the stated anxieties of "conservative" readers. But they also generalize the debate so that one can turn away from the embarrassing and perhaps disruptive details of Kinsey's two books.

Trying to summarize the religious judgment on Kinsey, Daniels writes that the arrogant scientist's philosophy is "atheistic, materialistic, evolutionary, 'animalistic.'"[22] It is aligned with every other menacing ideology, with every portent of cultural decline. Many of these movements come from Europe, but they are threats now to America—and especially America's youth. The causality of the threat need not be established with any specificity because it is caught up in a larger narrative of national struggle. The grand narrative in Daniels resembles a religious plot of judgment and redemption, but it operates on the level of civil reasoning.

This doubling of voices in response to Kinsey is clearer in a short piece that Daniels inserts into his text as an unimpeachable authority. It is the text of a radio broadcast from Billy Graham's *Hour of Decision*.[23] Graham's message is divided more neatly than Daniels's scatter into social commentary and a call to repentance from sin. Whatever Kinsey says, "the Bible" has condemned sexual immorality unflinchingly and unchangingly for two thousand years. Its law pronounces dreadful condemnation from which the only escape—under which the only hope—is faith in Jesus Christ. This is the end of Graham's message. The beginning is a sociopolitical reply to Kinsey's second report that employs many of the devices also seen in Daniels. Graham denies the accuracy of Kinsey's sample. He contrasts the virtue of "born-again Christian women in this country" with the untypical, the unblushing women who confide their sexual secrets to Kinsey's interviewers, those "secret agents." At a moment when American discourse was spooked by Communist conspiracies, to call the interviewers "secret agents" makes them spies of a foreign power. It is not only Kinsey's sampling technique that is suspect, it is his patriotism.

Graham emphasizes the dangers that Kinsey poses to American youth. Kinsey wants to teach "our" young people "how to indulge in premarital relations and get away with it." He corrupts them and removes them from effective parental control. Once they sneak out to fornicate, he will corrupt their moral sense by suggesting that "what so many people are doing must not be wrong." Then he will introduce them to "terrifying perversions that they have never even heard of before." American adolescents, removed from parental surveillance and dazzled by pimping numbers, will fall prey to unnamable deviations of an incomprehensible allure. They might never have heard of them before, but they will fall for them on first hearing.

In Graham as in Daniels, the cultural risk posed by Kinsey is situated within a culture-spanning disintegration. Its springs from foreign soil. More coherently and learnedly than Daniels, Graham names Nietzsche, Freud, and Schleiermacher as authors of a triple corruption of the mind. Kinsey is their American successor—and perhaps dupe. Against this cultural collapse, Graham opposes the unchanging word of the Bible, which he quotes verse by decontextualized verse in the reassuringly archaic English of the King James Version. The Bible's immutability is demonstrated by its resonant language, familiar from childhood, and by its immediate applicability, without need of cultural translation. So much of the Bible's felt authority is the acoustic illusion of immutability. This always-present Bible speaks directly to and against Kinsey and his European tutors—as if it had known all along that they were coming to threaten American teenagers. The King James Version is the American mother tongue—the native speech of truly American mothers.

The juxtaposition of scientific counterargument, patriotic alarm, and the intuitive application of ancestral verses will characterize the "biblical" response to sexological research down to our present. But the negative response to Kinsey's second report took other forms—and came not just from evangelicals. Equally opposed were figures who had been at least moderately favorable to the first report or else kept silent about it.[24] These later reactions rewrote the early toleration of Kinsey's work, as if his research with women had revealed a secret suspected all along. If Kinsey could publish the second report, then the first report must be discreditable as well.

Consider a scathing review of the second report by Reinhold Niebuhr. Niebuhr was then widely regarded as one of the most important Protestant theologians in America. He had appeared on the twenty-fifth-anniversary cover of *Time*, which described him as one liberal Protestant who heard the voice God reserves for addressing prophets. Niebuhr's *Irony of American History* had just appeared. His magisterial *Nature and Destiny of Man*, adapted from wartime Gifford Lectures, lay a decade back. So much gravitas in a book reviewer. A final blow: the review of Kinsey appeared in *Christianity and Crisis*, the influential biweekly that Niebuhr helped edit.[25]

Niebuhr first professes a lack of surprise at Kinsey's findings, though he deplores the figures on adultery as "further evidence of the decay of the family." The problem is not with Kinsey's results, but with his presuppositions or presumptions. He reduces human beings to animals and then wants to abolish any restraints on their sexual activity: for "Kinsey's consistent naturalism and its logical fruit of a crude hedonism," "sexual pleasure becomes the *summum bonum*," the highest good. Hence Kinsey is incapable of judging the morality of his interview subjects: "he is not concerned with the fact that some of these cases may be pathetic men or women who are so obsessed with the sexual function and satisfaction that they have become incapable of any creative relationships." Kinsey is "[blind] to the central problem of man's sexual life," which is intimacy between persons.[26]

Niebuhr is equally severe in dismissing Kinsey's complaints against repressive sexual codes. Beyond social conditioning, beyond the relativities of the moral code, the "essentials" of ethical prohibition "[approach] universality" and arise within an individual as "the expression of his essential being against acts which he feels to be violations of his essence." To confuse this ethical essence with mere prudery is to miss everything. So, of course, Kinsey's treatment of religion is marred by stupid confusions. Yet his figures show, despite themselves, that "religion has an effect beyond and above specific requirements of moral law, upon conduct, particularly upon sexual conduct." Niebuhr suggests that preserving the ethical core is more important than punishing individual lapses, especially in the young. "Modern parents will generally be concerned to prevent an undue sense of guilt [over masturbation, especially among boys] rather than to accentuate that sense."[27] Other socially produced tensions may be addressed creatively. The long periods of education required in modern life, for example, can be assuaged by marrying while in college and having children early.

The conclusion of the piece is a three-paragraph peroration in which Niebuhr first suggests that the root problem with Kinsey is an overzealous application of scientific methods to the humanities. Kinsey is ignorant of basic problems in his presuppositions and value judgments because they do not fall within his dogmatic biologism. His clumsy attempts to critique sexual codes only reinforce them. Next Kinsey turns out not to be such a good scientist. Better scientists, such as serious psychiatrists, side with religious leaders against Kinsey. Then the final paragraph, in which Niebuhr poses a question to himself: Why complain of one man's mistaken presuppositions about sex when signs of "the decay of the stability of the modern family" are so evident around us? When children and "adolescent delinquents" suffer in different ways the multiplying consequences? Niebuhr replies to himself that Kinsey's popular success in the guise of sex scientist is as telling a sign of cultural decay as one could wish. He concludes: "A culture has to reach a pretty low level for such pretenses to be at all plausible."[28]

This is a master's invective—for which the model is not Juvenal, but the biblical books of Proverbs or Ecclesiastes. Niebuhr's essay characterizes Kinsey's comprehension with elegantly varied pejoratives: blindness is the recurring insult, but uncritical anarchism, vulgar hedonism, and crude physiological naturalism are added on top. The rhythm of adjectives becomes an accusatory refrain. The essay then impugns Kinsey's moral character, though rather more by implication: he is accused of tolerating "every type of sexual promiscuity" and of "rejoicing" over the decay of the family;

he allies himself (unwittingly?) with social menaces, "the unscrupulous male," and the Soviet destruction of family.[29]

The editors of *Christianity and Crisis* invited Seward Hiltner to write a reply to Niebuhr's piece. They chose him because of his reputation for work in psychosexuality, but also no doubt because he had been a qualified advocate of Kinsey in official Protestant circles. Hiltner replies timidly: perhaps Niebuhr has been unfair. Kinsey is sometimes betrayed by his devotion to science and his ignorance of anything outside it, but he is only concerned to abstract certain aspects of human behavior, not to describe the whole of it. Hiltner corrects Niebuhr's endorsement of Kinsey's findings about the importance of religion, but he ends with diffident requests for Niebhur to clarify his own, doubtless authoritative position on sexual ethics.

Niebuhr is not mollified. His reply to Hiltner is sharper than his original review.[30] Niebuhr announces that he sees no value at all in Kinsey's reports. Kinsey's work is "absurdly hedonistic," "ridiculous and ignorant." Niebuhr introduces more acerbic ad hominem attacks: "one must come to the conclusion that an apprenticeship in investigating gall wasps is not sufficient preparation for guiding mankind in a very complex problem." Even Niebuhr's "exasperation with Kinsey's ignorance" is made to prove his point. "An ignorant approach to a complex issue cannot be creative. It prevents rather than encourages a consideration of the real issues." The only response can be sarcasm.

Despite these excuses, the energy of Niebuhr's invective cannot be explained from his stated motives. If Kinsey is only an ignoramus who has blundered into a field about which he knows nothing, why bother with him? It must be because of his extraordinary popularity. But is the worry that Kinsey's popular success will dangerously miseducate people? Or that his statistics will give ammunition to the conservative legalists, who will call for a crackdown? Or does Niebuhr really fret that Kinsey will spoil the chances for more expert critique? That assumes that a properly theological or historical critique couldn't distinguish itself from Kinsey in its sources, scope, or implications. None of these motives is quite convincing. The actual motive for the polemical tone seems rather to be betrayed in the opening gesture, the refusal to be surprised. "We experts knew it all along—and more besides." Only the experts didn't say it loud if they said it at all—and never before the great reading public. Kinsey's sin is to have breached an expert silence. He published a reputable-looking book, complete with statistical tables, in which all the forbidden words appear right before your eyes.

Outrage over Kinsey's indiscretion links Niebuhr back to Graham. However much they differ on religious matters, in cultural position, by choice of style, the two authoritative responses to Kinsey resonate unexpectedly with each other—without sounding in unison. Graham denies the truth of Kinsey's generalizations in the second report by denigrating the normalcy and patriotism of the respondents. Niebuhr agrees at least that Kinsey failed in psychological and moral evaluation of those he interviewed. Graham worries that American youth will be led astray by news of unfamiliar and putatively widespread perversion. Niebuhr concurs at least in distinguishing the ethical core of sexual regulation from its neurotic excess in "an undue sense of guilt"—though he would not agree with Graham about where neurotic guilt begins. Finally, Graham contrasts the plain, unchanging (English) scripture with the flood of fancy foreign ideas. Niebuhr is much more the expert advocate of those ideas, but he is not above appealing to the "simple words of Jesus," especially when writing invective.

These resonances across such cultural and religious differences should make us wonder about the circulation of rhetorical arguments. One reading of this comparison would conclude that there is only a small number of Christian rhetorical devices for sex. They are combined or nuanced by diverse authors without substantially increasing their stock. Another reading of the comparison might look instead to the representation of dangers in the two authors. They agree, for example, that Kinsey's uncensored speech threatens the social orders of self, family, nation, by upending authoritative knowledge and its controls. The important thing on this reading would be how they elicit and direct fear. I suggest that no rhetorical comparison should omit a third level—for me, the most important. It is the projection of the character of the speaker through what I can only call the tones and gestures of the text.

The speaker's implied character not only wins trust and secures conviction, it provides the standard against which any other characters mentioned can be judged. In these two pieces, the most evident contrast of character is between the knowledgeable, concerned, responsible speaker and Kinsey, who is ignorant and irresponsible, whose indiscreet speech creates innumerable risks. But the speaker also stands in contrast to a number of other characters—to the abnormal or morally broken informants willing to talk to Kinsey, to faltering American parents, to imperiled youth. The character of the speaker persuades not just by argument or emotion, but by constant juxtaposition with every other character. After reading Graham or Niebuhr, you are expected to be willing to rely on them rather than on Kinsey, but also to desire to be like them—or at least like the characters that they commend. Becoming acquainted with the character of the author, you are introduced to a whole troupe of ideals.

The contrast of two fairly simple polemics shows the layers of rhetorical operation, but also challenges the tendency to read polemic only for argument or evidence or the manipulation of emotion. Even simple polemic is rhetorical in the deeper sense: it is about the making and staging of character, the elicitation of character. Elicitation occurs not only when characters are described, but when characters are performed by the authorial voice. All the more interesting then to discover similarities of voice and gesture between two authors who stand at opposite ends of churchly or cultural scales—or to notice that their performed characters share most of all an outrage over breached silence.

The silence evidently covered a secret. It was not a simple secret—some act or feeling kept hidden without leaving a trace on the surface. It was no open secret—something that everyone knows, but no one says. The silence that Graham and Niebuhr accuse Kinsey of breaching concealed a paternal secret—that is, a monstrous secret. The rhetorical characters enacted by Graham and Niebuhr, like stern fathers, admonish their readers not to look down that alley, not to go into that abandoned house, not to open that attic door. There are monsters there. (I, your father, am strong enough to meet them and lock them up. You are not.) This paternal authority extends indefinitely. There is no growing beyond it. The religious expert is always father—and a better father than your unaccredited begetter. These expert characters claim an enduring paternity. But there are so many fathers presiding over the secrets of sex.

THE PASTORAL USES OF (AMERICAN) PSYCHOANALYSIS

Karl Menninger seeks to explain the change of attitude about Kinsey in an article for *Saturday Review* that was widely noted and reprinted.[31] For Menninger, Kinsey's figures only show what Freud and his followers had long known. Because Kinsey suffers from a "hysterical antipathy" to psychiatry, he refuses to recognize this priority or to accept correction from psychiatric specialists. Many psychiatrists were originally sympathetic to Kinsey's efforts to speak frankly and tried to help him by correcting his mistakes. But Kinsey, like some brash adolescent, refused their help. So now psychiatrists join with religious figures in condemning the two reports' premises and conclusions—including their efforts to normalize homosexuality. Many of the early reactions to Kinsey from progressive church authors claim or suppose just such a strategic alliance between theology and psychoanalysis on homosexuality, whatever their other disagreements. The alliance may have appeared more desirable for church authors than for analysts. But the analysts had their own war with Kinsey.

The reports become an occasion for hardening psychoanalytic claims about homosexuality and its treatment. A telling example of the analytic reaffirmation is Edmund Bergler's *Homosexuality: Disease or Way of Life?*[32] Discussed in journals of pastoral counseling, Bergler still survives in many seminary libraries—not to say, in the citations of the contemporary ex-gay movement and its scientific authorities.

According to Bergler, Kinsey had not only produced "wildly exaggerated" statistics, he had armed homosexual predators with a new means of seduction. Bergler posits as a new diagnosis "the tragic and pitiful spectacle of the '*statistically induced homosexual.*'"[33] Reading Kinsey—or listening to an old queen lisping his bogus numbers—can turn you queer. Follow these errors far enough and you will begin to think of yourself as a member of a *minority* that deserves some legal or political recognition. What is of more direct concern to Bergler, these numbers arm patients against effective treatment. He quotes a patient's appeal to Kinsey—and his own reply, with its acid analytic orthodoxy.[34] Kinsey's fantasies about sex can be corrected simply by distinguishing early adolescent sexual exploration from real homosexuality.[35] They are easy for analysts to correct, but quite powerful in popular influence. Hence the importance of devoting an entire chapter to refuting Kinsey's amateurish attempts to treat heterosexuality and homosexuality as alternatives.

Bergler ignores on every page Kinsey's linguistic proposal about homosexual responses and acts. For Bergler, "homosexual" is most definitely a noun, the name of a distinct pathological type. To eliminate any confusion, Bergler even dismisses the possibility of bisexuality: the bisexual does not exist except "as a flattering description of the homosexual who is at times capable of mechanical heterosexual activity."[36] The psychoanalytic habit of personifying symptoms has a complex genealogy. It reaches far beyond Bergler into many other sources—passages in Freud, but also the diagnostic history of the clinic. Still Bergler's vivid personification of the homosexual and his emphasis on the way in which homosexuality distorts the whole personality are also part of popular schemes for sexual characters. The inability of so many readers of Kinsey even to hear the point that there are no homosexuals, only homosexual responses or acts, shows that characters are indispensable to any rhetorically charged stigmatization of sexual acts. It is rhetorically impossible to stigmatize statistically tabulated responses. You have to consolidate responses into characters before you can mock them, blame them, or warn against them. Bergler's attacks on *the* homosexual show something about the history of medico-legal constructions of perversion, but they also and perhaps more immediately concede a rhetorical necessity.

For Bergler, the homosexual can be identified by ten negative traits.[37] He demonstrates these traits by quoting from analytic sessions—if, indeed, these are excerpts from transcripts rather than amateur fiction. All the exchanges show Bergler, the scientifically armed champion of healthy adulthood, in close verbal combat with invariably unpleasant homosexuals. They love to lie, to manipulate, to deceive. When they are caught out, they instantly take offense or wallow in self-pity. No matter their ages, they are all frozen in a petulant adolescence. With a teenager's self-absorption, they ruin themselves and their families, undoing their mothers with grief and their fathers through their mothers. Bergler does his best to speak vanquishing words to these masked changelings, but many are too far gone to be cured. The only hope is to spread the news of cure while training a nationwide cadre of therapists to help those who still want to make an effort. The rest, the resistant, must be left to thrash about in self-inflicted misery.

Bergler backs this program of mass analysis with social warnings. "Without being an alarmist, or sounding the alarm" (by which he sounds it), Bergler names homosexuality "a serious social problem" in "urgent need" of public education.[38] The problem causes much private grief, but it also distorts public life. There is an "invisible influence" of homosexuals in many professions.[39] Not only fashion designers and hair stylists, but novelists, playwrights, and screenwriters are consciously or unconsciously inflicting their homosexuality on an unsuspecting public. Normal reviewers who know authors' secrets must find ways to alert the unsuspecting public. There is no hope for homosexual reviewers. They will toe the party line. "Homosexuals, though overflowing with malice toward one another, form a solid and unbroken front when it becomes necessary to defend or promote one of themselves. The reputation of many a writer, especially in France, has been constructed in this way."[40] It is not only Kinsey who perverts his readers: Proust and Gide are guilty too. For Bergler, as for many of the Christian clergy, bad reading poses real dangers. If you can be perverted by Kinsey's statistics, how much more by trendy novels promoted through Gallic conspiracies?

Remember that these clichéd slanders are being pronounced in the tones of medical authority, by the rhetorical figure of the physician of psyches. The authority justifies its own cruelty, its punishing control over the bodies entrusted or remanded to it, in the name of individual health and social utility. Bergler's voice enjoins the reader—and especially soft-hearted mothers of homosexual sons—to become like the analyst in severity. He appeals to the sadism of orthodoxy. Or he offers a share in the sovereign power over bodies entrusted to him by the state. The power is never crueler than when it is exercised on the bodies of the young. In those moments, it also feels most righteous.

SEX AFTER CHRISTIANITY

Five days after the publication of Kinsey's first report, Gore Vidal published his third novel, *The City and the Pillar*. As Vidal tells the story, publishing it meant abandoning a political career and entering a sort of internal exile— six years during which major reviewers refused to recognize his work.[41] What made the novel so threatening? In part it was having a famous young war novelist almost "come out," as people would learn to say twenty years later. In part it was the novel's depiction of homosexuality as something natural—though not necessarily happy. But the shock of the novel, like the shock of Kinsey's numbers, is the discovery of a network of homosexual acts and desires spread through every layer of the "normal" world—sportsmen, sailors, soldiers. The network is discovered through that most masculine of activities, a worldwide war. It dissolves inhibitions, but it also discloses homosexuals to each other: "the war has caused a great revelation."[42] The novel is another report of disconcerting news. You think you know he-men, it whispers. You don't know them at all. "Sometimes it seemed as if the surface of the world was a fragile porcelain affair easily shattered, and that beneath the surface the real, the strange life of people went on."

The reader gets a glimpse beneath by following the young protagonist. Jim has a single sexual encounter with his high school friend, Bob, before the latter leaves for life at sea. A year later, having just graduated, Jim takes off to find him. He is driven by Bob's memory, which prevents him from desiring women or giving his heart to other men. (The power of the original, teen lover is a frequent piety in early gay novels: a first sexual experience in adolescence, no matter how violent, is magically decisive, but also unrepeatable. Homosexual desire is the failed repetition of an adolescent original.) Jim's pursuit of the indelible memory-image takes him through many homosexual "worlds." He becomes entangled with a Hollywood movie star, a masochistic novelist, a fellow army recruit, Manhattan art collectors, and anonymous patrons of innumerable bars. Pursuit ends when Jim and Bob meet again in New York—just as Bob is trying to decide whether to abandon the sea for his wife back home. The two retire to Bob's hotel room. As they finish the night's drinking, Jim finds out that Bob, the pursued-image, has never had sex with another man. At first Jim disavows his recent past in homosexual circles. When imperious instinct leads him to reach out across the shared bed in the dark room, Bob recognizes him as "a damned queer" and orders him to leave.[43] In the novel's

1948 version, Jim strangles Bob.[44] He then wanders off to a bar where he baits, then insults another queer man. The book ends with Bob confusedly plotting to escape the city by ship, registering the end of "the dream," "the legend" of his unique passion for Bob.[45]

Vidal's title is biblical. Its city is burning Sodom; the pillar is Lot's wife, who is changed into salt when she disobeys the command not to glance back at the divine destruction her family flees (Genesis 19:17–26). Over a millennium the story of Sodom was made into the expansive warrant for Christian condemnations of same-sex desire. The fantasy of Christian theologians extracted from it not only the medieval category of sodomy, but the lesson that tolerating sodomites would bring natural disasters and civic destruction on any city foolish enough to risk it. The image of a figure unable to flee, frozen eternally by a backward glance, applies in several ways to the novel's depiction of homosexuality. Yet the biblical reference seems curiously out of place. One thing Vidal's novel does not treat is religion.

Neither Jim nor Bob seems to have received a religious upbringing. Neither mentions religious judgments on same-sex desire. The only theological thought attributed to Jim is his disbelief in a heaven or hell; "both places seemed rather silly and somehow pretentious."[46] He already inhabits a world after Christianity. Other figures in the novel are not quite so cleanly removed from it. The melancholy writer, Paul Sullivan, is a former Catholic. In adolescence, he prayed to God to free him from homoerotic desire. When God failed, he performed a Black Mass in hopes of better results with the devil. Getting no response, Sullivan "discarded all religion."[47] Rolly, the sybaritic art collector, converts temporarily to Catholicism for its delicious liturgies, but after a few disappointments shifts his aspirations to Vedanta. In this novel, Catholicism is crushing guilt or optional accessory, and there is no Christianity but Catholicism.

The novel's only references to religion as a numinous force are pagan. Jim and Paul travel to Yucatán with Paul's friend, Maria (whose name should be noted). There Paul cultivates his misery by staging an affair between the other two. For the culminating scene, they enter the Mayan precincts of Chichén Itzá after nightfall. Beside the ruined city, in it, Maria becomes "the Death Goddess." She and Jim stop suddenly, as if magically, to sit on "a giant carving of a plumed serpent."[48] Among the pagan dead, they share a moment's lucidity and a kiss. (The affair is never consummated; Jim cannot perform.) The only divine power in this novel is exotic, ancient, and deadly. Perhaps it is also misogynistic: the woman who comes closest to initiating Jim must be figured as death. She confesses that the only god she can conceive as existing is "vindictive."[49]

The absence of any domestic religion in Vidal's novel may be connected to its elision of childhood and adolescence. For Vidal here, as for many gay narratives, Christianity's force lies in the past, in its oppression of childhood and early adolescence. But those periods appear in the novel only through flashback, only retrospectively, and then together. Vidal begins at the end of high school, at a moment of freedom from the parental home and the original community. Paul's Black Mass is a quick summary of an abandoned past. Jim's own childhood appears only in a moment of self-analysis, as a sort of diagnostic recall. The repudiation of childhood and adolescence goes along with the absence of histories, personal or collective, in the homosexual worlds through which Jim travels. You enter the secret world by trying to cut yourself off from family and home (except perhaps so far as you need to retain an inheritance). If your desire for a particular male image was burned into you back there, all you carry forward is the livid brand as present desire. You drop other memories. Your new world has only the archive of gossip. There are no written records and no need for historical authorization. "New Sodom" has its own language, its "expressions," which can be learned only from native speakers.[50]

Or from this novel—which is part of its audacity. A number of code-terms are documented and explained: queer, gay, fag, fairy, pansy, queen. Despite Vidal's later scruples, and against Kinsey, "homosexual" is used as both an adjective and a noun. "Normal" typically means heterosexual, as it does in outsiders' speech, but "nature" or "natural" can refer to being either straight or gay. To be homosexual is natural for some, and it is against their nature to attempt to be heterosexual. The clinical terms are entirely appropriate. They figure in the inner and outer dialogue of the novel's characters as part of a larger importation of psychological and psychiatric terminology. The reader hears of "neurotics" and "latents," of the grand theory and interminable practice of psychoanalysis. The novel also flirts with psychological explanations for the origin of homosexuality. Paul Sullivan sketches a typical adolescence in which an original feeling of difference passes through sexual experimentation to fixation in one of a "dozen types."[51] To "know more of himself and of others like himself," Jim reflects on the psychodynamics of his family and his adolescent fantasies.[52] Elsewhere he scrutinizes his dreams. He frequently conceives of Bob as his twin, brother, or mirror image—all images susceptible of analysis into narcissism.

The mirror implies a face to be seen—but perhaps only in a private space. However wide the network of dreamlike desires, heterosexual conventions require that it remain hidden. There may be "a well-organized homosexual world" in places like New York; its borders may even offer a "half-world where normal and homosexual people" mingle with some candor.[53] But in most places, queer desire must play a game, go constantly in disguise, wear a mask, perform a masquerade, tell necessary lies. Homosexuals find themselves living in the midst of their enemies, as if in an endless, worldwide war. The only escape from this hostile territory is to be cured of haunting memory-desires by falling in love more conventionally. Sullivan urges Jim toward an affair with Maria: "She could rescue you from this world." As soon as Jim admits that he may not want to be rescued, he recognizes himself "as a member of the submerged world of the homosexual."[54] He cannot, in any case, love Maria in the way required. He will continue to live underwater while enemies control the surface.

However much it insists on a submerged world hidden from sight, approachable only through special gateways, Vidal's novel speaks the secrets of that world plainly—for anyone who can find his book. If there are interesting parallels between Kinsey and Vidal on the neglect of religion or the importance of adolescent experimentation, their most striking agreement is in being able to talk publicly about what has not yet been spoken.

WITH KINSEY, AGAINST VIDAL

Not everyone swimming in the submerged world was grateful for reports about it in an accessible novel or statistical tables. One prominent homosexual writer attacks both Kinsey and Vidal on medical and moral grounds. "Donald Webster Cory" was the pseudonym of Edward Sagarin, who would later and in his own name espouse reactionary views of same-sex attraction. In 1951, when he published *The Homosexual in America*, Cory appeared much more liberal—if still in need of the pseudonym. In the preface, he justifies its use: "I am convinced that, in the present cultural milieu in the United States, the pseudonymous or anonymous writer can be more outspoken than one who is willing to place a signature on a subjective analysis of homosexuality."[55] The sentence gives much more than the justification. It tells us that the book will be a "subjective analysis," that is, a supplement to the "objective" analyses that frame it. The subjective recital often bows and sometimes cringes before the presumptively objective, positivist sciences of sociology and psychology, of psychiatry and jurisprudence. It requires a preface by Dr. Albert Ellis, whose words and name place the book in the genealogy of scientific sexology. Only after such a preface can Cory present himself as a talking specimen.[56]

The specimen talks at length about Kinsey. Cory praises Kinsey's method and reiterates the extraordinary effect of the first report on the American public. But he thinks that Kinsey's terminology and scale are both mistaken. Cory acknowledges that Kinsey is describing only acts, not individuals, but then falls back into his own habit of speaking about individuals. "The homosexual" in Cory's title and text refers to a kind of person. "I would call any person a homosexual who feels a most urgent sexual desire which is in the main directed toward gratification with the same sex."[57] Cory stresses the difference between his definition and Kinsey's measurement of acts, but he does not dwell on the definition's limits. The definition not only suffers from vague conditional phrases ("most urgent," "in the main"), it insists on conscious, felt desire, apparently ruling out many cases of deep denial. Indeed, Cory proposes to replace Kinsey's scale with a distinction between "compulsive" and "facultative" homosexual. The compulsive homosexual experiences "an urgent drive, or a compulsion, for this type of gratification." By contrast, the facultative homosexual can take or leave same-sex activities and for that very reason "should probably not be termed a homosexual of any kind or type."[58]

The most important conclusion for Cory is that homosexuals constitute "a minority involving millions of people in the United States."[59] The repression of such a minority is a pressing social problem. It cannot be addressed by trusting in cures. Cory does present a (modified) Freudian list of the causes of "homosexualism": unbalanced family dynamics, often aided by "faulty sexual education," "predisposition to effeminacy," and adolescent success in same-sex "pursuits."[60] But Cory calculates, rather archly, that the country couldn't possibly produce enough psychoanalysts to cure all the homosexuals. So Cory's advice to parents is the opposite of Bergler's: no minister's preaching or prayer will cure these tendencies, and any reputable psychologist or psychoanalyst will only encourage adjustment.

Cory's interspersed anecdotes of homosexual characters further reveal a large, secret world of homosexuals. It is a world characterized above all by "pretense and the mask." Looking out through the mask determines attitudes toward all "phases of life," including religion. Some homosexuals embrace religion as a consolation. Others reject it because it has rejected them. If homosexuality is not antireligious, Cory explains, religion is certainly antihomosexual. Cory means by religion both Judaism and Christianity—Christianity as the inheritor of Judaism. What unites homosexuals in their response to religion? "Only . . . that their homosexuality is the chief factor in fashioning their attitudes toward this aspect of our culture."[61] Religious or irreligious, the homosexual's engagement with religion is fundamentally homosexual.

So much for Kinsey. Corey judges *The City and the Pillar* a "disappointing failure not at all comparable to [Vidal's] other work."[62] The novel may accurately represent a certain phase of homosexual life, but it offers no solution to the homosexual situation—except violence and despair. It dwells on promiscuous sex with married men and cheapens the notion of "falling in love" by applying it to one-night stands. Like many novelists writing on homosexuality, Vidal overstresses adolescent suppression and late development. So much then for Vidal.

Cory illustrates the obvious point that is ever so easy to forget in organizing the archive: gay men can be the harshest critics of representations meant to free them from social oppression. Bergler would understand this as malice of gay men toward each other. I would suggest that it shows instead how tense are negotiations over group representation—especially when a group is constituted by negative representations, by stigma. But Cory illustrates as well the unpredictability of representation. A negative utterance is still an utterance. When it breaks into a silence, it can provide words—categories, plots, characters—where there had been none before. Not quite two decades after its publication, Cory's book would come into the hands of a young Pentecostal clergyman in southern California. That man, Troy Perry, would find in the book the absolute conviction that he was a homosexual.[63] He would then go on to unite homosexuality to Christianity for the sake of liberating both. This is not the result that Cory wants. Make that a general caution about intentions in the staging of rhetorical characters. Someone may fall in love with the villain.

Foucault sometimes speaks of reverse-discourse or return-discourse (un discours "en retour"). He uses the example of the shift in the nineteenth century from the relative silence around sodomy to the clinical prattling around the new species of same-sex desire. The multiplication of clinical speech brought new forms of lifelong control, but it also permitted or provoked a reply. Homosexuality "began to speak about itself, to defend its legitimacy or its 'naturalness' and often in the vocabulary, with the categories by which it was medically denigrated."[64] Elaborating a technical vocabulary of medico-religious control invites a counter-elaboration, a counterspeech. Indeed, the improvised reactions of aggrieved church leaders and psychoanalysts to Kinsey curiously anticipate the reaction of denizens of the hidden world to their condemnation. The silence has been broken. Let us speak back.

PULPS FOR DELINQUENTS

Talk about reverse-discourse may sound abstract and remote. It is easy enough to make it concrete and local by thinking about the circulation of books. Fifty years earlier, the restricted distribution of copies of Ellis or the translated Krafft-Ebing put expert discourse about sex into libraries, where it could be discovered by an adolescent brave enough to stare down disapproving guardians or cunning enough to sneak around them. In the 1950s, detailed discourses about sex began to appear on local bookracks. Many of the texts in this chapter were carried in the great wave of paperback publication that we call "pulp." That format is important both for their circulation and for the freedom of their interpretation.

Mass-market paperbacks had appeared well before World War II. The famous Penguin series, for example, began in the mid-thirties. But the war's enforced exiles recommended reading as a solitary way to kill time by inhabiting imaginary elsewheres. It was officially encouraged fantasy. Soldiers' experiences also associated well-thumbed paperbacks with single-sex institutions and their pent-up erotic energy. Discharged back in the States, many veterans brought with them a habit of paperback reading as private erotic reverie. They had come to expect that paperbacks could provide pleasures.

Most of the titles I have discussed so far were published as pulps. Kinsey's volume sold so well in hardcover, and at short discount, that it was not released in paperback, but early responses to it were quick into paper covers. Geddes and Curie's *About the Kinsey Report* appeared as a Signet Special in 1948, under the blurb: "New Light on Sexual Knowledge." The light on its cover falls upon an abstract, apparently naked male torso mostly hidden behind a graph. *The City and Pillar* was republished as a Signet paperback in 1950, behind the image of a voluptuous woman hovering about a brooding man seated in the booth of a bar. This is the opening scene of the novel, but also one of its few moments of heterosexual ambiguity. The blurb is only a bit more revealing: "A Masterful Story of Personal Tragedy." In the language of blurbs, "personal" means sexual, and "tragedy" suggests homosexuality. Still Vidal's blurb is the essence of restraint in comparison with many others. Indeed, the blurbs say it all— and often despite the books they tout. When *Better Angel* reappeared under the title *Torment* in the 1950s, its blurb asked, "Is it evil for one man to lavish affection on another? Torn between the boy who cherished him and the girl who struggled for his love, Kurt Gray could not be sure" (Universal 1951). The cover shows a redheaded, buxom woman in low-cut green satin. She reaches ineffectually for the back of a man in a gray flannel suit as he disappears through a doorway. Other novels from the 1930s repackaged for the 1950s include Blair Niles, *Strange Brother* ("The story of the men who are different," Avon 1952), and André Tellier's *Twilight Men* ("They lived in fear, loved in secret," Pyramid 1957).

The reappearance of these older texts in mass-market format—with frequently misleading covers and new titles—shows again the complication of readers' reception and the possibilities for reverse-discourse. Readers may read texts into their lives quite against authorial intention. But they may also read them quite out of authorial sequence—against the timeline of the culture of which they are supposed to be uniform members. Old speeches in obscure books—whether "literary" novels or treatises of moral theology—can be deployed unpredictably. Their rhetorical patterns and proposed characters, suddenly spoken into new controversies for other audiences, produce new effects. The publication of the first Kinsey report or of Vidal's queer novel obviously doesn't erase the earlier speeches. The later books may in fact direct new attention to the older ones—by opening semipublic space for discussion, by making new, if furtive markets. The rhetoric of the old books is not retrieved so much as reactivated or reperformed with unpredictable variations.

Whether they are new or old, and whatever exactly they mean to say, the pulps imply a reader with suspect tastes, with a fondness for sensational scandal and shocking truths. They fancy themselves as readings for and about delinquents. But the pulps can no more control how they are read than Cory can. However carefully it is marketed, the paperback cannot determine how it will be picked up—by whom, in which time and place, with what effects. They mean to titillate, but they may inspire. One man remembers finding *The City and the Pillar* in a drugstore. Raised Methodist, he had fallen in love with a young veteran at a church camp during high school. Like Vidal's protagonist, he graduated and went in search of that first love. Their single encounter was disastrous. So he began to pray that his desires would be taken from him. Then he found the pulp edition of Vidal on the rack. "I stood there for three hours and read it. I could not believe what I was reading."[65] But he did believe it, and went to find other books that would help him be a homosexual man, sexually and emotionally.

3

A SOCIAL PROBLEM

Churchly responses to Kinsey are only the edge of a much larger section of the archives for the same years. From around 1950 on, officials in Christian churches began to write about homosexuality more volubly, more publicly as a problem. In one sense, they were responding to Kinsey, to Vidal, to the whole astonishing roar of new speech about the homosexual. But they were responding by elaborating what could pass as Christian speech on this new topic. Their committee reports, background studies, and position papers wanted to continue or extend the libraries that begin with the earliest Christian codes for sexual purity or with the successive elaborations of languages and punishments for same-sex desire. But they found themselves caught in a divisive renegotiation of Christian teachings on all kinds of sex. The renegotiation begins under the banner of "social problems."

A clear example, now largely forgotten, is the relatively quick change in church teachings on contraception. In 1920, the official position of the main Anglican and Protestant churches was what it had been since the Reformation: marriages were supposed to produce children, and it was both sinful and socially irresponsible to frustrate that procreation. By 1960, the Anglican Communion and most of the major Protestant denominations had come to teach that contraception was an issue to be decided by the married partners—and that there were a number of acceptable and even compelling reasons for spacing or limiting births. Even churches that refused to go this far were led to significant modifications of their positions. The Vatican, which notoriously rejected "artificial" means of contraception in 1968, conceded the morality of contraceptive intent under certain conditions and for an indefinite period of time. The dispute by then was only over means.

What happened in those forty years between 1920 and 1960? One early document that hints at the change is a resolution of the 1930 Lambeth

Conference, the worldwide meeting of bishops of the Anglican Communion. In that conference's Resolution 15, the assembled bishops teach that when there is a "clearly felt moral obligation to limit or avoid parenthood, the method must be decided on Christian principles." The "primary and obvious method is complete abstinence from intercourse," but "where there is a morally sound reason for avoiding" abstinence, "other methods may be used, provided that this is done in the light of the same Christian principles."[1] The statement is guarded and ambiguous, but it departs from traditional teaching, which Lambeth conferences had reaffirmed as recently as 1920.[2] Statements from other denominations followed quickly and gave their reasons more fully. A committee report for the U.S. Federal Council of Churches (forerunner of the National Council of Churches) argues in 1931 that births should be spaced or limited for the health of the mother or child, for the stability of the family, and for strengthening the bond between the parents. It further acknowledges the danger of "overpopulation." Though this report was not endorsed by the whole council, a number of Protestant bodies issued individual statements concurring with it.[3] They asserted both that Christian couples had the right to regulate the number of their children and that they could do so using the best medical methods.

Official Protestant statements from the 1930s through the 1950s repeat similar arguments in favor of contraceptive intent and the use of artificial means to attain it. They share a growing recognition that human overpopulation raises acute moral issues of its own. Children should not be born for starvation, and families should not be formed only to be torn apart by harsh economic necessities. The statements also agree in appealing to ideals of health—of the child, the mother, the family as a whole. Advances in medicine have made contraception more reliable. Christians should use these discoveries or inventions just as they would any other for morally good ends. Procreation is mentioned less and less as the single or highest purpose for Christian marriage. It is balanced against intimacy between parents and adequate care of the children. Some denominational statements begin to assert distinct moral values in sexual relations, such as freedom or spontaneity. So far as artificial means of contraception increase those values within legitimate sexual relations, they are good.

Even this abbreviated history makes clear that social problems—overpopulation, familial and community health—are cited to argue for change in long-established Christian sexual teaching. In the 1950s, something similar happens with homosexuality—and also for reasons of health, if not of overpopulation. For some theologians and church officials, the personal and social consequences of the cruel criminalization of homosexual acts become an occasion to reconsider homosexuality itself. The visibility of homosexuality after World War II may have given the topic urgency, but it was analyzed as a response to a social problem—with special attention to the effects of criminal laws. The first analyses come from the Church of England, but they were quickly received by American readers and they appear in many American archives of church speech.

THE MORAL WELFARE COUNCIL

In January 1951, a correspondent wrote to the Anglican monthly review, *Theology*, about church silence on homosexuality. He noted that while the secular press was debating the inequity and uselessness of laws against homosexual acts, "no Christian comment is to be found."[4] "Is it to much to hope," the writer wonders, "that the light and fresh air admitted, perhaps too freely during the last fifty years to the problems of sexual morality in general may be extended during the next fifty, and as soon as possible, to the particular problems of the homosexual?"

In the next month, the same journal offered a short article in reply. The article was written by Sherwin Bailey, central lecturer for the Church of England's Moral Welfare Council. Bailey had a longstanding interest in theological issues of love and marriage.[5] One of his decisive intellectual experiences in theological college had been a lecture on romantic love by Charles Williams, eminent writer, friend of C. S. Lewis, Tolkien, and T. S. Eliot. Bailey began to publish his own views on the issues even before his ordination.[6] After service in a small parish and as chaplain to the Anglican students at the University of Edinburgh, he was offered an appointment as a traveling lecturer on sex and marriage for theological colleges and other church schools. Originally disinclined to accept the post, Bailey reasoned to himself and his future employers that he brought to it not only psychological interest, but historical expertise. He had after all written a dissertation on an early English reformer who dealt "at inordinate length with compulsory celibacy and the abuses and immorality it was held to have occasioned among clergy, monks and nuns."[7] So when the open letter about homosexuality appeared in *Theology*, Bailey was the obvious respondent.

Bailey's response is entitled "The Problem of Sexual Inversion"—an echo of Ellis, but also of the letter to which he replies. The title is tied to one of his main claims: the term "homosexuality" confuses different sorts of lives and conditions that must be carefully distinguished. Bailey notes that Kinsey's percentage for men who have male-male sexual experience is not a figure for homosexuality. Indeed, the percentage "tells us comparatively little about the real problem."[8] Bailey himself is most interested in the problem of "the 'natural' invert," "the homosexual who cannot help, and did not choose, his condition." He mentions two significant sources on the problem. He commends Anomaly's *The Invert* as a "wise and sane discussion." He also notes his disagreement with Northcote, *Christianity and Sex Problems*. Here and in his later work, Bailey takes the category of inversion, but then corrects at length Northcote's scriptural exegesis, history, and jurisprudence. One conclusion is also constant across Bailey's writing: while inversion's causes are unknown, this condition is clearly not in itself a crime and ought not to be treated as one by British law. "It is, without doubt, a Christian duty to press for the removal of this anomalous and shameful injustice, which has done untold harm and has achieved no good whatever."[9] Bailey also suggests what he will later argue at length: neither the Christian scriptures nor older theological traditions recognize the existence of the "natural" invert. Whatever the story of Sodom is about, it does not treat "genuine inversion, or take into account the psychological and pathological aspects of homosexuality, as we are now aware of them."[10]

The invert is not the sodomite—not scripturally and not in the intention of criminal law. Bailey justifies the decision of the letter writer to dispense with the traditional terminology. But he is equally clear that the invert is not an alternate heterosexual. Against Northcote, he is quick to deny that decriminalizing same-sex acts would imply recognition of same-sex marriage.[11] Bailey insists that same-sex love can never be equivalent to real marriage. "While gladly recognizing that a genuine homosexual love may have elements of beauty and altruism, there seems no reason to believe that homosexual intercourse has any quality which makes it strictly comparable to the intercourse of husband and wife."[12] The invert is no longer the sodomite, but he is not (yet) husband to another invert.

Bailey's response to the public letter was a promissory note. He knew that the rising public debate about the sodomy laws would require better answers from Christian churches. He undertook to secure them. In April 1952, Bailey proposed to his employers a study group on homosexuality. A group was called together, though its work was technically both private and unofficial. Still, by the end of the year an officer of the Moral Welfare Council had endorsed the idea of a governmental study, and its working group was named as part of the Church of England's response to the perceived social crisis.[13] When the council's executive decided to publish an "interim report" on homosexuality, it officially ascribed authorship only to "a small group of Anglican clergy and doctors, with legal advice," who were "alone . . . responsible for the views . . . expressed."[14] In some contexts, it was an expert committee of the church; in others, a small group of individuals speaking for themselves. There is a similar ambivalence about the status of the text. Technically, the small pamphlet was printed "For private circulation," as the cover page cautions. A red stamp repeats the warning: "PRIVATE: Not for publication." Any reader is warned: this is private and expert speech that solicits comments from other experts on the problem of (male) homosexuality. It is speech still behind Hall's curtain of expert silence. But copies were sent to every member of the Parliament, and the pamphlet's publication was reported instantly in the *Times*, which announced its sale to the public at Church House in Westminster.[15] The pamphlet both is and is not a church document: it is deniable whenever expedient. When it is not denied, it is an effort to speak against certain social constructions of the problem of homosexuality.

Bailey was only one of many authors for the report. As it was being finished, he was already preoccupied with historical studies of church views on homosexuality that would be published separately. But many passages in the pamphlet echo or agree with Bailey's first reply to the open letter. The interim report immediately adopts Ellis's distinction between the invert and the pervert. It understands homosexuality not as conduct, but as condition. A person who suffers the condition is an invert. He is to be distinguished from the bisexual and the pervert.[16] The pervert, according to the report, is "a heterosexual who engages in homosexual practices."[17] Inversion cannot generally be altered, either because there is no therapy for it or because therapy is resisted. The condition arises in adolescence most probably from psychological causes rather than from inheritance. Many adolescents feel homosexual tendencies. They are apparently normal. The desires can become abnormally and tragically fixed when there is an "unsatisfactory parental relationship": an absent father, a smothering mother, or the retreat of both parents after divorce. The psychological damage done in parental relationships will then be precipitated by failed attempts to date women or experiences at school or the solicitations of an older man confirmed in his vice. The report here excuses itself for a moment to consider women, noting the particular problem of schoolgirls who fall in love with their teachers—and teachers who reciprocate. Fixation in adolescence "will exempt an invert from responsibility for his homosexual condition *but cannot absolve him from responsibility for immoral homosexual practices.*"[18]

The report stresses at several points that it is merely preliminary and it ends by calling for a full, official study of the whole matter. But the pamphlet is clearly arranged to favor decriminalizing consensual homosexual acts between adults—Bailey's view and that of others on the council. The pamphlet's authors insist on the state's obligation to protect the young, but note that the current criminal regime may actually endanger them by driving adults away from settled relationships with their peers. There is a list of legal anomalies in the criminalization of male-male relations and "subsidiary considerations" of its consequences, which include suicide, blackmail, social isolation, moral deterioration, restricted diagnosis or therapy, and police brutality or complicity. Addressing these anomalies and consequences would not endanger the young. Indeed, the authors urge that a higher age of consent could be set for homosexual activities since homosexuality is unnatural.[19]

The appearance of that old Christian accusation reminds the reader that these arguments in the pamphlet are not particularly theological. They could have been written by any group of socially minded legal reformers. The pamphlet's theological content is, in contrast, entirely and severely "traditional." "Homosexual acts are sins against God, whether or not they are also crimes against the State." The pamphlet uses "sodomy" as an appropriate and perfectly general term with which to condemn all such acts as "the physiologically unnatural use of non-complementary organs within a relationship which is not that of man and woman." Homosexual acts are rejected as "deflecting the activity of the sexual organ from its proper end (*finitum proprium*)."[20] They cannot be excused on a plea of love any more than sexual acts between other unmarried lovers. The only space for erotic life among Christians is in marriage. Since inverts should not marry partners of the other sex, and since approving same-sex marriage would undermine society, those who suffer the condition should follow the example of (heterosexual) women who cannot find a husband: they should "*accept their condition, and by seeking to sublimate their sexual lives in various socially useful ways achieve personal fulfillment.*"[21] They should avoid homosexual bars, form chaste friendships, and rely on the sacraments while society tries to correct the causes that produced them.

The report offers what sounds like very traditional advice, but it fails to recognize or to admit how antitraditional its narrative of inversion is.[22] What biblical basis is there for distinguishing between inversion and perversion? For Paul in Romans 1, same-sex desires are a universal consequence of gentile idolatry. Later tradition did elaborate the sodomite as a distinct and especially hideous figure of sin, but that figure emerged by a mysterious spiritual contagion, not because of parental problems during adolescence. The pamphlet wants to maintain traditional Christian judgments on homosexuality while replacing the traditional understandings of what homosexuality is. It is no wonder then that the parts of the pamphlet do not cohere. The theological judgments, with their biblical and traditional allusions, cannot rest on the psychological narrative of inversion or justify the social arguments for decriminalization.

A MAGISTERIAL SUPPLEMENT—AND REJOINDER

The report's incoherence at just these points is tacitly addressed in Bailey's historical supplement. After the study group published its short report, and with its knowledge, Bailey offered to a general audience his monograph, *Homosexuality and the Western Christian Tradition*. Bailey frames the book as a study of how church history contributed to contemporary attitudes about male-male desire.[23] Because Bailey thinks that Christian tradition was settled on the question by the end of the Middle Ages, he concentrates on scripture and on earlier theological or legal texts. But his punch line is entirely contemporary: he reiterates the call to decriminalize homosexual acts in private between consenting adults, but only after explicitly detaching it from the biblical and traditional citations with which the pamphlet ornaments itself.

Bailey argues from history that Christian tradition about homosexuality "can no longer be regarded as an adequate guide by the theologian, the legislator, the sociologist, and the magistrate."[24] The tradition erred in making the biblical story about Sodom and Gomorrah into a condemnation of homosexuality. That meaning was added to Genesis 18–19 only much later, under the influence of confused, nonbiblical notions. (So much for the pamphlet's use of "sodomy" as a general term for male-male sexual activities.) This decisive misinterpretation has had innumerable theological consequences, not least on the reading of other biblical texts about sexuality. The Christian tradition has also been "defective" so far as it did not recognize the distinction between inversion and perversion. When Paul condemns male-male relations in Romans 1, he is attacking "male perverts," that is, heterosexuals who engage in homosexual practices. Bailey's application of the pamphlet's terminology here may seem ridiculous until one recalls the Pauline passage—the whole passage, not just the verses on men who burn for lust with men. Paul is describing a disorder of desire as a consequence of idolatry. Because human beings exchanged the glory of God for idols, "God gave them up" to desires and passions (Romans 1:24, 1:26). For Bailey, this confirms a distinction between heterosexuals who succumb to perverted desire "against nature" and inverts who have no choice over their desires— for whom such desires may even be called "natural." So far as the Christian tradition does not recognize a condition of inversion, so far as it confuses inversion with perversion, it has "but an indirect and dubious relevance" to contemporary debates over homosexuality.[25]

Bailey's historical arguments have been taken up time and again since 1955. Indeed, his book inaugurates a chain of historical studies into the exact contents of Christian teaching on homosexuality and their current implications. The genre returns to public attention at regular intervals— most notably in the books of John Boswell, whose famous *Christianity, Social Tolerance and Homosexuality* was published exactly twenty-five years after Bailey's monograph. Bailey is many ways the patron saint of gay-friendly church history. But he is something more. Bailey's book is distinguished from many of its scholarly successors by its association with church and state reviews of decriminalization. It is, as it were, a quasi-official pleading and recommendation, a sort of brief amicus curiae or— more precisely—a minority report. His care to stress his private standing only emphasizes his public office. His decision to publish a book rather than circulate a confidential pamphlet effectively upstages the original church study group. Bailey is thus also a patron saint for clergy who advocate homosexual inclusion.

It is important then to remember that Bailey is not an advocate for homosexuality simply speaking. His book pronounces no blithe endorsement of homosexual love.[26] So far as this text is concerned, inversion is a "mysterious and unfortunate condition," an "abnormality" and "peculiar handicap" due at least in some cases to childhood maladjustments.[27] Instead of punishing inverts with criminal penalties, society ought to admit its responsibility for the conditions that bring them into existence; it ought to improve marriage and family life in order to reduce inversion. "Society . . . has a heavy responsibility towards the inverts whom it creates by its relational failures and its wars."[28] When Bailey calls for education to correct prejudices against inverts, he likens them to other socially stigmatized groups, to those whose upbringing or biology has handicapped them for social life. Even if private acts among consenting adults are decriminalized, inversion itself will remain a social problem and perhaps even an index of the prior decay of marriage and family life.[29] The invert, so carefully distinguished from the pervert, still serves with the pervert as a social symptom.

Still there is Bailey's willingness to challenge established readings of scripture, to reread authoritative theology. He reinterpreted the authorizing story from Genesis at a time when biblical experts were still arguing, for example, that the angelic visitors to Sodom must have appeared as attractive adolescents to lure the city's notorious pederasts.[30] Bailey is also rhetorically careful when arguing that the tradition has missed certain things. He is not making an argument from Kinsey in which all traditional authority is debunked. He is constructing an internal critique—in relation, as it were, to an independent history of discourse. The argument is precisely not, "There is no homosexuality, but a lot of homosexual activity." It is rather, "There are inverts, and the theological tradition is defective so far as it fails to recognize such a category, such an entity."

Bailey's argument would go on to an influential history in churchly, activist, and academic discourses. He was less successful in his immediate labors. He edited the Moral Welfare Council's final submission to the Wolfenden committee and oversaw its publication in 1956.[31] The departmental committee's own report appeared in 1957. Its recommendations on decriminalization could be supported by the Archbishop of Canterbury, no doubt in part because of the arguments laid out by the pamphlet. Parliament was not persuaded. The recommended change in legislation would come only a decade later.

The two reports by the working group differ from Bailey's monograph at many points, but all three texts agree in attempting to divide or cut discourses of homosexuality. The report wants to cut debate about legal reform from Christian ethical teaching. The church can support decriminalization, so the argument goes, while reaffirming its traditional moral condemnations. Bailey's monograph wants to cut Christian tradition from the present. Because they fix on the (un)scriptural figure of the sodomite, the most vocal theological traditions have little to say for present debates. These cuts are motivated by admirable concerns for the well-being of homosexuals, but they also embody a rhetorical strategy of public persuasion. The strategy did not work—at least not immediately. It also risked oversimplifying the complicated circulation of speeches within and without the churches. The difficulty for Christian homosexuals is not just that they constitute a social problem, but that they have absorbed into themselves the shame of the old traditions. Changing the criminal laws has many positive effects, but it cannot erase shame—or prevent its further production in the young. For adolescents, the risks are not only sexual predation or broken family, but the active teaching of the languages and bodily habits of sexual nausea. Religious teaching does not take place in the stratosphere of parliamentary committees and church councils. It happens in spaces much nearer to home—at home.

FROM THE ARCHIVE OF RELIGIOUS EDUCATION

There are many ways to produce religious guilt, not all of them within the control of religious organizations. Family violence or social stigma often authorize themselves by appealing to religious principles, but without seriousness or consistency. Even within Christian churches, many unChristian motives instruct preaching and teaching. There are also slips or gaps between official teaching and local congregational pedagogy. A pastor may disagree with denominational creeds or particular scriptural verses. A Sunday school teacher may be better or worse educated. Even in the most tightly controlled denominations, there is a permissible variety in teaching emphases or textbooks.

Curricula for religious education are for these reasons always utopian documents. If they were followed to the letter, their effects would still be conditioned or thwarted by dozens of more immediate circumstances. When churches attempt sex education, these circumstances multiply. So do the secret or not so secret motives that run through them. A tone of voice, a grimace, a burst of irritability or anxious humor may do more to teach sex on Sunday morning than pages of carefully calibrated prose—with all their perky illustrations and fun-filled exercises. Looking at a workbook for "youth" or "young adult" classes on marriage will not tell you much about what was actually taught or how it was received—though the illustrations in particular are always worth a second look.[32]

Religious education documents do say something about how churches articulated the tasks of sex education for themselves. They also illustrate the tensions that pull churches in different directions. For the postwar period, a contrast between two books will make the point. The first is *Modern Youth and Chastity*, a Catholic manual for college freshmen written by Gerald Kelly on behalf of a committee of American Jesuits. Drafted in 1940–41, it was tested in classrooms before being published in 1943. The volume was frequently reprinted here and abroad. It was translated into Dutch and German, before finding its latest avatar in a Greek version published in 1994. My contrasting selection is Evelyn Millis Duvall, *Facts of Life and Love for Teenagers*. Originally published in 1950, it was regularly reissued, including as a mass-market paperback, before being substantially revised in 1963 as *Love and the Facts of Life*. Duvall's book was also translated into German and Dutch. It took other forms in filmstrips and workbooks.

Kelly writes inside the walls of Catholic moral theology. His ideals are chastity and purity, and he understands them as mediated through the exemplary confessor. But he is also a specialist on what we now call "medical ethics"—that is, on *Medico-Moral Problems*, to quote the title of another of his books. He is, then, by Catholic standards, negotiating conflicts between modern medicine and sexual law. By contrast, Duvall is associated with modern Protestant movements, especially Family Life Education, with its focus on social behavior in the larger contexts of family systems. She is a leader with the Institute of Family Living, which stresses the need to bring expert guidance to child rearing—a program that goes back to Hall. A few years later, she will help the American Social Hygiene Association shift to personal and family life, with a strong emphasis on heterosexuality.[33] So while it is tempting to contrast Kelly and Duvall as theological reactionary and sociological progressive, it is fairer to read them as two different understandings of the relations between sexual science and churchly teaching on sex.

Kelly's book, aimed at a slightly older audience, presents a system of numbered moral principles that can be combined to yield judgments on particular cases. It prepares for these chapters by stressing the richness to be found in love, friendship, and "companionship of the sexes."[34] But when it comes time to render moral judgments, the book adopts an almost geometrical casuistry. Here is the "First Practical Principle": "Every directly venereal action is against the law of God, and a serious sin of impurity."[35] The principle is set in boldface and centered on the page so that the negligent eye cannot miss it. From it the conclusion follows: "willful approval of unchaste actions" is a mortal sin.[36] The principle excludes from further consideration any action outside of marriage that has "the single purpose of stimulating or promoting the generative function," including "unnatural acts such as self-abuse or sexual intimacies with a person of the same sex." Outside of marriage, these "directly venereal actions" cannot be excused for any reason. "The law of God in this matter is absolute, and to do such things for some so-called good purpose is simply to do evil in order to obtain some good."[37] No further discussion is required—or permitted. Religious education about sex proceeds rather to consider such questions as how a heterosexual couple contemplating marriage may kiss or what a pious Catholic can read. One sort of thing he or she cannot read is "the pseudo-scientific trash printed today which is really nothing but a sugar-coated allurement to vice and perversion."[38] The steady reasoning of Catholic casuistry, based on immutable divine law, will not waver before the prurient sciences of modernity.

The contrast with Duvall couldn't be clearer on this point. Her book places itself on the side of recent science. Indeed, Duvall dismisses most traditional teaching about sex as so much prescientific miasma.[39] The spirit of new learning seems at first to animate the treatment of homosexuality. Duvall approaches it within the chapter on "Sex Troubles and Worries," but she begins by chasing away anxieties: "When you stop to think of what homosexuality means and how frequent it is, some of the fear drains off and you want to understand what it is all about."[40] You want to *understand*. You are animated by innate scientific curiosity. You begin by discovering that homosexuality is not one thing, but a range of feelings and actions, "what might be considered a *scale* of homosexuality-heterosexuality."[41] Indeed, its basic division is between latent and overt. Neither condition can be diagnosed by public inspection, and neither implies gender deviation or inversion. Something like homosexual attraction is to be expected when growing up. Many boys and girls go through stages in which they disdain the opposite sex and have crushes on each other. Duvall expresses no particular concern with this, so long as it is a passing phase and does not proceed to physical expression. When it comes to acting on these feelings, especially with older men, she becomes strongly disapproving. "In every community of any size there are men who desire contact with other men and boys. Some of these men actively seek sexual outlets with each other and with younger boys."[42] "Outlet" is one of Kinsey's favorite words, but the warning here is much older than Kinsey. It is for boys (not girls), and it is a warning about predators: teachers, coaches, leaders (but not, apparently, clergymen) can carry a sort of contagion from which recovery is doubtful.

Boys and girls who escape adult seduction or any of the other traps in development should look forward to marriage with a member of the opposite sex. The entire arc of Duvall's narrative moves from adolescent discovery to fulfillment in heterosexual marriage. If she allows in theory that some people may be constitutionally homosexual, she is ready to attribute its origin to unhealthy circumstances: "Sometimes our earliest experiences with people give us little faith in them or in ourselves or in love itself, and so we may develop distorted feelings about others and distorted ways of responding to them."[43] Distortion can deprive a person of a normal, happy life: "Some persons are so attracted to members of their own sex that the other sex does not appeal to them. When this condition becomes chronic, that person is unable to fall in love, get married, and lead a normal life as a man or woman usually does."[44] The best hope is to seek counseling while in one's teens in order to get back on the track of healthy development.

Read at one level, the contrast between Duvall on development and Kelly on moral principles mirrors a distinction between persons and acts. Duvall is worried about blocked development, while Kelly judges unnatural, illicit acts. For Kelly, there is no need to dwell on scales of homosexuality or theories of its genesis. The focus is on the unchanging divine condemnation of certain genital intimacies, of "directly venereal actions." Duvall, by contrast, has learned from Kinsey—from Freud, from Hall—about adolescent sexual development and its possible deviations. Except that she too gives great weight to acts—to the distinction between latent and overt, say, but especially to the deeds by which a young man is "inducted" into homosexuality. If Duvall is more sympathetic and better informed than Kelly, it is still not clear that she ends by being any more encouraging to young homosexuals.

Whatever her authorial intentions, her book had unexpected fates. Its discourse could be reversed or overwritten. One man was given a copy of Duvall's *Facts of Love and Life for Teenagers*.[45] At six or seven, he had been told not to touch his friends so much and not to play with girls unless at least one boy was present. Otherwise people would think that he was a sissy. At eight, he had stopped writing poetry and begun to overeat. Duvall's book, coming later, was meant to convince him that same-sex desire was an illness. One day he found a gay novel dropped on the street. Reading it, he masturbated. All that expert knowledge, that carefully plotted religious education, undone by a pulp—and by desire.

It doesn't even take the happy discovery of a dropped novel. Desire can find its way under the strict supervision of religious education. Another man, the son of a Baptist minister, remembers that he liked "pictures from biblical times because they so often showed legs, bare arms, sometimes there'd be a bare chest."[46] Books of bible stories teach more than they intend. At fifteen, he had an erotic dream of "something wonderful coming down the hallway towards our bedroom. I felt the presence [of] something strange and glorious." It was Jesus. Is this the failure of a religious education or its culmination?

A CONFERENCE OF THE SOCIALLY CONCERNED

In late April 1961, representatives of mainline Protestant churches gathered in Wisconsin at a Baptist retreat center, once a lakeside resort, for a "North American Conference on Church and Family." The meeting was chaired by Evelyn and Sylvanus Duvall—she the author of *Facts of Life and Love for Teenagers*, he a sociologist of religion. Another couple edited the volume of proceedings—he a staff member of the American National Council of Churches, she a volunteer member of YWCA's national board. A prominent marriage counselor led the worship, but he was of course introduced to the assembly alongside his wife. At every step, the meeting affirmed its pastoral concern for the imperiled family, which it acknowledged was "subjected to greater stresses and strains than ever before."[47]

The family's fragile state—that too was a social problem. Among the threats to it were newly nagging questions about sex. So the conference announced as one of its tasks the development of "a Christian ethic of sexual behavior" that will "answer persuasively the questions of this generation."[48] One of the organizers put it more plainly: the task was nothing less than producing "a valid sex code for our day," one that would eliminate venereal infection and unwanted pregnancy, recognize the equality of women, and reconcile old ideas of sin with a fresh conviction that sex can be wholesome.[49] Often enough in the proceedings, it sounds as if the answers for this generation will be very much like the answers for the last. The volume croons familiar pieties. In conference worship, for example, bits of Christian scripture are mingled with excerpts from world poetry to reaffirm the complementarity of the sexes, the stages of happy marriage, and the spiritual significance of every piece of family life. Even when preaching platitudes, the conference tries to reckon with new knowledge about sex. The worship leader intones, "The Bible lays down many detailed rules about sex. These rules were appropriate to the society of the time. Some of them are equally appropriate to our time. Some of them are not at all."[50] Detailed rules must be subordinated to the greater commandments of love. So the proper response to the sexual "waywardness" of others may not be condemnation, but blessing and transformation.

For the conference to answer new questions about sex, it must first "listen hard to what the medical and social sciences have found to be true."[51] Indeed, the briefing book distributed to all participants attempts a crash course in sexual science for church folk.[52] It remedies the "uncomfortable silence about questions of sex and family life" that has been maintained until quite recently in Protestant churches.[53] But even behind the closed doors of the rural encampment, even in the sober company of visibly married church leaders and their scientific tutors, there could be "some understandable discomfort about the array of challenging topics (some of them quite distasteful) that confront us in the week ahead."[54] None perhaps more "distasteful" than masturbation and homosexuality. For these topics, the organizers invited the most accredited specialists: Wardell Pomeroy, Kinsey's associate, summarized the study of masturbation. (Kinsey himself had died in 1956; Pomeroy was the obvious substitute.) The Los Angeles psychiatrist Evelyn Hooker presented homosexuality.

Hooker was less famous than Pomeroy, though her recent work was no less controversial. Since 1953, she had been conducting comparative studies of heterosexual and homosexual men. At a meeting of the American Psychological Association in 1956, she presented the results of a striking experimental comparison.[55] Scrutinizing the results of various personality tests without identifying information about sexual orientation, experts found no association between homosexuality and pathology and were unable to distinguish between heterosexual and homosexual men otherwise alike. Hooker suggests the strong inference: if these tests are an adequate measure of adjustment, "then clearly there is no inherent connection between pathology and homosexuality."[56] At the end of the paper, Hooker allows herself to suggest "*very tentatively*" that "homosexuality as a clinical entity does not exist. Its forms are as varied as are those of heterosexuality."[57]

In the briefing book for the church conference, Hooker summarizes recent research on homosexuality and offers a thorough bibliography, both scientific and religious.[58] She does not highlight her own work, though she does refer to unpublished studies on the fixation of homosexuality

in the young and on homosexual groups. Her written report begins with
Kinsey, but also surveys psychoanalytic theories and recalls the British
Home Office study, the Wolfenden report. The tone throughout is neutral
and impersonal. In the conference proceedings, Hooker's voice is sharper
and more emphatic. She begins personally, with a reminiscence of her
one meeting with Kinsey and of the prurient reactions to it from acquain-
tances. The story leads her to reflect on the costs and commitments of
research on sex. "All of us work in an area which is heavily laden with
the emotional burden and tragedy of our society. I find that the only way
in which I can do research in this field is to also be a helper to carry the
burden."[59] Hooker means by help not the proffering of doubtful cures, but
assistance with the "legal, psychiatric, emotional" problems encountered
in a persecuting society.

Only after affirming her solidarity with her homosexual subjects does
Hooker turn to the evidence. Having summarized Kinsey's statistics on
frequency and endorsed his reluctance to define a homosexual person,
Hooker rebuts five "myths" about homosexuals, including the notions that
they are easily recognizable and confined to certain professions. She takes
the assembled church leaders to task for their hypocrisy in treating homosexuality as something to be found only outside the church. "Whether
recognized or not, the problem of homosexuality is prevalent among [the
churches'] own members."[60] The invisibility of most homosexuals—of
those who are never caught by the police, secular or ecclesiastical—is no
accident. It is the result of daily efforts to keep themselves hidden. That
is why most people do not see long-term, well-adjusted male couples, for
example, but fix on those who run afoul of the law.

Although Hooker considers treatment possible in some cases, she emphatically denies the effectiveness of coercion. "In our society, in all probability there is the strongest condemnation which has ever existed." How
little it succeeds is apparently clear to all. But Hooker's point is larger:
homosexuality "is multiply caused. It is a universal phenomenon at the human level and we cannot prevent its occurring, all we can do is to attempt
to reduce it."[61] To do that, you must intervene early and without any hint
of horror. But there will always be some men who are homosexual, and for
them the best policy would be to change social conditions so that they are
encouraged to form stable relationships of the kind one encourages among
young heterosexuals. So far as society forces homosexuals into promiscuity, it condemns them to psychological pathologies. The promiscuous male
homosexual does fulfill many of the stereotypes: he is "lonely, isolated,
compulsive, driven . . . , somewhat schizophrenic, somewhat suicidal."[62]
But the promiscuous homosexual is also in the minority.

During the question period, some of the assembled church leaders want to know when and how exactly to intervene with teenagers for the best chance of success. Hooker responds that the most productive interventions will occur between thirteen and sixteen, when some homosexually inclined men may be turned toward heterosexuality if they can be brought into the "male alliance," the network of masculinity-forming activities and relationships, at the same time that they are given opportunities for heterosexual dating. The challenge is to introduce male bonding and contact with young women at the same time. As the leader of a national church youth agency confesses, growing up in church delays contact with the other sex, depriving pious college students of a definite sex role and confidence in their gender. Hooker agrees: postponing chances to associate with girls beyond fourteen or fifteen creates "a good breeding ground for homosexuality."[63] If the churches want to help youth, they can train sympathetic counselors and not delay dating. They can help parents to avoid divorce and to maintain a proper balance between mother and father. They can abandon the language of condemnation, since church attacks together with other societal labeling force people to identify as exclusively homosexual.

Every afternoon at the 1961 conference, the participants met in small groups to discuss the morning's proceedings. A brief summary of workshop discussions shows a wide range of views after Hooker's presentation. "Answers to this question [about homosexuality and the church] do not fall into any readily discernible pattern."[64] An understatement: the reported views range from traditional language about sin or worries about protecting teenagers from seduction to criticisms of the church's taste for punishment and self-righteousness. What should churches do? Reaffirm the prohibition on sex outside marriage *or* call homosexuals anew to the "saving message of Jesus Christ" *or* give up hypocritical moralizing. Things are no clearer when the conference comes into plenary session. While there are strong recommendations for the churches to face scientific facts and to undertake theological reflection and religious education based on them, homosexual acts remain a "problem." Churches should "work for positive legislation" about it and should "stop applying out-dated moralism," but they should also refer homosexuals to "rehabilitation facilities."[65] The main theological question is articulated only to be left hanging: "What revisions in attitude and treatment does new research data suggest?"[66]

THE CIRCULATION OF EXPERT OPINION

Research data, clinical treatment, legal reform, curricular revision, official church teaching: some coordinates of homosexuality as a social problem.

Framing it—whatever exactly it was—as a social problem, churches sought both to borrow specialized knowledge and to reject moral or creedal revision. Homosexuality is a social problem to which the church responds— not least by distinguishing its inward moral discipline from its outward social advice.[67] For some church writers, homosexual acts remain sin, but the church need not require that they also be crimes. For others, the quasi-natural condition of inversion may fall outside the criminal law, but not outside therapy or spiritual correction. Treating homosexuality as a social problem is an effort to differentiate realms of speech through which Christian speakers could move without being accused of self-contradiction.

The spheres could perhaps be distinguished by disciplinary prescription. They were hard to keep apart in rhetorical fact. The "confidential" pamphlet from the private and informal study group circulates through Parliament as a church document and is then advertised by the *Times*. Both the pamphlet and Bailey's monograph were reported in the new magazines of the American "homophile" movement. The monograph was reviewed within a few months of its publication by *ONE: The Homosexual Magazine* and by the *Mattachine Review*.[68] After wondering whether Bailey tries too hard to exonerate the Christian church, *ONE*'s reviewer judges his book "perhaps the most important . . . yet published on homosexuality" for "the intelligent religious reader."[69] In the next year, the retiring president of the Mattachine Society urged it as required reading for those who want to pursue "a fuller spiritual life."[70] The carefully distinguished spheres now frankly overlap. Of course, they had been in contact for some time.

4

SPIRIT OF THE HOMOPHILE RACE

During the same consequential decade, the 1950s, the rhetoric of the American homophile movement runs alongside both church responses to reports of homosexual life and church efforts to discuss it as a social problem. By the processes of reverse-discourse, or colonial imitation, homophile speech draws on the same scientific and medical sources; it conceives of social problems with social solutions; it even embraces the ends of moral advancement through sustained education. But if it copies and approaches the other, more powerful rhetorics, the homophile movement also struggles to distinguish itself. It is preparing a troupe of alternative characters for same-sex desire. Some of them will be religious, if not yet recognizably Christian.

To begin, the strange word: "homophile." It was coined at least twice. First, in Germany during the 1920s as part of a psychoanalytically inflected model of gender polarity meant to replace models of inversion, like the one in Ellis. Then the word was coined again, in Los Angeles soon after 1950, when Harry Hay was trying to describe homosexual community as more than a desperate sexual market.[1] For Hay, it was important to recognize homophiles as a distinct subculture, bound together by political, ethical, and ritual needs. Behind the concealing mask society forces them to wear, through the very roles society compels them to play, homophiles constitute an "androgynous *minority*." Describing them as a subcultural minority, Hay inscribed them in Stalinist social theory, but he also placed them within familiar American narratives of race and ethnicity.[2] The "like race" analogy is an essential element in Hay's invention of homophile character—even as it is a retrieval of much older language about sodomites.[3]

The invention authorized homophile organizations to engage in political and educational work—a version of "racial uplift." From the beginning, some of their prominent members held that the work had spiritual dimensions. "Spirituality" is their preferred positive term. The term carries its interesting history in male-male literature, but it is also a privileged term in American racial contexts.[4] The race analogy authorizes attention to spiritual concerns in at least two ways: by drawing on the cultural stereotypes of "Negro spirituality," and by recalling an older tradition of homosexuals as a separate and more spiritual race—or as the more spiritual portion of the human race.

However many troubles there are in the analogy to race, it helped some homophile leaders not only to organize homosexuals, but to name a space in their organization both for reforming churches and for inventing new religions. Even so dilute a notion as spirituality remained controversial, of course, given both the reality of churchly persecution and the ardently antireligious views of other members.

THE PROBLEM OF BEGINNINGS

The homophile groups of the 1950s are now named as the beginning of significant or persistent homosexual organizing in the United States. That story fits not only with the known archival sources, but with the larger narrative of the upsurge in homosexual networks after World War II. The archives also record scattered efforts at establishing something like homosexual churches after the war. There are doubtless many more groups that we do not know. All the church efforts in the late 1940s and early 1950s, known and unknown, cannot be counted simply as the beginning. Various kinds of evidence suggest that there have been same-sex counterchurches or parachurches for many centuries. Consider the homoerotic haunting of ordinary Christian rites. Recall Ellis's case of a woman who wanted to be confirmed alongside her female partner in order to mark their relationship. There is good evidence of a similar use of communion between women in the nineteenth century, and it can be tied to a longer tradition of Christian friendship rituals.[5] There are also much older uses of marriage rites, though here the evidence verges into the scandalous.[6] Or consider the appropriation of religious spaces. Certain congregations or kinds of churches disproportionately attracted members who were other than good married folk. Some of these sites were the great urban churches in "disreputable" precincts—prostitutes' churches or sailors' churches. Others were protected collegiate and monastic chapels or the dedicated parishes and private oratories supported and shielded by wealthy patrons. Most of this earlier history will remain unknown. What is clear is that after World War II, American memories and American archives begin to register the scattered appearance of sexually marked congregations—not the first simply, but the first we can see.

In 1945 or 1946, for example, a young man returned to Atlanta from a Vincentian seminary south of St. Louis.[7] George Hyde, a recent convert to Catholicism, had been expelled from its collegiate program because of an accusation of homosexual activity. He was nineteen or twenty. Outraged by the accusation, especially given what he regarded as the seminary's entrenched hypocrisy and punitive policing around sexual behavior, Hyde denounced Roman teaching on homosexuality. Much later, he recounted his views in these words:

I told them this: "The Church is the House of the Lord . . . a home for all men and women, but you would not have it so. You have built closets in every corner in which to hide the homosexual out of sight and out of hearing of the Word. This is wrong. The Church is the House of the Lord, and in His House there are no closets."[8]

Hyde found work in St. Louis, but he was sacked once the department store received a reference letter from the seminary.

Back in Atlanta, he helped at various Catholic churches while he stayed at the cathedral. Another young man at a downtown church suddenly became notorious for refusing to repent of his "unacceptable form of . . . lovemaking," to borrow Hyde's euphemism, complete with its significant pause. When the young man stubbornly insisted that it was not wrong for him given who he was, the priest yelled from the confessional that he should get out of the church and not return. The following Sunday, the young man approached the communion rail. The priest refused him communion. So too on the next Sunday—only the young man stood stubbornly at the rail. Gossip spread. When Hyde heard it, he volunteered to join the young man. They were both denied communion. After five weeks, eight people were standing in silent protest.

Since the numbers continued to grow, and since there was no sign of the parish priest's relenting, Hyde suggested that the group hold its own meetings. Beginning in April 1946, they did—as a racially integrated group that included both straight and queer-identified people, single, married, coupled. First the group met for "bible study and [its] own church service." Then Hyde was ordained for sacramental ministry by an exiled and renegade Greek Orthodox bishop. He was twenty—too young for ordination as a Roman Catholic. He was ordained not for a new homosexual church, but for a church that would not exclude homosexuals from the sacraments. "We were not trying to start up a separate church for people of the same gender sexual and affectional orientation. That's wrong . . . We were concerned with a person's spirituality. Not the . . .sexuality."[9] The telltale word "spirituality" is here coupled with earnest sacramental practice. The new group was called originally Blessed Sacrament, then Holy Eucharist. The name emphasizes what the church meant to offer: "Blessed Sacrament because the sacrament was being denied to certain people. But now we *had* it."[10] Hyde stresses "had," but the last sentence can also be read with the stress on "we." The first publicly announced Eucharist was celebrated by Hyde on Christmas Eve, 1946.[11]

Later Hyde's group divided to pursue different possibilities. Hyde himself joined Clement Sherwood's Orthodox Catholic Church of America, which ordained him as a bishop in 1957.[12] The legal documents, the name, and even the vestments of Hyde's Atlanta church finally passed to Robert Clement and New York's Church of the Beloved Disciple in 1972.[13] But that is another epoch. At present I underscore some features of Hyde's original founding. Though not explicitly homosexual, the new church was rather more than accepting. It had been founded to provide sacraments and ethical instruction to those who acted openly on same-sex desires. The congregation violated other social taboos, not least by mixing races. Moreover, Hyde was not fastidious about denominational boundaries. Members of various denominations attended his services, and his message, to judge from early newsletters, was broadly biblical and ethical—if it was also sacramental.[14] Hyde's congregation protested in a number of other ways against what he called "all that institutional stuff," but it did so by establishing a parallel institution. In all of these ways, it was much like a homophile group—though the word had not yet been retrieved.

A CHURCH OF HOMOPHILE BROTHERHOOD

In 1950, in Los Angeles, a small group of "homophile" men began meeting with Harry Hay, who did reinvent or retrieve the word.[15] After trying unsuccessfully to promote discussions around the first Kinsey report, Hay's lover Gernreich brought together a group around Hay's early drafts of a homophile manifesto for the androgynous minority. They formed the Mattachine Society, a secretive support network. It was secretive partly from Hay's notions about communal bonding or ritual, but mainly because of police persecution and the enormous cost of being branded a "homosexual." "Mattachine" referred to roving troupes of medieval performers, but also to the common notion of homosexual life as masquerade.

One member of the original group was Chuck Rowland, who had just moved to Los Angeles from the Midwest. Rowland had been raised a devout Methodist, but he became disgusted by church hypocrisy on social issues. At thirty, he was attending district rallies of the Communist Party USA, but he still associated singing the "Internationale"—the Communist anthem—with memories of singing "A Mighty Fortress Is Our God" or "Holy, Holy, Holy."[16] Rowland brought both his commitment to reform and his Christian upbringing to Harry Hay's new society, not least as convictions about the interaction of cultural consciousness with ritual. In 1953, Rowland gave a fiery speech at the Mattachine constitutional convention, which had been convened in part to rebut charges that the society was a Communist front organization. Rowland urged that homosexuals be understood as an oppressed social minority with its own culture.[17] The speech was not generally accepted by the members, who fled distinctness to profess their patriotism—their faith in "the American creed."[18]

Rowland transferred his energies to a new venture: *ONE Magazine*,[19] which counted Alfred Kinsey among its early subscribers.[20] The magazine was its own corporation, and the corporation initiated a number of activities.[21] By early 1956, Rowland was conducting Sunday evening meetings on religious themes. The meetings were surrounded by misunderstanding or disagreement from the start. The board of ONE approved them as "religious group-therapy meetings," on the model of Alcoholics Anonymous, for people who were working through religious issues. They describe the program entirely in therapeutic terms, and entrust it to Rowland as "Director of the Guidance Center."[22]

Rowland himself had been thinking rather of a religious group, in part because of his involvement with a Universalist congregation. Its pastor, Wallace David de Ortega Maxey, "had all kinds of ideas about a gay congregation that was to arise within the Unitarian-Universalist organization."[23] Maxey had followed a path something like Hyde's, though in the reverse direction and through more jurisdictions: he was ordained or consecrated many times by various "American Catholic" or "Old Catholic" prelates, some of whom he consecrated in turn—just to insure the apostolic succession for everyone. In 1949, Maxey joined Universalism, and it was as a Universalist that he met Rowland and other homophile leaders. Indeed, Maxey's church served as the site for the Mattachine constitutional convention in April of 1953.[24] But Rowland's relation to him awakened or prolonged churchly interests. Instead of leading group-therapy sessions, Rowland began to conduct his meetings as the worship of the "Church of ONE Brotherhood." He and three others were consecrated as bishops by a leader of the Christian Spiritualist Church of Los Angeles.[25] During the spring of 1956, the little congregation grew steadily.[26] Sometimes Rowland spoke of it in Christian terms. At other times, he conceived it as a "new RELIGION."[27]

Either way, the other members of the corporation were not pleased. The corporation's newsletter published a cruel description of Rowland's services. Jim Kepner ("Lyn Pedersen") claimed that Rowland "met GOD . . . just a few days after someone on ONE magazine made the careless remark that a 'homosexual church' could be a lucrative racket, if we were looking for rackets."[28] In a letter to "Archbishop" Rowland, the board adopted the cruelty as its "unanimous opinion concerning your church and its methods," which it declared "definitely damaging to the homosexual minority as a whole."[29] Rowland was thrown out of the corporation. The church collapsed a short while later, because Rowland's own life collapsed, financially and psychologically. With bus fare from his sister and travel expenses from Evelyn Hooker, Rowland fled Los Angeles for the Midwest, where he lived for two decades a hermit's exile.[30]

Through his correspondence, Rowland appears neither as a conman who sought profit from religion nor as dogmatic Communist who hoped to cure addiction to the churches' opiate.[31] Although he left few records of his religious views in 1956, there are some clues—and they can be expanded by reading underneath the satire on his worship service. In a survey of "Possible Courses of Action," Rowland ticked off the forms a homophile religious ministry could take.[32] They include a lecture series, nondenominational services, the formation of new congregations in existing churches, or the formation of the new (Christian) church. He speaks of another possibility with enthusiasm: "a new RELIGION with a new God—the God of our people—with a symbolism and ritual tailor-made for our needs." Kepner's caustic description of Rowland's service suggests that he in fact combined the notion of a new church with that of a homophile religion.

The service that Kepner describes is attended by several dozen people, mostly young, with a "high percentage of 'androgynous' types."[33] The service is conducted by an acolyte, "a slender and a spiritual youth," an archbishop (namely, Rowland), and at least one other bishop. (This enacts Wildean fantasies about priests and acolytes while fulfilling Hall's fears about liturgical "patheticism.") The service's language mixes the King James Version and the 1928 Episcopal prayer book with Romantic medievalism. A recited catechism affirms one's whole self "in the presence of thy brothers." There is a reading from Whitman. The Lord's Prayer is recited with joined hands. When the archbishop speaks, he "intones most devoutly that homosexuals were now all marching on a common path toward a united goal." Listen through the sarcasm: this is a ritual with some Christian reminiscences, but it is mainly a new liturgy for casting out self-loathing by the power of community. It harkens back to the spiritual socialism of Edward Carpenter—not only in the fondness for Whitman's notion of male comradeship, but in its seeking to build a community of such men with shared ritual practices. But the service also echoes Hay's own notions of ritual—as it anticipates Hay's return to new religion in the 1970s through the radical faeries.

The leaders of ONE may have cast Rowland out for taking religion too seriously, manipulating it too crudely, or having bad liturgical taste, but their own publications attested to its importance. For example, the June 1954 issue of *ONE Magazine* is devoted to religion. It reports excitedly on the Moral Welfare Council's interim report, from which it quotes at length.[34] Other pieces denounce the evils of churches, but they also attest the need to move beyond them to a personal mysticism or genuinely supportive small groups. Most interestingly, the issue contains a piece, "Thorn in the Spirit," that offers an "effeminate," homoerotic portrait of Jesus against muscular, "masculinized" Christianity.[35] Following Kinsey, the short essay shows vividly how the churches have distorted the Gospel image of Jesus in their hypocritical and uniquely violent denunciation of male-male sex. The piece is by Jim Kepner, Rowland's satirist. Perhaps Kepner's complaint against Rowland is not that he has fallen back into religion, but that he hasn't fallen passionately enough. Kepner, at least, wants something more—from and about Christ.

CHRIST MEETS THE HOMOSEXUAL

In the spring of 1960, the second issue of the *Dorian Book Quarterly* featured a clergyman on its cover. The *Quarterly* was a project linked to the "new" Mattachine—relocated to San Francisco and purged of its Communists. It was published by Pan-Graphic Press, which also published the *Mattachine Review*. Its editors included Hal Call and Don Lucas, officers of the Mattachine. This particular issue of the *Quarterly* features Robert Wood's *Christ and the Homosexual*. The magazine reprints a mixed notice of the book from *Mattachine Review*.[36] The reviewer pronounces Wood the new Edward Carpenter. The magazine's Book Service, for which it serves as informative advertising, summarizes the book with enthusiasm: "Of special interest to the highly religious homosexual troubled by the apparent irreconcilability of active homosexuality and devotion to Christian dogma. The author calls for social recognition of love relationships between members of the same sex in unmistakable terms, and castigates his fellow clergymen for their incredible ignorance of things sexual. Thoroughly excellent."[37] If only the book were thoroughly one thing or another.

Wood's book is at once courageous and equivocal, bold and self-concealing. The authorial voice has no consistency. It rambles and repeats itself. It veers from borrowed psychological jargon or earnest social concern to a clunking and incoherent pulpit oratory. "Woe, woe, woe to the homosexual who loves and lives for his homosexuality, for he is doomed to a wasted, unfulfilled life on this earth, not to mention the possibility of the closed doors of eternity."[38] How does the prospect of an "unfulfilled life on earth" add to the terrors of eternal damnation—unless, of course, the threat of eternity is an obligatory insincerity? Wood's voice often speaks against itself in this way—speaks contradictions, evades frank declaration. The effect is at once incoherent and inadvertently, painfully confessional.

Wood does not name himself a homosexual. He takes care to speak of homosexuals as others and to address them accusingly. "It is too easy, you homosexuals, to blame your homosexuality for your failure to establish a meaningful relationship with Christ."[39] Yet Wood's detailed knowledge of queer life betrays him. He knows how much this season's trendy coat costs and how often in the past gay fashions have passed into straight markets. He writes passionately and frequently about the plight of gay clergymen. In the most awkwardly revealing passages, Wood returns to sadomasochism in gay life. If he ends by condemning these practices as sin against the "holy temple" of the human body, the reader may remember a much more striking passage near the book's beginning.[40] It describes with a pulp's relish for detail an SM party in a private residence.

Wood writes the description in the second person: "You have not been to this house before nor do you know your host."[41] The rhetorical device is supposed to increase the reader's sense of immediacy—like a point-of-view shot in a film. "You" are there! But "you" are curiously like Wood's "I." You are obsessed with details of props and costuming, about which you are astonishingly well informed: the *cowboy* boots tied to a slave's testicles *with rawhide* and slowly filled with water as his back presses against the *roughened* plaster of the wall. (How did you spot rawhide and roughened plaster across a room? Didn't "you" have to move up close to see—to touch?) You profess in theological language to be overwhelmed with horror at the sights, sounds, and smells: "you wonder if Dante himself had ever experienced such a horror." You insist that you departed as soon as you were urged to join the infernal scenes. You assuage your sleeplessness later that night by recalling biblical passages from Romans on human depravity. The conceit is paper thin: "you" is "I" in this text, and the text's devices are borrowed from pornographic literature. From Sade, as from so many others, we learn to hear certain professions of horror as whimpers of desire—or mumbled vows to participate tomorrow. We learn too that theological learning can increase the pleasure of transgression. This displaced narrator, this "you," resembles our ordained author also in erudition. Conventionally, members of the Christian clergy can visit the haunts of sexual sin without being dirtied. They are expert observers of sexual transgression who never transgress. But the claim is multiply undone in Wood's text. None of his masks will quite stay in place, least of all the mask that says Aloof Minister.

The confusion of claims or purposes repeats itself in Wood's responses to his central question: "Can one be both an overt homosexual and a Christian?"[42] Wood means to answer with a resounding and unqualified yes that explicitly includes sexual activity.[43] To do so convincingly, he feels that he must demonstrate theologically the moral worth of male-male sexual activity. He offers three explicit arguments. They fail to cohere.

Wood's first explicit argument is that Christians should see homosexuality as a divinely created response to overpopulation. As a standalone argument, this does nothing to justify homosexual genital activity. Celibate homosexuals would serve the divine purpose just as well. But Wood is trying to find a reason for the divine creation of homosexuals. Why would God make some human beings who can only have sterile sex? Overpopulation was increasingly invoked by churches to justify another kind of deliberately sterile sex—sex with artificial means of contraception. Rethinking contraception means exploring the possibility that human sexual activity is not always about procreation. The possibility invites a larger reassessment of Christian restrictions on sex. (Only a few years later, the inference from approved contraception to approved homosexuality would bedevil Catholic deliberations—and help Paul VI overturn his own commission's recommendation of a change in official teaching.)[44] Wood hasn't got the argument right, but he does see that he needs to find a reason why God might have instilled desires for nonprocreative sex.

Wood's second and third arguments head in another direction—and should be read together. The second argument is that homosexual relations can be "sacramental" for those who cannot find heterosexual love. By "sacrament," Wood means "an act blessed by God and enriched by His mysterious presence."[45] The argument is a claim that God does sometimes bless sexual love between two men who cannot find sexual intimacy with women. The unstated premise is that sexual love is divinely intended for all kinds of human beings. Wood's third argument shifts from sexual love to the more encompassing category of self-*expression*. Kinsey's first report described homosexual act or desire as "an expression of capacities that are basic in the human animal."[46] There the term carries a biological aura and is not too far from Kinsey's notion of sexual *outlet*. Genital expression seems the inevitable result of a latent desire, the eruption of an unacknowledged disposition. But Niebuhr had also used the term in rebuking the biologists: he wrote of the expression of a person's essential being. For Niebuhr, the term is the opposite of biological: it carries the aura of high culture and ethical integrity, of fully human action emerging from the core of a human life. Wood means to sound like Niebuhr rather than Kinsey. For Wood, part of having "a sacred human personality" implies being able to express it adequately, not least in sexual activity.[47]

Reviewing the trio of explicit arguments, it is not clear whom they are supposed to convince. They are not arguments from traditional Christian ethics for the approval of male-male sex. Wood tries instead to find some moral content in male-male sex that could be attributed to divine creation or present blessing. There must be something to raise homosexual activity above the bestial and demonic scenes of SM or the idolatry of endless cruising. Wood is not saying, The pleasure in this sex is a created good. He claims instead that there is something in it beyond mere sexual pleasure. He props up the claim by an appeal to love or human self-fulfillment as higher than mere self-gratification, than couplings and rubbings—not to speak of rawhide straps.

It is easy enough to see Wood's reasoning as the sort of fuzzy optimism that reduces Christianity to a silly confidence in human powers. But Wood is not so quickly typed. Other arguments implied by the book point elsewhere. For example, Wood regularly identifies homosexuals as members of a minority group deprived of its rights by prejudice. The effects of prejudice are so indiscriminately destructive that Wood compares them to a hydrogen bomb's blast.[48] This cluster of images associates homosexuality with iconic political struggles—with the struggle over racial integration, of course, but also with the campaigns against nuclear destruction. To prejudge homosexuals is to become a dangerously ignorant bigot. As Woods presents it, the racial analogy steps *from* race *to* homosexuality: 'You used to persecute black people the way you now persecute homosexuals. You now concede that you shouldn't persecute black people, so stop attacking homosexuals.' Rhetorically, claims for racial equality precede and justify claims for sexual equality. Of course, a rhetorical narrative is not intellectual history. Minority logic was applied to homosexuality outside the American racial dichotomy of white/black, and the logic itself stands in some sense before both race and sexuality.

Wood often has in mind other models of minority status than racial ones. For him, the homosexual is like a paraplegic or someone blind, other handicapped people who struggle against their afflictions to become constructive members of society.[49] These analogies do not fit with Wood's moral justifications for male-male sex, but they do activate another set of religious arguments. Someone who cannot see the love or self-expression in a male couple might perhaps be moved by seeing them as poor wretches who deserve the consolation prize of mutual support. They cannot really love, the dears, but they can help each other through a crippled life. The tacit appeal by Wood for Christian sympathy undercuts his arguments for condoning same-sex genital activity. Sex among the handicapped is often viewed as freak sex—to be regulated, if not prevented by the institutions that a benevolent society creates to confine them.

Wood's turn to images of handicap and affliction brings into view deeper confusions about what homosexuality might actually be. He recites half a dozen definitions, misunderstanding some and leaving others un-criticized. Wood makes his own the text from Cory that defines the homo-sexual in terms of an *urgent* sexual desire *mainly* directed to persons of the same sex.[50] Though he promises not to treat the question of causality, Wood shares with Hooker and many other writers a desire to harmonize competing causal theories. But he can settle on no single account of the origin of this desire. He blames it on problems in the home—especially an imbalance between father and mother. When mothers attempt to dis-cipline boys, instead of leaving it to Father Who Knows Best, the result is an upsurge of homosexuality—in the young, of course, not in Father. But there may also be genetic factors. A bachelor uncle is a bad sign. So are an aunt's "three henpecked husbands."[51] The role of inheritance is also sug-gested by the label "sex variant," which Wood borrows from Henry. But then he invokes a theory of homosexuality by contact. Wood worries about teenage boys who are seduced by older men—though he adds immediately that it is often the teen who does the seducing and that there are many other sources for stimulating "erotic feelings" in the adolescent. "The flow of physique photos and homosexual pornography, not to mention toilet-room art, is so prevalent today that if a boy of high-school age has not seen a picture of a nude male he is indeed living a sheltered life."[52] But surely the picture of a nude male—or the glimpses afforded in the locker room—will only have powerful effects on those who are already so inclined.

It is the inclination that makes the homosexual. Wood is clear at least about that. Clear too that a homosexual is something that a person can *be*. "You are a homosexual," he declares forcefully as preface to a frank pep talk.[53] You may try to hide it for years—from yourself, from those around you. But it will track you down, even in an apparently heterosexual middle age. It can be felt as nagging loneliness, a recurring sense of social displacement. "Then the bombshell explodes! Something occurs, usually unnoticed over the years, to bring his latent homosexuality to the fore."[54] A man discovers that he is a *real* homosexual and so becomes an *overt* one. Hopefully he will be one of the *more normal* homosexuals and avoid the self-destruction of promiscuity, of flinging himself into the whirl of gay life. But whatever he chooses, he has his fate. The most important "decision" has already been made for him by unknown causes. He awakes, sooner or later, to find himself stranded in that "abysmal loneliness."[55] Note how this narrative differs from many we have heard about the invert. In them, the same-sex attractions of adolescence, instead of dissolving at the entry to adulthood, are prolonged into it. Inversion extends a feature of adolescent time into adult life. Wood's story of latency, by contrast, interrupts the time of adulthood with an unexpected return to adolescence. Indeed, it takes some adult males back to the adolescence they should have had. If Wood doesn't apply this story to all homosexuals, he recognizes in some of them a punctuated identity—an identity marked by belated discovery.

What is the church to do for homosexuals, whenever or however they come to be? It must speak about them and to them. Homosexuality should be discussed in sex-education classes, in marriage counseling, in seminary classes on sexual ethics. There should be homilies against the mistreatment of homosexuals, but also ministries aimed at their conversion. Churches should offer safe social space for homosexuals—dances and amateur theatricals. They should also establish a national institute for the study of homosexuality, to follow up on recent studies by the Church of England—that is, by Bailey and the study group to which he belonged. But Wood's list of policy recommendations culminates in an altar call for the homosexual. He cannot resist the preacher's impulse—or he has no better gift to offer. The homosexual must not let his condition become an obstacle to seeking Jesus. He must join the church. Room will be found for him—on the pews, but also in the choir, surely, and even in the clergy, if he has the call. "The alternative is a half-fulfilled life, deserted, distorted, lacking in creative purpose. It is a life that is already half-dead."[56] Christ welcomes the sexually active homosexual, but only after normalizing him as far as possible.

Neither Wood's moral arguments for homosexuality nor his policy proposals were favorably received in the Protestant press. Though Hooker recommended his book to the church conference, it was not widely reviewed in church periodicals.[57] His moral arguments were hardly received at all. Some of the "homophile" organizations, by contrast, welcomed them. In April 1964, Wood spoke to the New York chapter of the Mattachine Society. A published version of the text presents twelve points for dialogue between Christian churches and homosexuals.[58] Wood lists a range of issues, from criminal law reform through military service and ministerial ordination to same-sex marriage. Youth appears only near the end, in a discussion of the shifting moral attitudes on college campuses. Wood again urges the denominations to revise their religious-education materials to include homosexuality. He ends as before by calling on homosexuals to be active participants in their local congregations because they too need the saving power of Jesus—though they do not need to give up their homosexuality. Speaking to Mattachine, Wood speaks as if to homosexuals at large about homosexual youth. But youth beyond homophile groups was already being claimed for different purposes—and under a different theology.

A NEW DIVINE COMEDY

Not long before Evelyn Hooker spoke to the church leaders assembled by the lake in Wisconsin, she sought out one particular subject in Los Angeles for her studies of homosexual men. His Anglicized name was John Rechy, and she had heard—from no less an authority than Christopher Isherwood—that he was a smart young man who was hustling on the streets.[59] Rechy filled out Hooker's questionnaire as a research subject, but he was already known for other writing. Since 1958, he had been publishing short pieces in literary magazines about life in the underworld of male hustlers. These pieces would reappear, transformed, as his first novel, *City of Night* (1963). The novel became a bestseller, no doubt because it seemed to offer prurient glimpses of forbidden sex. It marks an epoch in writing about gay lives, but also in the representation of gay adolescence. What is more frequently forgotten, it is one of the great works of gay religion—precisely because it is a prolonged meditation on adolescence. In Rechy, as much as in Hall, adolescence is the period of religious and sexual epiphany. Then it must be the period through which a new theology can be prophesied. In Rechy's novel, the hustler experiences and announces divine revelations.

When *City of Night* appeared, John Rechy was in his early thirties. Internal references and biographical evidence place the novel's main events between 1954 and 1958, when Rechy was in his mid-twenties—when Bailey's book appeared, when Chuck Rowland started his Church of ONE Brotherhood. The book is *not* a record of street life in the early 1960s. Indeed, it is no record of street life at all. Thoroughly autobiographical, it is also a carefully constructed pilgrim's narrative, with well-plotted shifts of voice and a system of motifs or symbols. Rechy later professed himself surprised that the novel was ever read as unadorned autobiography or as "a social protest novel."[60] Much of *City of Night* is a visionary journey through moralized landscapes in which people are compelled to confess their sins and—what is more painful—their hopes. It is, as Rechy suggests, another telling of Purgatory—which is to say, an account of sanctification and the near approach to Heaven.[61] Except that in this undivine comedy, *Purgatorio* is indistinguishable from *Inferno* because there is no further paradise. The novel's epigraph points to James Thomson's poem "The City of Dreadful Night," which begins in its turn with a quotation from Dante:

"*Per me si va nella citta dolente*," the opening words of the inscription over the gateway to hell (*Inferno* 3.1). Rechy's readers enter the novel under them. The only hope in the city beyond is to bless one's suffering by speaking it as revelatory.

The action of the novel ends on Ash Wednesday in New Orleans, the epilogue of a Mardi Gras of demonic visions. That morning the narrator visits one Catholic church after another to talk with a priest. Most rebuff him. When a young priest does finally agree to listen, the reader hears nothing of the narrator's confession. Or rather the reader has heard it all, in its more ornate form throughout the novel. Here, as in Augustine, confession rearranges memory until it discloses a hidden trajectory toward the divine. Rechy reminds his readers that every remembered telling has its forms, and that imposing form—or searching for it—is often the main purpose for the telling. From that Ash Wednesday confession, the novel records only the priest's absolution: "'I know,' he said. 'Yes, I know.'"[62] In Rechy, absolution is recognizing the form of another's telling. To read *City of Night* as straightforward autobiography is not only to ignore its elegant structure and its extravagance of styles, its made-up words and bent rules of grammar, but to forget how imperceptibly self-narration becomes theodicy.

Rechy means to write against Augustine and Dante, against their canonical Christianity, by reversing religious language. *City of Night* is overstuffed with Christian topics, images, and allusions. The title borrowed from Thomson originally applied only to the stream-of-consciousness segments that punctuate, like hymn refrains or antiphons, the remembered confessions of other characters encountered on the journey. Rechy considered various titles for the whole novel, including *Ash Wednesday*, *Shrove Tuesday*, or *Storm Heaven and Protest* (the last a quotation from a remarkable drag queen). Under two of the alternate titles, the novel would have been a long entry into Lent. Under the third, it would have appeared as a reverse theodicy, in which the Christian God is compelled to produce some justification for having created and then let fall.

Whatever its title, the whole book meditates on divine incarnation, that is, on divine articulation in our flesh. As a pious and fearful boy, the novel's narrator watches during the weeks that his father builds the family's *nacimiento*, a traditional nativity scene that models the Catholic cosmos in fanciful miniature. The older man hangs "angels from the elaborate simulated sky, replete with moon, clouds, stars."[63] Other days his father abuses him physically and perhaps sexually (the narrative is deliberately unclear). So of course the boy throws rocks at heaven hoping to make it fall down; he searches for a stick big enough to puncture it. Later, already hustling, he imagines a God so overcome with sorrow at creation that He plunges into Hell. (Rechy's God is still a capitalized male.) But God in Hell is still recognizably God. Heaven fallen to earth is heaven in pieces. A reverse-discourse of Christianity moves still within the Christian imaginary. The sexual underworld through which the narrator makes his pilgrimage is one enormous *nacimiento*, much bigger than any built by his father for Christmas in El Paso. Its angels and devils, saints and sinners, surround the makeshift bed(s) where the divine might take flesh tonight.

The story writes its Christianity directly onto sex. The narrator's violently Catholic childhood gives way to adolescent rejection of the church. He stops going to Mass, stops praying. But his first experience of sexual intercourse takes place under a hilltop crucifix bearing *Cristo Rey*, Christ the King. When he finally leaves El Paso to wander the night cities of America, he wants, of course, "some substitute for salvation."[64] A man picks him up in Times Square. Their exchange—the "score" pays to fellate him—takes place as the narrator projects "a shawled Mexican woman" into a landscape painting on the wall.[65] Our Lady of Guadalupe watches over his initiation—or baptism—into hustling. A while later he enters an arrangement with the invalid Professor, who proves to be the theologian, the *doctor ecclesiae*, of the hustlers' heavenly hierarchies. The Professor conducts multiple inquisitions, monologue-interviews, before assigning each hustler to his proper angelic choir—as earthbound or seafaring or ethereal. (The simple conceit of *Better Angel* has become a scholasticism.) The narrator learns that the "good," "fairytale" God of Christianity is in reality a voyeur—or rather a fickle, sometimes malicious woman.[66] To rebel against Her is, in a curious way, to turn back by reversal toward the truly good.

The extraordinary drag queen Miss Destiny offers another theology. She asks the narrator whether he believes in God. He replies that "God" is only "a cussword." Miss Destiny corrects him. There is a God—a jokester deity who traps human beings in a world that is a drag bar. "But one day, in the most lavish drag youve evuh seen—heels! and gown! and beads! and spangled earrings!—Im going to storm heaven and protest! *Here I am!!!!!* I'll yell—and I'll shake my beads at Him. . . . And God will cringe!'"[67] Miss Destiny's theology embraces the world in order to embarrass God when she delivers it to heaven.

For Rechy's novel, the only convincing theology comes out of drag bars in high heels. Certainly it is camp theology in that sense: Miss Destiny offers an articulate reverse-discourse to Christian theology, a counter-theodicy. But Rechy's novel is camp theology even when Miss Destiny is offstage. In its stylistic excesses, its montage of cultural citations, its passion for hyperbole, the novel performs camp from page to page. It is "the theatricalization of experience," but also the mannerist redemption of whatever is most stigmatized.[68] Rechy stages gutter-baroque theology: he affirms hungry flesh while styling its subterfuges.[69] In Rechy, the sexual underworld is the one place in which God can still become incarnate. It is the only cradle, the only *nacimiento*, in which God can be born.

Sexual desire opens a space for incarnation and epiphany—but only, it seems, until the moment of orgasm. While in New Orleans for Mardi Gras, the narrator meets Jeremy. As the carnival rages outside, they conduct a holy conversation on the white sheets of his rented bed. It is something like a retreat—or, more exactly, an examination of conscience before a general confession and a change in state of life, the sort of confession one would make before professing vows to a religious order or to a partner in marriage. On one level of the plot, the narrator refuses Jeremy's offer of unpaid mutual relationship and engulfing love. On another, he encourages Jeremy's desire, claims a part of his own, and goes beyond fellatio to anal intercourse. But then, necessarily, "the orgasms have made us strangers again." The narrator stands over Jeremy, who lies smiling on the white sheets. "That wry smile seemed to be a judgment on the world."[70] The narrator leaves Jeremy to rejoin the throng.

The throng—or rather the infernal city, city of night. "Then I had the feeling that I was in hell."[71] This hell used to be called Sodom. "The skeletons, the jesters, the cannibals, the vampires, the ragdolls, the witches, the leopard-people—I imagined the razing fire sweeping this rotten city. People scream! Attempt to Escape! Flee the holocaust!" It could be Lot remembering his angel-guided flight from the rain of fire over Sodom. Only it is a hustler who is tempted by the desire to become queer—by the seduction of love and mutuality. "The terrible apocalyptic fire" threatens "the dark masked Ritual." But there is no good God in the heavens to send the fire. It is the Devil who appears before him, who embraces him. The narrator escapes, only to "look at the ghostly steeples of the Cathedral. *I'll climb to that nonexistent Heaven!*" He remembers finally a deranged vagrant, a woman, who again and again shielded her eyes from the spectacle of Hollywood Boulevard only then to bless it. "Stupidly, now, I raised my hand as if to imitate that woman's benediction." Blessing Sodom is the spiritual condition for making a good confession at the start of Lent.

Inhabitants of Sodom: in *City of Night*, the reader sees only a few "homosexuals" up close. The narrator's neighborhood doesn't welcome them except as transients. He acknowledges that there are suburbs elsewhere for mutual homoerotic love, for settled relationships and something like marriage. *City of Night* offers a more local classification. It divides its denizens into queens, scores, and youngmen; or, more tersely, queens and their trade mock-husbands; or, more structurally, painted manikins with their middle-aged pursuers and tough hustlers with the much larger crowd that pursues them. The hustlers are expensive objects of desire for scores, that is, for queers, fruits, fags, cocksuckers. Officially, hustlers feel no desire for their customers. They allow themselves to be sucked and fondled, but they reserve their desire for young women—officially. The narrator follows the hustler script in not having sex with a man before he has it for money. His first homosexual experience is also his first commercial sex. There is no homosexual childhood, no troubled foreshadowing of misdirected passions to come.

At the same time, being a hustler is performing a role. Every citizen of *City of Night* has a role to play and a mask to wear. The masks go with costumes—as elaborate as High Drag or fetishwear, as severely simple as blue jeans and white t-shirt. Wearing the mask requires dissembling self and past. It is unclear which language might describe what lies behind the mask: an inverted Christian language, perhaps, or the terminology of psychiatry. The narrator repeatedly diagnoses his own narcissism and explains it as the effect of a "childhood-tampered ego."[72] Miss Destiny reports that a psychiatrist once claimed to cure her, and after her disappearance from the night-world there is a rumor that he has. But the Professor mocks the voyeuristic desire of one of Kinsey's assistants who comes to interview him. He longs so badly to see a wild gay party that they stage one for him. "In the future, you will see life imitating science!"[73] Because life is a masquerade—and science wants ever so much to be tricked by clever disguises.

If there is no describable reality under masks, if there are roles and costumes all the way down, some events or relations do impose incontestable restraint. The night-city acknowledges hard realities in the orders of violence and poverty. Its citizens are delinquents exposed alternately to society's neglect and punishment. They are denounced as "perverts and tramps," "hobos! homos! and momos!" (no one quite knows what the last insult means).[74] They belong to the underworld of delinquency: "hoods, hobos, hustlers, homosexuals." Menaces to society, they belong with the outcasts and vagrants, their hustler bars next to the hobo cafeterias.

The hustlers in particular condense the category of delinquency because they are "youngmen." The narrator writes the word as a fused noun, the name of a distinct species or category of creature. He also capitalizes the word "Youth." The night-city is the network of delinquent youth. Youth means running along its streets—from home, from the law, from dangerous scores. Youth is the norm of same-sex desire, its object and its judge. The hustler is the emblem for desire, but also its reversal—its rejection in a required straightness, in mimed butchness. The earliest part of the novel to be published, a version of the Mardi Gras section, appeared in an issue of *Evergreen Review* with a cover story about James Dean. Its opening paragraph places the narrator's cross-country hustling under "the shadow of James Dean because of the movie."[75] "The movie" is, of course, *Rebel Without a Cause* (1955), with its iconic costume, its laconic style, and its homoerotic subtexts. The theology of Rechy's novel appropriates and recirculates discourses of delinquency, but also the popular codes for representation of sexually ambiguous adolescence. In 1955 or 1963, there can be no movie advocating same-sex desire in teens, much less arguing that it discloses a more plausible theology. But what you can suggest with a white t-shirt, a leather jacket, and Sal Mineo's eyes! In *Rebel*, Mineo's character is nicknamed Plato. Say no more.

HOMOPHILE PENTECOST

Rowland, Wood, Rechy: three rhetorical possibilities in relation to the spiritual. Rowland's liturgy makes a pastiche of Christian liturgy, homoerotic poetry, and socialist sentiment, but his ideal is a religious language for homophile people, a ritual that will both express and advance his kind. Wood's arguments in favor of sexual love between men are a rejoinder to churches, but even more an effort to save the heart of Gospel language for homosexual men. While in the infernal city, Rechy learns or overhears fragments of languages for sexual damnation, but not any redemption other than mute blessing of the throng.

Rowland, Wood, and Rechy are also three claims on the place for religious language about same-sex desire. Wood writes in a version of traditional Christian genres, and some of his pages sound very much like moral theology or homily. Rowland moves religious language into worship—also a familiar gesture. In Rechy, the place to speak theology is a novel about hustling. That is a claim both about the revelations of stigmatized sex and the possibilities of the modernist novel. Rechy's double claim is worth taking seriously. I count him into the archive of church debates, but also into the canon of theological writing about same-sex desire. He is, to my mind, a much more astute theologian than Wood. At a minimum, I want to include works like *City of Night* in any story about the religion of nonheterosexual Americans.

Rowland, Wood, and Rechy can also be names for three social spaces: homophile groups, churches, and the streets as sexual marketplaces. Individuals regularly travel between them, but the spaces are not supposed to touch. That rule is taught by Rowland's failure, by Wood's masking, or by Miss Destiny. But they do touch—and not only in the lives of Rowland,

Wood, and Rechy. Some of their most important contacts begin around figures like Rechy's protagonist and in neighborhoods like those he worked. In San Francisco, for example, downtown churches began to open coffeehouses for runaways who had fled to the city from a hundred situations of violence or neglect. Those coffeehouses, like tentative missions in exotic lands, brought unexpected consequences for the missionaries—for the churches and the homophile groups. Perhaps they also helped some of the young.

5

MEETING FACE TO FACE

Within a decade of its retrieval or reinvention, "homophile" was mostly stripped of the mythological or ritual connotations Harry Hay had given it. The word now served more mundane purposes. According to an anecdotal etymology that doesn't mention Hay, "homophile" was coined in opposition to Kinsey's preference for "homosexual" in order to emphasize that it wasn't all about sex.[1] Later promoters of the term stressed its human breadth: "'homophile' . . . puts the emphasis on love and friendship, rather than on sex. Sex is only a part of the attraction between persons. To put the sexual component in perspective is not to denigrate it, but to imply that all homophile feelings are merely sexual seems to us to cheapen such relationships."[2]

Organizations that continued to describe themselves as homophile shared a political program and not just a fondness for friendship. In her 1968 dissertation on networks in San Francisco, Roxanna Thayer Sweet quotes a 1965 definition from Schur: homophile organizations "seek to create better understanding of the homosexual, to work for legal reform, to aid homosexuals in trouble with the law, and to help homosexuals themselves come to grips with their own problems."[3] On this and similar definitions, homophile groups are clubs of social reform rather than cells in a revolution or temples of new mysteries or way stations on a nocturnal subway. Their preferred language relies on moral ideals, psychological or sociological standards of adjustment, and political analogies to other cases of reform—especially to the plight of other minorities.

The homophiles' own plight was frequently represented in terms of the sufferings of adolescence. The troubled adolescent forced to suicide or to delinquency remained a potent emblem for what was wrong. But homophile projects of reform also required a scrupulous avoidance of the appearance of corrupting the young. The adolescent could be an emblem, but not a member. The minute and still fearful homophile groups needed

the political clout and intrinsic respectability of the churches for general
social purposes, but even more for any outreach to actual teenagers. Happily the churches were realizing that they needed homophile groups if they
were going to carry forward increasingly public dialogue about social reform—and if they were going to minister to youth on urban streets.

Before there were official meetings, there were private tokens of good
faith. In 1960, according to the *Dorian Book Review*, James Pike, the Episcopal bishop in San Francisco, refused to be drawn out in print on the merits
of Wood's *Christ and the Homosexual*.[4] But that same year he sent a representative to meet with the Daughters of Bilitis. Two years later, another
chapter of the Daughters invited Evelyn Hooker to chair a panel on religion
and mental health at a Los Angeles meeting.[5] The homophile groups and
publications formed a small but reliable network for discussing such topics.
Mimeographed lectures on church teaching or scriptural interpretation
passed from hand to hand. Related articles had appeared in the homophile
press since the beginning, but their tone changes after 1960. If the earlier
issues held out little hope of gaining anything by attending to the details
of Christianity, ten years later there is an eager readership for new books
or pamphlets, including from England, where the struggle was considered
to be more advanced. American readers were interested not only in publications associated with the Church of England, but with the work of the
Wolfenden Committee and church-supported progress toward decriminalization.[6] It is not clear at this distance how much they knew of more private
conversations overseas. Once published, the results of these conversations
were immediately imported and emulated by American church groups.

SOME QUAKERS' VIEWS

In 1957, a group of British Friends quietly began a Quaker inquiry into
homosexuality. According to one account, the conversations grew out of
concerns over student suicides at Cambridge in the wake of widely reported sex scandals and a national police crackdown.[7] Anna Bidder, a
distinguished zoologist and later founding president of Lucy Cavendish
College, was also mentor to young Quakers at Cambridge. So she gathered
a group to proceed with the conversations. If deaths at Cambridge were an
urgent motive, there were other and more general ones. The Moral Welfare
Council and Bailey had already published their work, and the governmental review was proceeding apace. The topic seemed to be everywhere.

The Quaker group was mixed. It contained the predictable combination of psychiatrists, psychologists, counselors, and educators, but there
was also one homosexual man, a lawyer. The group met regularly for seven

years. Different members were assigned to draft sections of a report. The lawyer was asked to write the section on homosexuality. But the whole text was thoroughly reviewed and revised by the whole committee. The report finally appeared as a pamphlet in February 1963 under the title *Towards a Quaker View of Sex*. It was published by the Literature Committee of the Friends Home Service Committee, but with a very pointed disclaimer: "the views expressed are those of the authors."

Seen from certain angles, the Friends' pamphlet resembles the interim report of the Anglican committee circulated almost a decade before. Indeed, *Towards a Quaker View* is sometimes understood just as the Friends taking up for themselves a question that the Anglicans had already considered. But the Quaker authors, perhaps because they are not driven by a legislative agenda, understand how large the question is. From the beginning, they see that "the study of homosexuality and its moral problems could not be divorced from a survey of the whole field of sexual activity."[8] Their report is not about the problem of homosexuality, but about the problems that sex poses to churches. Indeed, it means to "question the whole basis of judgment as to what is right and what is wrong. We shall have reason to say that sexuality, looked at dispassionately, is neither good nor evil—it is a fact of nature"[9] The questioning is sharp because "many professing Christians are themselves no longer certain what are the true implications of Christianity for sexual relationships."[10] The pamphlet attributes its own boldness to features of Quaker witness—to the equality of women and men over three hundred years, but also to steady confidence in examining empirical truth under the guidance of the ever-present God.

The empirical appears in the pamphlet chiefly as a model of "normal sexual development." Heterosexual attraction is "normal" only in the statistical sense: it is where most human beings end up.[11] Normal development includes masturbation, both during infancy and adolescence. The horror many feel at masturbation is a result of parental or social instruction, not of any natural repugnance to an evil act. Whatever damage is caused by masturbation comes from imposed guilt. The prohibitions against premarital intercourse must also be rethought—especially in view of changing social relations of the sexes.

Homosexuality is added to the model of normal development in a separate section. The section uses the abstract nouns, but begins by criticizing them. "People are not either homosexual or heterosexual. Most people are *predominantly* one or the other."[12] "People" is not a euphemism for men. The pamphlet is an attempt, however uneven, to treat women's same-sex relationships as both important and different. The discussion begins as always with male homosexuality, but it ends with female homosexuality—which it treats more or less as unknown territory. For men, the territory is a bit more familiar. According to the developmental model, "homosexual orientation . . . is actually usual among boys in the 11–17-year-old group, and may frequently find physical expression."[13] Many expressions are casual; a few, heartbreaking. The "sensitive boy," in particular, may be permanently affected by the callousness or cruelty of adolescent sex play—or by a first love abruptly broken off. More important for the pamphlet is the principle that adolescent contacts do not predict adult sexuality. Even experiences of seduction by an older man can be forgotten unless they are seared into memory by parental or social shock.

For most males, the experiments of adolescence "flow naturally into heterosexuality and even marriage."[14] The pace of development varies widely, and many who are still in male-male relationships during their twenties will be married later on. But some will not turn to women—or at least will not turn to them under present social arrangements. "Of those now becoming permanent homosexuals, many would not do so did not pressures of law and of public opinion drive them into the only society where they can find acceptance, sympathy and apparent security."[15] The law and society make permanent homosexuals out of slow learners. Or, by implication, make permanent adolescents of them. Men of this kind are a remnant or reminder of male adolescence for all. Others may revert to strong homosexual feelings later in life, after marriage—as if in a return to adolescence, an atavism. (Here the pamphlet joins Wood and others in adopting the narrative of latency.) Husband and wife can manage the consequences so long as they deal with them and each other candidly. Of course, "a substantial minority" of men may never marry—may indeed end up with other men. They can attempt "long-term homosexual 'marriages,'" sometimes with "quite impressive" results.[16]

For this model of development, most male adolescents are having same-sex relations or thinking about them. Bit by bit, most of them shift over a decade or more to heterosexual relationships. Some do not. The process is not so much an expression of nature as of circumstance or even chance. Indeed, the Quaker pamphlet accepts more fully than any earlier church text not just Kinsey's terminological suggestion about how to speak of homosexuality as outlet rather than ontology, but his notion that homosexual acts vary with time. To think of yourself as a homosexual should mean no more than observing where you are in the arc of your life and with whom you are now spending it. For the pamphlet, images of the homosexual as a garish alien are the unfortunate result of social conditions of visibility. The only homosexuals most people see are flamboyant effeminates or denizens of "'queer' society."[17]

The Friends' pamphlet then tries to give some sense of what it is like to be a homosexual. It proposes the now familiar thought-experiment of reversing the social field: imagine the world if *heterosexual* relationships were stigmatized. It points to contradictory social demands: Don't have anonymous sex in public! But don't move in as a visible couple next door! The pamphlet even provides a list of suggested readings, including Vidal's *The City and the Pillar* and Bailey's historical monograph. These paragraphs, like those that describe the life of the "sensitive boy," try to depict something of the emotional quality of male-male desire. They almost lend voice to the male homosexual—not as a criminal defendant or psychoanalytic case, but as a suffering, "sensitive" person. The evocation succeeds best, I think, with adolescence. The longer the story of development runs on, the less evocative the prose—and the more desire is said to be determined by compromise, by management. The group's concern for the young is shown not only in the developmental narrative, but in a nostalgic tenderness for the moral space of male adolescent sexuality as normally homosexual.

After a survey of the legal situation, the pamphlet turns to "constructive thinking." It asserts as fundamental a principle of equal moral evaluation between heterosexual and homosexual relationships. "We do not regard the standards of judgment relevant here as being different from those that apply to other sexual problems. Surely it is the nature and quality of a relationship that matters: one must not judge it by its outward appearance but by its inner worth."[18] But what "standards of judgment" are then relevant? Having cut the contemporary situation off from tradition (with and after Bailey), the group of Friends tries to offer some moral guidance. They affirm, emphatically and perhaps a little defensively, that "*there must be a morality of some sort to govern sexual relationships*."[19] They then insist that family life should be defended and that sexual impulses find freest expression in marriage. Deliberate, coherent action without coercion is a high moral good. By contrast, sexual sin is the exploitation of another person. Acts that involve "any element of force or coercion, or abuse of some superior position," must be condemned.[20]

The pamphlet's authors anticipated negative reactions. They got them. The report was brought to the Meeting of Sufferings, a sort of standing executive committee. It was reviewed at various monthly and quarterly meetings. The authors were often asked to speak in explanation or defense. There was press coverage in print and on television, including a satirical skit on *That Was the Week That Was*. News also traveled quickly through American homophile networks—into their publications and meetings, into their lists of resources. The pamphlet became a model for an American deliberation that began with outreach to street youth and ended with clergymen and homophile leaders on retreat—together.

THE CHURCH MEETS THE HOMOPHILE

Already in the 1950s, various San Francisco churches were engaged in outreach or youth programs that brought them into contact with young homosexuals, especially where they fell under the law. One of these was the Glide trust, endowed in 1929 to support a church presence in the Tenderloin. In 1962, partly at the urging of John Moore, the church's pastor, the trust decided to expand its work by creating the "Glide Urban Center." It appointed the Methodist clergyman Lewis Durham as executive director of the Glide Foundation and leader of efforts for urban change. Durham in turn brought in three younger ministers, including Ted McIlvenna, who was to manage the San Francisco chapter of American Methodism's outreach to young adults. During his first year, as McIlvenna recalls it, he had a sort of conversion with regard to homosexuality when he was called in to help a young man who had been beaten by the police and refused treatment at a hospital.[21] He began to minister to young gays on the street, then to establish contacts with the city's homophile organizations—not only the Daughters of Bilitis and the Mattachine Society, but the Tavern Guild and the League for Civic Education.

By 1964, McIlvenna was ready to try to bring together this newly discovered world and the much larger Protestant world for which he worked. With the sponsorship of the Methodist church's Older Youth/Young Adult Project and its Division of Alcohol Problems and General Welfare, he began to plan for a "Consultation on Religion and the Homosexual." It would bring national and local Protestant leaders to meet with representatives of the local homophile organizations. Note that the sponsoring church agencies are not the ones concerned with doctrine and ethics. They are rather agencies for social problems, especially the problems of youth. "Social problems" is still the safest rubric for churches to talk about homosexuality. McIlvenna himself would later serve for several years with the national Methodist youth ministry in Nashville and would be cited as something of an authority not only on homophile rights, but on ministerial immersion in urban youth cultures.[22]

The "consultation" (or "the retreat") brought together sixteen clergymen and fourteen members of the local organizations.[23] McIlvenna could rely on his own contacts for church leaders, but the invitations to homophile organizations were influenced by his acquaintance with two women, Del Martin and Phyllis Lyon. Martin and Lyon were among the original founders of the Daughters of Bilitis in 1956. They had presided over the launching of *The Ladder*, a lesbian magazine. By 1964, Martin and Lyon were most definitely included in the small group that ran the homophile network in San Francisco. They insisted to McIlvenna that he must include more women in the conversation—and from the homophile side, since women were evidently not going to be well represented among the Christian clergy. Martin and Lyon also brought their considerable energy to organizing the event—as they would continue, in the next few years, to provide a sort of organizational center for the elaboration of homophile Christianity.

The motives of the two women have been variously interpreted, but it seems fair to say that the main motive was neither active piety nor the wish to make peace with a deeply religious girlhood. Martin and Lyon were persuaded that contact with the churches was required both by the needs of some (other) lesbians and, perhaps more sharply, by the political agenda of the homophile organizations.[24] In this, they were not untypical of the Daughters. At a meeting just before the consultation, only two of the twenty-five women present reported still attending church.[25] (That figure is much lower than the ones given by Sweet for the male-dominated organizations: she reports only a quarter of each men's group "as having no religion or as being atheists.")[26] Perhaps an untypical group attended the Daughters' meeting that night—or, as seems more likely, homophile men retained church affiliation in greater numbers than homophile women.

The 1964 consultation was scheduled to meet May 31 through June 2 at a retreat center north of the city in Marin County, on the slopes of Mt. Tamalpais. Or rather its conversations were held there: the event actually began Saturday night at a church-sponsored coffee shop on Bush Street. According to the report by Don Kuhn, head of Glide's communications center, the pilgrims first visited a variety of men's bars—preppy, leather, faux elegant, drag. A newspaper account some time later would refer to this as "pub-crawling in 'gay' bars."[27] Bars were visited—and their habitués followed out into the streets. "When San Francisco's bars closed at 2:00 a.m. the remaining unmatched men [presumably the observed homosexuals, not the observing clergy] moved to coffee houses where they joined teenage boys restricted from bars by ever-cautious owners intent on keeping their beverage licenses."[28] But an account by a homophile participant stresses that the evening also included meetings with homophile leaders and members, as well as visits to long-term male couples.[29] Sunday afternoon offered a clandestine picnic several hours outside the city with the League of Civil Education. By Sunday evening, the (exhausted? scandalized? titillated?) group met on the mountain slope under the leadership of

Lewis Durham to hear Ted McIlvenna articulate the purposes and hopes
for the consultation.

In the original plan, Monday is devoted to listening to reports, Tuesday
to small-group discussions in pursuit of agreed statements and plans. The
presentations turn out to be uneven, of course. The churchmen speak generally and carefully about the church of today, the possibilities for reinter-
preting St. Paul according to the existential ethics of Paul Tillich, and the
symbolism of basic doctrines. The message is to forget the church past in
order to look toward the church future. The homophile leaders are rather
more sober about churches, past and present. The most direct challenge
to the clerical assumptions comes from "Billie Talmij," the regular pseudonym of one of the Daughters.[30] She invokes homophile claims to minority status and cultural distinctness in order to disrupt the consultation's
model of encounter between two social groups.

Talmij circulates a list of seventy numbered statements, which she describes as "demolition fuses" for blowing down the walls of mutual ignorance and prejudice between "the Gay and the Straight."[31] She offers in
fact, and in pure '60s idiom, aphoristic challenges to the imagined opposition of churches and homophiles, even as she claims the ground on which
the churches want to stand. Her text ends by calling the clergymen to follow the homophiles into an exodus from organized religion. Homophiles
have been compelled to discover "an approach to spiritual things" beyond
the official God.[32] Talmij solicits the clergy—sometimes mockingly, sometimes teasingly—on behalf of a divinity that forsakes dying churches. She
aligns homophiles with the movement of spiritual history and so refuses
either to disconnect the past or to repeat it.

In her "fuses," Talmij plays with categories of gender and desire in relation to assigned identities. She wonders whether God is a woman; she
jokes about traditional female roles in church.[33] Talmij also explicitly arranges her multiple identities in an "order": human first, then woman,
then lesbian.[34] In this she expands on homophile theories of the mask and
the role.[35] At times Talmij seems to adopt the consultation's logic of representation, of opposed identities. She speaks self-consciously for homophiles, for lesbians, for the Daughters of Bilitis, but she adopts the roles
precisely to draw their anarchic spiritual lessons. For Talmij, homophile
and Christian interact as alternate and simultaneous spiritual characters.

I can find no record of reaction to Talmij's efforts at demolition. It may
be that she was too far ahead of the purposes of all participants, ministerial
and homophile. The stated interest of the homophile leaders was not to
reclaim Christianity for their purposes, but to enlist the churches as allies
in the struggle for decriminalization or at least the curtailment of police

harassment. But a summary of the group conversations by Del Martin suggests another set of issues. None of the three groups could agree on a statement, much less an essay like the Quaker pamphlet, but group 1 came closest to finding some agreeable language. It "expressed deep concern for the plight of the homophile teen-ager. Since the homophile organizations may not legally deal with minors, the group proposed that an educational program be started so that clergymen at the parish level could deal knowledgeably with teen-age homosexuals."[36]

The homophile groups need church youth ministry to reach their own young. The stated reason is a legal prohibition: homophile groups are not permitted under law to deal with minors. But there are many unstated reasons. Sweet's study of the San Francisco groups two years later uncovers strong prejudices against hustlers and smear campaigns against leaders who were interested in dealing with them. She explains this as typical of stigmatized minorities, which tend to be conservative—and often decidedly prejudiced—both to protect themselves from police action and to reassure themselves of their respectability.[37] Homosexual youth—especially young male hustlers—challenge both the security and the respectability of the homophile organizations. To reach them, it would be safer to go through the officially straight ministries of a Christian church.

Martin's record of group conversation also highlights an otherwise unremarked absence in the 1964 consultation: the only voices of the young that are heard in its conversations come in a report of a survey conducted by Don Lucas. The plight of the young may have been the occasion for the meeting, but they had to be kept away from it for any number of reasons. They are to be talked about, not to talk.

THE LUCAS SURVEY

In preparation for the consultation, Don Lucas used his position as executive secretary of the Mattachine Society to circulate a questionnaire to its national mailing list. The membership of the Mattachine Society was not all of it "homosexually inclined," but most members were, and so its roster offered the best hope of getting a quick national sample. Lucas was hardly a social scientist. He supported himself for many years as a bookkeeper while he gave his energies to Mattachine and associated enterprises. With Hal Call, he set up the Pan-Graphic Press to print troublesome material (including the *Mattachine Review*), then the Dorian Book Service to educate homophile readers.

The idea of a sex-related survey was by then pure cliché. Surveys still retained for homophile activists the magic that Kinsey had conferred on them. A survey could produce revelations and spark social change. Many years later, Lucas would add to precedent the motive of curiosity: "I was just very interested in seeing . . . what problems [homosexuals] had with the church and . . . how it affected their beliefs."[38] It is worth taking the statement at face value. The leadership of San Francisco homophile organizations might know each other too well, but ignorance about the varieties of homosexual life at large challenged them as it did other homosexuals. In the cover letter accompanying the survey, Lucas writes only that he has been asked to present "some of the problems and conflicts that the homosexual finds in regards to the Church . . . In talking with hundreds of persons over the years I have found that a great number do have definite conflicts in regards to Religion and the Church."[39] The language of the survey presumes Christian or formerly Christian respondents. Indeed, the questions are written in high-church idiom—and not only because of relentless capitalization ("The Church").[40]

The survey was mailed or otherwise distributed to some 150 homosexuals with assurances of confidentiality. Forty written responses were received to the eight questions. The respondents provide autobiographical material most often when answering the fifth question: "What denomination, if any, were you raised in and what influence, good or bad, did it have on you in your childhood or now?" (Note that the interest focuses on "childhood," not adolescence.) All responses to Lucas's survey remain in the archives. I follow the printed transcripts Lucas later published, except where noted.[41] My few tests of accuracy show that the transcription is a good copy of the responses. Lucas does provide a variable summary of information about his respondents, but it includes no information about gender. To judge from internal evidence, most of the respondents (at least) are male.

Lucas prints twenty-two responses under question 5.[42] He appends five "complete essays" and eight shorter pieces that refused the question format, most of which discuss church upbringing. Taken together, thirty-one of Lucas's forty respondents comment on growing up in a Christian church. The denominational range is wide, from Roman Catholicism to Unitarianism and Christian Science. By the roughest division, there are sixteen Protestants, seven Episcopalians, and seven Catholics. There is no clear correlation between denominational background and character of experience: equally anguished incidents are recounted from Catholic, Methodist, and Unitarian upbringings. In general, the responses offer little evidence of current church practice. Only a few respondents make a point of mentioning their present affiliations or rejections.

Lucas's respondents do try to name both positive and negative effects of growing up in the churches. Some of the positive effects are specifically

religious. "I am glad that I at least had the training which has permitted me to know Christ and the BIBLE."[43] More often, the reported effects are moral, in one sense or another. "[The Methodist church] taught
me Christ's principles which was good."[44] "I am firmly convinced that
what good qualities of character that I may possess were partially the result of the Catholic church's teachings, which are of the most unselfish
and noblest behavior, and of the practice of this religion by those closest
to me."[45] "[The influence of a childhood Congregationalist church] was
rather vaguely good in morality if we define morality as possessing a positive view toward one's society."[46] For other respondents, the chief favorable
impression is social: "I recall in my [Protestant] childhood that church was
primarily a place for social gatherings, parties, picnics."[47] Finally, and perhaps too predictably, some respondents emphasize the aesthetic: "Church
buildings with organ music (which I love) and stained glass windows gave
me from childhood to this day, a kind of exhilaration."[48]

Among negative effects, the most frequently mentioned is some kind
of sexual shame. "The confessional brought built-in guilt, shame and ridi-
cule. So I had to discontinue it to remain an individual and escape with
sanity."[49] "The influence [of the Methodist church] as far as my being
homosexual was all bad. They had nothing but condemnation for us."[50]
Some recollections of negative teaching are accompanied by repugnance
at church hypocrisy. For other respondents, the problem is not thundering
condemnation, but silence. "Homosexuality was considered apparently to
be so horrendous that it was mentioned only in whispers and fraught with
terror and denial."[51] The silence on homosexuality, combined with male
privilege in scripture and church life, could lead children to draw odd conclusions: "All the teachings I had received as a child were forceful against
adultery. If I did not get involved with females it would be impossible to
commit this 'awful' sin of committing adultery."[52]

Complaints against churches are not confined to homosexuality—or
even centered on it. One respondent writes: "My childhood experiences
as far as religion is concerned: I was taught to fear physical expression
of what was natural to me; I was put in mortal dread of death; I was not
instructed to understand the beauties of my religion, merely to echo the
meaningless words and definitions; I was taught naught but conformity in
living, thinking and dying and more sorrowful of all I was led to believe
that I was an abomination in the eyes of God who created me."[53] The same
words could be used to describe many adolescents' experience of heterosexual awakening in strict churches, but they might also cover any sensual
or physical aptitude at odds with a preached asceticism.

The survey responses contain some striking stories of homosexual youth inside Christian churches. I quote from two printed in full by Lucas.[54] The first response comes from respondent 24, a psychiatrist of about forty-seven—that is, someone who was an adolescent in the early 1930s. He describes a churchgoing Methodist youth in Kalamazoo, Michigan— not far from the setting of *Better Angel*, though about twenty years later. Here is the heart of the narrative, somewhat condensed:

When I was about 11 or so I was elected president of my Sunday school class. At the same time I began to accumulate little colored medals or pins for consistent attendance. When I was about 14 I finally received the gold inlayed pin indicating several years of unbroken attendance. I was very vain about this achievement and wore the pin for quite a long time . . .

In the meantime I was undergoing sexual awakening and it wasn't on the heterosexual side . . . Nothing had ever happened in my life to hint to me that sex in any shape or form wasn't utterly evil. Thus I knew in no uncertain terms that I was utterly evil. Being an extremely sensitive and thoughtful boy, I realized that I was an abominable monster. As my desires increased my agony increased. I knew that there was nobody like me in the whole world . . .

About this same time my Sunday school teacher who must have been at least a latent homosexual himself felt compelled to steer his young pupils away from the path of evil. He related during the lesson that day a horror he had recently heard of. Two men employed by a local factory had been found playing with each other and taken away by the police . . . That beautiful Sunday morning I got home in a kind of daze. Now it began to come to me. There was no longer any question about it. For some reason that I couldn't understand I was in league with the devil . . .

I can still remember that final Sunday about 32 years ago [when he was fifteen]. We now had a new Sunday school teacher, a middle-aged man, a good and saintly man, at least he appeared to be. Our lesson that morning was on the subject of making our lives worthy of the church. That did it. I went home and after an hysterical session with my mother, I gained the concession that I did not have to go to Sunday school or church anymore. With the exception of a couple of weddings I have never been in a church since then.

This is in many ways the most familiar narrative of traumatic churchly rejection. Hatred of sex is proclaimed by churchly hypocrites with the force of social and judicial judgment. The solitary boy finds no help, no understanding, and so must carry the terrible secret of monstrousness until he just can't. It is a pre-Kinsey narrative in the sense that there is no contrary body of evidence with which to address condemnation, and preanalytic in the sense that a prospect of medical cure does not appear. There are traces in the retelling of categories learned later on: the Sunday school teacher is "at least a latent homosexual." Traces too of decisions confirmed by the intervening decades: "I have never been in church since." The break has been reiterated with the help of later science and the apparent absence of regrets.

Lucas prints in its entirety another response, from a sixteen-year-old Catholic on the East Coast (respondent 2). I have quoted from it already, in the introduction. I now rehearse parts of it again, in order. The first section describes the confusion of churchly teaching:

one priest tells me "go see a doctor," another tells me, "forget the whole matter and don't think about it," another tells me that "your inclinations are abnormal because carnal love should only result in offspring" and another tells me that "you can desire latently but it is a sin to follow through overtly!" This makes me come to the conclusion that church is only for the majority and THAT CHURCH is ALWAYS MEASURING UP TO *CONFORMITY*!!

These lines summarize the range of views around 1964, from the medico-psychological (consult a physician, don't obsess) through natural law (sex is for reproduction) to a "liberal" distinction between tendency and act. (A little later, the respondent will stress that when he uses quotation marks, "I quoted from the actual words of people.") The lines also show both the acceptance of the majority/minority distinction and the criticism that the church is an agent of social conformity. The response concedes the Catholic Church's influence over law and public opinion, but despairs of any effectual change in teaching: "if the Dogma was changed, churchmen would still want us to change our ways." He can't imagine himself changing—and yet he can't feel confidence in his own conviction.

I don't have visions. I don't see and converse with Christ every night before I go to bed. How am I supposed to know what my Creator thinks of me? The Church says that God thinks I am a "monster." Throughout my whole life I've received the sacraments, done good and bad things, sinned and confessed. Now—since a couple of months ago, I am "against nature, which is the law of God, and unless you [referring to me] don't change you are doomed."

The letter ends with pleas for understanding and even mercy.

How is the church to know how an invert feels? . . . In other words, a person or group should experience the feelings of a "monster," and an "abnormal, diverse degenerate" before judging it. . . . . I don't want to be condemned. Please don't make me feel I'll go straight to Hell—at least send me to Purgatory, then I'll have a slight chance to progress.

These two accounts describe adolescent confrontations twenty years apart, in opposed denominations, at distant points in the country. Condemnation is collaborative in both accounts. In the first, judgment is pronounced by God, the police, and Sunday school teachers. In the second, God, nature, doctors, and priests join in condemning. The collaboration increases the sense of isolation and so despair. It magnifies the gravity of the sin: to be a homosexual is to be "doomed" as a "monster" or to be "utterly evil," "an abominable monster," and "in league with the devil." Both respondents describe themselves as monsters—the one because of a marked silence, the other because the silence has been broken. For the sixteen-year-old, the newly imported scientific vocabulary lies over the other accusations, the horrors produced in sightless silence. Certain entries in the church lexicon circulate before and after Kinsey, as in a separate history. Others take over scientific terms or actively import them to speak the old lessons. We are not yet to the point where frequent, loud repetition has reduced the medico-scientific terminology to banality.

Or a frozen history. The tone is equally intense in both of the accounts, though one is written in the present tense (by a sixteen-year-old) and the other in retrospect (by someone approaching fifty). The distinction between narration and recollection may not be so significant because of the function of "timeless" religious locutions in both. Even though church teachings do of course change, especially around sex, they are taught and learned as timeless, as divine, as scriptural and natural.[55] So much of learning a religious identity is acquiring old languages—or new languages made to sound old. The rhetorical illusion may be reinforced by the curious timelessness of a violent rejection or loss. I can only wonder whether the sixteen-year-old wouldn't tell the story of those last few months the same way today—if he is still alive.

There is a difference in agency between the two accounts. In the first, there is no personal condemnation. A general lesson is applied by the hearer to his secret. In the second, the young man makes the rounds of priests looking for an answer—and he has gotten too many. The first is a self-imposed exile; the second, an as yet unfinished quest for acceptance. The two accounts share the sense that whatever comes next, comes after this church, will have to be as strong a church. The sixteen-year-old reports this as a felt need: "every guy has got to have some place to go, even if he is not a devout and saintly person. Going to church or confession sort of makes a person feel that he isn't alone. After all, a bed partner is only for a couple of minutes, hours or for a whole night—but God lasts for ever." The place he means is not a homophile strategy meeting. It is some new kind of church—or, in Talmij's language, a site for spirituality more authentic than what the retreating churches have on offer.

COUNCILS AND DENOMINATIONS

The weekend consultation led within a few weeks to the founding of a Council on Religion and the Homosexual (or CRH) that undertook a range of activities, educational and political, in San Francisco and elsewhere. Two months after the first consultation, Billie Talmij, Del Martin, and Phyllis Lyon were holding a community discussion on "Homophile Religious Experience and Expression."[56] The main text for the discussion was Wood's *Christ and the Homosexual*.

Later that fall, the CRH was inspired by the success of a local Halloween dance to think about sponsoring a sort of homosexual church social and fundraiser. The council negotiated an understanding with the Alcoholic Beverage Control Board and the city police under which the CRH could sponsor a "Mardi Gras" costume ball on New Year's Day, 1965.[57] Lewis Durham remembers Ted McIlvenna and Cecil Williams trying to negotiate with members of the vice squad, who quote Bishop Fulton Sheen to them.[58] Whatever the authorities agreed, they changed their mind in the event. Pictures tell the story—pictures taken by the police and pictures taken of the police. The police photographed anyone entering the premises, and then repeatedly demanded access to the hall. When lawyers with the CRH finally asked to see a warrant, they were arrested, along with the two gay men accused of disorderly conduct and a woman collecting tickets.[59] This would be just another incident of oppression except for what happened next: seven straight-identified clergymen called a press conference at Glide Memorial Church to protest police intimidation. A photo of them—an impressive row of clerical costume—appeared on the front page of the *San Francisco Chronicle*. There is no better image of the hopes for a homophile Christianity: the church stands up at last to defend the civil rights of homosexuals.

For the rest of the sixties, the CRH worked energetically—not least because Phyllis Lyon continued as McIlvenna's assistant.[60] The CRH published broadsides, pamphlets, and short books on legal, social, and religious matters. In 1967, to take one example, it produced a little anthology of quotations on decriminalization from progressive church leaders. The pamphlet begins by retelling the story of the Moral Welfare Council and Bailey. It then goes on to quote "the Quaker Report."[61] The CRH hosted conferences on Christian theology and the homosexual lifestyle. In August 1966, for example, it convened at Glide a "Consultation on Theology and the Homosexual" as part of the larger homophile event, "Ten Days in August." This consultation promoted an annotated bibliography with notes on Bailey, *Towards a Quaker View of Sex*, and Wood, but also Don Kuhn's 1964 report on "the dramatic meeting between a group of clergymen men and a group of homosexuals."[62] One participant remembers more simply how important it was to hear Evelyn Hooker and others whom he had only read in *ONE Magazine*.[63]

The CRH organized public outreach and protest. When its request for a booth at the state fair was denied, pickets were mustered at the front gate.[64] There were programs of outreach in gay and lesbian bars, which sometimes met with angry objections.[65] It helped establish sister organizations in Los Angeles, Washington, and elsewhere. The council's members were sent out as ambassadors. Don Lucas presented his survey results at a number of venues, including a conference in London organized by the Alban Institute. There he met Anna Bidder, the moving force behind the Quaker pamphlet, and was invited to tea by John A. T. Robinson, author of *Honest to God* and Anglican Bishop of Woolwich.[66] Back home, Lucas accepted the offer from James Pike, then Episcopal bishop for Northern California, to join a new committee on homosexuality. Pike had changed his mind decisively after hearing a description of the 1964 retreat.[67] There was a sense that real progress might be possible through the denominations.

News of progress came. In April 1969, the Council for Christian Social Action of the United Church of Christ passed a resolution on homosexuals and the law. It could have been written by the CRH. The resolution acknowledges "new insights" about sex from both science and biblical exegesis. It adopts the language of "socially rejected minorities." It calls for decriminalization, for an end to discrimination in government hiring or military service, and for the abandonment of police harassment and entrapment. In its last clause, the resolution encourages all levels of the church "to hold seminars, consultations, conferences, etc. for honest and open discussion of the nature of homosexuality in our society." This is the program of the 1964 consultation written into denominational policy—and it is only the first of a string of statements from various denominations in favor of legal reform and social recognition.

After the 1964 consultation, McIlvenna continued his work with gay youth. In 1966, he helped organize Vanguard, an organization for hustlers and others on the streets. It held Sunday evening meetings and dances. For a time, it even published its own newsletter. The first issue—mimeographed, then folded and stapled into a pamphlet—is full of the language of trampled human rights and churchly hypocrisy. Its editor adopts the French Revolutionary pseudonym "Jean-Paul Marat." But it also includes an article lamenting the departure of Edward Hansen, a minister at Glide who helped in founding a number of projects for the Tenderloin and its youth. "Once in a while a certain breed of minister arrives on the scene and brings about some real changes for the better."[68] Vanguard soon fell part, in part because it never succeeded in establishing alliances with the other homophile groups. But this organization of street youth did suggest, for those who had eyes to see, the possibility of another kind of homosexual movement. It would organize itself not according to the associational patterns of the homophile networks, but loosely, ephemerally, "radically." It would seek a way out of its solitude not by looking to the old churches, but by refashioning itself in view of a revolutionary future.

According to one historical reconstruction, the skirmish with the police at Stonewall was provoked by young hustlers in the crowd of onlookers.[69] They proved in New York, as they had in San Francisco, the uncontainable element. They were locked out of the bars by their age—and kept out of homophile organizations for their dangerous criminality. In New York, if not so plainly in San Francisco, they also announced the birth of homosexual politics without benefit of clergy.

6

CHURCHLY LIBERATIONS

The glossy pages of a soft-core gay magazine from 1970 are one montage of the institutional end of homophile projects in religion. The magazine is *Vector*, published by the Society for Individual Rights (SIR), a San Francisco homophile organization that participated in the church consultation during 1964. Following the consultation, SIR or some of its members pursued the possibilities of homophile engagement with the churches. SIR letterhead was used in December 1964 to announce nonprofit status for the CRH. Following the New Year's Day dance in 1965, SIR established a "religious" committee of its board, chaired by Don Lucas, for which the charge included "liaison with established religious groups; referrals to ministers; research and surveys into religious attitudes; . . . and participation by homosexuals in church and religious activities."[1] The committee began immediately to plan an orientation for ministers or congregations and conversations with a variety of clergy. By 1967, SIR was reprinting articles by friendly clergy from mainstream church publications.[2] Religious news appeared regularly in *Vector*, SIR's best-known publication. In October 1970, the magazine's list of contributors includes national homophile notables like the Mattachine's Frank Kameny, and at least two writers of erotica, both under their pseudonyms: "Phil Andros" and "Richard Amory." Equally notable among the contributors is Del Martin, who has been writing for the magazine on issues of police harassment. The October issue will be her last, for reasons she explains in it.

A news story in the issue provides the context. In August 1970, SIR hosted the meeting of the North American Conference of Homophile Organizations, founded in 1965.[3] The meeting never quite took place. The self-baptized "Radical Caucus," a group of "gay liberationists" and "revolutionaries," prevented it from opening officially by insisting that it be open to all. The proceedings jumped back and forth between the announced agenda and public spectacles of "revolutionary" protest. Del Martin was invited to speak on women's rights as part of the official agenda. She did, but disruptions swirled around the speech—even though her session would have been congenial to the rebels. Finally, the Radical Caucus agreed to wait outside while the official delegates debated their inclusion. After two hours, tired of waiting for a decision, the caucus led a large group back into the hall, chanting "Power to the People." The last reported "actions" taken by the meeting were an approval of open voting, "support of the aims of the Black Panther Party; a national 'gay strike' day; and a call for women's liberation."

In the issue of *Vector* that reports the failed NACHO meeting, Del Martin publishes her last column.[4] She describes the meeting as one that "displayed vividly our divisions rather than our unity."[5] Any proposed unity risked excluding or subordinating women and youth. Having "been forced to the realization that I have no brothers in the homophile movement," Martin identifies instead with "her sisters"—specifically including young women. She then bids caustic farewell to homophile organizations and platforms, to their nude-adorned magazines, to bar-based gay social life, to the defense of public sex, and to women who are still willing to abide or abet any of it. In the string of angry farewells, Martin includes her own work with the churches: "Goodbye to the various Councils on Religion and the Homosexual . . . There is no place for women in the Christian and homophile brotherhoods. Be warned, my sisters, CRH only spells purgatory for you."

This issue of *Vector* and others just before and after make many of Martin's charges credible. Indeed, the editor concedes as much even as he tries to explain the reasons: "But [SIR's] membership is 85% male and [*Vector*'s] readers are 95% male . . . so we have a male-oriented magazine."[6] He begs for more contributions by and about women. There is no making excuses for the magazine's condescension to the young liberationists, which is evident not only in the report on the disrupted NACHO meeting, but at many other points.[7] More interesting is the question of religion. Like much of the homophile press before it, *Vector* around 1970 printed a lot of religious news.[8] This also reflected its membership. A survey of SIR conducted in 1968 found that slightly more than half of the men responding "claimed some religious affiliation."[9]

Not just affiliation, but leadership. The NACHO meeting witnessed clergy on both sides of the growing split between homophile and liberationist. Troy Perry, the founder of the Metropolitan Community Churches, spoke in favor of widening participation. Another clergymen, Michael Itkin, spoke as a liberationist and for the cause.[10] Indeed, one reader recalls that Itkin stripped in order to dance nude with three other protestors on the head table.[11] Taken to task by another reader for being "snide" about Itkin's standing as a bishop, the editor of *Vector* replies, "There are so many people around S.I.R. Center these days with clerical collars and titles that we haven't time to figure it all out."[12]

Del Martin rejects all of those collars and titles as another form of "male privilege."[13] Her gesture of abandonment is striking because of her crucial role in CRH and related movements. But it is curiously doubled with another gesture of rejection or dismissal—by the liberationist rhetoric itself, which wants to erase not only the homophile past, but the claims of religion to be anything other than oppression. Martin is an experienced, middle-aged activist refusing any longer to be used by organizations she helped to found. The liberationist rhetoric is the claim of a new birth without religion—and also, inevitably, a new variation on potent religious rhetorics.

MYTHOLOGY OF STONEWALL

In February 1970, half a year before the NACHO meeting in San Francisco, a mimeographed pamphlet entitled *Gay Liberation* was circulated in New York by Red Butterfly, "an association of gay men and women who as revolutionary socialists see their liberation linked to the class struggle."[14] The pamphlet narrates the origin of a new liberation movement in resistance to the police raid on the Stonewall bar during June 1969. The resistance is described as a spontaneous public uprising against "the pigs." "We consider the Stonewall Riots to mark the birth of the Gay Liberation movement, as they were the first time that homosexuals stood up and fought back."[15] The fight would have gone further except that it was betrayed by the compromised leadership of "the gay establishment," especially the Mattachine Society. The pamphlet calls for solidarity across all movements and convokes those interested to the "nationwide" celebration of "Christopher Street Liberation Weekend" in order to commemorate "the birth of the Gay Liberation movement."[16]

The pamphlet shows why any meditation on recent gay history in America has to contend with Stonewall. It was from the beginning not so much an event as a political emblem imposed on an extraordinary play of contradictory principles and contending actors. Notice just one of its limits—or results: Stonewall as emblem excludes religion. The exclusion is both theoretical and tactical. The largest part of the Red Butterfly pamphlet is an argument for the naturalness of homosexuality from anthropological and sociological evidence. Kinsey's results are summarized; anthropologists, including Ruth Benedict, are quoted as authorities on the truth of human life. Friedrich Engels is the expert on the critique of the family. Ethnography and social history are applied to the American political moment through vaguely Marxist assumptions about the reducibility of all oppression to economic structure and the urgency of revolutionary solidarity. In such analysis, which wants also to be humanitarian and democratic, "organized religion" appears only as part of the oppressing establishment. It actively slanders "gay people" while reinforcing "the prevailing myth system or ideology" that underwrites their legal oppression. So of course Red Butterfly announces that it is "engaged in study and writing projects to develop analyses relating Gay Liberation to radical critiques of religion."[17]

The homophile movement was an uneasy coalition of religious and antireligious groups, comprising antireligious Marxists or Communists, religiously indifferent socialists, and religiously motivated activists. With the liberationist symbol of Stonewall, antireligious or nonreligious groups gained greater control over politically effective representation of lesbian and gay history. This is a remark about a symbol, not about the membership or social interconnection of liberationist groups. On the ground, in messy fact, the groups overlapped not only with homophile organizations, but with religious congregations or denominations. But in their rhetoric, many liberationist authors agreed with Red Butterfly in declaring a new beginning, a new birth, the only religious rite for which was "the baptism of billy clubs."[18] The revolutionary rhetoric of gay liberation depended on the promise—the illusion—that a new generation would bring revolutionary change. The change was *rhetorical*. Liberationist rhetoric is new in its theoretical dogmatism, its eschatological claims, and its prophetic self-righteousness. But many would consider those to be features of religion gone bad. Indeed, in its reversion to the image of "baptism," but also in its messianic expectations of the newly born, Red Butterfly suggests some of the ambivalences of any clean break with religion—especially when it comes to the regeneration of sexual identities.

A GAY MANIFESTO

The ambivalences are clearer still in a text that stands behind Red Butterfly's pamphlet—and that was being written just before the police raid on Stonewall. It allows a glimpse of liberationist rhetoric without the overlay of Stonewall as symbol and in closer proximity to homophile conversations with Christian churches. It more clearly plays out the liberationist ambivalence toward religion. The text I mean is the widely circulated "Gay Manifesto" by Carl Wittman, first published in December 1969 in the Bay Area.

Wittman "came out" as a homosexual in print during 1968, though his sexuality had been an issue during the many years of his involvement with "new Left" organizations, including the SDS (Students for a Democratic Society).[19] By 1969 he was involved with the West Coast's Committee on Homosexual Freedom.[20] He participated in the group's unsuccessful picketing of States Steamship Line for its dismissal of a gay employee.[21] Wittman was sketching ideas for a manifesto in May and June of 1969, that is, in the weeks just before the street events in New York. His finished piece was first published in the year-end issue of the *San Francisco Free Press*.[22] Its full title was "Refugees from Amerika: A Gay Manifesto" ("Amerika" with a *k*, of course). The text was widely reprinted in the underground press, including in 1970 by Red Butterfly, which added its own commentary.[23] Less predictably, the manifesto was also taken up by Christian groups in the Bay Area.[24] A few months after its first publication, Wittman returned to the text to revise it for a new printing by the Council on Religion and the Homosexual.[25]

Wittman opens the manifesto with an image of refugees fleeing the rest of the country to find an exile's shelter in San Francisco. They flee threatened lives in small towns, flee disowning families and employers who fired them or schools that expelled them. They come at many ages, but most especially when young. They find some space by the bay to rest, though they realize soon enough that they are trapped in a ghetto run by their oppressors. Their only way out is to organize and educate themselves, to cultivate the consciousness of gay liberation as radical refounding of community. Flight teaches them at last to claim some land as their own.

Who are these exiles? In the manifesto's first sentence, they are simply called "homosexuals," as if no further label were needed. But the manifesto goes on to give them special powers and pasts. Powers, because "homosexuality is the capacity to love someone of the same sex" (all in caps). Pasts: "As kids, we refused to capitulate to demands that we smother our feeling toward each other." But in other passages the cultivation of homosexual feelings becomes a sign of loss. The original openness of sexual feeling in childhood is disciplined by compulsory heterosexuality—that is, by the binary opposition between successful heterosexual and failed homosexual. For the present, under ghetto conditions, the best hope of the exiles is some return to a childish freedom for loving all. "We'll be gay until everyone has forgotten that it's an issue. Then we'll be complete," that is, sexually open to both male and female.[26]

On Wittman's telling, the radical transformation of human life does not require religion. The manifesto never refers to churches or other religious organizations. The closest it comes to the topic is in two references to spirituality. Wittman writes that the beauty of young bodies is "inspiration for art, for spiritual elevation, for good sex." Again, he suggests that some paraphilias (like bestiality) may enact "spiritual or important things," like interspecies communication or sexual activity as "highly developed artistic endeavor."[27] In the manifesto, as so often before in gay letters, the spiritual is allied with art, beauty, intensity of pleasure, and breakthroughs of consciousness, but never with institutions.

This is hardly surprising given Wittman's biography and intellectual commitments. Raised by Communist parents, he was taught early on to conceal both the family's politics and its theoretically dictated atheism. Concealment went along with critique. Wittman notes that it was difficult in later years for him to listen sympathetically to stories about justice work in Catholic schools, since he had been trained to see them "as a central source of evil."[28] Intellectually, he operates within a frame of vulgate Marxism, which he gradually extends to include gender and sexuality as objects of revolutionary struggle. But exclusions of religion are hardly simple in American contexts. The manifesto's occasional mentions of the spiritual resonate both with the narrative of exiled pilgrims and with their avowals of utopian longing—ideals at once, always, secular and sacred, so far as those terms can have separate meaning. They are also terms haunted by present fallenness. Male chauvinism and sexual objectification are more daunting enemies than Wittman had imagined. Neither demonstrations nor copulations will be enough to undo them. "The defining of sexual liberation as 'doing your own thing' without guilt doesn't begin to deal with the crippling of our human and sexual potential."[29] There follow allusions to Marcuse and Reich. "In short, another of our imperatives is to question the emptiness of our personal and social relationships, even *after* we have come out."[30]

To question, then to rebuild. In the manifesto itself, Wittman gestures toward "free territory" beyond the ghetto. "To be a free territory, we must govern ourselves, set up our own institutions, defend ourselves, and use our own energies to improve our lives. The emergence of gay liberation communes . . . is a good start."[31] So too would be "rural retreats." In the year after the CRH republished the manifesto, Wittman moved onto acreage at Wolf Creek, Oregon, his own bit of free territory. A few years later, he would become involved with *RFD* magazine and the radical faeries, antiurban gay ritualists.[32] Wittman undertook spiritual experiments: rereading the Tarot as gay code, writing about forest magic. The trajectory of Wittman's future will take him away from his Communist youth and into communities that ritualize male-male desire.

How far can his future trajectory be discovered in or around the "Gay Manifesto"? It was first published in an issue of *San Francisco Free Press*, embellished by idyllic pictures of young men on a beach. On the cover, they stare pensively into the rising (or setting?) sun. At another moment, they gather around a rough altar featuring a dildo in order to perform a laughing rite of worship. The photographer, "Marcus," writes a brief gloss in which the apocalyptic collapse of America is followed—is redeemed—by rural communities where young men are taught "the arts of love" by omni-sexual wise men.[33] This utopian fantasy frames Wittman's manifesto—and not inappropriately. Wittman earnestly imagines a life outside, beyond sexual binaries, after enforced social roles, on land unpolluted by the economic tyranny of cities. In the manifesto, he dispenses with existing religion and speaks of spirituality as synonym for art or higher consciousness. But perhaps that is because other texts around him—texts echoed by the photographer "Marcus"—had already spoken his gay utopia in quite religious language. Or they had sung it.

SONG OF THE LOON

Song of the Loon was published in 1966 by a pulp house as part of an effort to improve its list. This is pulp with a difference, "a Greenleaf classic," high gay literature in convenient pocket format. The novel's wraparound cover shows a Caucasian in buckskin staring down upon an "Indian" (as the novel calls them) who plays a flute.[34] They are grouped intimately against an empty mountainside of aggressive green. The blurb headline promises "A Shocking and Enchanting Underground Best-seller!" It was indeed a bestseller by pulp standards, though exact sales figures are as always hard to establish. The title page gives the author as Richard Amory. Pulp fans might assume that this was a pseudonym. Attentive readers of the novel— we have already been lured inside—will find the pseudonym's key: one character, originally called Tsi-nokha, is renamed with various conjugations of the Latin verb *amare*, to love.[35] Sure enough, "Richard Amory" is the pen name for Richard *Love*. Love wrote the book in his late thirties. A married man and father, a high school teacher in Oakland, he had returned to school for graduate study in Spanish. The privacy of a campus office allowed him to write gay erotica. Four years after the novel's publication, in his early forties, Love would divorce his wife and assume a less ambivalent identity as a gay activist, writing for *Vector* and trying to organize his fellow writers against pulp publishers. Liberation of another sort.

Song of the Loon follows the adventures of Ephraim MacIver in frontier Oregon. (Readers of the Hebrew bible will remember that Ephraim, second son of the patriarch Joseph, gives his name to one of the most prominent Israelite tribes, which is often made into an emblem for all of Israel.)

MacIver has fallen tragically in love with another white man, Clarence Montgomery, who has to drink before he can act on his urges for love. Montgomery abuses MacIver and abandons him to despair. A local Indian (but with an inexplicably Mesoamerican name) rescues MacIver by sending him on a trip into the wilderness, where he is to find an Indian visionary, Bear-who-dreams. (All "bear" puns fully intended: the novel features several bears, that is, hairy men of a certain size.) Bear-who-dreams is, *of course*, the chief of a semisecret brotherhood of gay Indians and their admirers. Traveling up river, chased (he thinks) by the vengeful Montgomery and the chilling local missionary, Ephraim meets his teachers in the lessons of gay love. He learns, roughly in order, to voice his desires, to give and receive fellatio, to overcome the sickness of possessive monogamy, to distinguish gayness from effeminacy, to give and receive anal sex, and to divide his life between coupled winters and orgiastic summers—summers of love. He also receives instruction in woodcraft, new dance routines, and the making of poems. If the lovers in a Broadway musical break unexpectedly into ballad, Amory's lovers register their passions in poems that are called songs—very gay poems in a variety of forms and tones.

"Gay" is the important word. This is a Men Only pastoral. No women appear in it. Neither do children. Young men appear out of nowhere, around the age of fifteen, at a forest encampment where they can apprentice in free love. They experience the variety of body types and what can be done with them. They then take off down the river to put their learning to practical use. (I resisted the verb "cruise," but evidently not long enough.) *Song of the Loon* imagines a communal society that can defend and sustain itself by welcoming those who have been cast out by the larger (homophobic, reproductive) world. They are welcomed by being educated. The initiates must also have a lot of sex without any guilt or shame. The descriptions are not quite anatomical. They are decidedly not vulgar. They deploy flocks of metaphors, similes, tropes, and images to represent bodily acts. Indeed, the book's literary genealogy must include *Fanny Hill* or other works of English literary pornography in which the poor penis is draped with a hundred gilded metaphors, and the anus—oh, the anus ever remains a cave of indescribable mystery. In Amory, the metaphors are not always quite right: "Singing Heron gazed casually at Ephraim's cock, thick and *muscular like an oak tree*."[36] O muscled oaks of yore! Other descriptions recur: buttocks are constantly flexing, penises regularly swelling. The ornate language cannot quite distract from the basic premises of pornographic narration. Everyone is always eager to copulate. Attractive bodies abound. Clean-up takes place in handy streams. There is no clumsiness or chafing or disease.

Song of the Loon is not all about the body. It is a classic, after all. Ephraim's sentimental education must also be a spiritual awakening. He flees the "missionary Way" in favor of an earth-based, spirit-worship liberally adapted (or, rather, fantasized) from Native American religions. The missionary who pursues him is named, *of course*, Mr. Calvin. Mr. Calvin tries to make gay Indians into his property by baptizing them and putting them to work. Only by running away from him may a man return to the true religion. (Mr. Calvin also turns out to be a pathetically repressed gay man who is humiliated into confessing his love for the abusive Montgomery.) The true religion entails morning hymns to the earth, the passing of intoxicating pipes or heady (but natural) liquors, and vision-quests that reveal which partner you should take for the winter. Suffering is homophobic illusion, to be cured by speaking desires honestly—by coming out. Even Mr. Calvin and Montgomery are redeemed by plain speaking. They become properly gay lovers and may eventually join the Loons.

Read in one way, *Song of the Loon* transports the fantasies of an urban gay enclave to an imagined frontier—where American boys have often gone to play. The novel is life on Polk Street performed in David Crockett hats against leafy backdrops. Read in another way, the pastoral in five books with an interlude yearns—as Wittman himself does—for a life outside, beyond the gay ghetto that is never more than a refugee camp. Outside, there might be authentic community—and real religion, which not only liberates homosexuality, but reveals it as a sacrament. Gay pastoral is the sequel to the gay manifesto. Amory, writing before Wittman, writes his conclusion.

I have retrieved *Song of the Loon* as a piece of camp. It offers itself for that retrieval and is content, I suppose, to contribute to the complex pleasure of the camp collector. But there is something more here—as there was in Rechy. Amory claims an erudite stylistic genealogy: he subtitles the novel "a gay pastoral in five books and an interlude." A prefatory author's note insists on the genre. Amory "has taken certain very European characters from the novels of Jorge de Montemayor and Gaspar Gil Polo, painted them a gay aesthetic red, and transplanted them to the American wilderness."[37] But why implicate Montemayor and his continuator, Gil Polo, Renaissance founders of the Spanish pastoral? Because Amory too is playing with and at a pornographic neobaroque, a mannerist announcement of a new religion of the flesh. If you read the text as mere pornography, it turns to poetry. Read it as merely bad poetry, it mocks you for taking it seriously. Read it as a particularly convoluted camp, it reminds you that language fractures when it strains to speak new revelations. *Song of the Loon* is pornographic and religious, serious and mocking, passionate and self-observing, pulp and treatise. It is camp—that is, gay neobaroque—that is, theology after the triumph of sexuality.

An epilogue to the pastoral: bad books get read alongside good ones. Both kinds have unpredictable effects on earnest readers. A man, with Mormons on both sides of his family, makes his way from Utah to the gay neighborhoods of Los Angeles. A bartender at The Gauntlet recommends that he read *The City and the Pillar*. On his own, he finds *Song of the Loon*. He remembers that reading them together was the turning point for his life.[38] Critics, beware.

LEARNING TO TALK LIBERATION IN CHURCH

The assumption in Wittman, the conceit in Amory is that Christian churches are either irrelevant or safely remote. But churches continued to stand, and some pastors or congregants who had been involved in conversations with homophile groups took up dialogue with liberationist groups—when they did not house them, feed them, and do their office chores. Indeed, some progressive church groups simply read across the liberationist break to make a continuous story of ongoing engagement between churches and lesbian or gay groups. Del Martin may have repudiated the CRH and stopped writing for *Vector*, but others—including other feminists who were explicitly indebted to her—were willing, at least for a while, to carry on.

Loving Women/Loving Men carries the subtitle *Gay Liberation and the Church*. Published in 1974, the anthology explicitly connects liberationist rhetoric with the older homophile conversations about Christian churches. The book was produced by Glide Publications, the printing arm of the church that started the 1964 consultation, and one of its editors was executive director of the CRH at the time of publication. He was also widely regarded as the first openly gay man ordained in a mainstream Protestant denomination—by the UCC, on June 25, 1972, the third anniversary of Stonewall.[39] The other editor would also serve as co-chair of CRH for some years in the '70s, but she was much better known as a lesbian activist. Coming to the Bay Area in 1970 after teaching in Methodist and Lutheran colleges, she moved decisively into the streets—and into more pointed confrontation with the churches.[40]

Their book is an experiment in talking across the new divides; it also embodies them. Sally Gearhart confesses to worrying about publishing "through an establishment press," but even more about working with a gay man, given her "staunch separatist feelings—for I had long believed that at this point in history it was impossible for women and men to work together constructively." Experience shows her that it is possible to have "'careful coalitions'" even with gay men. William Johnson, on his side, admits that he was "apprehensive about Sally in the beginning, mostly because her feminism precedes her by about a quarter of a mile." He finds that they share a "common concern for Gay people and for church people." In the end, he finds his collaborator "prophetic and loving." Yet the two voices enact so many oppositions. Older lesbian/younger gay man is only one of them. Another is the distance between the homophile groups, still continuing, and their liberationist opponents. Most interesting is the opposition between the woman who is leaving churches and the man who has stayed in them to be ordained. The book repeats its juxtapositions without being able to make them more than juxtapositions.

It begins with Don Kuhn's account of the 1964 consultation and a version of a paper on biblical exegesis originally read there by Robert Treese, a Methodist clergyman and professor. The third piece is a history by Gearhart and Johnson in which they try to tell the story about the churches and homosexuality from the late 1960s on. Their frame is entirely liberationist. The title speaks of "the Gay Movement in the church," but it means mostly events after Stonewall. It claims that "the Stonewall Rebellion gave birth to the Gay Liberation Movement."[41] Liberationist claims determine not just the chronology, but the characterization of relations between "Gay people" and Christian religion. After alluding to the CRH, Gearhart and Johnson concur that "the majority of Gay people in 1969, activists and non-activists alike, viewed the church as hopelessly homophobic and anti-life."[42] That is an unsupportable claim historically, but an important tenet in the new rhetoric. It is quickly applied to analyze American religious history: "As Gay consciousness has evolved, individuals have begun to understand the direct relationship between traditional Judeo-Christian attitudes and Gay oppression. The legal sanctions against the expression of Gay love are rooted in religious doctrine."

Most of this joint essay chronicles not so much consciousness raising as denominational actions. The most dramatic action it mentions must be the founding by Troy Perry of the MCC (Metropolitan Community Church)—which preceded Stonewall by more than half a year, though Gearhart and Johnson don't emphasize that point. Another founding makes the Roman Catholic Dignity "the first organizing effort of Gay people within a particular tradition." Equally striking are the efforts to ordain honestly gay and lesbian seminarians, with Johnson's own ordination as the signal victory.[43] But much of the chronicle is rather less interesting—as denominational histories tend to be. Caucuses form, committees meet, conventions vote. There are losses too: ordinations refused or rescinded, advocates leaving ministries or denominations in despair.

The next essay, by Johnson alone, opens with a clarion call: "There comes a time in the collective life of every oppressed minority when passive acceptance of injustice is no longer possible."[44] The central category is "oppressed minority" and the general theory is collective revolution. In the present moment of Christian churches, revolution means a list of nonnegotiable demands. Johnson's piece is a revolutionary manifesto, though less visionary than Wittman's. It describes the crisis of its moment in order to lay out the urgent, the necessary, the correctly political actions required.

Johnson offers a number of arguments meant to contest established positions: Jesus wants freed response in discipleship; the prevailing exegeses of Pauline passages cannot be sustained; neither can the most familiar homophobic condemnations. Yet the heart of his challenge is a series of claims that psychosexual integration, covenanted same-sex love, and gender fluidity are more likely to embody Christ's ideals for human relationship than the presently prevailing models.[45] Johnson's challenge to the churches is an argument for the religious and moral superiority of lesbian or gay relationships, families, and gender expressions. He integrates liberationist discourse into the church by recognizing it as more essentially Christian than what is now found in the churches. Gay men are better witnesses to Christ's original ideals than many church officers or policies are. Liberation is not so much baptized as transfigured: it is recognized as divine teaching all along.

Gearhart's essay goes in the opposite direction. It is a leave-taking, an explanation for a decision to abandon churches, but with some compassion for those who remain. Gearhart performs at greater length, and with more specifically religious citations, the gesture of Del Martin's angry valedictory in *Vector*. Gearhart addresses her preferred reader in the second person, and her "you" is female.[46] A woman speaks to women, calling them out of the churches in which they find themselves. "The Christian church by its very structure and by the very assumptions on which it is founded is in direct, fundamental, and irreconcilable conflict with feminism." Some pages later she says again: "We realize that no matter how hard we work to alter it, the church *to be the church* must continue its dehumanizing practices." It follows that "a womanization, a Lesbianization of theology is not a reformist move to 'incorporate a woman's point of view.' *It is an absolute and uncompromising denial of what has gone before*." Gearhart imagines a general exodus from the churches that would bring them to collapse, but she recognizes that many women, many lesbians, will stay in for one reason or another. She specifies concrete practices and criteria for staying in without being destroyed. She sums these in one place by saying:

"Every day leaving must be seen as an option; and every day the price of our staying and the price of our leaving must be calculated."[47]

Gearhart's passion—her rhetoric—is with the call to come out of the churches in order to find the "woman-god" who speaks within, "the sharing of our new-found gospel-selves with other women." Again: "We maintain that the gospel message calling for love of our whole self as well as of others does not and cannot live within the Christian church . . . If [the church] continues, then we will not survive. If we allow it to continue, we do not deserve to survive."[48] Indeed, a few years later she would picture this kind of life in a utopian fantasy called *Wanderground* (1978), one of the many instances in which science fiction imagines homoerotic religion.

Gearhart's novel describes a community of lesbian separatists who are trying to heal the earth after it has been poisoned by patriarchy. There are still men on the planet, but most of them are trapped in decaying, totalitarian cities; neither their machines nor their penises function properly outside them. A few other men, "gentles" or "unmanly men" who "touched no women at all" because they recognize that male touch is inherently violent, live both in the cities and outside. Inside they have male lovers; outside, they seem grateful for impotence.[49] The "essential fundamental knowledge" of gender is that "women and men cannot yet, maybe not ever, love one another without violence; they are no longer of the same species."[50]

Mentions of Christianity in Gearhart's novel are equally divided into female and male, peaceful and violent. There were once "vigilante Christian groups who patrolled the parks with clubs looking for queers." "People, particularly religious fanatics, were outraged against the women." Yet "Lesbian Priest" appears in a flashback of headlines illustrating the women's progress.[51] Christian terms have also carried over into the Wanderground's language, though their original meaning has been forgotten: "This was the grace-making, the creation of extra attention and love, either toward one woman or toward a number of them. Zephyr did not understand what *grace* meant: it was now an archaic word." Archaic, but apparently unforgettable. So too are some church institutions. The women's central council turns out to be "Long Dozen," members of an apostolic college.[52] And so on.

I do not want to assimilate Gearhart's rejection to Johnson's ordained ministry by saying that they are both equally within the church. They are not. Nor is Gearhart's later turn to the imagination of a fantastic religious community exactly the same as Wittman's trajectory after the manifesto. Nor is *Wanderground* just the *Song of the Loon* with changed gender and no room for camp—though the novels' resemblances are worth exploring. I do want to argue that the liberationist rejection of churches is never as complete as it wishes, in no small part because utopian and separatist imaginary is, in America, typically Christianized. Going off into the woods to found a pure community is the originary story of American Protestantism and a repeated event in its church history. Liberationist rhetoric that wants to ignore churches, to denigrate them, or to abandon them to their own collapse, is not so far from the rhetoric that wants to establish purified church groups of which lesbians and gays are full members—of which they are, indeed, the revered founders.

TROY PERRY'S TESTIMONY

The first alternative to churchly oppression mentioned by Gearhart and Johnson is Troy Perry's "founding a Christian church that would welcome Gay people."[53] Two years before they published their anthology, Perry had already published his own testimony about the founding. He would write about the story on other occasions, and he still tells incidents from it when he speaks, because the story is in no small measure the source of his apostolic authority. Faced with this proliferation, I remind myself and my reader that I restage texts for their rhetorical patterns—texts, not lives. I am not reconstructing a composite history of the group's founding, balancing Troy Perry's various accounts against other reports, records, or memories. Nor am I attempting biography. I only want to read one autobiography—or, rather, one religious testimony that recalls and justifies a church founding. So I choose the original edition of *The Lord Is My Shepherd*, published less than four years after the first public worship of what would become MCC.[54]

Here in outline is the sequence of events that leads to the founding and secures it. Born in Florida in 1940, Troy feels a call to ministry as a boy. He is encouraged to preach by his relatives and begins to do so in public in junior high school. The teenager is quite literally the messenger of God. At fifteen, he is licensed as a Baptist preacher. But Troy is also having sexual experiences with other adolescents, and their discovery gets him sent home from a church summer camp when he is sixteen. Just before he turns nineteen, Troy marries a pastor's daughter with a view to a church career. Shortly after the marriage, the couple moves north to Chicago so that Troy can attend Bible college while ministering in a Pentecostal church. When a former male lover reports him to local church leaders, he gets sent back to Florida. The couple has their first son. Troy is outed again in Florida and moved to an independent church. He goes back to Chicago to study at Moody Bible Institute. The plastics company at which he works transfers him to southern California in 1962. At twenty-three, Perry becomes pastor of his own church there. But the sexual awakening continues, this time with the aid of books. Confronted again by church leaders, Perry is again forced out. He separates from his wife after five years of marriage. In 1965, in his mid-twenties, he is drafted into the army for two years. On his return to LA in 1967, he enters some of the networks of gay life, meeting a lover and falling away from God. He returns to interrupted adolescence—to take the path he "ought" to have taken in adolescence. Adolescence is detached from biological chronology to become a repeatable ritual of character—to become the ritual by which one can perform a change of character. But this means undergoing the traumas again too. In 1968, Troy attempts suicide after a disastrous break up. In the emergency room, he hits bottom—and remembers God. Through the long purgatory of his recovery, he relearns habits of prayer and bible study. He is led by many interventions to consider a ministry for homosexuals. In the final one, a friend declares angrily that God doesn't care about homosexuals. Following "a still small voice," Perry places an advertisement in the *Advocate*, then still mostly a local publication, and announces a date for the first meeting of a church that would show God's care.

Let me stop the testimony just there, before the first MCC service, in order to notice how many kinds of story it is—and how it is transforming those kinds even as it cites them. Most obviously, Troy's first book is a roughly "evangelical" testimony of fall and redemption. What most evangelicals would consider the sin turns out to be part of the redemption. The lowest moment—the suicide attempt in LA—comes not because he is homosexual, but because he has forgotten God by falling into a damaging relationship from which God is excluded. Turning back toward God doesn't mean renouncing homosexuality, but affirming that one can be a Christian homosexual.

The book is also a Pentecostal testimony of direct call to ministry by various signs—by education under a charismatic elder (his aunt), by early anointing as a boy-preacher, and even by "New Age" discernment that his spirit guide wears a clerical collar. The book is filled with anecdotes and expressions of direct divine guidance. They authorize Perry's ministry, and they give him a model of church within which a new founding is not unexpected. In his narrative, denominations and theological traditions are entirely subordinated to the direct guidance of the spirit. Perry's Pentecostal tradition makes it relatively easy for him to become a founder—and to claim legitimacy for the founding by providing testimonial evidence of the Spirit's call.

Finally, the book is a coming-out story, with predictable stages: clandestine play in adolescence, marred by fear of exposure and confusion about implications; overcalculated efforts at straight dating; an early marriage required for career, followed by the return of old desires and old partners. After waves of increasing troubles, career, marriage, and social respectability collapse all at once. Then Perry discovers through reading the language of another world and the claim of his true identity. "Coming out" no longer means announcing what you have been doing in private, bringing your desires and acts out of hiding for the world to see. It means overcoming inward resistance to the truth that you have been denying. "Coming out to yourself" is not an act of publicity. It is an act of conversion. It is also a narrative of rebirth—of one's sexual character. So it requires going back to the moment in which sexual characters are born, to adolescence.

Perry's rhetorical feat is to combine the familiar Christian narratives of personal salvation and call to ministry with coming out. The combination modifies all three genres. For example, evangelical testimonies accustom their hearers to episodes of sexual sin on the way to conversion. A vivid tale of how low one fell shows how much God has done in bringing one back. Perry relies on that custom in telling his sins, but then turns the story of conversion so that he repents not for having sex, but for concealing his true sexual nature. Again, Perry's narrative includes typical scenes from evangelical narrative: teary confrontations with wives and mothers, angry accusations before church elders, drunken encounters in bars, desperate hours in police stations. There are lucky discoveries of books bearing truth (in the bookstore), and angels of divine grace (an African American woman in the hospital). But these familiar elements end with an unexpected divine command. He is not told to abandon bars, foreswear homosexual contacts, return to his wife, and embrace a life of penitential service in an established congregation. The still, small voice says: go and minister to homosexuals as one of them.

Perry's coming-out story also twists its genre. It narrates the usual forms of denial, including attempts at suppressing the unwanted feelings and at accommodating them in bisexuality. But then, reading Daniel Webster Cory's *Homosexual in America* in his early twenties, Perry reaches clarity: "I knew without the shadow of a doubt that I was a homosexual; I was gay."[55] Being a homosexual is a matter of nature—which is to say, of creation. In some passages, Perry is emphatic about the created basis of homosexuality. "I'm sure that homosexuality was in my genes, and in my soul, from the very beginning."[56] The word "genes" gives the claim of nature a recognizably biological basis, but "soul" moves it into the realm of divine creation. So too Perry's claim of a "total sense memory" from before conception, of his being somehow already a soul in his father's semen.[57] This "metaphysical" conviction of a divine origin overrides other possible interpretations that occur to Perry for religious reasons, including the notion that these were demonic temptations to be overcome: "God just doesn't seem to understand, or he doesn't answer my prayers about this for some reason."[58] Certitude about being created homosexual is confirmed not just by the divine silence, but by the divine call to ministry.

The call led Perry to announce the first service of a new church. The date was October 6, 1968—chosen not for its liturgical significance, but in view of the *Advocate*'s publishing schedule. The service attracted twelve people—not a bad number for founding a Christian ministry.[59] Perry made several choices about worship that proved consequential. He announced that while the ministry would "serve the religious and spiritual and social needs of the homosexual community of greater Los Angeles," it would soon enough "reach homosexuals wherever they might be." Perry then "made it clear that we were not a gay church, we were a Christian church." This may sound like a casual contradiction, but it is the heart of Perry's inspiration. Having suffered such bitter exclusion from churches, he was not about to establish a new church on the basis of a reversed exclusion. Given his background, he could never conceive church as anything other than intrinsically expansive. If Perry imagined a movement that would reach homosexuals everywhere, he equally insisted that it could not be confined to the homosexual ghettos that Wittman had described and deplored. Spreading everywhere, it would spread even into other churches. The gay ministry must become a general church reform—and not only on issues of sexuality. The reform would take place in Christian churches everywhere—not in a utopian community on some imagined frontier.

Perry's second choice at the service was to declare the ministry a sort of ecumenical movement in miniature: "I also told them that we would be a general Protestant church to be all-inclusive." In fact, "all-inclusive" quickly overtook "Protestant." So the impulse to minister to the homosexual community of Los Angeles began almost immediately to undo the old divisions incised into Christian history.

The third decision at the inaugural service is the most powerful symbolically and pastorally. After the sermon, Perry declared that any of those present could come forward to receive communion. He writes: "There wasn't a dry eye in the place." Everyone in that place sympathized with what it was to be denied communion, to be debarred from communion, for being a homosexual.

Perry goes on—in his first book, in his other writings or speeches, in later books—to narrate the growth of the fledgling church. I turn aside from the story to note a few circumstances and to draw a few conclusions. It is important to remember that Perry encountered opposition from early on not only from outside but from inside, that is, from other gay activists and, as we have seen at the NACHO meeting, from other gay clergy. At NACHO, another "local minister," Ray Broshears, argued that "MCC is trying to ghettoize the homosexual by creating a homosexual church."[60] In private correspondence, sharper things were said. Writing to Broshears, Michael Itkin urged, "the more that can be done to end Perry's sexist separatism and attempted monolithic control of the Gay religious scene, the better."[61] For the activists, at NACHO and elsewhere, Perry sometimes seemed a Southern preacher trying to reassert a particularly unsophisticated Christianity into gay life. A gay detective novel by Joseph Hansen ends with a hustler's beauty pageant at a bar in LA. One of the judges is introduced in this way: "a minister, complete with dog collar, though he'd gotten his training in backwoods Baptist seminaries in the deep South."[62] A few minutes later, the "pastor of gay sheep" prays: "Head thrown back, eyes closed, hands folded demurely at his crotch, he told God what had happened . . . The prayer ended. An electronic organ with bronchial problems and a subnormal pulse began 'The Lord's Prayer.'" Perry's first book provoked equally harsh judgments from some activist readers. Under the headline "Gay Sheep," Merv Walker, writing in Toronto's *Body Politic*, professes to be surprised that Perry "has not seen through the church. He can see it as an institution of inclusion-exclusion: an instrument of power, but does he not recognize the human genesis of that power?"[63] Walker ends: "We are left to assume that [Perry] really does believe in God, and the institution of the church as God's representation on earth . . . Confronted thus, I can only throw up my hands and slide the Lord and his sheep back on the shelf with the dust and the pope."

Perry's answer to competing clergy and critical activists is a fusion of Christian and liberationist rhetoric—or, more precisely, the fusion of unedited Pentecostal language with street actions. Perry sets his church down in the middle of the gay sexual marketplace, eager to take up its fights while receiving its members. At the first service, Perry promised to meet "the religious and spiritual and social needs." He could have added "political" and "sexual." Perry's ministry addresses the liberated world—in order to free it again.

DIGNITY AND FATHER MCNEILL

Shortly after Perry held his first service, another group was founded in southern California that would attract large numbers of gay Catholics and ex-Catholics. Dignity began as a support group run by an Augustinian priest, Pat Nidorf. Nidorf advertised for "Catholic Gays" in the San Diego "underground" newspaper in 1969.[64] Frustrated by the lack of response, he placed ads in the *Los Angeles Free Press* and the *Advocate* (where Perry had first advertised). Response increased sharply. Some people who had been attending the new MCC began making the drive to San Diego for the meetings. After alternating between San Diego and LA for a time, Nidorf moved the meetings to LA to be nearer most of the membership. In early 1971, a letter was sent to the archdiocese asking for recognition. The response was predictable: Timothy Manning, then a co-adjutor (or deputy) to the archbishop, rebuked Nidorf for working in the diocese, judged the principles of Dignity "untenable," and ordered him to stop ministering to the group. In response, Dignity installed lay leaders and began a campaign of national outreach. A New York chapter was founded in 1972. The first national meeting was held in Los Angeles in 1973, with a dozen recognized chapters and another dozen in formation.[65]

The "untenable" principles of Dignity were expressed in its "Statement of Position and Purpose." The statement claims, among other things, that "homosexuality is a natural variation on the use of sex. It implies no sickness or immorality. Those with such sexual orientation have a natural right to use their power of sex in a way that is both responsible and fulfilling." The document also asserts, "We believe that gay Catholics are members of Christ's mystical body, numbered among the people of God. . . . We believe that gays can express their sexuality in a manner that is consonant with Christ's teaching."[66] The statements resonate with what Troy Perry was preaching, but the idiom and the institutional logic are different. Most early members of Dignity in LA did not understand themselves to be separating from the church. Meetings were held on Saturdays rather than Sundays and members were encouraged to be active in their home parishes. Dignity Masses were celebrated only rarely, and then to mark special occasions. But there were members who had grown up in more political organizations (Mattachine, Catholic Worker) and who were more at ease with the language of "oppression" and "liberation." The political rhetoric carried over into the national organization. In 1975, for example, and as a national group, Dignity approached the American bishops asking for the appointment of a committee to address "the oppression of the gay Catholic."[67] Some members were also willing to use civil disobedience or other forms of street activism. When Brian McNaught was outed in 1975 as gay and as president of Dignity's Detroit chapter, his regular column was cancelled by the diocesan newspaper.[68] He began a fast. He was then fired from his job as staff writer, but under the glare of national publicity. Twenty-four days later, two auxiliary bishops delivered a letter undertaking as a serious obligation "to root out structures and attitudes that discriminate against the homosexual as a person."

There is much more to the early history of Dignity—including many more examples of creative resistance. I am now interested in it as a setting for the writing of John McNeill, then a Jesuit of the New York Province. His early articles contributed to Dignity's original self-understanding—indeed, to its founding statement.[69] During Labor Day weekend 1973, McNeill spoke in Los Angeles to the first national meeting. He summarized for those present his book-in-progress: *The Church and the Homosexual.* Publication of the book would be delayed by several years while he sought approval to publish, and McNeill would revise parts of it in answer to objections, official and unofficial. But when finally published, the book did not retreat from the main claims of the speech to Dignity.[70]

McNeill's book is often identified as the first extended affirmation of homosexuality by a Roman Catholic theologian writing in English. That judgment is largely justified, though McNeill himself points back, especially in the introduction, to some of the earlier voices. Certainly he makes a number of distinctively Catholic arguments in the book. McNeill appeals to traditions of natural law as support for a model of psychosexual development in the direction of mature freedom. Homosexuality properly speaking is a "psychic condition of the individual" that determines the capacity for sexual love. Mature human beings are called to express sexual love in responsible freedom. So the true homosexual must be reconceived as a developing erotic agent whose particular sexual desires are justified by the general obligation to find "interpersonal love."[71]

This is, of course, exactly the "plea of love" that the Anglican pamphlet had rejected in 1954 on the grounds that licit sexual activity for Christians must be confined to marriage. McNeill's counterplea is to present the dilemma of the Catholic homosexual: either be celibate, which will destroy you, or leave the church, which has been your home.[72] A choice between two forms of self-mutilation cannot be the last word morally, because morality cannot aim for the destruction of the moral agent. To say this less abstractly: McNeill's pleads that since sexuality is an important part of forming loving relationships for most adults, and since most human beings cannot be celibate without severe damage, homosexuals must have a moral right to sexual expression as part of their moral development. This is the best of Wood's arguments in *Christ and the Homosexual*, formulated more coherently and with psychological precision.

McNeill's accomplishment in comparison with earlier entries in the archive, including Perry, is to articulate an argument for homosexuality as a divine creation from traditional moral sources. He does it in steps. First, he argues from the experience of pastoral counseling that converting to heterosexuality or achieving celibacy is impossible for most homosexuals.

What the Anglican pamphlet recommends and many later texts echo cannot in fact be accomplished—and so cannot be a plausible pastoral ideal. Second, McNeill reasons from his "personalist" philosophy that the love of God is inseparable from the mature love of other human beings. He insists, third, and from psychology, that mature human love normally finds erotic expression in committed relationships. The psychological conclusion is then corroborated by the scriptures. The "positive ideal" of the New Testament, McNeill writes, is that "all human beings . . . [must] struggle to integrate their sexual powers into their total personality, so that their sexual drive can be totally at the disposition of their desire to achieve union in love with their fellow human beings and with God."[73]

In this scriptural claim, as in the other arguments, McNeill locates the character of the homosexual within the arc of normal human development. The homosexual is not a violation of nature, a deviation from nature, or a pathology afflicting nature. The homosexual is natural. McNeill knows and even approves the older distinction between pervert and invert, and he identifies the latter with the true homosexual.[74] McNeill recharacterizes the word with something like its original, neutral meaning—though within a much simplified range of characters. Recall Kertbeny: homosexuality was originally conceived not just in opposition to heterosexuality, but alongside monosexuality (masturbation) and heterogeneity (bestiality) and in relation to other terms like pygism (preference for anal intercourse). A pathological connotation is clear, but an identity is not. In Kertbeny, for example, monosexuality, homosexuality, and heterogeneity could perfectly well be found in the same person. For him, homosexuality does not define a species. According to McNeill's new narrative, by contrast, homosexuality is not a symptom of abnormality, much less of racial decay or oedipal failure. Alongside the heterosexual, the homosexual participates fully in the universal human striving for fulfillment through community in divinity. The "true homosexual" is for McNeill a fixed type of person defined as equal and opposite to the heterosexual.

The claim that the homosexual is a regularly occurring variation within human nature allows McNeill to find some support for his arguments within Christian tradition, rather than in its repudiation. He knows that natural law teaching is a corollary of the doctrine of creation. When he presents the true homosexual as a created type, he gains a foothold in natural law—a foothold for the new character of the Christian homosexual. If homosexuals are created by God, then homosexuality is called to a share in divine life by its very constitution. The Christian homosexual becomes not just a habitable identity, but a commanded one. Whereas some church progressives (like Charles Curran) had argued that adult homosexual relations might be pastorally tolerated as the lesser of evils, McNeill argues in effect that the *repression* of homosexual desire in a true homosexual would be the violation of nature. Trying to be celibate when you are not especially called to celibacy is a rejection of the order of nature—that is, the order of creation—that is, the will of God. Church proscriptions of homosexual acts in a loving relationship are the real immorality.

McNeill has the confidence to appropriate the tradition in this way not least because of two experiences of divine providence, only one of which he names in the book. In it, McNeill identifies "the emergence of a visible homosexual community both in society and in the church" as a "providential" witness to the created variety of human sexuality and its future possibilities.[75] Ethics cannot ignore this new act of providence. We learn from other, later texts that for many years before the speech to Dignity, McNeill had been a sexually active gay man, driven almost to suicide by his inability to remain celibate. In that moment of despair, and then more intensely in prayer about a committed erotic relationship begun in 1965, McNeill reports discovering an assurance of divine approval. He tested the discovery by applying Ignatian rules for the discernment of spirits.[76]

McNeill does not make such testimony the basis of his original argument. He wants instead to argue from traditional sources of Catholic moral theology the possibility of being a sexually active gay Christian. Where Perry claimed this from an inner conviction of divine creation and spiritual guidance, McNeill—in this book at least—argues it from rational conclusions about nature as corroborated by the New Testament ethical imperative. Both agree on the possibility of the gay Christian. Both embody it as founders—though differently, since McNeill was for years bound not only by his public celibacy, but by his obedience.

THE SUCCESSES OF ARGUMENTS AND OF FOUNDINGS

Perry and McNeill are both theological writers and religious reformers. They pose together and in acute form the question of how to judge the success of an argument for religious reform. Even if the standard for success is the flourishing of the new religious group, the results are ambiguous. For a long time, MCC certainly seemed the more successful venture—much larger than Dignity, it often drew more Catholics than Dignity. In the last twenty years, especially, Dignity has hovered near extinction as MCC has grown. But the growth of the denomination has also stopped, at least for the moment, and some doubt its long-term survival as a free-standing group.

Whatever the historical survival of the two groups, they clearly represent different strategies for supporting LGBT Christians. MCC is in some ways a separatist model—and so might recall Gearhart or Martin. But MCC has also and from the beginning wanted to be accepted as real church, to take on many of the trappings and the privileges of other denominations. Dignity by contrast is a model of working from within—and so might recall Johnson's ordination. Except that Dignity was never really incorporated into Catholic structures, even when it was permitted to use Catholic property for its meetings. Nor has Dignity succeeded in modifying official teaching by force of argument. Quite the contrary: official Roman teaching has only become blunter in rejecting McNeill's position.

Because of delays in publication, McNeill's book actually appeared after a Vatican document on human sexuality that contained what many regarded—what some still regard—as an important paragraph on homosexuality. The 1975 *Declaration* from the CDF (Congregation for the Doctrine of the Faith) is not primarily concerned with homosexuality. Its purpose is more all-encompassing. It wants to reassert what it considers to be "natural law" arguments against a variety of sexual sins, including extramarital sex, homosexuality, and masturbation. The *Declaration* sometimes claims that the teaching of the Catholic Church on sexual matters derives from unchanging principles discoverable by human reason apart from divine revelation. The "natural wisdom of reason" can discover the requirements of human nature, at least "in the order of things proper to it."[77] These requirements are not historically or culturally conditioned. Catholic sexual morality is founded upon the "nature" of the "human person," upon the "constitutive elements and essential relations of each human person," upon the "norms" or "precepts of the natural law," upon principles contained in the "divine, eternal objective and universal law" of God.[78] This may sound like McNeill's language, but it intends the opposite conclusion. As regards "the sexual inclination of man and the human reproductive power," the "natural law" precepts teach that genital acts "do not have their true significance or moral force outside of legitimate marriage."[79] Any other genital activity, including any activity involving "artificial means" of contraception, is an abuse of human sex. It is not hard to predict how this teaching will apply to "homosexual relations." Both the "perpetual teaching" of the church's officials and "the moral sense of the Christian people" refuse to excuse "the homosexual relations of some persons."[80]

The *Declaration* does allow that there may be some reason to distinguish between curable and incurable homosexuals, between those who have a homosexual "proclivity born from bad education or damaged sexual maturity or habit or bad example," and those who are homosexuals "in perpetuity" because of "some kind of almost innate impulse" or "a vitiated constitution."[81] But this distinction speaks nothing to homosexual acts. "According to the moral order of objective things homosexual couplings are acts that are deprived of their necessary and essential ordering." Again, "acts of homosexuality are disordered by their very nature, nor can they be approved in any way whatever." Those are the closing words of the *Declaration*'s paragraph on homosexuality.

If this is an advance, it only brings the CDF up to the late nineteenth century, to Ellis's distinction between incurable inverts and punishable perverts. The *Declaration* does seem to make a point of admitting or approving the nineteenth-century categories of "sexuality" and "homosexuality," and their appearance in so authoritative a document is significant. The *Declaration* begins, for example, by telling us, "according to the opinion of the learned men of our time," that "sexuality" is to be counted among the most important elements of human life.[82] But whatever science appears in the *Declaration* is Edwardian—and subject to Vatican correction. If scientific evidence shows how typical masturbation is in adolescent development, so much the worse for scientific evidence. "Facts do not give us a rule by which the rightness of human acts can be judged." Neither do the arguments of "contemporary psychology" or the findings of "sociology."[83] If the document speaks of certain scientific characters, it does so for its own purposes.

When Vatican offices change teaching, they do not trumpet it. Continuity is a central justification for continued authority. A change from "sodomite" to "homosexual" would not seem such a significant change in any case—not to contemporary Catholic readers and perhaps not even to the dicasterial officials who drafted the document. The officials could have pointed to earlier Catholic documents, though not of such authority, in which the new term appeared. At least from the late 1950s, for example, the Vatican's appellate courts for marriage cases had used the category "homosexuality" (*homosexualismus*), and at least since the late 1960s some verdicts held that "perpetual" or "incurable" homosexuality made one incapable of consenting to marriage or achieving its union of souls and bodies.[84] The category and the principle seem to have entered the proceedings through the reports of psychiatrists or psychologists brought in as experts.[85] Earlier matrimonial jurisprudence, both in Rome and in the United States, shows a mixture of categories, including sodomy, sexual inversion, perversion, neurasthenic sexuality, and pederasty (applied to men). In 1975, the *Declaration* reduces this confusion of names to *homosexualitas*. At last, Kertbeny finds readers in Rome.

Changing names has consequences, but not always at once and not at first in the political order. Using the newly approved category and

McNeill's arguments, Dignity set out to build a network of chapters that increasingly celebrated separate Masses. Its members undertook to write tracts and to revise liturgy. Dignity and MCC both could draw on a growing body of scholarship—most notably that of John Boswell, a brilliant and charismatic young professor at Yale. During August 1976, Boswell spoke in Washington to the General Conference of the MCC. He "presented an overview of the relationship of gay people and the Christian church and [he] will soon publish an as-yet-untitled book on this subject."[86] In 1979, he addressed the fourth biennial meeting of Dignity. A version of the talk is still posted on the web.[87] When Boswell's *Christianity, Social Tolerance, and Homosexuality* appeared in 1980, it enjoyed an astonishing success. Reviewed by *Newsweek*, it sold so quickly in the early months that the University of Chicago Press struggled to fill orders. A year later, it won an American (now National) Book Award.

The new moral arguments, the innovative liturgies, the renowned erudition fortified Dignity, but they did not persuade the "competent authorities," to use the canonical phrase. In 1986, the CDF issued a letter on "the problem of homosexuality." The title seems to cite the Anglican pamphlet from three decades earlier, but the meaning has changed. Homosexuality is now not a social problem, but a theological and political problem—the occasion for confusion and organized resistance among the faithful (especially in America). The *Letter* reprimands Catholic bishops, priests, and laypeople who have been taken in by movements for homosexual rights, even to the point of arguing for them within the church. Only the official teaching authority may judge such matters, and it judges that the "peculiar propensity of the homosexual person" inclines the person "more or less strongly" to do something that must be considered "objectively evil" in the "moral order." So "the propensity itself is to be judged objectively disordered."[88] As proofs, the *Letter* appeals not only to nature, but to the string of familiar biblical passages. It does not hesitate to read the story of Sodom or Paul's diatribe against idolatry as condemnations of homosexuality. So much for Bailey, so much for Boswell.

Having settled the moral issue and interpreted both scriptural and scientific evidence in its favor, the *Letter* performs two other rhetorical gestures. It threatens gay activists by reminding them that the unsurprising consequence of pressing their groundless claims will be to strengthen irrational, violent opposition. Then, almost as if in ironic fulfillment of that prediction, the *Letter* orders bishops to expel Dignity and any similar groups from church property and to deny them any support.[89]

The efforts to bring gay liberation into the church did not convince many church authorities. They also failed to convince many gay liberationists.

John Lauritsen, among others, wrote severe criticisms not only of Boswell's book, but also of Bailey and every effort to make Christianity seem friendly to gays.[90] Arthur Evans begins his influential collage of liberationist and neopagan discourses by accusing Bailey of whitewashing "the church's atrocities against Gay people."[91] In the 1970s, as now, to be a gay Christian is to double occasions for insult.

Still there are larger ironies that catch up all these discourses, including the liberationist critiques. The liberationist movement is supposed to be a youth movement—a movement of the young against the old. But in fact its discourses quickly lose sight of the teenager, especially the teenager who is still subject to parental religion or who finds in it some real consolation. "Liberated youth" referred in fact to twenty-somethings, most of whom were not involved with raising children. In this way too, adolescence is cut from chronology and fused with the ritual of coming out. There is no true adolescence until you are free to avow your true self.

The same is true of most religious authors. If churchly liberation is the sequel to the conversations between homophile groups and the churches, it changes those conversations in one important respect: it abandons teenagers, at least as objects of discourse. The theory of homosexuality as maturation was not quite a charter for all-age community. Enthusiasm for Boswell's historical research was not enthusiasm for age-graded models— or even for love among the young.

Teenagers, abandoned by liberation, become the preoccupation of the most effective counter-rhetoric to claim the name of Christianity. It sought to undo the very possibility of conversation between churches and homophiles or homosexuals or gays. Liberation or no liberation, the issue was going to be "the children."

7

SAVING THEIR CHILDREN

Anita Bryant is the icon of a backlash against homosexuals that was so effectively political because so ardently religious. Journalists, historians, and screenwriters return to the episodes of her 1977 campaign as a turning point, a moment of political invention.[1] But Anita Bryant is better understood as a figure of rhetorical accumulation and new discharge, like a battery in a system of switches. Or else she is a figure of vivid recapitulation and reenactment. She gathers into her public character decades of church debates around homosexuality.

Here Anita Bryant is not the woman, whose life derailed so sadly after the campaign, but the rhetorical performer, whose strategies, whose scripted self has gone on to the success of endless reiteration. She may now appear as a ghost in old headlines, in fuzzy newsreel footage, or badly dubbed TV commercials, but she still haunts our religious debates, especially when we conduct them through headlines, news clips, and commercials. Anita Bryant, the Christian mom who beat the homosexual recruiters of Dade County in 1977—and whose rhetorical performance is used to beat them back—or beat them up—again and again, before the cameras, for the sake of the cameras. The Anita Bryant I am about to present is no more than this public performance, which was perfected through her.

Bryant's performance is not pure invention. Most of the elements of her speech are familiar from earlier "evangelical" reaction to Kinsey or to developments in liberal churches. Bryant reperforms the elements to stunning effect because she speaks them through a new character. She shifts the speaking voice from male pastor to female congregant—indeed, more importantly, to suffering Christian mother. She then points a row of rhetorical devices used earlier on other targets (Communists, sex researchers or educators, juvenile delinquents) right at the single figure of the gay male predator. Bryant fixes or fixates on the threat of homosexual recruitment, with all of its contradictions. Because they are sterile, homosexuals must recruit to reproduce themselves. But they can recruit only because mascu-line heterosexuality is curiously vulnerable, unstable—liable to destruction by a single encounter or image, by a single suggestion. An embodiment of feminine fertility rises up in defense of a fragile reproductive cycle. It's the mother who must protect husband, children, and church—because there are some things only a mother can say. This mother was made to say them for the news cycles because she had been made in news cycles.

MAKING ANITA

Long before the public struggle of Dade County began early in 1977, Anita Bryant had been fashioned and refashioned as a public figure, though not explicitly a political one. Her innocence of politics is part of how she wants to tell her story. Of course, the politics of a certain brand of patriotism are there all along. So are the politics of gender. Once Miss Oklahoma (1958) and second runner-up for Miss America (1959), Anita began as a singer with a predictable mixture of patriotic songs, romantic ballads (*In A Velvet Mood*), and hymns. She joined the Bob Hope Christmas Tours to American soldiers overseas and sang frequently at the White House for LBJ—indeed, she delivered her signature song, the "Battle Hymn of the Republic," at his funeral.[2] In the same years, she appeared in the Billy Graham Evangelistic Crusade. Then she began to write—her Christian testimony, of course, but also "inspirational" books, many with her hus-band, including a "Christian" program for physical fitness. Her husband did not coauthor her Christian cookbook.[3]

In attributing these books to Bryant, I consent to a sort of authorial fiction. Many of her public statements, including her books, were ghost-written by others, and there is internal reason to conclude that the most political books were pasted together by several hands from various sources. There is no need to decipher this authorship, because I am only interested in the character Bryant presents rhetorically—in Bryant as a papier maché torso fashioned out of scraps of speech. I am interested by the rhetorical work, the extraordinary performance that this figure can accomplish de-spite the evident flaws in the speech assigned to it. Like Anita herself, the books overcome defects of form by the melodrama of their appeals and the menacing certainty of their convictions.

In the autobiographical books that tell segments of her "story," Anita's Christian testimony is wrapped from the beginning around gender—though not around sex. She was raised in families that were significantly matriarchal. Her father left the house twice through divorce. Her maternal grandfather, though present, had been blinded in an oil field accident. The strong figures are the women—mother and grandmother. Faith comes by matrilineal descent. Anita was saved at the age of eight after she showed herself, like the young Jesus in the Temple, able to stump her elders with her scriptural wisdom. Her mother asks, "Don't you want to wait until you're older before you take such an important step?" The child Anita answers, "Can you show me in the Bible where it says how old I must be before I can be saved?"[4] Mother is convinced—and mother must be convinced, because she is the spiritual authority much more than the minister. Retelling the story, Anita immediately projects this line of maternal transmission forward to her own children: "Now that I am a mother, with children approaching the age I was that Sunday night I remember so well at the Church of Christ in Velma-Alma, Oklahoma . . ." The long line of mothers nurtures young souls so that God, who is very much Father, can be reproduced in them. Maternal authority comes by delegation from God. A few years after her baptism, right relationship is "restored" when her mother slaps Anita for being rude. Her mother explains, "The good Lord provided a place for me to smack you when you need it." Anita understands and agrees: "She is my *mother*."[5] But maternal authority goes along with wifely subjection—at least, in theory. "Mother almost worshiped Daddy," Anita assures us, the "almost" reminding us that Daddy is not quite God the Father.[6]

Submission to God: the refrain in Anita's testimony. But submission is curiously paired with worldly advancement. God has not only given Anita a voice with which to sing, He hears Anita's prayers about becoming a star and actively manages her performing career.[7] Of course, God's gifts some-times call for a little improvement. Anita sings notes that have "always . . . been there, just as God gave them to me," but a high school vocal coach is needed to add two or three steps to the top of her range for a role in *South Pacific*.[8] Prayer and hard work combine; together they "pay off." When it comes to difficult career choices, Anita discovers the same profitable combination. At a crucial moment, she must decide whether to accept the invitation to go to New York for an appearance on "Arthur Godfrey's Talent Scouts." Her pastor and other church members are worried about Anita in the big city. But she really wants to go! Mother, as always, pro-vides the decisive advice: Anita must seek God's will with the promise that she is sincerely ready to obey it. "Feeling more rebellious and troubled" than ever, Anita kneels and weeps.[9] Then "a tremendous, indescribable peace descend[ed] upon me . . . Suddenly I jumped to my feet. I felt ab-solutely washed with relief and joy." God wanted her to go to New York all along, but first demanded her "submission," so that she would "perform and act in full obedience to my inner guiding from Him." The language is that of her earlier baptism: "I felt so clean inside, as though my sins were washed away. And as I walked down the aisle . . . I felt the Spirit of God Himself leading me there."[10] Baptism and career choice: in both cases, submission is answered by consolation—without interfering at all in the forward march of the successful life. Her performance is her testimony.[11] Her testimony underwrites her performance. Melodramatic submission is the prelude—or price—for both.

Anita's performed graces make her more and more famous. She scales the celebrity ladders: from small church worship services, local television, and high school musicals through state and national beauty pageants to broadcast and recording contracts. But there is so little time along the way for boys—and so many girls and boys of the wrong kind. Luckily she meets a DJ, Bob Green, at a recording-industry convention in Miami. She rebuffs time after time, yet still he pursues her. Anita learns that he neither smokes nor drinks and that he seeks "simpler, more solid values" than show-business success. Bob even aspires to be a dad, hoping to "establish a home with a wife who possessed high moral standards—the kind of woman he wanted to rear his children."[12] Anita finally falls in love with him, though the pursuit is all his. They are engaged when Bob slips a ring on her finger while at dinner with his parents. But Anita remains adamant on one point. "Bob had not been saved; he frankly admitted to being just a nominal Christian, and even looked somewhat puzzled when I tried to explain what I meant by being saved though Christ." So on the night before their wedding, the couple kneels down alongside one of Anita's close friends, her "spiritual sister." Between these two women, Bob finds God. "The Spirit of God descended upon us. Bob felt led to confess Jesus Christ as his Lord and Saviour."[13] Female intervention once again opens the way for divine action—once again shores up faltering masculinity. The next day—June 25, 1960—Bob and Anita are married. She is twenty.

During these same years, from the late 1950s on, Anita became a corporate "spokeswoman"—that is, an advertising icon. She did a series of television commercials for Coca-Cola that chart her progress from beauty queen to perfect mom. It is hard now to retrieve these spots except as camp artifacts, but even in context they seem to flirt with her double role as sex kitten and suburban goddess. In one ad for Coca-Cola, from around 1960, Anita frolics at the seaside with the Brothers Fours, a singing group that looks and sounds like the chorus in a beach-blanket teen romance. We get to see Anita dash up the sand in a one-piece bathing suit, then sing and swig framed by bared male chests and panting abs. Backed by beefcake, in a moment of thirsty consummation, she even winks at the camera—if not quite at us. Then she is carried into the waves on a lounger, since she may not be manhandled, not even by the Brothers Four. Anita disappears into the foaming water, her legs kicking, with a strangely throaty yell. Aphrodite tossed back into the waves. She is not yet tamed.

In later Coca-Cola ads, Anita is more fully domesticated. The domestication is complete after 1969 in television spots for the Florida Citrus Commission. One of them shows her waking the children at home, then tending to them in a bright, sinless kitchen—her real kitchen, her new stage, new cage.[14] If the other Anita sometimes peeks through, she is quickly muzzled. In one famous spot, Anita does a sort of dancer's fall from a ladder in an orange grove. Imagine Marilyn Monroe being carried as she sings "Diamonds Are a Girl's Best Friend"—or Madonna's final, swooning fall in "Material Girl." Anita falls like that into the arms of an attending man. He seems at first glance the very type of the Broadway dancer. But it turns out to be only Bob, her husband, who pecks her on the cheek and stands her on her feet—so that she can serve breakfast to him and the kids in the middle of the grove.

Anita's televised conversion from beach-party star to nurturing mom prepares her final transfiguration into antihomosexual evangelist. Before the fight in Dade County started, she had already been refigured as a still slender Mother Nature, proclaiming sun-based slogans: "Put a little sunshine in your day!" "A breakfast without orange juice is like a day without sunshine!" Before the sun turns into the Son (of the thundering God), Anita is already a public priestess of the bountiful earth. She makes families by feeding them. Reproduction requires suckling at the carefully veiled breast of the chaste mother. How many times she says or sings the words "natural" or "naturally" in those citrus ads. In some print ads for the campaign, "natural" is underlined.

Alongside the impossible fictions of the ads, Anita was living more painful episodes of motherhood, but they too were incorporated into her public character. The most anguished episode of her public life before the battle over homosexual rights showed her poignantly as a mother suffering for her children. Early in January of 1969, immediately after doing color commentary for the Orange Bowl, Anita went into labor prematurely. She delivered a boy, the first of twins, but a Caesarian was required for the second, a girl. Anita hemorrhaged. The newborns hovered near death; so did she. The *Miami Herald* picked up the story immediately and kept to it in vigil. Bulletins went out on the wire services. Messages of support arrived from LBJ and Billy Graham. Public prayers were offered at a "Christian convention" in Honolulu and by the employees of Holiday Inn, after urging by the corporate chaplain. But the crisis continued: the twins were moved to another hospital for more intensive care while Anita herself was kept under treatment.

Anita narrates this "drama" in the longest single section of her first autobiography. She tells it as a sequence of providential miracles that supplied the right doctors and the right equipment just in time. She details the urgent requests for prayer made of "everybody . . . who stays close to the Lord."[15] Unbelievers too offer their help and profess their admiration for Christian fidelity. Since faith and popularity remain intertwined for Anita, this story must demonstrate the rallying of popular support, of "a nation's love," to quote the chapter title. But Anita also frames the story as a trial of faith: is God punishing her? Her pastor assures her that the babies are innocent; they suffer for the sin set loose in the world. "It's sin in the world that brings on disease, sickness, heartbreak, and disaster." But God does require that she surrender her babies to Jesus. They must be offered up in order to accomplish "His perfect will for them."[16] Once the words of oblation are stammered out through tears, peace returns—and the babies improve. After two months they are strong enough to come home. That same month, Anita appears in public for the first time since the difficult birth— at the "Miami Youth for Decency Rally," an evangelistic protest against the onstage antics of Jim Morrison of The Doors. Reduced to tears, Anita manages to say to the crowd, "As a mother of four, I am deeply grateful to you young people."[17]

Tears over babies surrendered to God, tears of gratitude for youthful decency. Already before the "battle of Miami," Anita is at once reformed starlet, patriot, evangelizer, purveyor of natural goodness, and iconic mother. She lives the story of sex tamed by marriage for the sake of the children. In the early '70s, she returns to the Billy Graham Crusade, but also to the televised spectacle of the Junior Miss Pageant.

As the topic of homosexuality filters into the news, she is already associated with many church figures who will speak against it. But her relationship to the issue is more complicated, at least for some of her fans. Through the passionate possessions of camp desire, she had already become an object of shameful adulation for some boys. Anita Bryant was Julie Andrews in the sunbelt. If some tender-hearted boys grew up having memorized every line in *The Sound of Music*, others practiced singing "Come to the Florida Sunshine Tree" and dreamed of falling from orchard ladders into the tanned arms of a Broadway dancer—I mean, of a solicitous husband. As the fantasy of a certain style of womanhood, as gender caricature, Bryant was perfectly available for gay inhabitation. Not a few "good Christian" boys moved in.[18] All of this *before* the fight in Dade County. The carefully publicized narrative of the starlet become our mother endowed her with special powers for that fight. So did her camp attractions.

THE BATTLE OF DADE COUNTY

In December 1976, the Dade County Metro Commission passed unanimously on first reading an ordinance banning discrimination on the basis of "affectional or sexual preference" in employment and housing.[19] The commissioner proposing the ordinance was Ruth Shack, wife of one of Anita Bryant's booking agents. Indeed, Anita had recorded radio spots for Ruth's election campaign. After the resolution passed, a local attorney, Robert Brake, decided that because the nondiscrimination ordinance contained no religious exemption, it would force local churches and their schools to hire avowed homosexuals. The fear from the first was about gay men, though television reporters would later explain, with the pedantry of new learning, that "by 'homosexual' we are referring to both men and women."[20] Already an advocate for conservative causes, Brake began to use political and church networks to organize a petition drive that would force a popular referendum on the ordinance. It was no longer enough to declare religious space exempt from civil rights regulations. Religious values had to be proclaimed to the world—and imposed on it in the name of religious exemption.

In January of 1977, when the ordinance came back for a second reading and what was presumed to be automatic passage, the noisy commission meeting was filled with "Christian" protesters—including Anita Bryant, who had been recruited to lead the campaign by her pastor after the mortifying discovery that she had endorsed the politician behind the ordinance. Despite the protests, the ordinance was approved, though only by a vote of 5–3. So the petitions were circulated in earnest, especially through churches. Six times more signatures were collected than required by law. Given the option of repealing the ordinance or scheduling a referendum, the commission set a special election for June. The ensuing campaign drew national attention and organizational support for both sides. In its last weeks, Anita appeared frequently—in a debate before the Kiwanis Club, where she sang the "Battle Hymn of the Republic"; handing out pamphlets to the morning shift at Eastern Airlines; taking calls at her campaign's phone bank. There were full-page newspaper ads and television spots.

On June 7, the ordinance was overturned decisively by almost 70 percent of those voting. At the victory news conference, Bryant intoned, "Tonight the laws of God and the cultural values of man have been vindicated." She spoke for the no longer silent "normal majority": "Enough, enough, enough." Her husband kissed her twice for the cameras, saying, "This is what heterosexuals do, fellas." Bryant went on to other campaigns in other cities, the once and future icon of the intractable opposition between Christian decency and homosexual filth.[21]

The Bryant campaign shows something of the techniques and the stages through which the "Religious Right" came to dominate American electoral politics by defending the family, that is, fatherly (or Fatherly) regulation of sex and gender. It should be no surprise that Anita's immediate supporters included the televangelists Jim Bakker and Pat Robertson. Jerry Falwell not only invited her to his show, he lent her campaign experienced staff. Dade County was a laboratory for the Religious Right, in which it learned the usefulness of homosexuality as a wedge issue for both churchly and secular politics—or rather for the fusion of the two. But the Bryant campaign has also been read in the opposite direction, so far as she provoked a new rhetoric of national gay and lesbian politics not quite a decade after Stonewall.[22] During the campaign, activists claimed that Bryant provided a national rallying point around which various queer groups could converge—including, importantly, both lesbian and gay groups. The electoral defeat over the ordinance led to much more important electoral victories, including the defeat of the Briggs Initiative in California in the fall of 1978. Or so the stories go.

I am more interested in how the Bryant campaign clarifies the continuing history of church debates over homosexuality. It rearticulates decisively the rhetorical devices that some Christian groups had used for decades to "battle" sexual danger. Bryant's performance displays in their mature forms many features of churchly condemnation of homosexuality. She quotes scriptures and rehearses what are supposed to be arguments. She lends her considerable stage presence to the repertoire of inherited topics. But more importantly she performs a rhetoric of compassion and cursing that claims the vulnerability of the young as justification for waging war on homosexuals. The Bryant campaign deploys the professedly, aggressively "Christian" rhetoric that still surrounds us, that still works in us and on us.

ANITA'S VINDICATION

The fullest specimen of Bryant's campaign rhetoric is a mass-market book written right after the Dade campaign and subtitled *The Survival of Our Nation's Families and the Threat of Militant Homosexuality.*[23] It rehearses a script that proves remarkably easy to take on the road, to perform in other contexts, to translate into other Christian dialects.

The shape of the book is not easy to describe, because it has no single shape. Or rather it belongs to the evangelical genre of the deliberately disordered diatribe that we have encountered before, beginning with Daniels.

Bryant's thin narrative is interlarded—interrupted—with exhortations, observations, and too many quotations. The book keeps breaking its own plot line, jumping forward to its conclusion, because the reader is supposed already to know how the story ends. The reader buys the book or borrows it from the church library because she or he has already read the headlines. Indeed, a collage of selected headlines fills the back of the dust jacket. The collage is a sort of picture of the whole: it is a scrapbook that overpowers any expectation for coherence by a mounting insistence—by saying to the reader, page after crowded page, "No, here's a better picture of the wedding."

While there is no clear plot in Anita's book on the Dade County campaign, there are evident motives. She is eager to correct misinformation and to combat slanders. She will vindicate her benign intentions and her reasonableness against charges that she is prejudiced, stupid, silly, or crazy. Anita emphasizes her own gentleness and meekness, but also her lack of prejudice, even toward homosexuals. Indeed, she frequently confesses her love for homosexuals and her desire to bring them back from their sin. She also praises legitimate racial minorities (as opposed to the false minority claims by homosexuals), and she reports cooperating with non-evangelicals and even non-Christians.[24] Anita is no bigot.

Christian love—and Christian rationality. The book insists on the perfect clarity of the Bible's condemnation of homosexuality, but it cannot let biblical authority stand alone. The Bible's clear commands are supplemented by a host of historical, legal, and even scientific claims. Across history, Anita tells us, the acceptance of homosexuality has led to social disaster.[25] More strikingly, she cites "a wealth of anthropological, economic, social, and psychological data" to show that "family breakdown is the chief cause of the problems that have come down with such force upon our country in recent years."[26] Scripture is clear, and its lessons are backed by history and science. What could be more rational? Then, of course, there is God's continuing speech to those with ears to hear. Lest this last claim raise fresh doubts about Anita's rationality, she explains very carefully that when she says that God speaks to her, she is certainly not referring to "a supernatural audible voice." God speaks to her through her "thought patterns."[27] Anita is certainly not a crazy person who hears divine voices.

If the book is anxious to refute slanders against Anita, it is also eager to stir up complacent American Christians—especially those in misguided, "liberal" churches—and to warn all patriotic Americans about encroaching dangers. Here Anita's ambivalence toward the media becomes plain. She wants to reveal that the media, various levels of government, and even some benighted churches have been taken over by homosexual activists and their supporters. She attacks national print and broadcast media for their distortions. But then she cites newspaper coverage to show her own importance, quotes praise from conservative pundits to prove the cogency of her case, and recalls with pride her victories during television broadcasts. She exhibits the same ambivalence toward the political. Anita repeatedly contrasts her spontaneous, grassroots campaign, which claims to operate entirely on unsolicited donations, with the political machinery of the militant homosexuals—even as she recounts strategizing by her allies and boasts of meeting Ronald Reagan at the Florida Conservative Union.[28] Yet Anita stands above politics.

There are other ambivalences or contradictions in the text, but cataloguing more of them would not disclose the sources of Anita's rhetorical power. The ambivalences lie on the surface of Anita's speech, not far below her avowed intentions and self-vindications. The rhetorical power lies further down—or, rather, right on the skin of her constructed rhetorical body. Bryant's script works not by arguing from evidence, not by appeal to scriptural authority, not even by manipulating combative emotions, though there are frequent cues for anger and fear. She beats back the homosexuals by performing a soliciting narrative, a morality play that assigns roles to various members of its audience and to all who surround them. The morality play is meant to capture all of us—not least when it assigns some of us to a fixed role of demonic opposition.

ANITA'S HEART

Consider the opening sentence of the book—which is set off as a separate paragraph. Let me lay it out as the hymn verse that it almost is.

> Because of my love for Almighty God,
> because of my love for His Word,
> because of my love for my country,
> because of my love for my children,
> I took a stand—one that was not popular.[29]

Note first the ritual repetition. This is the language of worship, of creed, litany, psalmody. Note next the elision of the four objects of Anita's love: God, His Word, country, and children are gathered into one object of devotion. To love God is to revere the Bible *and* America *and* America's children. To defend America's children is to save the country, but also to stand up for the Bible and for God. Being an American mom is being a servant of God. Being antimom is both unpatriotic and irreligious. But these things shouldn't be said—indeed, the fundamental elision of objects can't be said, because it might sound blasphemous even to Anita's intended audience. The elision of objects works best when performed.

The most insistent phrase in the opening sentence isn't about the objects, but about the subject. "*My* love," repeated four times. Then the punctuating declaration—with its echoes of Martin Luther at the mythological moment of announcing the Reformation: "I took a stand." Our eyes are on Anita—as reformer, but even more as mom. A mom with a loving heart that wicked people are breaking. Here are some things we learn about Anita's broken heart.

God has put a flame in her heart and impressed truths upon it. God also hears the cries welling up within it. Anita *knows* things by heart—especially the Bible, which speaks to her plainly from within. But she also groans in her heart—groaning that only God can answer. Anita's heart is troubled. She cries often: out of a sense of her own unworthiness, for fear of what homosexual teachers will do to her children, over America, from fatigue during the campaign, for the poor homosexuals themselves. There is hurt in her heart and agony in her soul. She is sickened and repulsed by the sexual suicide caused by homosexuality and feminism. She agonizes over the damage to children from filth. In short, her heart suffers a woman's pain, a mother's pain, that even her husband can't understand.[30]

If Anita were Roman Catholic, we might say that she is narrating herself as the *mater dolorosa*: Mary the mother of Jesus at the foot of the cross, her heart pierced by the blade that pierces his side. Bryant actually performs a more complicated alignment with scriptural types. She explicitly likens herself to strong Israelite women, especially Esther and Deborah. She identifies with Jesus: "whatever I have suffered has caused me to identify more closely with Jesus' sufferings."[31] If men can't understand a woman's heart, Jesus can. God can too—He can understand, but perhaps not wholly identify. (I continue to copy Bryant's language, in which God is definitely and deliberately "He.") God is bound to enforce His absolute moral code. He cannot tolerate deviations from it.[32] So it is left to Anita and other American moms to stand as intermediaries, weeping for the homosexuals, toiling for their conversion—or public reprobation. Anita is the dutiful daughter-wife-mother who tries to soften the understandable severity of Father's law. The tender chambers of her heart can accommodate any good thing, but they must expel whatever is evil. This heart swells to embrace everything decent, everything holy, but it cannot embrace what God the Father commands her to repudiate.

The appeal to Anita's heart is as much artifice as affect. She has been coached into it. The performance falters when she is tired or surprised.

Then she sounds and looks vindictive—or worldly. While on tour after the referendum vote in Miami, Anita and Bob conducted a news conference in Des Moines. The cameras were rolling. Suddenly a protester stepped into the frame to hit her in the face with a cream pie.[33] In fuller video records of the event, Anita shifts awkwardly from one character to another—slips from the script only to be coached back to it. At first Anita says, with an aging showgirl's weary self-possession, "Well, at least it's a fruit pie." Next Bob cues her to a more appropriate speech: she wants to pray for those who have attacked her. Finally, and while praying, Anita begins to weep— from being startled, no doubt, but also because her role in the campaign is to seal scripted words with iconic suffering.

HOMOSEXUALS AS PUBLIC ENEMIES

Through her tears, mom can speak honestly—must speak honestly—about the dangers of homosexuality. Anita repeats that she loves homosexuals and that she never resorts to name-calling.[34] She manages nevertheless to present a vivid picture of what her God-fired heart must expel.

Mom says: homosexuals have organized themselves into a widespread and well-financed militant organization. Although few in numbers, they attempt to terrorize opponents by telling the big lie and by making themselves appear more numerous than they actually are.[35] Many of Bryant's terms and images—indeed, the reiterated word "militant"—derive from American anti-Communist rhetoric. Presumably that militancy justifies her repeated use of war metaphors and her appropriation of the "Battle Hymn of the Republic" as a campaign jingle.[36] This is not a simple application of Red-baiting rhetoric to homosexuals. After all, homosexuals and Communists were already explicitly associated by McCarthy. Bryant does something more. She reverses McCarthy's accent: homosexuals, not Communists, are now public enemy number one.

The mother's heart speaks on: homosexuals are abnormal, aberrant, irresponsible, rebellious, deviant, abominable, guilty of gross moral perversion, unnatural, and ungodly. Bryant associates them with the uncleanness that destroys empires and likens them to an aggressive social epidemic. They are radically selfish: they give priority to money, careers, power, and any pleasure rather than to God and family. Homosexuals cannot even conceive self-sacrifice, as they can be neither clean nor healthy. That is why God has condemned them for five thousand years as unnatural, unproductive, and sinful. They flagrantly violate both God's law and the laws of the vast majority of mankind across the ages.[37]

Despite being radically antisocial, homosexuals have managed to band together into secret networks to feed their appetite for political power. They know how to maneuver the media and government; they can mobilize cadres of sympathizers. Using their preferred devices of stealth and camouflage, they spread their insidious lifestyle.[38] Homosexuals are quite willing to resort to violence: they have threatened with physical harm Anita's campaigners, a Christian bookseller, and several Christian bookstores. More: they have menaced Anita's life, even on stage, and made her fear for the physical safety of her children.[39] With his arm around Anita at a Miami rally, Jerry Falwell tells the crowd, "We are dealing with a vile and a vicious and a vulgar gang. They'd kill you as quick as look at you. If you don't think that, you don't know the enemy."[40] Homosexuals, like Communists before them, become the very type of the bloodthirsty enemy—the Enemy. Unlike Communists they create a world of secret pleasures for themselves. Every American city now has its own bars, hotels, baths, publications—even travel guides. Not content with secret temples for their abominations, they demand the right to have sex in public.[41]

In one way this litany of attributes is very old news for churches. Something like it goes back at least nine hundred years. In Peter Damian's *Book of Gomorrah*, a reader can see the same accumulation of moral, medical, and political charges against the sodomite.[42] But one striking difference is that Bryant unknowingly rewrites the traditional condemnations of the sodomite within the modern, medical dichotomy of homosexual/heterosexual. As much as any progressive theologian, she is appropriating the modern clinical identities. While Anita sometimes emphasizes—rather more than Peter Damian—the possibility of repenting from the sins of weak flesh, she names that redemption clinically as a "return to full heterosexuality" and so a reversal of the "choice" for homosexuality.[43] It's a choice, not a birthright, she repeats. She bewails the urban enclaves that reinforce homosexuality rather than pointing a way out, and she praises those "exgays" who have ended their homosexuality by coming to Christ.[44] She appropriates the clinical terms, but twists them according to her own deep narrative of willed conversion.

Bryant is not trying to use the new identity of the "homosexual" to draw a distinction between the *condition* of homosexuality and its *expression* in acts. As we have seen, progressive theologians had been doing that since at least the 1950s. Bryant heads in the opposite direction: she assimilates the acts to the identity, she thinks of the acts only in terms of the identity. Indeed, when she wants to talk about these sexual acts, she uses the odd locution "the act of homosexuality."[45] Not "homosexual acts," but the "act of homosexuality"—as if these acts could only be defined as acts of the identity. She doesn't want people just to restrain themselves from the acts; she wants them to stop being homosexuals. Hence the importance of the emphasis on the "return to full heterosexuality," from which the homosexual has strayed by choice. Bryant repeats the old clichés about the unhappiness of homosexual relationships: they are agonizing for most participants, and so it is no wonder that homosexuals are desperately lonely and given to suicide.[46] The repetition is not meant to engender sympathy. Her point is that those wretches should stop being homosexuals. She accepts the medical category, then reconfigures it as selfish choice. She assimilates the category to voluntary malice—to a chosen demonic state. In the end, homosexuality is worse than much Communism, which can be excused in many cases on ethnic or nationalistic grounds. An American homosexual—like the WASP Communist—is the ultimate traitor. All those cute, blond boys on Miami's beaches, looking just like the Brothers Four, like extras in any wholesome beach movie, but carrying treasonous poisons inside their tanned chests.

The emphasis on choice allows Anita to contrast as pure opposites God and homosexuality. One urgent task for her melodrama is to make it impossible for the two to overlap. Anita must silence anything that might sound like a gay or lesbian Christian voice. When she must mention such voices, she does so quickly and without serious engagement. During Anita's appearance on the Phil Donahue show, a woman calls in to identify herself as a Bible teacher and a lesbian.[47] This is one of the few "abnormal" *women* who appears in the text, though there are general condemnations of lesbian feminists who destroy the gender order. Anita replies to the woman caller only by scolding her for picking and choosing Bible verses. There is no mention of her claim to share Christian faith, to be a Christian while being a lesbian.[48]

A bit more extended and more interesting is the depiction of John McNeill, who also appeared on the Donahue show.[49] Bryant first mentions McNeill after talking about "theologians and scripturally uninformed church men" who diverge from the Bible. She then names him as someone who has been misled by psychology into false tolerance. Later McNeill is described as the author of a "very controversial" book. He does not appear in Bryant as a gay man because he was not yet out. He is rather an emblem for misguided liberals who reject God's word—that is, who are not true Christians. By their refusal to trust and obey God, they are putting both the churches and American society in peril.

Lesbian Bible teachers and Jesuits who excuse homosexuality psychologically have fallen away from Christian faith into the abyss. They have joined battle against God, whether they know it or not. There is no middle ground between Christian and homosexual. There is no civil or religious argument that can justify a Christian in supporting homosexual "rights." Anita emphasizes support for her position across Christian denominations and non-Christian religions in order to reinforce this stark binary: God or the homosexual. That is also why she likes to highlight the "anti-God" statements of gay writers.[50] Anita insists that they are all joined in a "disguised attack on God." The voice of any countertestimony from Christian homosexuals is ruled out of hearing. It would be too dangerous to listen. A believer might begin to be persuaded.

HOMOSEXUAL RECRUITMENT

The cruelest homosexual danger circles around the weakest members of American society. The original and strongest emphasis of Bryant's campaign was the threat posed to children by the Dade nondiscrimination ordinance. The slogan "Save Our Children from Homosexuality!" appeared on bright posters and on the cover of a widely distributed pamphlet. Inside the pamphlet, there is a collage of newspaper clippings about child abuse and child pornography. The first headline announces, "Teacher Accused of Sex Acts With Boy Students." The pamphlet's text encourages the reader to "scan these headlines from the nation's newspapers—then decide: Are homosexuals trying to recruit our children?" It concludes with a boxed quotation of "demands" from a 1972 convention of gay organizations. Under the heading "What homosexuals want," it lists the "repeal of all laws governing the age of sexual consent" and federally funded sex-education classes that would present homosexuality "as a valid, healthy preference."[51]

Anita emphasizes the danger to her own children in the scripts for her speeches and her interviews. After passing out pamphlets, she explains herself to one interviewer in broken phrases: "as a mother" she seeks "the protection of my four children," especially since the ordinance would (allegedly) install openly homosexual teachers as a "role model" for them in their "private Christian school."[52] She is more didactic with the Kiwanis Club: "the danger of the homosexual becoming a role model for our children" is not just "the physical," but "psychological molestation, which is even more detrimental."[53] The television ads produced by the communications director for Save Our Children were more emphatic. In the most famous, footage of the Orange Bowl parade, "Miami's gift" to the nation of "wholesome entertainment," is intercut with footage from a San Francisco Pride parade. The narrator intones, "But in San Francisco, when *they* take to the streets, it's a parade of homosexuals, men hugging other men, cavorting with little boys."[54]

"Little boys." Anita's campaign was called "Save Our Children." When she conducted it, her oldest child, Bob Junior, was thirteen. But he had to be read down into the category of the child. The campaign performed the same sleight of hand on the newspaper headlines it cites. Of course the pamphlet omits any mention of men preying on girls or young women, and then it generalizes its hand-picked cases to all homosexuals. Just as importantly, it has to confuse the question of age. Whenever the adolescent is an innocent victim, the adolescent becomes a child. But the transformation is unstable, because the adolescent is not always assigned the role of innocence.

What exactly is the danger that Anita Bryant decries? She once characterized the threat as malnutrition or insult to the growing body: "If [my children] are exposed to homosexuality, I might as well feed them garbage."[55] She has a mother's obligation to protect their tender and unknowing bodies. The language of malnutrition merges with that of contamination: "garbage" goes along with the repeated references to "filth" and "sickness." Anita is still the purveyor of natural goodness. The advertising scripts slip easily into the political campaign. More often Anita describes the physical threat not as latent toxicity, but as active aggression. Exposing her children to homosexuality would be like force-feeding them garbage. There may be an unconscious allusion to fellatio, which she once likened to "eating life" because of the ingestion of semen.[56] But the quite conscious association is with sexual violation. Homosexuals hunt for "boys" because they prefer the young, because they get bored in adult relationships and seek new thrills. The result is rape or sexual slavery—though Anita uses neither term, and relies mostly on the words of expert others to describe such outcomes. These things are too terrible for her to know or to tell—except by extensive quotation.[57]

The threat of physical violence passes over into the stranger threat of the "role model." Here the image oscillates between deliberate contagion and cunning persuasion—between bodily infection and spiritual recruitment. Anita explains the homosexual impulse to recruit in two ways: as fulfilling an unmet childhood need and as overcoming sterility. The first explanation: deprived of role models growing up, homosexuals want to provide role models for *our* growing children—where "our" refers to parents and children who are, of course, presumptively heterosexual.[58] On this explanation, recruitment seems almost a byproduct of modeling—as if the main point were to become as an adult what one lacked as a child. But the second explanation secures the image of recruitment directly:

homosexuals can't reproduce, so they must recruit in order to survive—
not as individuals, but as some unnatural quasi species, some alien army.

There are immediate difficulties with both the metaphor of recruitment
and its explanation. Sometimes recruitment is reduced to infection by
contact. One gay organizer spoke of "Anita's vampire theory."[59] The analogy is exact: homosexuals, like vampires, somehow change the innocent
young against their wills, through their bodily vulnerability. At other times,
Anita seems to mean recruitment more strictly. She supposes that "our
children" are susceptible of persuasion, that they are confused or impressionable. Anita quotes a psychological authority who worries that a gay
Pride parade poses a threat to millions of young men with precarious masculinity. She shares the worry—and not only about gay Pride parades. Just
having a teacher in a classroom who is known to be gay, who represents
gayness as an acceptable alternative, is enough to endanger "our children."
Any public approval of homosexuality encourages more homosexuality.[60]

What accounts for this tremendous susceptibility in "our children"?
Anita is not clear, though she suggests that it has something to do with
the troubling boundary between childhood and adolescence. Sometimes
she concedes that sexual orientation is not fixed for an indefinite period
of childhood or adolescence. At other times her worry is that the "young
person," the adolescent as opposed to the child, is prone to rebellion.[61] But
she prefers to fall back on the model of passive suffering: falling victim to
the advances of a homosexual or being exposed to the unforgettable, the
mind-molesting image of the act of homosexuality. In one of the campaign
book's most vivid passages, Anita recalls opening an anonymous letter that
contained a photograph of—the reader never learns. We are told only that
it was the "most hideous thing [she] had ever seen; a picture of two nude
men committing an act of homosexuality. The letter that accompanied it
was filth—just filth."[62] The image sticks in her mind and keeps recurring,
so that she finally has to cast it out by the power of the blood of Jesus. If it
has that sort of effect on a famous Christian crusader, imagine the effect
on a defenseless child!

Recruitment turns out to be not so much a consequence of thwarted
queer reproduction as a persistent flaw in straight (masculine) desire. Heterosexuality is precarious, perhaps especially during adolescence. It can
be unsettled by a Pride parade, an out teacher, or a filthy picture. Anita
blames homosexual recruiters for exploiting—for exposing—this flaw in
the young, but her accusation enacts a contradiction of agency. The account of the passive origin of homosexuality in the young cuts against the
call for adults to leave their homosexuality actively. You were insidiously
seduced into it—you were molested, you were possessed by an image, you

succumbed. Now, years later, you are obliged to choose to make a "return to full heterosexuality." But when did you ever have full heterosexuality? It would make no sense to call you back to the vulnerable heterosexuality you possessed as a defenseless child or uncertain teenager. You must be called to some new heterosexuality, now confirmed because chosen as an adult. This is something like the basic narrative of innocence, sin, and acceptance of salvation from Jesus. Recruitment to homosexuality must be reversed by recruitment to Jesus—since recruiting for Jesus is, after all, the daily work of Anita's style of evangelism. Yet recruitment through Jesus to heterosexuality cannot be done, like Anita's own conversion, in precocious childhood. It can only be done after a certain treacherous vulnerability has passed with the end of adolescence.

Homosexuality, like sin, is loose in the world. Babies and children are innocent yet vulnerable. They must be protected so vigilantly because they can be corrupted so quickly. They deserve all the outraged tenderness of Anita's heart. For the adult, by contrast, homosexuality is culpably unnatural. It must be actively rejected—by the sinful individual, by the vigilant society. Homosexuality must be an unnatural choice for the adult or else God's judgment will seem unreasonable—and Anita's heart not so tender after all. But homosexuality must not be a choice at all for the child—or else it is not entirely the fault of the recruiters, not just a suggestion from the wicked world outside. The agency demanded of the adult contradicts the blameless passivity required in the child. In between, there must be the figure of the adolescent, who must sometimes be as innocent as a child, sometimes as wicked as an adult. But Anita prefers not to talk about troubling adolescents. She wants either innocent children or sinful adults, but not changeling adolescents, half victims, half predators.

The central accusation against homosexuals—the accusation of recruiting—undermines the foundations of a heterosexuality to which they are, in gentler moments, commanded to return. We could say that the paradox of homosexual agency is underwritten by the performed paradox of Anita Bryant herself. She takes religious agency as a woman only because men won't; she gains political force only by denying political motives; she gathers evidence in support of authoritative lessons in the Bible even as she claims to know its clear teachings in her heart; she hears God in her thoughts, but His most repeated message is opaque, "Trust and obey."[63] The paradox of homosexual agency (childhood innocence, youthful rebellion, adult culpability) is no greater than—and perhaps no other than— the paradox of Anita's own gender, rescued from those now suspect boys on the beach so that she can serve breakfast in her very own kitchen— morning after morning. Trust and obey: the deep code of her performance of Christian womanhood. You cannot reply to her rhetoric unless you can reply to her self.

CAMPING ANITA

Anita Bryant's rhetoric works when you are brought to inhabit the morality play that surrounds her public character. You inhabit it when you accept it, but also when you fight back in the ways that it expects and predicts. Every morality play assumes that some or many of its hearers are sinners who may well not be turned. It assumes their resistance and discounts their demonic arguments in advance. You cannot win against a morality play by better scriptural exegesis, better ethics, better jurisprudence, or better science. The most effective answer is always a counternarrative. One effective counternarrative reveals the silliness, the shrillness of what the morality play urges so melodramatically.

In her book about the campaign, Anita makes clear that the response she most dislikes is mockery, especially the mockery—call it camp—that exaggerates her own artificial stylization. Anita has long been a camp target or inspiration. She has been done in drag at innumerable demonstrations, but also parodied in theatrical productions, on t-shirts, in mocking rituals—that pie in the face, of course, but also the coy invitation to "squeeze a fruit for Anita." "Stop Anita the Hun." More serious protests against her have that fierce exaggeration that is one description of camp "sensibility." Anita's picture was carried in Pride parades alongside those of Nazi leaders. Anita in a Nazi uniform over the slogan: "Hitler is alive and well in Florida." "From Dachau to Dade." That too is camping Anita.[64]

The camp response to Anita Bryant activates a potentiality that lurks in her public character. The slightest deflection of that old Coca-Cola ad on the beach, and our Anita becomes Donna Loren in *Beach Blanket Bingo*, singing "It Only Hurts When I Cry." One slight twist, and the tears of Anita become the tears of Tammy Faye Bakker, who passed smoothly from being a televangelist's songbird to sharing a daytime show with a flamboyantly gay co-host. All those protoqueer boys singing along with television commercials weren't wrong: turn your head just a little and Anita Bryant is disclosed as pure camp—and never more than when she is leading the Dade County crusade.

Anita at the lectern, reading didactically from 1 Corinthians: she sometimes seems to be a drag queen herself. The helmet of hair and the suburban outfits are too perfect. The voice betrays its lessons in elocution. The eyebrows are penciled to symmetry. Clearly this womanhood was learned as a role. When the performance falters, when she loses her place in the script, Anita sometimes seems sweetly vacant, but more often angry. The costumes, the diction, the makeup, the studied sweetness hide not a sex kitten, but a mother lion—lanky, leathery, ferocious. Anita Bryant is easy to do in drag not just because her gender is already a caricature, but because she is so *fierce*. It is as if she had learned to be a woman by copying drag queens. So of course she is ready for politico-religious campaigning as maudlin, menacing spectacle.

To say that Anita's performance of Christian womanhood lends itself to camp is not at all to suggest that her power is therefore negligible. There is, as Foucault has remarked, a grotesque power that makes us laugh even as it judges our life and orders our death.[65] I would say there is a kind of power over gender and sex that prefers to be laughable—partly to disarm resistance, partly to confuse refutation, but mostly to show how little it cares for the games of rationalization. Camp responds to that grotesque power by the attentive repetition of caricature. It takes into itself the full range of the grotesque, the laughable, in order to display its influence over bodies. Camp is a mode of rhetorical analysis, and it is particularly useful where religion and popular entertainment meet sex. Where did they not meet in Miami during the spring of 1977? Or in church debates before and after?

In another way, the camp responses to Anita reactivate or extend the efforts at indigenous gay religion that we have seen in Rechy's hustler theology or the pagan Eden of *Song of the Loon*. Dragging Anita mocks her. It exposes the artifice of her own womanhood. But it also takes her over, puts her on. Dragging Anita hollows out a space for the queer in the middle of homophobic evangelism. It reminds everyone that queer boys have always found space there. But it also hints at the fabulous outfits that can be produced by recutting church material. As Anita knew only too well.

Many gay activists did not respond to Anita in the spirit of camp. Bryant sometimes succeeded in polarizing the rhetorical field between gay and Christian. Only a few weeks after the June 7 vote, a contingent at Boston's Gay Pride parade marched under a banner that read "Christianity is the Enemy!"[66] Once on the speakers' platform, its leader, Charles Shively, burned in succession his Harvard doctoral diploma, a dollar bill, an insurance policy, a letter refusing his request to teach gay studies, and the sodomy statute of Massachusetts. At the climax of the speech, Shively read out Leviticus 20:13 and its death penalty for those Israelites guilty of male-male intercourse. He then dropped the Bible into the flames. The crowd erupted. A man jumped on stage to pull the book from the flames. Shively was compelled to yield the microphone to Brian McNaught, one of the best-known gay Catholic activists. But Shively's point had been made:

during that June, the most audible versions of Christianity had become the most dangerous rhetorical enemy. His rhetoric met Bryant's midfield by demanding an anti-Christian political allegiance for anyone truly committed to liberation. For Bryant and Shively both, there is no middle ground. You must speak as gay or Christian, you must *be* militantly gay or fervently Christian.

8

COMING OUT OF HOMOSEXUALITY

After the "battle of Miami," Anita Bryant looked for ways to capitalize on her religious notoriety and to replace the income that was lost because of it. Within a year of the vote, she announced that she and her husband, Bob, would be opening a network of centers "to help homosexuals who want to be delivered from that kind of lifestyle." Another year on, she was claiming that two thousand people "have not only been rehabilitated but they have been transformed."[1] Anita Bryant Ministries applied the claims about "returning to full heterosexuality" or becoming "exgay" that she made during the Dade campaign and the book about it.

The most visible ex-gay organization is now Exodus International, and so the origin of the ex-gay movement is sometimes fixed to the founding of Exodus at a meeting in Anaheim during September 1976.[2] But Exodus was originally a council of ex-gay ministries, and that meeting was an effort to coordinate those already involved in the work. Like the new church groups that sprang up in the early 1970s, ex-gay ministries were widely scattered, almost simultaneous responses to the proliferation of public speech about homosexuality and religion. The 1976 meeting was called because staff members at Melodyland Church who had started an ex-gay hotline met with Frank Worthen, leader of an ex-gay ministry in the Bay Area. The two groups had been established independently. So had a number of the other ministries represented by the five dozen people who gathered in Anaheim.

The group decided to call itself Exodus because winning freedom from homosexuality was like the Israelites escaping from pharaoh. The Exodus metaphor was already being used by progressive theologians to describe or justify emancipation of homosexuals within Christian churches.[3] In its emphasis on freedom from bondage, "Exodus" also appropriated the main image of gay liberation—returned, as it were, to its scriptural roots. The conception of being gay as a false identity from which one must be liberated is only the logic of coming out turned back on itself, applied a second time. The act of coming out is vulnerable to revision: like any nonbinding declaration of a hidden self, it can be undone or overwritten by another declaration. Exodus: liberation from Liberation, but only at the price of citing Stonewall. An ex-gay ministry that promises freedom for a true self will always recall that other, prior claim of liberation, to which it reacts, on which it depends. There is no ex-gay without gay.

The ex-gay group usually named as first in the U.S. is the (original) "Love in Action." In its later form it would mount the Refuge program in Memphis to which Zach, the sixteen-year-old from our introduction, was sent. But it began in the Bay Area, growing out of a tape ministry started by Frank Worthen in 1973. There were, of course, evangelicals at work back in the 1960s among urban homosexual populations. In some notable cases, the work led to a change of heart about homosexuality.[4] In the 1970s, gay-identified evangelicals would also organize a ministry—not of conversion, but of mutual support.[5] Worthen himself was associated early on with two ministries that welcomed homosexuals. What marks out Frank Worthen is his position as a once-gay man who promises that a truly loving Christian community can help men exchange their homosexual identities for something better. Over the years, he alters his theories about the origins and prospects of homosexuality, but he never abandons the originating promise.

BROTHER FRANK'S TESTIMONIES

Any effort to retell Frank Worthen's ex-gay ministry is interrupted by his prior claim on that history as testimony. He has long narrated the ministry's beginning as the outcome of his ex-gay conversion. Here, as with Troy Perry, the testimony justifies the ministry as the divinely prompted result of the conversion it announces. The experience is certified as a conversion when it is successfully narrated under a standard form before an expectant community. Of course, the communities differ starkly in the two testimonies. By contrast with Perry, Frank Worthen becomes ex-gay when the orthodox church accepts his testimony. Public hearing bestows the change of character conceived only as an identity.

With Brother Frank, as with Anita, it is imperative to read the testimony as rhetorical performance rather than biographical data. The testimony is a vivid script. In a ministry as long as Brother Frank's, the script changes with time. Some of the changes are dictated by shifts in audience expectations or proprieties. He can say some things to gay men in a charismatic, upstart congregation near San Francisco that he can't quite repeat twenty years later to the suburban audience of the Religious Right. The testimony also changes through repeated telling: embellishment or condensation make the story better. Or the testimony changes with the succession of theories about the origins and prospects for homosexuality. Finally, toward the end, the successive testimonies are driven by journalistic or historical accounts of the events of Frank Worthen's life. The more that is written about him, especially by those skeptical of his work, the more carefully his testimony must control the telling of his life. The rhetorical function of the ex-gay narrative is to move certain biographical events from one plot to another—that is, from one reduced or caricatured character to another. So ex-gay testimony watches over the susceptibility of those events to alternate interpretations. An ex-gay plot slips too easily into the plot of a failed gay life or a celibate homophile life. Conversion risks becoming reversion: a man who haunts churches while he struggles with same-sex attractions is either ex-gay or in desperate need of liberation. If most coming out stories retell adolescence, if most coming out processes restage a new adolescence, ex-gay testimony must do so with particular concern for counterinterpretations. It is not just a narrative of conversion and consequent ministry; it is polemical exegesis, not so much of scriptures as of youths past.

Given the multiple versions of Frank Worthen's testimony, a reader must choose. I collate two printed testimonies: an interview made public in 1977 by the pastor then sponsoring his ministry and a monologue written almost twenty years later, just after his tenth wedding anniversary in 1994.[6] I combine plot elements from these two accounts and other sources, but I separate the accounts at crucial moments to illustrate the changed narrative impulses.

Born in 1929, Frank Worthen grew up in the Bay Area.[7] In the interview, Frank remembers "being sort of homosexual-oriented back to about three years old, playing with the neighborhood kids and so forth." He implies: and not before three, since the orientation must not be created or irremediably innate. In the later testimony, he adds that he was mocked during his boyhood for being a sissy.[8] Frank "received the Lord" at thirteen because of his piano teacher, who took him to her church. He played the organ. At the same time, according to the interview, he began "to realize that maybe things weren't quite right," that he was "different." In both accounts, but especially the later monologue, the "homosexual" minister at the church is blamed for encouraging him to think that it was fine to be homosexual. Indeed, the later testimony begins with the pastor diagnosing Frank as a homosexual.[9] It then explains that Frank didn't date in high school, had no friends, didn't play sports, and spent a lot of time with his music—which means, he spent a lot of time in church. The later testimony offers a portrait of failed adolescent masculinity. When he was eighteen, in 1947—in those years when the urban gay networks were expanding so rapidly through the Bay area—Frank dated a young woman for about a year. To his proposal, she replied, "There are only two things that I love: horses and other women." Devastated, Frank went back to his pastor, who explained that Frank had actually been attracted to her masculinity. "I left the church that day, making the decision to accept my homosexuality. Since 'God's man' had convinced me that I was homosexual, I hoped that God would accept me. I entered the gay life-style at that time."[10] The 1977 interview omits the high school narrative to emphasize that the culpable pastor "painted a very beautiful picture of homosexuality." So, after graduating high school, Frank moved to San Francisco, where he continued to work as a church organist. In those churches, homosexuality was condemned. Frank began to suffer "conflict" between his "engrained" gayness and the church messages. He became "nervous" and had difficulty with his music. So he "dropped the church . . . at about twenty-two." He felt anger at the church for rejecting him "along with homosexuality."

Let me pause the testimonies at the moment of rejection in order to underscore their differences. In the 1977 interview, a misguided pastor, himself homosexual, presents a false picture of homosexuality. Frank takes up that "life style" in his late adolescence because of the pastor's encouragement. When other church leaders condemn homosexuality, he experiences conflict between his life and the church. He leaves the church for the expanding gay networks of San Francisco. This earlier version of the story is eager to stress two ways that Christian churches can fail with regard to homosexuality: by liberal encouragement of homosexuality or by conservative rejection of homosexuals. The first is more serious, but the second is also sinful—because it forecloses the possibility of ministry. Elsewhere Worthen says that he was sexually abused by the homosexual pastor.[11] That would make the liberal betrayal complete: unbiblical theology goes along with sexual predation by a closeted homosexual. Bad theology justifies and perhaps implies sexual abuse. But the first account insists that Frank kept an inner, "closeted" relationship with God, despite leaving churches.

The 1994 monologue turns the explanation in another direction. It conceives Frank's childhood as an experience of difference because of gender deviation or reversal. Homosexuality becomes a defect of masculinity— linked to withdrawal from a dysfunctional family and an absent father, whose death also falls at the crucial age of thirteen. Even before the father's death, something has gone wrong in little Frank's being a boy. The precipitating event is rejection by a lesbian woman. Many years later, the final proof of healing will be acceptance by a woman who agrees to become his wife. A child's gender is broken by a failed marriage. The gender is repaired by the grown-up child's own marriage. Gender is performed and redeemed within the space of marriage. The later testimony insists on that—no doubt in celebration of the tenth wedding anniversary.

In both accounts, if for different reasons, Frank's choice to accept homosexuality is a choice to leave the church and to enter the gay lifestyle. Accepting homosexuality is not just performing certain sexual acts. Accepting homosexuality means switching community membership, putting on a new identity. Character in the reduced sense of identity is the main concern and the raw material of the ex-gay ministry. It is tied to adolescence as a period of stark choice between opposed identities. Adolescence is the fatal crossroads between Christian and gay. One road or the other, but never both. The decision is dreadful, but fortunately it can be taken more than once.

Frank's story now skips twenty years. In the 1977 interview, he describes his recent misery upon turning forty. "Reaching forty is a very difficult period in anyone's life," but it is gruesome for homosexuals. "As you get older, anything good about homosexuality passes away and you are left with all of the bad things."[12] The bad things include prostitution, the loss of looks and of love, the choice between utter isolation or heartless male hustlers. Frank notices that a young man at work is changing before his eyes—first in being saved, then through the indwelling of the Holy Spirit. Here as at other points in the earlier interview, Frank praises charismatic churches and faults churches that reject the Spirit's gifts. Day after day, the joy of the young "charismatic Christian" reproaches Frank's middle-aged misery. At last there comes the moment of decision. Frank is about to leave the office to go to "a disreputable house of sin," to add a "new lower experience" to his moral slide. We learn elsewhere that he was going to a bathhouse.[13] "The Lord 'touched me' and gave me a sort of ultimatum. If I was going to do this, I felt God was saying to me that He would not protect me as He had my whole life."[14] Frank abruptly asks the young man, "the boy," to take him instead to church. They go together, and "the boy" leads him through a prayer of repentance.

In 1994, Frank tells both the change in the young man and the decisive moment differently. Frank notices that Michael, the "'hippie' boy," appears at work with "short hair" and "properly washed." He has become "efficient": "the customers loved him, and he smiled all the time."[15] Michael provides a living example of the sudden changes that come with conversion, but he also illustrates how far conversion implies conformity to prevailing social norms, especially those of gender. Michael cuts his hair, which is what men are supposed to do. More striking is the new narration of the decisive moment. Where Frank had earlier said that God "touched" him and gave him "a sort of ultimatum," now he hears God speaking to him: "Today I want you back." So Frank runs to ask Michael for advice. Michael takes him to his empty church, where he leads Frank through a confession of sins—including some he hadn't committed. "When the prayer ended, the Lord's Spirit came alive in my heart. I came out of the church a changed person!" Frank then learns that Michael's church community has long been praying for him. After his conversion, members of the church come to visit Frank every day for a year and a half. "That accountability kept me from going back to the homosexual life-style."[16] There is no mention of the bathhouse or of the implied threat of heavenly judgment. Instead of a premonition of divine abandonment, Frank receives a direct and articulate declaration of personal love—a reliable, divine proposition.

The emphasis on the direct divine call is emphasized by something that the two accounts share: this conversion is a scene of male bonding. Michael, "the boy," is straight and doesn't know much about the gay life-style. Despite that, perhaps because of that, he appears to Frank as an object of attraction and an occasion for submission. Michael doesn't persuade Frank by giving him arguments or scriptural verses. Frank is not turned back to God by poring over the scriptures. He is attracted by the change in "the boy." God speaks. Then "the boy" leads Frank though a life-changing prayer. Their relationship may reverse a traditional homoerotic pattern by which a middle-aged man leads someone younger into the ways of gay life, but it is still a scene of same-sex instruction. Ex-gay conversion, like coming out, cannot be performed in solitude. Both God and "the boy" are there to hear.

The boy is the guide and the audience, but also the figure of returning adolescence. In his own transformation, and even more in his youth, he represents adolescence as the moment of sexual/religious choice. He takes Frank back to the crossroads, then points to the proper road—the road that Frank should have taken then, but can still take now. Coming out typically means returning to possibilities abandoned or suppressed in adolescence. Becoming ex-gay means returning to reiterate the abandonment, to strengthen the suppression. Or, more precisely, to commit oneself to an endless, adolescent discipline of self-control. "Ex-gay" sounds as if it marks a decisive departure—like leaving a marriage or the Communist party. In fact, it is an indefinite prolongation of adolescent tension. You are always at the crossroads.

How exactly was Frank changed by the episode of prayer with "the boy"? In the earlier interview, Frank says that the prayer "worked" to lift the burden. He was immediately "relieved from the homosexual life," taken "out of homosexual life." This did not mean a change in desire. There were recurrent temptations. Indeed, having earlier assured the interviewer that middle-aged gay men can only buy sex, he now describes being offered "easy sex with beautiful young people" after his conversion. These offers come from Satan, the great guide to the other road.[17] God gives strength to resist them while Frank labors to learn scripture and to build fellowship in his church, just as if he were an adolescent. Once he is able to tell some of his new friends and his pastor about his homosexual past, they replace his entire network of gay friends, many of whom had already turned away because of his conversion. Frank is further held in place by a fear of divine rejection. "I didn't know if God would take me back a third time."[18] Resisting homosexual temptation, replacing gay networks, staying close to God—all of this makes Frank happy, but it does not make him a heterosexual. He is a "new creation in Christ," but that means that he is "ex-gay" or "ex-homosexual."[19] He is happy to remain single and celibate forever, though he is also happy to consider marriage if God brings that about—which God apparently did.

In the later testimony, more emphasis is put on Frank's incredulity about the possibility of change. "I told myself, 'No. God has never changed a homosexual person.'" After the penitential prayer, the Spirit comes alive in Frank's heart and he leaves the church "a changed person."[20] Changed how? The main change seems vocational: Frank launches his own ministry and devotes himself to it full time. There is no mention of persistent temptation. Frank is "secure and complete, able to settle into a life of comfortable celibacy." A decade later, Frank begins to pray for a "mate" to ease his loneliness. God arranges for one. In this account, Frank is changed from a homosexual person to a contented celibate, then to a husband with a wife.

Still his performance of heterosexuality remains tentative—or unusual. Frank's future wife, Anita, is a woman who is passionate about his . . . ministry, which by this time has expanded to include a round of meetings, a list of publications, and a residential program. When Frank and Anita decide to marry, he is already fifty-five and "uncertain that I could consummate our marriage."[21] They decide that even a sexless marriage would be a boon. Sex matters little in definitions of identity exchange. What matters is the marriage, even if has to be without sex.

Marriage without sex means marriage as a social unit, as the building block of congregational life, but especially marriage as the declaration or performance of correct gender. What matters is being the proper sort of man, even if one can't have sex with a woman—or sex at all. Frank comes out of the lifestyle, is changed from a homosexual person, but he is not having sex. He is a celibate whose life is taken up by ministry. Sex is not required for Frank to be a real man. What *is* required is that he enact the right gender relation to women, with whom he might or might not have sex after marriage. Of course, there is another gender relation in Frank's new masculinity—namely, his relation to other men, with whom he cannot have sex and cannot be married. Look more closely. Frank Worthen passes from "the lifestyle" to a ministry in which he spends all of his time talking to gay or ex-gay men. He passes in his mid-forties from homosexuality to celibate homosociality so that he can be restored to the rightly ordered politico-social space of the church. Frank's exodus is a return from the false gay community to the true church community. In both, he is surrounded by men who desire other men, but they do so under different identities. The identity is the thing—not the sex; the identity and its community.

FROM TESTIMONY TO PROGRAM

In his formal testimony, Frank reports that soon after his conversion, "the boy," Michael, suggested that he should make a tape for people who were "trapped in the homosexual lifestyle." Or perhaps the suggestion came from the pastor of Agape church, which Frank attended.[22] Late in 1973, Frank took out a classified ad in the *Berkeley Barb* to sell a tape of his testimony. The ad read: "FIND Homosexuality and Christianity incompatible? Send $8.00 for a new Christ-centered tape: *Steps Out of Homosexuality*."[23] For Frank and his successors, 1973 marks the beginning of his ministry, Love in Action (refounded as New Hope in 1995).[24] There are other accounts. Kent Philpott describes the origin of ministry to homosexuals in his own counseling practice at Open Door church. The earliest newsletters from Love in Action (beginning in December 1975) were written not by Frank, but by Bob, a schoolteacher neighbor of Kent's.[25] Yet Philpott seems to recognize Frank's special role in starting a ministry as an ex-homosexual for ex-homosexuals.[26] Here, as with the founding of Exodus, I am less concerned with anniversary dates or institutional lineage than with Worthen's progressive articulation of programs and the theories that would underwrite them. So I note that Frank began fulltime ministry in 1977 and opened his first residential program in 1979.

Offering to sell testimony tapes is a familiar evangelical gesture. So too is running weekly meetings—though with them the ministry begins to blur into church-sponsored recovery groups. Setting up a residential program moves more fully into the model of recovery or, as Anita Bryant would say, rehabilitation. The blur from Christian testimony to counseling group to residential clinic is one the most elusive features of Frank Worthen's speech. It is suggested in his testimonies, but it is shown most plainly in the first book he wrote in his own name, *Steps Out of Homosexuality*. The title echoes the original ad, and the contents develop its contradictions.

The ad assumes that some people are troubled by the opposition of homosexuality and Christianity. The two identities are somehow symmetrical. Homosexuality is not a statistical inference from a set of reported desires or behaviors. It is chosen as a complete way of life in opposition to Christianity, which is another, equally complete. The ad offers steps out of homosexuality toward Christianity. By offering "Christ-centered" steps, it simultaneously cites the call of evangelical ministries and the stages of AA or other recovery programs. Christ can change the suffering person by divine power from one way of life to another, but Christ will do so according to fixed steps: a calibrated miracle. This is the basic narrative contradiction. It shows itself at many points. For example, hearing about Christ on a tape, like hearing recorded sermons or testimony, might make sense as an incitement to immediate conversion, but it is not clear how the steps could be practiced by the solitary listener.

Worthen displays the steps in a book published about a decade after the tape ministry had started. It draws on the residential program of Love in Action, which had then been in operation for about five years. Worthen describes twelve steps, the canonical number since AA. He makes the comparison explicit in likening his first step to that in AA.[27] The comparison extends beyond the steps into the rich history of American church wars on alcohol. In many ways, the ex-gay movement is temperance for modern times.[28] But the comparison is limited. For example, Worthen's steps trace no clear arc. The recovering alcoholic is lead from recognizing powerlessness and surrendering to a higher power through a "fearless moral inventory" and the making of amends to those harmed. The AA steps end with continuing moral evaluation, seeking God's will, and a commitment of service to other alcoholics. Worthen's steps begin with a decision in brokenness, but then move to the need for a savior and spiritual combat. He replaces moral inventory and the effort to make amends with cognitive acts: holding a correct image of God, self, and others. His penultimate steps include submission to God and displacing all aspects of the earlier lifestyle with elements from the new community. It is not clear whether Worthen is deliberately revising the AA sequence to make it more Christian. He is quite clear that he differs from AA on the crucial point of identity. Whereas a recovering alcoholic is still and always an alcoholic, an ex-gay is no longer gay.[29] Otherwise, Worthen would have nothing to offer.

Worthen's book deliberately juxtaposes scriptural, theological, and scientific languages. He takes pains to rehearse and refute liberal reinterpretations of biblical passages. He paraphrases bits of Bailey, McNeill, and Boswell, but then he dismisses them as the kind of false teachers predicted in scripture. He points to the scriptural readings of Scanzoni and Mollenkott with the stern warning that they can seduce. They are aligned with Satanic forces active in this world.[30] Satan's agency is specific. Worthen catalogues the various forms of Satanic attack on the vulnerable ex-gay.[31] At the same time, and often without a pause, Worthen invokes scientific authority both to disprove any genetic basis for homosexuality and to supply the real explanation: gender disorder. His scientific authorities range from the authoritative to the idiosyncratic. Worthen will argue from authority that homosexuality cannot be constitutional because no sexual orientation is, then immediately assert from Genesis 2 that heterosexuality is fixed—by God.[32] The highest scientific authority is Elizabeth R. Moberly.[33] She provides Worthen with the key therapeutic insight: "Homosexuality should not be defined, except secondarily, as a difficulty in relating to the opposite sex. Essentially, it marks a difficulty in relating to the same sex."[34] Deprivation of appropriate same-sex bonding leads to distancing, then to eroticization. On Worthen's retelling of the theory, the real problem is absence of approval from a properly masculine father.[35] The "root causes" of homosexuality, which can evidently do their work by the age of three, are "non-sexual": they arise from a deficit in gender. Therapy must fill up the gender deficit in *nonsexual* ways, so that sexual desire—whatever's left of it—can be directed properly, appropriately, in godly fashion, to the other gender.

The model has no biblical basis. Indeed, if one tries to construct biblical models for the origin of same-sex desire from the texts that Worthen cites, they hardly have to do with gender deficit. For example, if you believe that the story of Sodom is about homosexuality, then you could conclude, from the very explicit interpretations of the Sodom story in the Hebrew prophets, that the cause of homosexuality is arrogance, luxury, and inhospitality (Ezekiel 16:49–50). Again, if you believe that Romans 1 is about homosexuality, then you would conclude that the occasion of homosexuality is pagan idolatry—and that the immediate, precipitating cause of homosexuality is God's abandonment (Rom 1.24, 1.26, 1.28). Worthen adopts neither of these biblical constructions of same-sex desire. He turns instead to Moberly's pastiche of psychoanalysis—or, rather, her "more thorough elucidation of the implications" of "existing psychoanalytic data."[36] It is worth meditating on the cultural incongruity: an ex-gay evangelist from a charismatic new church quotes a compendium of psychoanalysis as the authority on the nature of same-sex desire.

In the same way, Worthen's therapy for gender disorders combines explicitly Christian practices with mock-clinical languages and techniques. His book stresses the need for prayer, scriptural study, pastoral supervision, worship, and Christian fellowship. It also undertakes behavioral modification, with a system of surveillance not only for sexual sins, but for any contact with the former identity. The languages of grace and of the clinic are held together by redefining identity. A change of identity becomes a change of community. Being a homosexual person is understood as entering a lifestyle. The lifestyle is defined by opposition to church, dedication to hedonism, and rejection of decency. The lifestyle negates human order— political, social, personal. Coming out of the lifestyle requires reaffirming the triple order. The change of reference community much more than the change of sexual partners constitutes the ex-gay experience. So long as you remain a member of the ex-gay group or of a ministering church, you are declared to have changed identities. Weekly meetings, weekend retreats, national conventions, and live-in programs are so many spaces in which to put on the ex-gay identity by participation. The lamented ex-gay "ghetto" is not a failure for the therapy, but its very condition. Ex-gay ministries create a mirror image of the social networks of gay life because they redefine sexual identity by reference to group membership. It's not your desires or your genital acts, it's the company you keep.

That view of ex-gay identity depends on liberationist claims about gay identity. Declaring gayness is moving into an alternate social order, because your sex must be your politics. Indeed, your politics may run far ahead of your actual sexual experience. The ex-gay movement accepts exactly this liberationist notion of gayness. It agrees with early liberationist models that stress political pronouncement over genital activity, that make gayness a form of political consciousness. The essential ritual of liberation is not a sex act, but a speech act: the act of coming out. So the essential act in becoming ex-gay is the speech act of repudiating your former coming out. You perform this speech act formally to God, but materially to new Christian buddies, your pastor, and then your church.

Speech acts undoing speech acts: a familiar American theology of how to be saved. According to this theology, pronouncing the sinner's prayer sincerely or otherwise accepting Jesus into your heart makes a decisive break in your life. It does so because it changes God's view of your sinfulness. In the version of the prayer printed in Worthen's book, the person declares: "I am a new creature in Christ. I am no longer controlled by my past. I have been reborn. I have a new life. I have been freed from my sin." God responds: "All that lust, all those sex acts, all the shabby things you have done, I have thrown these into the sea of forgetfulness. I see you as pure; I have restored your virginity."[37] That's finished—and yet it's not. Your old identity is not erased. Rebirth only takes you from gay to ex-gay. God's "forgetfulness" only gives you a status that constantly reminds you of the supposedly forgotten past.

What exactly does God forget? The ascribed identity, it seems, but not the inner experience. "The ex-gay has a new position in Christ. . . . God views this person through the perfect sacrifice of Christ. God no longer sees him as a homosexual."[38] He is no longer seen as a homosexual even though the history and psychology that define the homosexual remain in him. A speech act decisively changes moral status, but only from one identity to its formal negation. Nothing else may have changed. Nothing else *need* have changed. You carry the same desires and aversions, and yet your moral standing is entirely different. You are no longer gay because you have renounced the name; God agrees not to see you through it. This is salvation as an exchange of names—or, to speak more technically, by extrinsic imputation of righteousness.

SELF-HELP HETEROSEXUALITY

Bob Davies and Lori Rentzel helped Worthen to produce his book. Nine years later, they produced one of their own with a major evangelical press. They dedicated the book to Worthen as "a pioneer in the ex-gay movement," and they quote him at decisive points.[39] They also share history. Davies, a Canadian, came to the residential program at LIA as a young man in June 1979 and was soon put in charge of the newsletter.[40] He would go on to lead Exodus over two decades, retiring only in October 2001. Rentzel had joined the LIA staff in January 1979—not as a struggling lesbian, but as a concerned Christian worker.[41] Davies and Rentzel descend directly from Worthen's ministry, but their book marks another stage in conceiving the possibilities for changing homosexuality. At the time of writing, they are happily married—though not to each other. They are also very careful in describing the exact limits of their heterosexual selves.

Coming Out of Homosexuality is a self-help book. The genre matters, because it intensifies the contradictions of causality latent in Worthen. This book constantly flirts with the paradox of do-it-yourself divine grace. It mixes counseling experience with expert opinion and true-life stories. Breezily written, it offers its readers practical exercises (the "Time Out" sections), study guides, and resources for further help—including counseling resources and residential programs. Like other books in the genre, this book lays out a narrative of sentimental progress, so that a reader can move through the emotions of healing just by reading. *Coming Out of Homosexuality* foreshadows what it promises, including the satisfaction of triumph. It refuses to argue about God's judgment on homosexuality, relying instead on a presumptive affirmation of the reader's commitment: "you want to overcome homosexuality and . . . you are looking for specific, practical help in finding freedom."[42]

A self-help book promises that new expert knowledge can make you happy if (and only if) you apply it in just the right way. Expertise must be explained by friendly advisers who have experience in applying it to people just like you. In fact, the author-advisers *are* people just like you, people who have struggled with what you are facing, though often not in its ugliest forms, because they are also a little better than you. After all, they are ahead of you in helping themselves. They can show you the way out because they have already taken it. Between them, Davies and Rentzel perform the insider-expert a bit differently, in order to reinforce the gender ideals they advocate. This is not only a self-help book, but a gender duet. It not only tells you how, it shows you the results in the relation of the two authors. Bob has been more burned by the flame of homosexuality—though it was more like a singe, because he never committed overt acts. The "gay" out of which he has so triumphantly come is a gayness only of fantasy and temptation. Lori discovered the "shakiness" of her sexual identity through her work with lesbians: "Though I have never been involved in a lesbian relationship, I did go through a period of several months during which I experienced strong sexual and emotional attractions to women."[43] Her "gay" is a brief period of attraction that God uses to make her a better counselor. Neither Bob nor Lori has had homosexual sex. It is also important that these two experts are not having heterosexual sex with each other: correct gender performance of male and female need not involve copulation. It may even be that their celibate partnership in ministry is marriage-plus, Christian marriage in its most ideal state.

More acutely than Worthen, Davies and Rentzel must negotiate the basic contradiction between the genre of the self-help book and the underlying call to conversion by unmerited grace. The more they follow the self-help genre, the more acute the contradiction becomes. On the one hand, they call readers to submit to God's power in everything, weeping over their impotence and brokenness. On the other hand, they urge readers to take control over life, to plan the next week, to change habits, to set up accountability groups, to keep journals, to monitor feelings minute to minute. Surrender to grace, but count on techniques of behavior modification. Two forms of expert knowledge collide. Biblical and therapeutic expertise not only push in opposite directions, they have opposite properties. Biblical expertise is supposed to be fixed, unchangeable: God has always condemned homosexuality. God condemned it even before the Bible was written, when He created the natural complementarity of the genders. New biblical interpretation, like the destructive "pro-gay" theology of the misguided churches, is culpable misinterpretation. At the same time, the book's therapeutic expertise is *supposed* to be new—very new and very specific to the ex-gay ministries. Other ministries and churches are faulted for not understanding its peculiar challenges, for not keeping up with the latest research, for not having up-to-date techniques.[44]

Davies and Rentzel do acknowledge some difficulty with the biblical basis for the central category "homosexuality." They admit that "homosexuality" and "heterosexuality" do not occur as such in the Bible, but then they go on to say that "the Bible distinguishes behavior from identity."[45] What they don't emphasize is that their central category "identity" is not biblical. Neither is the contemporary distinction in English between "sex" and "gender." Neither are "co-dependence," "defensive detachment," or "dysfunctional family of origin." The book's theoretical framework is being supplied not by the Bible, but by pseudoscientific discourses elaborated in reaction to the identity politics of gay liberation. But of all these borrowed terms in this allegedly biblical model, the most unstable may be the essential category of "sexual identity." According to Davies and Rentzel, sexual identity is so deep that it is hard to change. At the same time, it is unpredictably fragile. It is generated in the individual psyche by familial and cultural forces, but it is also tied to God's plan for "true, godly heterosexuality."[46]

What exactly is heterosexuality for this ex-gay model? Davies and Rentzel perform a more complete redefinition than Worthen does. They make very modest claims about the ability to change orientation, with many cautions against overconfidence and expected slips, with repeated emphasis on therapeutic process and continuing accountability. A *successful* ex-gay therapy may lead to celibacy, with recurring lesbian or gay fantasies, especially in connection with masturbation, and little or no erotic interest in the opposite sex. Or it may lead to a marriage in which there is some sexual interest, but never as much sexual pleasure as there was back in the lifestyle.[47] They define heterosexuality not in terms of sexual desire or orientation but as purity. "What do we mean by the word *heterosexual?* . . . Rather than opposite-sex lust, healing for both women and men means experiencing sexual interest in the opposite sex, as well as having healthy friendships with both men and women."[48] Heterosexuality only requires interest, because it is mainly about friendship—properly sorted by gender.

The ex-lesbian is a friend to other women, though always careful about emotional dependence and inappropriate intimacy. She no longer tries to pretend to be a guy; instead, she cultivates sexual interest in them. Ex-gay therapy reverses the polarity of sex and friendship without altering the emotional intensity at the two poles. You sleep with the people you used to hang with and cultivate friendship with the people you used to sleep with, but you don't much change your emotional satisfactions. This devaluation of sex is reinforced by Davies and Rentzel's adaptation of the liberationist model. For Davies in particular, the gay identity has no need of genital acts. A mere history of desire, a persistent longing to be involved with the subculture is enough to make you gay—or gay enough to then declare yourself ex-gay. In the closet, you can do, but not say. Out of the closet, you both do and say. In the ex-gay movement, you can't do, but you must say—while you continue to remember.

The redefinition of heterosexuality and the detachment of emotional intensity from rightful sex appear in all cases except the most important—the relationship with God. Davies and Rentzel conceive Jesus and God as heterosexual males who exhibit a proper father-son relationship in which an orderly transmission of gender identity has occurred. If they sometimes echo muscular Christianity from the start of the century, they go behind it in eroticizing or, better, "genderizing" the believer's relation to the divine persons. Early on, they quote Worthen as saying that ex-gay ministry is not a method, but a person. "Change is what *results* as we pursue a far more important and compelling goal: knowing, loving, and 'beholding' Jesus."[49] The quotation marks around "beholding" can't stave off the uncomfortable implications, which appear soon enough. It is not unusual for Christian writers to say that God desires us or woos us. Erotic vocabulary is the Christian vernacular for the soul's relation to the divine. But that vocabulary traditionally requires a scrambling of ordinary notions of gender. God or Jesus can become husband because every believer, male or female, is wife, just as the whole church is bride or body to Jesus as bridegroom or head. Not so in Davies and Rentzel. They emphasize the normative masculinity of Jesus and His Father even as they stress our intimate relation with them. They perform the normal, normative relation of man to woman before us even as they redirect erotic energy to God. Jesus is the "foremost model of godly masculinity." He is also the partner you invite to sit at the table with you when you dine alone.[50] One exemplary ex-gay describes giving up visits to his ex-lover in order to be with Jesus: "The security and peace I had in Jesus were more real to me than anything homosexual involvement could offer."[51] In traditional teaching, that comparison would hold for any human relationship, with woman or man, sexual or not. In this book, with the incessant emphasis on gender identity, it sounds rather as if Jesus were a more reliable and manly boyfriend. So, too, the reader must flinch when a former lesbian describes her newfound relationship with God the Father: "Daddy loves me! My daddy loves me!"[52] Daddy, we have heard, is the engine for the correct transmission of gender to both little girls and little boys. We have also been told that sexual abuse by men, including fathers, is a primary cause of lesbianism.

Too often in Davies and Rentzel, the only erotic intensity allowed to an ex-gay is in his or her relationship with God. With God, the ex-gay man can continue performing certain otherwise forbidden actions of male-male intimacy. Passivity is a problem for the male homosexual, but success-ful therapy requires decisive and then daily "surrender," "yielding," and submission to God.[53] Ex-gay men are warned not to tell their new straight friends too much about their homosexual pasts. The caution doesn't apply to God, who already knows everything. "He is not shocked by confes-sions of involvement in masturbation, pornography or other sexual sins. Nothing we do or say comes as a surprise to him."[54] The lesson is clear: "Ultimately our deepest needs are met through our relationship with God. He has created us that way; no human being can reach deep inside us like he can."[55] The claim and the image are perfectly common in Christian tradition. They are not so common in a discourse that insists on the nor-mative masculinity of Jesus and His Father—or the impenetrability of the masculine body.

Gender matters more than sex for Davies and Rentzel. Marriage is the highest accomplishment not because it allows you to copulate naturally, but because it gives you the best stage for performing gender correctly. If Davies and Rentzel refer the interested reader to evangelical pillow books meant to instruct and stimulate the properly married, Davies is just as con-cerned to recommend the sports pages to his male readers so that they can have something to talk about with the guys at church.[56] Indeed, ex-gays may actually be able to use marriage better for gender performance than heterosexuals can, since they are unlikely to enter it on account of lust.[57] Being married, like being ex-gay, is not about sex. It is about gender. The central category of "sexual identity" means in the end only "roles as men and women."[58]

FROM MINISTRIES TO SMEAR CAMPAIGNS

What is left of Frank Worthen's ministry in San Raphael is now shrink-ing. The offshoot that bears the name Love in Action (LIA) claims more success, but largely because of its change in therapeutic model. In recent years, under Bob Davies's successors, Exodus has become more successful as a media presence and coordinating agency, but not as a direct ministry. In many ways, the residential model of LIA seems to be yet another institutional form from the 1970s that has come to the end of its shelf life—or that can survive only by taking on a very different form. Even the genre of the self-help book seems curiously outdated, curiously private, in some of its promises and preoccupations—especially when compared to newer uses of ex-gay rhetoric.

The ex-gay rhetoric has become more consequential than ex-gay ministries, because the testimonies and theories have been taken up into the stridently political, apocalyptic scripts of the Religious Right. Some recent members of ex-gay ministries complained to Erzen about the appropriation of their programs for political ends.[59] The appropriation has been going on since the 1970s. Anita Bryant is one example. For another, pick up a relatively early book by Tim LaHaye, *The Unhappy Gays*. By the time of its publication, he had published at least nine other books on Christian psychology, marriage, and biblical interpretation. Having pastored several churches and run a small "Christian" college, he was employed largely as a lecturer with his wife Beverly for "Family Life Seminars," an extension of their television program, *LaHayes on Family Life*. He undertook the book on homosexuality, he reports in it, after returning from overseas ministry to find an America in which people were coming out on every side and Anita Bryant was drawing protesters after the Miami campaign.[60]

LaHaye's short book draws together many of the rhetorical strands from the 1970s. It lists sixteen religious, moral, psychological, and medical harms from homosexuality; eight physical, psychological, and behavioral predispositions to homosexuality; and eighteen steps (nota bene) to overcoming homosexuality. LaHaye attacks the Kinsey reports, and Ellis through Kinsey, but then cites C. A. Tripp, who uses Kinsey's data as part of an argument against any simple notion that homosexuality is a failure of development.[61] Irving Bieber is an "acclaimed" scientific authority, but so is Hippocrates, since LaHaye continues to promote a version of the ancient theory of four temperaments.[62] He handles biblical evidence with equal assurance: in order to have a chance at coming out of homosexuality, the repentant sinner must adopt without hesitation the antigay reading of all eight clobber passages in the Bible.[63] Demons are also treated authoritatively, though they get rather less space here than in some other accounts.[64]

The most telling thing about LaHaye's book is the way it cites evidence from ex-gay ministries to motivate an apocalyptic appeal for political action against homosexuals. The citation is anonymous. Although LaHaye refers to the "cassette tapes" produced the ministries, he doesn't name them.[65] He attributes the story of a boy shamed by his father only to "a former homosexual, now a minister who is effectively helping homosexuals out of their life style." LaHaye credits another "former homosexual" with an "effective ministry" to "over three hundred homosexuals." Neither the person nor the ministry is named.[66] In other cases, he speaks of hearing the testimonies himself—but, again, without citation.[67] Even when he is disagreeing with some of the ex-gay ministries, he does not name them.[68] Perhaps LaHaye hesitates to welcome such groups into regular churches; perhaps he is unwilling to advertise other ministries when he has his own books to sell. Whatever the motive for indirect citation, LaHaye wants the evidence of homosexuals healed through Christ to fortify his condemnation of those who refuse to be healed. If there is a way out, there is no excuse for staying in.

Anita Bryant had gestured at this argument on the way to attacking homosexual recruiters. LaHaye mimics the gesture and Anita's collage of threatening newspaper headlines.[69] He advocates "militant Christian compassion" in her style, a compassion courageous enough to speak out as Jesus would. "If our Lord were living in America today, I have no doubt he would speak out vigorously and frequently against this blight on humanity."[70] But LaHaye goes further into apocalypse. Homosexuality may have been one of the causes of Noah's flood.[71] More importantly, "the anti-Christ *may* be a homosexual. If he is, that would explain the significance of the influential group of international homosexuals who are rumored to be gaining worldwide political influence."[72] In order to save America, to keep it on the right side of God's final judgment, believing Christians must take action against homosexuals at every political level. "It is time for us Christians to lead this enormous majority of pro-moral Americans in reestablishing the values that earned for us the blessings of God on our country."[73] The moral majority: Jerry Falwell would soon enough make telling use of the phrase—especially against dying gay men.

9

POLEMIC IN A TIME OF PLAGUE

The coming of AIDS to America during the 1980s—or, rather, its American naming. We are supposed to know that history already and always keep it back in history. Conventions of silence, wounded or self-serving, discourage more talk: it happened, we protested, let's move on. The terrifying appearance of the virus suffers at once from overexposure and abolition of memory.

From the familiar and still unassimilated history, I take a handful of religious responses. They are responses to the epidemic, but also to its appropriation in Christian judgment. I concentrate on the first six or seven years after the disease was named in hopes of catching rhetorical reactions as they were improvised, before they could be prettied up or retracted. My selection is limited, as it has been everywhere in the archives. I hope that memory will supply other examples, especially counterexamples. Sometimes memory must supply them, because the archives are patchy and liable to interested revision. Many of the early words about AIDS were never recorded. Broadcast speech has passed away. Church speech that was recorded and saved has been erased. For example, it has become surprisingly difficult to recover outrageous pronouncements on AIDS in the 1980s by well-known Christian leaders. They or their successors no longer want to claim them, and so the words have been expunged from the websites. Today, when prominent evangelicals fly off to Africa for their favorite AIDS ministries, few want to lift up evangelical claims that God permitted or created AIDS as a gay disease to punish American immorality. Or the calls in the name of Christ for mandatory testing, tattoos, and quarantines. Or even the fear that kept many Christian pastors from visiting hospitals, performing funerals, or ministering publicly to the sick who were also gay.

From early in the '80s, other church leaders responded more generously, after some stammering. But the most constructive religious reactions came from within the stigmatized community. The early years of American

AIDS required harshly that gay men provide theologies and rituals for themselves. The disease demanded new religious reactions to Christian hostility. They are most interestingly religious when they claim not to be.

JEREMIAD AND DIVINE JUDGMENT

The first CDC reports on what we would learn to call "AIDS-related opportunistic infections" appeared in June and July of 1981. By August, there were already organizing efforts in gay urban areas, though there was little beyond fear to teach. Best known is the gathering at Larry Kramer's apartment that led to founding Gay Men's Health Crisis in New York.[1] In July 1982, at a national meeting that accomplished little else, the disease was named AIDS.[2] It still went by more menacing names in gay circles. On March 3, 1983, under pressure from the CDC, the U.S. Public Health Service urged "members of groups at increased risk for AIDS" to refrain from donating blood. Existing research had identified three such groups: "homosexual men with multiple sexual partners, abusers of intravenous (IV) drugs, and Haitians, especially those who have entered the country within the past few years." The government statement noted with concern unexplained cases among hemophiliacs and an infant who had recently received a transfusion. The bulletin offered this advice for prevention of sexual transmission: "Sexual contact should be avoided with persons known or suspected to have AIDS. Members of high risk groups should be aware that multiple sexual partners increase the probability of developing AIDS."[3] "Persons known or suspected to have AIDS," "members of high risk groups": new characters for compulsory performance by gay men.

In the second week following the Public Health recommendations, Larry Kramer published a sustained polemic in *New York Native*. The *Native* had broken the frightening medical news in 1981 before the CDC reports and despite CDC denials. It then reported regularly about the disease or diseases, under shifting names. Kramer's piece in March 1983 changed the tone of both debate and reporting around AIDS. I take it up for another reason: it shows what will become characteristic ambivalence in how AIDS activism speaks about and within religion.

Kramer borrows the form of an apocalyptic jeremiad.[4] In the manner of the Puritan preacher, who imitated in turn the Israelite prophet, Kramer hopes that arousing popular fear and anger will secure justice from those in power. He even delivers the standard prophetic warning: either do what I say or die. While the prophetic version of that warning is backed by a divine sanction, Kramer's jeremiad predicts destruction by an unchecked disease of "gay men" considered as a quasi species. "Unless we fight for our lives, we shall die. In all the history of homosexuality we have never before been so close to death and extinction."[5] The punishment does not come from God, but from the malice, incompetence, or apathy of a long list of culprits. It threatens to cut off the chronicle of men who are, like the sodomites, descendants of an ancient tribe: "*all* the history of homosexuality."

In this jeremiad, Kramer identifies himself with the sick and the imperiled. He reflects the prevailing medical ignorance. In 1983—indeed, before the wide distribution of the ELISA test in 1985—diagnosis of the underlying virus was largely symptomatic. You knew a gay man had AIDS when he showed certain symptoms. You expected, you feared that any gay man—that you yourself—could develop those symptoms tomorrow. Part of Kramer's strategy is to insist that every gay man is at risk, that any gay man can be afflicted without warning. He includes himself in that threat. But Kramer performs a more direct rhetorical identification. More than a dozen times in the jeremiad, he speaks the phrase, "I am sick . . ." He means it in the colloquial sense: I am fed up with . . . , I refuse any longer to tolerate . . . In a jeremiad about a fatal epidemic, to say "I am sick" invokes other meanings. So when he writes, "I refuse to die," it is not only a call to political solidarity, it is a protest from the deathbed. In Kramer's secular jeremiad, he is at once the accusing preacher and the threatened addressee. His plea is not just for prevention or palliation, but for a cure. Nothing less will prevent extinction—not least, his extinction. The identification of gayness with the threatened body is complete.

Despite its genre or its gestures of denunciation and conversion, Kramer's apocalyptic jeremiad makes only a few explicit mentions of religion. They are sharply divided between praise and blame, though religion as such is never praised. Kramer acknowledges that Beth Simchat Torah, "the gay synagogue," has hosted important community meetings, which had drawn, among many others, representatives from "Dignity [and] Integrity," that is, the Roman Catholic and Episcopalian lesbian/gay groups. His blame of religious figures is more animated. As part of an attack on a mayoral liaison to the gay community, Kramer complains that the man is also liaison to the Hasidic Jews. "Hasidic Jews hate gays."[6] Kramer refers twice to Jerry Falwell. Falwell is first blamed for influencing a politician to vote in support of retaining the District of Columbia's sodomy laws. Falwell's publications are then attacked for "printing editorials proclaiming AIDS as God's deserved punishment on homosexuals."[7]

If Kramer writes a secular jeremiad, Jerry Falwell had long been writing more traditional, theocratic jeremiads against homosexuals. From before his appearance onstage with Anita Bryant, he listed homosexuality as one of the social threats that would bring judgment on America—and so required ceaseless donations to fund political action. He followed Anita Bryant in describing it as a raging disease. In 1980, in a book that catalogues America's failings, Falwell devotes a chapter to homosexuality. "History proves," he intones, "that homosexuality reaches a *pandemic* level in societies in crisis or in a state of collapse."[8] The first example is Sodom and Gomorrah. Falwell explicitly reactivates ancient Christian rhetoric about same-sex desire. For more than a millennium, Christian preachers had warned that sodomites brought plagues. The surviving citizens of Sodom suffered uncountable deformities in their own bodies, then spread them as they fled divine judgment. God cursed their footsteps and destroyed cities that dared to harbor them. Falwell blames the American pandemic of homosexuality on the victimization of children and adolescents, the addictive character of sexual perversion, and the failure to follow gender roles.[9] Falwell even quotes the essential argument from Anita Bryant, while gesturing to her newspaper evidence: "Homosexuals cannot reproduce themselves, so they must recruit."[10] But the language of blame is perfectly consistent with reiterated medical metaphors. "Homosexuality is a symptom of a sin-sick society." For Falwell, as for Bryant, "sick" expresses disgusted moral rejection. Of course, in Falwell, as in Bryant, the medical metaphors also lead in another direction: toward the notion of a therapeutic cure for homosexuality. "I love homosexuals, but I must hate their sin."[11] Hate it and treat it. Hate it more confidently because it can be treated.

The increasing governmental panic about AIDS allowed Falwell to go further—and in a genre better suited for him. He did not innovate much in the long forms of antihomosexual harangue. That rhetorical invention—including the reactivation of old slanders across a millennium—had already been done by others, not least Anita Bryant. But Falwell possessed in abundance a rhetorical skill that Anita so awkwardly lacked: command of the outrageous and thus memorable sound bite. Four months after publication of Kramer's diatribe, in Cincinnati for a July 4th "I Love America" rally, Falwell referred to AIDS as a "gay plague" that was "a definite form of the judgment of God upon a society." He urged screening of blood donors, closing of gay bathhouses, and guidelines for service workers in contact with AIDS carriers.[12] One week later, he was paraphrased as saying that AIDS was "a holy punishment of homosexuals." He drew an analogy to the quarantine of infected cattle.[13] A few days after that, in a debate produced by the ABC affiliate in San Francisco, Falwell reminded viewers of the inexorability of divine judgment: "You cannot shake your fist in God's face and get by with it." Confronted over his lack of concern for homosexuals, Falwell replied that his church had a number of psychiatrists and counselors available to cure them—not of AIDS, of course, but of homosexuality.[14]

Though Falwell was repeatedly challenged about his pronouncements and sometimes sought to nuance them, he kept making them. In 1985, in remarks reported by the gay press and remembered by gay Christian circles, Falwell falls back on the same trope: "AIDS is a lethal judgment of God on the sin of homosexuality and it is also the judgment of God on America for endorsing this vulgar, perverted and reprobate lifestyle." He then makes the traditional, but unscriptural association of Paul in Romans with the story about Sodom: "God also says those engaged in such homosexual acts will receive 'in their own persons, due penalty of their error.' [Romans 1:27] God destroyed Sodom and Gomorrah primarily because of the sin of homosexuality. [Genesis 19] Today, He is again bringing judgment against this wicked practice through AIDS."[15] Within a year, Falwell would pretend to backpedal, but not really. In sermon from June 1986, as in other iterations, Falwell said: "There is hardly a press conference in which someone doesn't ask me, 'Do you believe AIDS is God's judgment against homosexuals?' I always say, 'No, I don't believe that. I believe it is God's judgment against America for endorsing immorality, even embracing it.'"[16] No, he didn't always say that, but when he did, he still plainly implied that homosexuality was an immorality worthy of divine judgment by plague.

Falwell insists on the link between gay men and the disease, though with different language than Kramer's and for opposite ends. For Kramer, the "epidemic" is gay because it disproportionately infects gay men, who are then callously abandoned by the government. They are likened to "lepers," but also to "guinea pigs."[17] For Falwell, this is a "gay plague" because God directs it at the perversions of gay men, through whom the laxity of American society and liberal government are chastised. Falwell's readers will hear in that charge the divine visitation on pharaoh. God afflicts the immoral, idolatrous Egyptians with seven plagues so that the chosen people may go free (Exodus 7–9). Indeed, in the sixth plague, the penultimate one, a cloud of soot blown over Egypt brings up boils. Even that is not enough to break pharaoh's stubbornness. Plague means, in Falwell's lexicon, a famous instance of divine judgment on stubborn decadence—almost as famous as the divine destruction of Sodom and Gomorrah. AIDS is a plague because homosexuality is already a plague—a "pandemic" that spreads as a precise marker of divine displeasure. The plague metaphor for AIDS rests within the plague metaphor for homosexuality itself.

For Kramer, the spread of the epidemic is a failure of medicine—and more specifically of public health policy. While he faults both doctors and hospitals, he attributes their failure mostly to lack of resources. More money would bring effective treatment, fairly distributed. Money will be allocated only if gay men organize themselves to apply political pressure. Kramer's voice is shrill and his devices histrionic. At the stuttering limit of his rage, Kramer lapses into clumsy insult: his gay readers are apathetic, stupid, sex-crazed. He calls them "turkeys," but also "faggots" (the title of his dyspeptic novel). He invites them, contemptuously, to "march off now to the gas chambers; just get right in line."[18] Falwell, by contrast, is famously modulated. His is the honeyed voice of the Southern preacher who smiles affably as he consigns you the eternal flames—or blesses a wind-borne plague. Falwell's rhythm, volume, timber, his analogies and images, his gestures and glances, are studied performances of righteous sincerity. But Falwell doesn't want only his preaching or his scriptures to carry the argument. After all, he is leader of the new evangelicals who have entered into politics. So he must also show himself an expert in public health policy. He has his own experts, who claim to conduct scientific research for the common good and God's punishing majesty.

SCRIPTURAL STATISTICS

In 1982, Paul Cameron founded the Institute for the Scientific Investigation of Sexuality in Lincoln, Nebraska. A former academic in private practice as a psychologist, he led opposition to a local nondiscrimination ordinance using some of the tactics tested in Bryant's "battle for Miami," including circulating unfounded rumors about mutilating assaults on children.[19] He had been speaking against homosexuality in his professional capacity for some years.[20] Fresh from victory in Lincoln, Cameron decided to redouble his efforts at politics-through-research and undertook the institute's founding. By the spring of 1983, he was directing a survey of homosexual behaviors and their consequences that would correct the errors of Kinsey and underwrite stricter legal regulation.[21] The results were published in August 1985, but Cameron hawked them to friendly audiences before that.[22] In July 1984, for example, he presented at the third "Family Forum" in San Francisco. Moral Majority was one of the sponsors for the meeting, and Falwell provided the opening address. Cameron was given a breakout session of his own that evening.[23] Less than a year later, he was assuring a reporter at the Conservative Political Action Conference that homosexuality was curable and that "AIDS was started and transmitted by homosexuals." They should be quarantined, he argued, and unless things improved dramatically "in three or four years, one of the options discussed will be the extermination of homosexuals."[24] Why wait

on the numbers when the inferences from them could be put to such immediate use?

What numbers they are! In one popular presentation, after warning that
the "extremely explicit" content will be "offensive to normal sensibilities,"
Cameron recites his results salaciously in answer to the apparently urgent
question, "What do homosexuals do?"[25] Homosexuals almost always fellate
their sex partners and then swallow the semen. "Thus gays are doing the
next thing to consuming raw human blood." Two-thirds engage in anilingus
(Cameron is more graphic) and so "ingest biologically significant amounts of
feces." Indeed, "the latest national random survey [presumably Cameron's
own] found that 17 percent of gays admitted to having eaten and/or rubbed
feces of partners." Most famously, Cameron claims that "a small propor-
tion of homosexuals" anally insert "animals—gerbils are commonly used."
He presents these and other practices in "developmental order." This is "a
ladder" (to hell?) down which homosexuals descend given time. "By age 21
most gays have adopted most of these practices." But with enough discipline
and enough religion, it is possible to break out, to stop the descent. "Homosexual habits are learned and homosexual habits can be unlearned."[26]

So far the voice of the self-proclaimed scientist or clinician. Cameron
goes on, in a voice that alternates between theology (or "Judaeo-Christian
philosophy") and civics. "What about the questions of homosexual behavior, activism, recruitment? . . . We not only have the right but a responsibility to fight such things, not only as orthodox Christians or Jews, but as
citizens of an endangered society." In America, homosexuals are behaving
more dangerously than at any time in history—not only in their admitted
sexual acts, but by their activist demands for legal recognition. "This kind
of outrageous assertion . . . demands harsh words and harsh measures, for
nothing else will expose it for what it is—pure malevolence, a cursing of
innocence and normality."[27] Harsh measures, Cameron has already explained, should include as least "soft quarantine" (with the real prospect
of "hard quarantine" if things get worse), nationwide criminalization of
"homosexual conduct," restriction on sex education, and immediate steps
in each family to limit contact with any dangers.[28]

Cameron's survey was criticized immediately in the very journal that
published it.[29] It has been refuted many times since. I am less interested
in the errors or fictions behind his "results" than in their rhetorical success, which is attested by their wide circulation (though often without attribution). What rhetorical functions do Cameron's numbers perform? A
first answer is that his science conforms to a certain model of scriptural
exegesis. I think of the so-called Scofield Bible, the preferred edition for
several generations of readers interested in prophetic denunciation and

apocalyptic prediction.[30] Scofield's elaborate annotations are famous for their improbable cross-indexing, their historical charts, and their running chronological computations. To study the Scofield Bible is to discover scriptural secrets by manipulating numbers. The scandals of the modern age and the coming of cataclysmic judgment can all be calculated. Cameron's obsessive production and rearrangement of sexual statistics fits this model of arcane knowledge.

A similar rhetorical effect—or evocation—can be seen in another volume to which Cameron contributed. *Special Report: AIDS* is a thick pamphlet published by Summit Ministries, "a religious, educational Christian Leadership Training Center."[31] The pamphlet makes fifty-two recommendations, ranging from a reaffirmation of "Western Civilization's theological, spiritual, moral and legal foundation" in the Christian Bible to a call for homosexuals to repent in the name of Jesus. Recommendations call for the government to shut down gay institutions, criminalize homoerotic sexual activity, mandate Christian teaching, and subject persons with AIDS or at risk of AIDS to various legal penalties, including quarantine. Each recommendation is supported by a string of quotations drawn from a range of sources: the Christian Bible, evangelical authors, "great" literature, medical journals, news reports, gay publications, and the studies of Paul Cameron. What remains constant across the sources is the technique of proof-texting: quotations taken out of context and identified only by brief citation are expected to produce conviction in the reader. The *Special Report* mimics a common form of argument from scripture.

Cameron writes in two languages at once—a superb bilingualism. He delivers knowledge in the form that readers of the Scofield Bible expect, but his numbers can be used where religious arguments can't to make exactly the same points. In a courtroom or legislative hearing, Cameron's survey substitutes for the numerologically enriched scriptures in order to urge scriptural conclusions. "What I have to say in the discussion that follows shouldn't be regarded as 'religious' at all, but rather as imminently [sic] scientific and practical."[32] The conclusions are *exactly* what the most ferocious preacher would want. This is secular jeremiad in a quite different sense than Kramer's denunciations: it is religious jeremiad that has learned to mask itself as secular. Cameron's speech promises to produce what preachers want—and even more. Unrestrained by even the pretense of pastoral charity, Cameron can make chilling policy recommendations with the impartiality of the scientist—or, more precisely, of a doctor complicit with the bloodiest reasons of state. Science can speak plainly when and where preachers cannot, and it can draw conclusions from which tenderhearted preachers might shrink.

Cameron's science reactivates the metaphors of plague as a double threat to individual bodies and the body of the state. He perfectly aligns bodily integrity with national security.[33] Homosexuality is an unnatural assault on wholeness of the flesh—not just by penetrating the supposedly impermeable male body, but by poisoning it with "raw blood" and feces. (Not to speak of gerbils, which one would have thought impossible, if one hadn't seen it done on *South Park*.) It simultaneously attacks the body politic when the nation lets down its moral defenses. Cameron's images of bodily purity and its defilement recall a library of nationalist and racist rhetoric. They activate fundamental images of moral pollution. When Anita Bryant tries to describe what she cannot speak—the letter accompanying a picture of the "act of homosexuality" mailed to her anonymously—she can say only "filth, pure filth." In that moment, she quotes centuries of Christian speech. However much influential Christian writers condescended to Judaism for its "legalistic" and "literal" attention to purity regulations, many Christian communities adopted both the images and the codes of bodily purity. From Paul forward, Christian condemnations of sexual sin have especially depended on languages of pollution and contamination. Preaching against sex catalogues the ways filth can touch, stain, smear, coat, or penetrate human skin. Christian authors use these vocabularies in a range of exhortations and condemnations, but they also rely on them to incite mobs or their rulers to violent reaction against those denounced as filthy. Cameron's preoccupation with feces may shock the reader, but it is hardly more graphic than the moral metaphors of centuries of church speech.

BECOMING PASTORS

Falwell and Cameron stand at one end of the range of denominational or other official church responses that appeared especially from the middle of the 1980s.[34] There are various ways of diving them into types, and such divisions were proposed soon after the responses themselves.[35] I sometimes sort them in terms of how they negotiate the competing figures of the suffering victim and the culpable sinner. For some church statements, gay men are not "victims" of AIDS so much as its bearers. For another set of statements, the urgency of the medical emergency means that we must respond to the suffering while suspending judgment on the sin. For a third group, the truly Christian response is to reach out to infected gay men as innocent victims in need of solace and embrace.

An insistence that gay men are not innocent victims is most associated with the talking mouths of the Religious Right, but it also appears in denominational documents. The Vatican, indirect as always, alludes to something like this in its 1986 *Letter* on homosexuality.[36] In June 1987, delegates to the national meeting of the Southern Baptist Convention adopted a resolution on AIDS criticizing educational efforts that ignore the "biblical standards of decency and morality" in favor of "infidelity and adultery, as well as perversion"; reaffirming "obedience to God's laws of chastity before marriage and faithfulness in marriage"; and deploring any widespread distribution of condoms that "seems to encourage an acceptance of immorality or deviant behavior."[37]

A suspension of ethical judgment under conditions of crisis appears in a number of the early statements, typically as the gesture of separating response to AIDS from judgment on homosexuality. In 1988, for example, the General Conference of the United Methodist Church asserts that "it is not helpful to speak of diseases in inflammatory terms like 'punishment for sin,'" but it also confesses that the UMC has "failed to offer a grace-filled alternative, consistent with an understanding of the whole Gospel of Jesus Christ."[38] The statement then outlines an ambitious program of pastoral, educational, and political response to AIDS. The same General Conference amended the church's Social Principles to read: "Although we do not condone the practice of homosexuality and consider this practice incompatible with Christian teaching, we affirm that God's grace is available to all."[39] The separate pieces of legislation mirror the separation between the disease and its alleged behavioral causes—between the gay man as suffering patient and the gay man as healthy agent who somehow brought it on himself.

Outreach to the suffering victims is the dominant tone in the last group of church documents, including some of the earliest. In 1983, for example, the General Synod of the United Church of Christ (UCC) passed a resolution indicting the U.S. government for inaction and calling the church to active, loving involvement—though it is a bit reserved in describing the objects of its concern. While it stresses the relative youth of the infected, the resolution nowhere refers to sexuality—or, indeed, to sexual transmission. The only clue is the declaration of "compassionate concern and support for all who are victims . . . , *their lovers*, spouses, families and friends."[40] Four years later, the UCC General Synod adopted a statement (or Pronouncement) that addressed the issue in greater detail. While stressing that anyone may be infected, it admits that "the number of cases in the gay, Latino and Black communities has provided an opportunity to fan the flames of prejudice. The church must counter this prejudice which has already been a serious barrier to an effective response to the pandemic."[41] Citing the example of Jesus, the statement repudiates the practice of "blaming the victim," and it calls the church to heal, whether or not "AIDS is the consequence of the patient's own behavior."[42] A somewhat different version of the same impulse appears in a 1986 "Report of a Study of Issues Relating to Homosexuality" prepared for the Lutheran Church in America, soon to be merged into the ELCA. A portion of the document deals with AIDS, inscribing it within the homosexual frame.[43] The Lutheran report unequivocally rejects the notion that "gay and lesbian people" are "suffering the wrath of God for their sexual orientation. Such accusations are repulsive and contrary to the gospel of Christ."[44] Reaffirming the Lutheran conviction that all are guilty of sin, it attacks any "moralism about homosexuality" that singles it out as uniquely deserving of blame.

This rough division of figurations and responses can be used to sort the dozens of church statements on AIDS from the 1980s, but like all taxonomies, it reduces. Favoring official documents, it can lead the reader to forget that some clergy and congregations in the most condemning denominations cared tirelessly for gay men with AIDS. Even for a particular document, the taxonomy describes only the predominant rhetorical figuration and response, since individual documents often register contrary impulses. For example, both the Vatican *Letter* and the Southern Baptist resolution urge a qualified respect for homosexual persons. Most of all, the taxonomy reduces the ways in which AIDS interrupted the settled presumptions of church rhetoric about homosexuality.

AIDS "outed" a lot of men, church members and church leaders. In too many cases, news that a man had AIDS—or had died of it—was also the first declaration that the man was gay. As the visible signs of AIDS became more familiar, it took rare courage for some sick members to keep attending their churches: their faces, their thinness, their tottering fragility betrayed them. Even those who stopped attending made a declaration, since rumors love churches. So a number of congregations and denominations that had righteously denounced gay men as alien outsiders suddenly had to confront how many of them were already inside. What liberationist calls to come out had not accomplished, the consequences of viral transmission did. Of course, the systems of silence that many churches had constructed around same-sex desire did not entirely break down. Concealment and denial continued, sometimes more energetically than before. But in other cases AIDS undid a compact of churchly discretion. The gays were no longer out there, but very much in here.

In church contexts, having AIDS often meant not just coming out as gay, but coming out as someone who actually had sex with other men. The distinction may seem odd to those who have not experienced how churchly discourses can "accept" homosexuality without mentioning sex. AIDS renders that politeness impracticable. Especially in churches that condemned it as punishment for perversion, the disease solicited detailed discussion of the most unusual practices of male-male sex. Cameron is a telling example, but the wide circulation of his views through religious networks shows the general appetite. Earlier antigay or ex-gay books included glossaries of gay terms to illustrate the emptiness of the "lifestyle" and to establish the author's expertise.[45] None provided the level of detail to be found in Cameron and those who quoted him. Even to debate condoms at a denominational convention meant thinking about what they would be put on and then in.

AIDS sexualized the gay body in church discourses, both "conservative" and "liberal." The rhetorical strategies of liberal churches have the effect of counteracting the sexual charge. Refusing to raise the moral question about AIDS or treating it as just a disease forestalls fantasy about its transmission. Please think about the results, not the preceding actions! Even church advocacy of condoms, which would seem to admit male-male copulations, can sound like a plea for sanitary separation: the condom becomes a cordon sanitaire, a hygienic separation of two bodies that ought not, after all, to be touching in quite that way. As if the condom could retrieve the gay body from discourses of penetration and ejaculation. As if the condom could divide not just the healthy from the sick, but the acceptably asexual believer from a slimy, sinful slough of despond.

I associate this latex dream with another wish for impossible separation, "love the sinner, hate the sin."[46] The slogan is supposed to safeguard moral principle while encouraging compassionate action. What the slogan counsels is either spiritually impossible or indistinguishable from the whole range of Christian life. It is of course possible to help someone through the consequences of error while reminding her or him that it was error. That is the task of much parenting or teaching, and there is nothing particularly Christian in it. It is also possible to love someone who is a sinner. In traditional Christian theologies, that is the predicament of every love between humans. But I am not convinced that it is possible to enact love for a dying gay man while denouncing him for bringing it all upon himself by a prolonged, sinful choice to be gay. In such a case, "love" means either a lure for deathbed repentance or a grudging duty despite the person on whom it must be exercised. As soon as the enacted love is something more than proselytizing or clenched obligation, as soon as it becomes love, it first mutes and then modifies the professed hatred of homosexuality.

Some early accounts record transformations when the practice of loving the sinner outruns the hate prescribed for the sin. In 1984, the pastor of a Baptist church west of Fort Lauderdale, William Amos, heard of two AIDS cases. The first was a gay grandson of a longtime member of the congregation. The second was a current member who had formerly used IV drugs. These are, in some ways, "easy" cases for a conservative church. The pastor is asked, after all, only to take care of the pious (straight) grand-father, and the person infected by drug use is both rehabilitated and mar-ried. Still the cases force Amos to confront difficult questions about when to mention the epidemic in the pulpit, and they lead him from his sub-urban church into predominantly gay networks of AIDS care nearer the cruisy beaches. In 1986, through another congregant, he joins those min-istering to a gay man, Larry, when he helps to break the news of Larry's ill health to his devout grandmother. Amos then enters Larry's final efforts to sort out his relation to the church of his childhood. Amos praises the predominantly gay church that had been nurturing Larry, but regrets that he cannot address its ministers at Larry's funeral because of the parents' insistence on concealing the cause of death—that is, the life of their son.[47] From these experiences, Amos counsels pastors to suspend judgment so that they can be present to whatever God is doing in the person's life.[48] Disconcerting advice for those who need the assurance of condemning.

The theologies of more "liberal" denominations or congregations were disrupted in other ways. Newly visible human tragedy raises old doubts about God's justice, providence, or existence. How can an all-powerful God let this happen? The most candid replies to that question are professions of ignorance. Theodicy—the effort to vindicate the provident Creator's good name despite tragedy—is often obscene. Even when theodicy is set aside, some theology sounds too much like naive boosterism. AIDS punctured naiveté. What could such theology say to the growing number of the stigma-tized facing cruel deaths at an early age? Or AIDS made horrors visible in churches that had perhaps tacitly assumed a privileged safety. What safety as the gaunt figures began to cluster at the back, along the aisles, up at the communion rail? John Fortunato writes eloquently of the ways in which AIDS disrupted theological fantasies of managed life and merely aesthetic religion.[49] He ends with a prayer—and a valediction—in expectation of re-union in heaven. The failure of ordinary optimism, of a theology of personal progress, calls for older rhetoric of consolation in the end-time.

In Falwell or Cameron, the epidemic gives occasion for eschatological warnings. In Fortunato and others, it leads to eschatological hopes—to unfamiliar thoughts of heavenly reunion or universal restoration. The film *Longtime Companion*, released in 1990, follows the spread of AIDS through a network of friends in New York from 1981 until 1989. It ends with an eschatological sequence: the dead are brought back into the unhindered light on the celestial shore of Fire Island. The sequence captures a turn in some churchly responses to AIDS. Theologians and pastors who had been raised on optimistic popularizations of the social Gospel or liberation theology, who had regarded themselves as part of an ethico-political struggle assured success, found themselves talking about final judgments, heavens, and the impossible yearning for restoration. Remember the slogan: "All I want is a cure and my friends back."

Restoration—and ritual. Grief is consoled and eschatology anticipated in Christian worship, by liturgy and sacrament. The turn to ritual appears in a volume produced by a study group of the Commission on Faith and Order of the National Council of Churches. The group decided to concentrate on AIDS and invited into its membership Ron Russell-Coons, an MCC minister who was living with its effects.[50] By the time the group published the results of its studies, he was dead. But his voice opens the book—in a sermon he preached in March 1989 at an ecumenical service in the Castro attended by members of the NCC commission.[51] One of the study group members responds to the singing of an old gospel standard by a congregation of mostly gay men, many with AIDS, as "a thundering affirmation of God." She sees the congregation as "a quasi-church in diaspora," tending to those "outside the camp," but also "an eschatological church. The members are living as though the reign of God has come; as though heaven has broken into earth and wrested from the very jaws of death, life; precious and profoundly God's."[52] The field is reversed: instead of coming from "the church" to observe people with AIDS, the commission members encounter the intensity of church outside, where they do not expect it.[53]

Times of plague are times of ritual. Some days, some places, the rituals are exorcisms: formulas of quarantine, exile, immolation. Other days see desperate rites for miraculous healing, ferocious penances. When a plague allows enough time, the demand is for rites that align lives in their last days with the divine order. AIDS brought a number of gay men back to church after long absences. They came in search of burials, blessings on their unions, or spiritual clarity. One work of religion is to make or mark families at births, marriages, and burials. Another is to configure bodies and souls for the transit through death. All of that had to be accomplished or improvised in the hour of these plague deaths.

Facing AIDS, a number of gay men went back to the Christian churches in which they had been raised—when they could get through the doors. Or to other, more accepting congregations. Or to mixed sacred spaces, the gathering of divinities. The member of the study group described MCC San Francisco as a "quasi-church." This may be gentle condescension, as if the congregation were only half a church. But it may also register puzzlement: MCC SF is evidently more than church, church augmented. In the study group's volume, the anonymous "John" writes of a dead friend: "Archie found his 'church' outside the church."[54] I would take away the cautionary quotation marks. Or I would say: in the first wave of deaths from the AIDS epidemic, some American gay men found that church was mostly outside churches.

There were many of these juxtaposed sacred spaces, private and public, explicitly temporary and doggedly permanent. The AIDS Quilt, begun by the Names Project in the spring of 1987, projected such spaces around itself. Stitching quilt panels in memory of the dead tapped into a number of church customs: the quilting bee in the church basement or classroom annex, but also the memorial plaque or stained-glass window in the sanctuary. Since many people stitched onto their panels favorite images or objects of those gone, the quilt became a reliquary. Blue jeans, scrubs, t-shirts, bits of drag costumes or uniforms, flags and patches, leather strips and teddy bears were movable relics. So of course the public displays of the quilt contained acknowledged and unacknowledged elements of religion. When it was first shown on the National Mall in Washington during October 1987, the volunteers who would unfold it stood in tight circles holding hands. At church, these would have looked like prayer circles. As Cleve Jones began to read out the names of the dead, the volunteers unfolded the panels to link them into the larger grid. Like setting up an altar for Eucharist. Or preparing for a sunrise service on Easter. The reading continued for three hours. When the quilt was done, some walked through the panels in stunned or reverent silence. But many knelt beside them to weep. Or reached out to touch the cloth, its relics. Or placed bouquets, mementos, messages.[55] They were pilgrims to a shrine. Their actions around the quilt enacted a religious relation to gay bodies with AIDS more emphatic than any of the designated religious events scheduled around the March on Washington.

I read in a similar way two other responses to AIDS in the 1980s. They are less well known, and when known they are generally not counted religious. They approach Christian churches in the rhetorical registers of parody and rage—or, rather, in the single register that oscillates between parody and rage.

SISTER TEACHES YOU SEX

According to the best legends, the Sisters of Perpetual Indulgence were founded in San Francisco on Easter weekend 1979. Three men, dressed in black habits of a style then disdained by most American nuns, processed through various gay neighborhoods and even onto the nude beach. (The habits, discarded by a convent in Iowa, had once been borrowed for a faraway production of *The Sound of Music*.) In the fall of that year, two of the Sisters attended the "Spiritual Conference for Radical Faeries" convened by Harry Hay and others—a conference that gathered scattered groups, including many readers of the magazine *RFD*, to which Carl Wittman had given his energies for a time. The Sisters attracted aspirants at the conference. Within a few more months, they had their official name and the seriocomic sense that they were founding an order of gay nuns devoted to expiating guilt. A more pedestrian description would say: a group that would use ecclesiastical drag for pleasure, but also for fundraising and protest.[56] Some of the protests supported progressive causes, like antinuclear activity or gay Cuban refugees. But others, from early on, were distinctly religious: the Sisters were known to chase antigay street evangelists out of the gay neighborhoods. An AP story on the San Francisco Pride parade in June 1981 referred to them as "a group of men who dress up as female clergy."[57] Catholic nuns are not clergy (as the Vatican will rush to remind you), and these men are not just playing dress up. Whether the Sisters are pronouncing salacious blessings, protesting bigotry, or tending to the dispossessed, they are post-Christian ritual specialists for gay spaces. They mark the confusing persistence of church after church has been denied.

The Sisters encountered AIDS early, not least among their members. Bobbi Campbell, diagnosed with Kaposi's sarcoma in September of 1981, joined the Sisters after he had already begun to write about the unnamed epidemic. In 1982, he collaborated with six other Sisters to produce one of the first safe-sex pamphlets, *Play Fair!* In May 1983, the Sisters helped to organize the first AIDS candlelight vigil. They produced the banner that led the procession: "Fighting for Our Lives." Campbell appeared out of habit and with his lover on the cover of *Newsweek* as the iconic person with AIDS.[58] The service of the Sisters to AIDS hardly stops there, but I pause to examine the original *Play Fair!* pamphlet.[59]

A nun hands you a tract, which you are supposed to memorize and obey. For Catholic men of a certain age, this is the basic scene of catechetical instruction. The Sisters play on that scene, play into that scene, with their pamphlet. The title itself echoes a nun's piercing admonition on the asphalt playground, backed by a pointing figure and a brandished yardstick. The cover here illustrates the brandishing of other objects in the vicinity of exposed asses. The pamphlet recounts a series of vignettes of life among the Sisters, and it is illustrated with scatological cartoons of convent life. Here is the premise: an outbreak of sexually transmitted diseases among the Sisters requires stern action from Mother Superior and an emergency subvention from the Vatican. The vignettes that follow are punctuated by surprisingly moralistic admonitions. "We are in for some harsh lessons in personal and social responsibility . . . We are giving these diseases to ourselves and each other through selfishness and ignorance. We are destroying ourselves." Among the diseases is "a mysterious form of cancer," later called "gay cancer," and "gay pneumonia."

The pamphlet parodies nuns' teaching, but it still demands the obedience of the good Catholic boy—and some godly fear. Mother Superior is a stern disciplinarian, who determines that poppers (amyl nitrate) are unhealthy and who gives permission for some sexual acts only to Sisters "in monogamous relationships." (In Catholic high schools for boys, that teaching would not have been entrusted to Sister, but never mind.) The pamphlet certainly celebrates pleasure. Guilt appears last in the list of STDs. The symptoms of guilt include "feeling bad after a trip to the baths, bushes or tearooms [public toilets]; low self-esteem." Guilt's symptoms appear "from 2 to 3 years of age and persist in many cases throughout one's life." You contract it from "Judeo-Christian tradition of morality, Catholic schools; 3 to 4 hours of TV a day when young." There are home remedies. If they don't work, "you can mail your guilt (in a plain brown wrapper) to the Sisters of Perpetual Indulgence, and we'll get rid of it for you." The church assigns purgative rituals and offers absolution. Some things never change.

The Sisters' pamphlet inverts memories of sisters from school, but it also suggests that teaching safer sex depends on something like sacral or ritual authority. As the gay community's emerging ritual specialists, but also as mimes of familiar religious authority, the Sisters can teach you how to have safer sex. They can also help you carry the accumulating grief of AIDS deaths. These Sisters care for the sick and attend funerals, but they also lead the candlelit political march behind a banner promising life. It looks like a Pride parade, but also a religious procession—say, the processions that used to wend through the Castro on Corpus Christi or that still mark the feast of Our Lady of Guadalupe two neighborhoods to the east.

It is hard to camp liturgy, because liturgy is already a camp performance—an improbable mimicry of divine persons and actions. Or it is easy for camp liturgy to become liturgy simply. A man in a discarded habit pronounces a blessing over the dying. Is that not a blessing? Or he cradles an emaciated body, like Mary in the Pietà. How is that not a religious icon, especially in a "post-Christian" society? Some of the early members of the order had tried vocations in more traditional forms of Catholic religious life. Becoming Sisters, they both abandoned and fulfilled that calling.

"STOP THE CHURCH"

On December 10, 1989, ACT UP (AIDS Coalition to Unleash Power) joined in organizing a demonstration at St. Patrick's Cathedral in New York. The action was known as "Stop the Church." Though ACT UP judged it a success, that first "Stop the Church" (there would be others) generated much censure—not least because of unscripted events inside the cathedral. I turn to it because of its ritualized rage and its refusal of any dichotomy between "the Church" and sexualized bodies, including gay men with AIDS.

Of all the activist organizations, ACT UP has done the best job of archiving its history. There is little point in retelling what the archives tell more vividly. I will only hurry through some of its earlier protests to notice encounters with religion before "Stop the Church." I concentrate on the work of artists, especially the group known as Gran Fury, since so much of what ACT UP wants to say about religion it shows instead.

ACT UP was founded early in March 1987 in New York. From its second demonstration on April 15 of that year, ACT UP used the image that became its emblem: a pink triangle centered in a black field with the slogan "SILENCE = DEATH" shining underneath. The image was designed by a coalition of artists now usually called the SILENCE = DEATH Project. Its members were present at the founding of ACT UP and lent their image to it.[60] The image is usually (mis)read as an analogy between the American treatment of people with AIDS and the Nazi control, confinement, and slaughter of Jews. Something like the analogy had been urged by Larry Kramer, but before him by others, including Harvey Milk. Perhaps ACT UP recalled it in creating an AIDS "quarantine camp" at New York Pride in June 1987.[61] But the pink triangle actually makes two precise historical references. It is a pink triangle, not a yellow star. The explicit reference is to the Nazi internment of tens of thousands of men convicted of homosexual acts or dispositions.[62] But this triangle is turned upside down from the display specified in Nazi regulations. It is now a symbol of militant resistance. It refuses compliance: we will not wear that patch again.[63]

Equally forgotten in the familiarity of the triangle's use by ACT UP is its original association with religious critique. The SILENCE = DEATH image from 1986, carried as a placard by ACT UP in April 1987, puts a block of much smaller type underneath the slogan. It begins with two questions: "Why is Reagan silent about AIDS? What is really going on at the Center for Disease Control, the Federal Drug Administration, and the Vatican?"[64] Religious authority is already named among the villains of the American neglect of AIDS. The fact that it is the Vatican rather than Jerry

Falwell may have something to do both with the personal histories of the
artists and with the religious imaginary of New York.

Falwell would not escape for long. Later in 1987, the curator of the
New Museum of Modern Art offered its front window on Broadway to
ACT UP for an installation. An ad hoc group produced "Let the Record
Show . . ."[65] Under a lunette with a neon sign of the pink triangle and a
ghostly white SILENCE = DEATH, the window's backdrop is a photograph of the defendants at the Nuremberg trials. In front of them, there are
six photographic silhouettes. Five of the figures are linked with a quotation
preserved in a slab of concrete. (The slab below the face of Ronald Reagan
is empty, a record of his silence.) The figures and their words are illumi-
nated in turn. Under Jerry Falwell, the quotation reads, "AIDS is God's
judgment of a society that does not live by His rules."

Falwell and the Vatican. Or more precisely, more personally, the pope,
John Paul II, and the Roman Catholic archbishop of New York, John Cardinal O'Connor. The pope was the obvious personification of Roman
Catholic authority, the figure that most people intend when they say, the
Vatican. O'Connor was not only the local Catholic authority, but a volu-
ble conservative. Over several years, O'Connor had blocked city efforts at
public health education about safe sex. In November 1987, while the ACT
UP window display was still in place, the administrative board of the conference of American Catholic bishops approved the release of a statement,
"The Many Faces of AIDS: A Gospel Response." The statement included
carefully qualified acceptance of educational programs that would include
information about condoms, but not their endorsement.[66] O'Connor issued a rejoinder: he disagreed with some portions of the text, threw confusion on others, and insisted that whatever it meant it wouldn't apply
to educational programs in the archdiocese of New York.[67] The following
May, O'Connor's public resistance was seconded and amplified in a letter
from Joseph Ratzinger, then head of the Vatican's chief doctrinal agency,
later Pope Benedict XVI. The letter from Rome strictly prohibited any
recommendation of condoms and scoffed at theological arguments from
medical crisis.[68] The American bishops retreated to the Vatican position—
and O'Connor's.[69]

O'Connor was the national face of the Vatican's "no" to condoms—
and the powerful leader of local Catholic resistance to safe-sex educational
programs in schools or other public settings. So he became the obvious
emblem of the murderous Christian refusal to contend with AIDS. The
artist and writer David Wojnarowicz was one of many to use him in that
way. Wojnarowicz, who spent part of his shattered childhood in Catholic
schools, labored to represent the assaults of churches on sexed bodies, the

iconography of old and new gods, and the quest for an obliterating spiritu- ality. For the moment, I concentrate on texts he wrote about the cardinal after his HIV-positive diagnosis and his involvement with ACT UP.

Nan Goldin invited some of Wojnarowicz's work for a New York exhibit scheduled to open in November 1989 under the title "Witnesses: Against Our Vanishing." Wojnarowicz contributed an essay to the exhibit cata- logue, "Post Cards from America: X-Rays from Hell." Cardinal O'Connor appears in it: he is "this fat cannibal from that house of walking swastikas up on fifth avenue [i.e., St. Patrick's Cathedral] . . . This creep in black skirts has kept safer-sex information off the local television stations and mass transit advertising spaces for the last eight years of the AIDS epi- demic."[70] When a proof of the exhibit catalogue containing Wojnarowicz's essay reached the National Endowment for the Arts in early November 1989, its chair, John Frohnmayer, rescinded a grant given for the show. News of the controversy appeared on the front page of the *Times* on No- vember 9.[71] Frohnmayer is quoted as complaining that the show is political because it makes "specific derogatory references" to Cardinal O'Connor, among others.

Cardinal O'Connor, the enemy of condoms—and, it goes without say- ing, of abortion. The action at St. Patrick's took place roughly a month after that news story in the *Times* as a collaboration between ACT UP and WHAM, Women's Health Action and Mobilization. The posters proclaim double reasons to "Stop the Church": "Fight its opposition to abortion. Fight its murderous AIDS policy."[72] They show the cardinal, smiling in profile. Other images, used in subways and on placards, are sharper. One says, in bright capital letters, "Know your scumbags." It juxtaposes the smiling cardinal with an extended (but empty) condom. Under the con- dom, much smaller type reads, "This one prevents AIDS."[73] Other posters quote the Vatican letter on homosexuality or reproduce a *New York Times* editorial on Catholic opposition to condoms.[74] Still O'Connor was the favorite target. He was quoted on posters as saying, "Don't blame the church if people get a disease because they violate church teaching." Mate- rial for the protest listed "The Seven Deadly Sins of Cardinal O'Connor and Church Politicians," beginning with "Assault on Lesbians and Gays." O'Connor is pictured with crazy spirals superimposed over his glasses, a ri- diculous and yet malign figure. The slogan says, "Public Health Menace."

The official plan for the demonstration called for ACT UP to conduct a legal picket outside the cathedral during a Sunday mass.[75] Penned into a small space and surrounded by police, the demonstrators waved plac- ards, shouted, gestured. Statements explaining the action were disguised as church programs and distributed to those entering. Inside the cathedral, members of "affinity groups" took a more direct role. There had been considerable discussion in public meetings about whether or not to enter the church and interrupt the service. Despite the agreement not to disrupt the service, these groups decided out of public hearing how exactly to do so.[76] They interrupted the liturgy with recitations of Catholic crimes. They blew whistles and cried out accusations against the cardinal. Protestors staged a "die in" across the aisles. Their limp bodies were carried out by police on orange stretchers. One protestor, "a former altar boy," received the consecrated host communion and deliberately spit it out. Between the cathedral and the street outside, more than a hundred demonstrators were arrested.

There had been disagreement within ACT UP before the demonstration about its usefulness and its target. Was it against "the Church" or against "this man," the cardinal? Once announced, the action was met with threats and political pressure. Though some claimed afterward that it was a success, if only in raising public awareness of the role of religion, the price paid in negative publicity was high. An editorial in the *Times* judged that the protestors "mostly brought discredit on themselves," offering "another reason to reject both the offensive protestors and their ideas." It singled out the "act of desecration that deeply offended worshipers."[77] The chaotic scene allowed the cardinal to appear as a suffering martyr. He addressed the congregation, holding his crosier, wearing his miter: "I always feel anguish when I meet people who hate for any reason. We must never respond to hatred with hatred, but only with love, compassion, and understanding." Not exactly the message ACT UP wanted to send about him or the Catholic Church.

"Stop the Church" can look like it simply reverses "Christian" attacks on gay men with AIDS—as if it reinforces the violent binary between gay and church. Both the images and the actions go further. Consider the effect of juxtaposing a condom with a cardinal, all to the moral advantage of the former. You mean to mock the cardinal by putting him next to the condom, of course. But you turn the honest, effective condom into a more reliable icon. What holds for the parodies by the Sisters of Perpetual Indulgence holds for some pieces of "Stop the Church": parody can be a way of transferring sacral power.

More importantly, the demonstration ignores boundaries around religion. It refuses to observe the curious immunity granted religious speech. Demonstrators interrupt the cardinal's sermon. This breach of good manners, so troubling to the *Times*, refuses to grant the cardinal's speech the kind of immunity it wants to claim for itself in the name of religion. Why, the unruly demonstrators ask, do we have to listen while clergy preach almost any violence in the name of God? Why should lethal Christian speech be able to deny responsibility for its consequences? The demonstrators ask the question that ought to have been asked of Falwell and Cameron and all the others—that ought still to be asked.

"Stop the Church" then crosses a physical boundary: it brings protesting gay bodies into sacred space—and, indeed, into contact with the ritually protected body of Jesus. Why, the former altar boy asks, is the desecration of a host so much more offensive to the worshipers—or the *Times*—than the desecrations of human beings for whom Jesus surrendered his body and blood?[78] Jesus was hardly so fastidious about his body. Its "desecration" in these circumstances can be read not as reinforcing the binary between gay and church, but crossing it decisively. The body of Jesus is spit out in church precisely as the body of the infected have been spit out by the church. The body of the protester at the altar rail, the bodies dropping onto the cathedral floor: the gay body with AIDS may be a plague body, but it can be a witnessing body, a martyr's body, a saintly body.

In "Post Cards from America," in a passage on imagination as the last remaining space of freedom, Wojnarowicz writes out a fantasy: "I imagine what it would be like if, each time a lover, friend or stranger died of this disease, their friends, lovers, or neighbors would take their dead body and drive with it in a car a hundred miles [an hour] to washington dc and blast through the gates of the white house and come to a screeching halt before the entrance and then dump their lifeless forms on the front steps."[79] ACT UP performed the fantasy in its political funerals, one of them David Wojnarowicz's own, and in the "ashes actions."[80] In the funerals, activists marched into the streets with the caskets of those who had died from AIDS—frequently in response to their final and explicit instructions. Or at least they tried to march: the police often formed a human wall to block them in. The ashes action of 1992 dumped cremated remains on the lawn of the White House. In the funerals and the ashes action, ACT UP takes on the priestly or ministerial role of journeying with the dead. It declares the religious rites always already political. "Political funeral": this funeral is conducted as politics because every other AIDS death is political. Because churches that refuse to bury these bodies or to tend them while living or to receive them once dead are playing brutal politics. There is no wall separating the religious from the political. A political funeral is a funeral. An ACT UP meeting to plan "Stop the Church" is curiously like a reformers' conventicle.

Wojnarowicz worries that those left behind will be consumed by "perfecting rituals of death rather than a relatively simple ritual of life such as screaming in the streets."[81] But screaming in the streets while pushing an open coffin or spreading ashes is also something that more demonstrative Christians traditionally do at funerals. When I was a boy in Mexico, coffins were pushed or driven in front of our house on the way to the cemetery. There was screaming. Drinking, too. And a band of mariachis. ACT UP's political funerals are folk funerals for this particular folk.

The direct action of invading the church is one of several moments in which ACT UP appropriated the occasions of religious ritual—not in Sisterly parody, but in furious protest. Protest against the divine is a familiar scriptural action. It can even be a form of petitionary prayer. AIDS moved much gay speech into religious forms: unaccustomed eulogies, spontaneous prayers, bedside vows, blessings and valedictions. The suffering refused to let religion remain the possession of those institutions that manage God for the sake of established powers. That is the essence of church reform.

RYAN WHITE; OR, THE MISSING GAY ADOLESCENT

In its early portrayals, AIDS especially ravaged young male bodies. Young, but still figured as adult. Because of the age stratification of gay social networks and the incubation period of the virus, the youngest of those infected were typically in their twenties. The iconic image of the young gay man with AIDS was not a teenager—and the single icon of the teenager with AIDS was decidedly not gay.

Ryan White was a young hemophiliac who was infected, along with many others, through contaminated Factor VIII, a blood product used to facilitate clotting. He was diagnosed with full-blown AIDS on December 17, 1984, just after his thirteenth birthday. He was not expected to live long, but he did—and so he wanted to go back to school. His public school in Kokomo, Indiana, refused him on public health grounds. The story might have stopped there, except that Ryan's mother was persuaded to fight back. The fight made his story public. Publicity divided the local citizenry and provoked attacks on the family. It also brought Ryan fame far beyond the steppes of central Indiana. He became the "boy with AIDS," pursued by the media and befriended by stars. He testified before a presidential commission. He helped in the production of a movie about his life. When Ryan died in 1990, his funeral was attended by First Lady Barbara Bush and telecast live on CNN. Elton John sang. Michael Jackson joined the final viewing of the body.

One version of the icon is the film, *The Ryan White Story* (1989), which takes Ryan through his acceptance at a new high school in a new town. Another version is the celebrity autobiography that Ryan wrote "with" Ann Marie Cunningham (whom he met while doing a television appearance). Since Ryan frequently confesses in the book that he cannot write well, and since the book itself conforms so tidily to the celebrity genre, I don't take its first-person narrative as his. Indeed, the words cannot be his, since the book continues, eerily, up to his last moments of lucidity. But then I am looking not so much for his innermost thoughts as for the construction of a public character. The construction emphasizes two things: that he only wanted to be "normal" and that he was definitely not gay.

"Normal" appears often in the book, and more frequently as Ryan's life is pressed both by the disease and by celebrity. The struggle for normalcy goes back to his diagnosis with hemophilia shortly after birth. From infancy, "Mom wanted me to live as normally as possible," and she succeeded.[82] Ryan grew up like every other boy in his version of Kokomo: he likes basketball and racecars; he is a daredevil who can't stand being babied; he collects comic books and G. I. Joe figurines. So it comes as no surprise that within minutes of receiving his AIDS diagnosis, Ryan wants to "just get back to being a normal kid."[83] Among other things, "normal" means not gay. Ryan has a girlfriend when we first pick up his story; he is twelve and a half. When he is not nursing a crush for Alyssa Milano, he is wondering about his present or future prospects. His social knowledge follows his desires. The book emphasizes that Ryan knows nothing about gay men except what he hears on news reports about AIDS. In Kokomo, he assures us, "ninety-five percent of the people are just like everyone else, and the other five percent lie pretty low."[84] As he becomes more famous, he sometimes gets information on new treatments from gay organizations and once on a trip a man comes over to shake his hand in a waiting room and express his admiration of Ryan's calmness.[85] "The thin man" is the only acknowledged representative of that other community to appear in the book—unless we are to understand between the lines that an unpleasantly solicitous correspondent in Oregon is a gay pedophile.

The book keeps Ryan far away both from gay men and the suspicion of gayness. When he is taunted with being a fag, a faggot, a queer, he replies by astonished denial rather than by rebuking the insult. During the film production, Ryan decides that he wants to get his ear pierced. The director forbids because people in Kokomo would say, "See, he's gay."[86] Ryan seems at times perfectly aware of the dangers of being a gay man with AIDS. When is he asked what would have happened to him if he had been gay and five years older, he makes the gesture of a firing handgun.[87] And if Elton John keeps vigil by his deathbed, the most Ryan will say of him is that "he wasn't afraid to be different."[88]

Some of the rhetoric used against Ryan echoes uncannily the rhetoric of Anita Bryant. The parents who wanted him banned from school deploy as one of their slogans "protect our children."[89] But Ryan is also represented as religious: he prays with his family, at home and in the hospital. His mother brings their minister when she must reveal the diagnosis. Ryan no longer fears death because he has a dream-vision in which God saves him from the devil in order to bring him to heaven. He is ostracized by the fearful in his grandmother's church, and he gently mocks the parade of faith healers that appear at his front door. But the book culminates with a triumphal return to church—in the nationally televised funeral.

Ryan White is not a redemptive icon for gay adolescents. When his mother hears that Falwell has accused her of using Ryan to give AIDS a good name, she is enraged.[90] But the accusation is wildly improbable—especially given Falwell's drumbeat identification of AIDS with gayness. If anything, Ryan White shows that the problem really wasn't AIDS after all. It was gay men. Once AIDS is put into a straight teenager's body, it can be accepted—even by a Republican First Lady.

But Ryan White is also not an icon for gay adolescence because he is curiously not adolescent. He is read down into boyhood. He is the "AIDS boy," one of the "kids with AIDS."[91] If certain features of his story reflect the mythology of the Midwest teenager, others do not. He looks still like a boy: small to begin with, he stopped growing at twelve because of the virus.[92] Moreover, while he regularly ponders girlfriends, he reports being asked about sex only to say how much he hates the question—and to set it aside without an answer.[93] Ryan White is the AIDS *boy*—normal, because he is not gay and is still an asexual boy.

One of the posters for "Stop the Church" carried a quotation from the *Times*: "The extent of AIDS among teenagers is going to be the next crisis." In much writing about AIDS during the 1980s, the adolescent body is spoken about, but not speaking. It is an object of concern, but not (yet) an agent—and certainly not a bearer of divinity. If some AIDS discourse from the '80s found ways to render the gay body sacred, it could name that body only this side of the legal age of consent. More than ever, the old compact seemed to hold.

IO

IN SEARCH OF NEW YOUTH

Out of the archives and into the present—or so we sometimes wish. The archive is never safely closed. No one can talk without memory of speech; to remember speech is to become its performing archive. The most consequential record of rhetoric is carried in the living memory of speakers, who consult it as they talk—especially whenever they try to persuade. They do not think of it as an archive. They call it their language.

I mark the move out from the archive only to declare a change in my practice of listening to speeches. Instead of restaging clusters of speeches, some of which have receded in memory, I now describe the interaction of important types of speeches still around us. I count them off one after another, on the assumption that their types will be familiar, even if my examples are not. In most cases, a single example will have to do—usually the clearest or boldest, not the most typical. I spend less time with topics that repeat older material, turning instead to the organization of new sites or topics of controversy. At every site, in every example, I highlight the representation of adolescents. One feature that seems to distinguish our present versions of the debates is a confused preoccupation with emerging characters of "LGBT youth." Some churches are eager to court them, but turn speechless once they arrive.

FAMILIAR SITES OF CONTROVERSY

Current church controversies over homosexuality are conducted around fixed topics. A topic in rhetoric is not a subject matter. It is a set of cues for composing and expectations in listening. It is like a checklist of moves in a game or prescribed patterns in a formal dance. Some topics in current controversy are so familiar that the sequence of moves, no matter how cleverly done, produces tedium. Other topics are newer and so more open to approved variation or even improvisation.

Two of the oldest sites of church controversy are scriptural interpretation and extrapolations from divine creation. They overlap: favorite biblical
passages are read as descriptions of God's plans in creating sexed bodies
(Genesis 2) or God's judgments on those who try to fit them together
improperly (Genesis 19, Romans 1). Many of the arguments declaimed
today about the most cited verses were already worn in by the 1950s. They
are repeated incessantly because of the supposed authority of the Bible
for Christian discourses, but also because they reinforce comforting divisions: the strict letter versus its modernizing adaptation, faithful submission against critical engagement, scriptural intuition before scholarship.
Changes in scholarly exegesis now do little to alter the outcomes of rhetorical combats over these verses. Often the point of repetition is not persuasion so much as reaffirmation of loyalty to a fixed reading—that is, to a
particular sect of readers.

Prolonged, partisan controversy over set verses produces usable rhetorical effects. For example, it creates tedium, then aversion. Repetitive
controversy prevents texts from being reconsidered while keeping them
in plain sight. Who wants to think again about Genesis 19, Leviticus 18,
Romans 1? We have heard it all before. Cycling controversy also leads reformers to cede the Bible to their entrenched opponents. The Bible becomes identified only with condemnations of homosexuality; arguments
for its moral goodness are typed as nonbiblical. News reporting picks up
this pattern: church debates over homosexuality are represented as the
Bible against human rights or love or some other abstract value. Telling
the story in this way ignores decades of scholarly exegesis and endorses a
partisan model of biblical interpretation. Many reporters end up agreeing
with "literalists" about how the Bible should be read. Their view is easier
to summarize, after all, and it conforms to journalistic conceptions of language. Reforming readers soon tire of explaining the alternatives.

Despite the calculated repetition, there are some changes in the topics
of biblical controversy. They may be easier to see in rhetoric directed at the
young. It is important to remember that it is directed at them without representing them. There are no figures of youth in the verses commonly cited
for debates over homosexuality.[1] The Hebrew Bible and the New Testament
do not know the modern notion of adolescence, much less the teen years.
They divide human chronology otherwise. But the debated verses are, of
course, taught to youth and applied to them. In a youth pamphlet offered
by Exodus International, the concluding section instantly settles the question, "What does GOD say about Homosexuality?": "The Bible clearly
states that the act of homosexuality is one of many sins against God (Leviticus 18:22, Romans 1:27), but notice that it is the act of homosexuality

that God doesn't like, not you."[2] Notice rather that the story of Sodom is omitted. It no longer serves as a principal proof text. Note next that in order to focus on "the act of homosexuality" (Anita's Bryant's phrase), the tract must read Romans 1:27 against its literal sense. Whatever Romans 1 is about, it describes acts that spring from the heart's deep disorder. The acts are only consequences, symptoms of inward idolatry. But saying that, or narrating the destruction of Sodom, wouldn't support the pitch Exodus puts to young American readers. At the most familiar site of controversy, underneath the rhetorically useful repetitions, there are interesting adjustments for the sake of today's youth.

Something similar is happening with the topic of creation. Scriptural and "commonsense" arguments about natural uses of bodies have changed little in the last half century. God created men and women to have sex with each other: you are supposed to be able to read that lesson both in God's word and in genital anatomy. But there are ongoing adjustments in the "scientific" arguments for and against churchly acceptance of homosexuality. As we have seen, the impulse to fight science with science goes back into the early 1950s—and, indeed, farther back to Hall on American adolescence. When reformers of church morals quoted Kinsey, opponents criticized Kinsey's motives, methods, and alleged results. The same impulse is applied to every new discovery that threatens to prove the naturalness of homosexuality: its results are absorbed and reinterpreted, then connected with what is supposed to be equally up-to-date biblical exegesis.[3] The debates have elaborated parallel bodies of evidence and hierarchies of scientific authority. The ex-gay therapies or Cameron's institute generate new research for the continuing effort to match antibiblical science with biblical science.

Literature from the Exodus youth ministry shows how the accumulated, alternate science is applied to the young. The pamphlet that ends with the assured biblical exegesis begins by explaining the acronym "SSA," Same-Sex Attraction.[4] It provides eight questions for self-diagnosis, then reassures the young reader, "If your answer to some or most of these was 'yes,' then you have good reason to believe you were not born gay." Exodus points to approved publications that present the alternate science at greater length.[5] In its conceptual frame and rhetorical deployment, the alternate science of homosexuality resembles nothing so much as the antievolutionary discourses of creation science or intelligent design that clamor for space on high school curricula.

Other sites of controversy may look newer than scriptural exegesis or divine plan, but they too are episodes in long-running battles. The battles over ordaining openly lesbian or gay candidates in major denominations move back and forth, like trench warfare, from season to season. It is worth remembering that they started in earnest in the early 1970s—and claimed decisive victories then. The decades have not changed the underlying arguments so much as the legal maneuvers, which track ever-mutating church legislation. The mutations drive significant shifts in the rhetorical field or backdrop. Because some efforts to ordain LGBT candidates can move through silences or ambiguities in older laws, efforts to prevent ordination rewrite the laws toward complete specificity. Not only the laws or regulations: in many denominations, fights over ordination have justified blunt revision or tendentious retranslation of founding documents, such as confessions and statements of social principles. The whole of Christian tradition must be reduced to enforceable regulation in order to block the approach of this new character. There can be no tolerance for silence, and no genre other than law.

Fights about ordination do not usually involve adolescents, but they have clear consequences for them, both disciplinary and rhetorical. Some adolescents who might have considered pursuing ordained ministry in less contentious times are dissuaded before they begin. Others shy away from church activities. The endless reports about denominational fights over homosexuality keep the topic unavoidably present and falsely definite. If LGBT people are excluded from church office by legal decree, then being an LGBT person must be something decidable, verifiable. So much for the inventive uncertainties of adolescence.

Something similar can happen with programs for "welcoming" churches. The programs are important efforts to help individual congregations discuss issues around sexuality in orderly and constructive ways. They try to move the site of controversy from national meetings or central denominational committees into local settings. The lesson was learned some years back: denominational statements are ineffective if they are not "received" by individual churches. So groups began to prepare that reception. The Presbyterian "More Light" movement traces its origins back to 1978. The Methodist "Reconciling Congregations" and the Lutheran "Reconciled in Christ" programs got underway about five years later. The United Church of Christ adopted its "Open and Affirming" resolution in 1985. Many of the programs grew out of earlier LGBT caucuses that had been formed to secure changes of policy, not least in regard to ordination.

Some congregations appear to move through the prescribed processes quickly, without stirring passions—and perhaps without lasting effect. Other congregations—including very progressive ones—can be painfully divided. Pastors and church teachers become confused about their roles: are they participants or neutral presiders? Congregants who once sat together contentedly or took communion kneeling side by side now find that they must move apart into rival camps. So too with the young people in the congregation, even if they are typically not given an official, deliberative role: they now inhabit a church space in which a vote must be taken. A congregation can welcome and affirm LGBT people only by singling them out. The processes reinforce the politics of identity. Indeed, they apply the politics of identity to whole congregations. A church becomes an affirming church precisely in opposition to others that are not. Apply that as a lesson for growing up in church.

Then the marriage debates. Veteran activists complain about the "sudden" emergence of same-sex marriage in the 1990s as a political goal. The salience of marriage on the LGBT political agenda may be somewhat new, at least for liberationists. But it is hardly a new topic in church controversies. Echoing Christian voices from nearer the century's start, Anita Bryant and her allies warned that homosexual marriage was bound to follow on the relaxation of societal standards.[6] They were not performing prophecy. Troy Perry began blessing same-sex marriages in the summer of 1970—that is, within a year and a half of the MCC's first service. The first Quaker minute for a same-sex marriage was recorded in 1973 by the San Francisco monthly meeting. The Unitarians endorsed the blessing of same-sex unions in 1984. And so on. More importantly, and over a much longer span, same-sex couples have claimed Christian marriage rites in secret (or semisecret) to formalize their loves. The new political energy behind same-sex civil marriage has of course changed religious rhetoric. Legal recognition of unions or marriages in a small number of states creates inconveniences for churches that want to be marriage agents for the state without having to marry everyone that the state would.

Adolescents are generally omitted from church debates over marriage as agents. Advocates of same-sex unions or marriages do not generally favor teen brides. Yet regularizing same-sex marriages does of course affect those too young to enter into them. It announces a more or less explicit goal toward which erotic relations should tend. When a church offers blessing or marriage to certain types of relationship, on certain conditions, it institutes a norm for judging other types. Marriage becomes the crown of contemporary gay adulthood. When a church extends marriage to same-sex couples, it drafts their loves into a well-established (and quite profitable) system of stages. If two women can get married in church, then two Christian girls know not only what they are supposed to seek, but how they are supposed to behave in the present. The stages leading up to Christian marriage are projected backward, and the great library of Christian courtship arrives to instruct beginners. Not to mention the wedding industry, bearing fabric swatches, illustrations of place settings, and honeymoon brochures. In debates over marriage, a few churches read LGBT adolescents up into married adulthood by anticipation.

In many more churches, adolescents are read back into passive childhood when marriage is up for debate. Anita Bryant's rhetoric of danger to children is nowhere more obvious than in political campaigns against same-sex marriage. Sometimes the threat is pictured as direct: same-sex marriages deprive children (but especially adolescents) of parental models for male and female, without which they are not supposed to flourish. But since children raised by same-sex couples are probably already damaged, and since they often speak in favor of their parents, it is safer to mount an indirect attack: if same-sex unions become real marriages, then public schools will teach children (and impressionable adolescents) that same-sex relationships are acceptable. So same-sex marriages must be outlawed for the sake of saving our children—in this case, from the lessons of democratic toleration. The argument appears to suppose that all children and adolescents are potentially heterosexual, since it omits from its calculus of harms the damage to the young of denying marriage rights—damage not just to those being raised in same-sex households, but to nonheterosexual children and adolescents who might expect to learn about themselves in the public schools.

The omission of these young from the assaults on same-sex marriage is hardly new. The queer adolescent has flickered around our path through the archives since the beginning, a constant preoccupation and a regular absence, a talisman and a scapegoat. But the ghost begins now to materialize. Indeed, if there is anything in our rhetorical present likely to change the near future of churchly debate, it is the appearance of characters for same-sex desire in youth. Such a character is implicit in the Exodus pamphlet—in its use of new "empirical" studies about the origin of same-sex attractions, but even more in its address to the young person experiencing them. The new character figures as well in controversies about the address and content of religious education—whether in the revision or church-sponsored curricula or in the operation of ex-gay ministries through church schools or youth programs. Certain of the young are now increasingly studied and taught, but also recruited as subjects of therapy and agents of ministry. Certain of the young, I say, without further specification, because the emerging topic, the new controversy is how to characterize these young people. Do they suffer curable same-sex attractions or do they bear a special identity, members of a new subspecies within adolescence?

AN LGBT YOUTH

The figure of the male adolescent who suffers because of his difference is as old as novels we might want to call "gay." We encountered it in the

archive with *Better Angel* and *The City and the Pillar*, but there are dozens
of other titles, from the most durable literary masterpiece to the flimsiest
pulp. The figure of the troubled male youth—or his delinquent cousin—
has also been a staple of clinical and pastoral concern during the last century. What distinguishes our moment is not the depiction or preoccupation
with sexually troubled youth, but efforts to narrate that trouble as the sign
of an alternate development. The new character is the Healthy Gay Teen—
or, for evangelicals, the Healthy Teen with Passing Attractions.

The character did not emerge first in church controversies. Indeed, it
appears as an exception or contradiction to church rhetoric. Consider just
one example of the relatively recent genre of handbooks for the gay or
lesbian teenager: *A Way of Love, A Way of Life* (1979). Its authors identify
themselves as long-term members of the "Gay Liberation Movement" who
want to use their experiences to help "young people who are either gay or
uncertain of their sexual orientation."[7] While they are tentative about de-
termining who is and isn't gay, they are not tentative about identity as such
or its presence in teenagers. The authors' main rhetorical effort is to point
the bearers of a gay identity to their proper future, their real home. The
book's refrain is the assurance that you can grow up into a varied world
of lesbian and gay adults happily connected by a network of institutions.
There are all sorts of normal lesbian and gay lives, including (occasionally) religious ones.[8] Of course, Christianity must be blamed for many of
society's negative attitudes about homosexuality, and the religiously inclined youth is assumed to need special support in overcoming them. In
other words, religion is a special impediment to healthy gay adolescence

The same point is made in other genres, like the anthology of teen
voices or the handbook for concerned parents.[9] More importantly, and
from the late 1970s, secular organizations spring up to protect the healthy,
if vulnerable LGBT teenager, not least from Christian parents and their
churches. Some of the organizations are continuous with earlier social centers for youth at risk. They are social service organizations, like New York's
Institute for Protection of Lesbian and Gay Youth (founded in 1979) or the
youth groups at Horizons in Chicago (begun in 1978). But other groups
are located in the schools, like Project 10, founded by Virginia Uribe at a
Los Angeles high school in 1984. Student organizations in particular high
schools linked LGBT teens with their supportive, straight-identified peers.
These gay-straight alliances have been organized into larger, now national
networks. They must defend themselves most often against religious opposition. Their representations of religion are accordingly defensive. In a
comic book aimed at teens by the successor to the Institute for Protection
of Lesbian and Gay Youth, Christianity appears, both in the narrative and
in the framing material, as violently dangerous for young queers. The main

figure of religious malevolence is an African American woman, Ramona's mother, who reinforces her lessons in Christianity with ceaseless verbal humiliation and frequent beating. In one scene, after discovering her daughter's journal, the mother hits Ramona until she draws blood, then forces her to kneel with the command, "Pray with all your heart—only then will your wickedness change. Only then will your soul be saved from eternal damnation!" The panel containing these words shows, in close-up, the head of a statue of Jesus.[10]

The recognition of the new figure of the healthy gay teen in popular genres, in social services, and in educational settings has been accompanied by research on this new type, this new identity. Some research carries forward early preoccupations with delinquency or prostitution. One study from 1972, for example, treats homosexual identity development in young men, many of whom are working on the streets in Seattle. What distinguishes the study is not the concern with adolescent sexuality, or even with hustlers, but rather the notion of identity formation.[11] Other studies followed, driven in large part by successive groups of "gay youth" that become visible, since the challenge was always to find a research population of teens so identified. The question of identity is not only a topic of research, but its precondition. Since the groups of "gay youth" that were easiest to study were also ones that had come to attention of various social management systems in one way or another, many of the studies from the 1970s and 1980s discovered high incidence of distressing behaviors or emotions, especially impulses to suicide.

In the same years, there appear models for the proper development of homosexual identity. The most famous is that by Vivienne Cass. It has gone through various iterations and modifications.[12] The original model has six stages that move in a narrative arc from confusion and comparison through tolerance and acceptance to pride and synthesis. Cass's first five stages correspond to the liberationist narrative of coming out: they culminate in a pride that expresses itself as solidarity with other gay people in confronting the nongay world. The sixth stage hopes to move toward "synthesis": being gay is integrated as one part of a larger human person. That too, as we saw in Wittman, is a liberationist dream. Cass's model has been supplemented by a number of others, with varying numbers of steps and of caveats on their wide application. Despite the caveats, the models have also been frequently and sometimes roundly criticized for pretensions to universality, especially across differences of gender, ethnicity, and culture.

I am more interested by the continuing disregard of religion in the models and studies based on them—especially since religious models for adolescent sexual development both precede and inform the psychological theories, as we saw in Hall. When religion does figure in studies of the homosexual adolescent, it is often and again a risk or threat. But the studies struggle even to conceive the effects on adolescent selves of religious languages and practices. Here is a handful of examples—which are precisely not intended to be a survey of the literature.

Religion can simply be missing from studies either because it never occurs to the investigators to ask about it or because it is (allegedly) negligible in their data. For example, one team developed a "Gay Identity Questionnaire" based on a model of adolescent identity formation.[13] The fifty true-false questions make no mention of religion. They speak of "society's treatment of gays," "heterosexual society," and "heterosexuals' oppression of me and other gays." They do not ask about God, scriptures, or churches as agents of oppression—or liberation. The questionnaire mentions work, school, and home as places of contact, or friends, family, and associates as the surrounding social network, but not religious school, congregational youth group, religious leader, or worshipping community. Of course, the reverse exclusion can be found in studies of teen religion. The monograph reporting on the "National Study of Youth and Religion" (conducted 2002–3) somehow manages to conceive teen sexuality as only heterosexual. Its highlighted respondents inhabit astonishingly straight spaces, and even its tabulated findings seem to measure responses by the prospect of (male-female) marriage.[14]

In another group of studies, religion appears principally or exclusively as a threat to queer adolescence. For example, one study concludes from earlier research that "religion" is "another significant risk factor correlated with suicidal ideation for gay and lesbian youth . . . Families often rely on religious doctrines for an understanding of homosexuality. Therefore, these negative views juxtaposed [sic] by religion may be internalized by families, particularly religious families."[15] The researchers do not differentiate within the blanket term "religion." Experience, anecdote, and the archive make painfully clear how particular religious rules, doctrines, or images increase despair for many adolescents. That is not the same as saying that "religion" as such is a significant risk factor for suicide.

Studies in a third group mention religion, but then deny any significant connection with homoerotic selves. For example, one team hypothesizes that the "religiosity of the adolescent's parents will be negatively associated with the expression of homosexual identity [in the adolescent]."[16] They cite studies showing that "conservative religious values are positively correlated with homophobic attitudes" and that "frequency of church attendance is also associated with homophobia." The researchers measured "religiosity" in adolescence with the question, "How important is religion to your immediate family?" For the lesbian respondents—drawn from a support group of thirty-five members between the ages of fourteen and eighteen—a higher score on this question went along with a lower likelihood of expressing lesbian identity. The same was not true for gay respondents. The gender difference is interesting, but the data won't support further reflection. The question is impossibly general, glossing over differences between groups (or syncretistic combinations of them) and lumping together creed with cult, public with private, familial with personal. The religion conceived in this study bears little relation to any lived religion.

The difficulty in hearing or seeing the operation of religious languages and practices in these adolescent lives may be the result of certain assumptions built into the models of development or the making of quantifiable questionnaires. But it also appears when the models and the questionnaires are criticized. Ritch Savin-Williams writes a sustained critique of the last decades of research on gay adolescence. He professes various motives. Sometimes he wants homosexuality to disappear as a significant social marker. Certainly he wants to undo negative characterizations of the "gay teenager" as suicidal and maladjusted. His main impulse is to assert the ordinariness of homosexuality, even its banality. The "new gay teenager" will be distinguished not by suffering, but by being mostly indistinguishable from all other teenagers except in the matter of sexual attractions and acts. Indeed, this new teenager will move beyond identity politics and even the need for sexual identification. As opposed to the tired old activists of 1970s liberation, the new gay teenager is the true revolutionary precisely in denying the need for revolution.

In one respect, at least, Savin-Williams carries forward the assumptions of the liberationists: he sees little need to consider the effects of religion on the construction, repression, or punishment of sexual attractions and acts. Religion appears only a few times, and then in lists of social attributes that may occur alongside same-sex attachments. Brief reflection will suggest how odd this is. For teenagers in America who are growing up as something other than heterosexual, religious voices carry the loudest condemnations and some of the most articulate characterizations of being gay. So far as our public discourse on religion is still dominated by avowedly Christian voices, *church* condemnations just are the salient interdictions. They are obviously more potent and more "internal" for adolescents raised in a church community—or converted to one. Still the church condemnations reach far beyond church walls and affect many more than believers—as our transit through the archives has shown time and again. So far as churches produce stigma around sexual difference, they would seem an essential factor in research on queer youth. Yet the conclusion seems to be that the "new gay teenager," like the liberationist of decades before, enters a world in which religion has no force, in which it has been neutralized, confined, vanquished.

One reply to my objection might be that Savin-Williams is following his interview data and that religion simply doesn't appear in them. Of course, and as he frequently remarks of other studies, it may not appear because it is not asked about. But even if we were to take the data as reported, we would need to consider another place in which religion can appear—namely, in Savin-Williams's own terminology or list of characters. He prefers to avoid identity language (as I do), and so he speaks of "same-sex attractions." That is exactly the preference of the current versions of the ex-gay therapy, as in the tract from Exodus. The acronym "SSA" appears prominently and regularly on the websites of any number of ex-gay organizations.[17] It is one of the main rhetorical devices for religious groups fighting legal and educational rights for teens struggling with homoerotic desire. The acronym authorizes a separation of attraction from identity in order to argue to the adolescent that a transitory or even persistent attraction need not imply acceptance of any identity—other than the unmarked and "natural" identity of the heterosexual. I am not suggesting that Savin-Williams has aligned himself with ex-gay groups or their purposes. I am not even suggesting that he cannot use the language because they do. My point is rather that no one writing about adolescent desire in contemporary America can write as if the religious discourses don't exist, because they have long since crossed the boundary between religion and politics, education, or science. The rhetorical forces in religious speech affect not only the construction of adolescent selves, but the supposedly political, educational, or scientific terms in which we talk about them.

Some researchers and their critics have been looking for religion in the wrong places when they have looked for it at all. But perhaps their misdirection can become a suggestion. Religion has in fact not performed one of its traditional roles around this emerging adolescent group. No immediately recognizable Christian character has been created for same-sex desire, much less for its anticipations in adolescence. No church has a shaping myth to tell about them. Not the "conservative" churches, for which the character is an illusion, a temptation. Not the "liberal" churches, which take over the character as defined by the sciences or enlightened public policy.

Historically churches make sexual characters in a variety of ways. They define them in biblical exegesis, moral theology, and church law. They extol them or (more often) condemn them in preaching, religious education, and penitential practice. But before they speak of them, they often evoke them in ritual, that is, in worship or liturgy and sacrament. But here the churches have lagged even further behind: theological or institutional acceptance of homosexuality has typically run far ahead of ritual recognition—much less, ritual creation. The rituals for creating queer characters are not found in churches.

RITUAL PLACES

Established in the early 1970s as a lesbian and gay social services center for Chicago, Horizons began pioneering adolescent coming-out groups in 1978. In 1987 and 1988, Gil Herdt and Andrew Boxer observed these groups and conducted interviews with about two hundred lesbian- and gay-identified youth, mostly male, aged at least fourteen.[18] They heard in the interviews a model for coming out into queer identity as co-created culture. The youth they studied did not pass into an undifferentiated future of the banal ordinary. They became citizens of "another country" that had "opened its arms to them: the gay and lesbian community." More: they were "brave pioneers" in the "very process that forges culture."[19]

Herdt and Boxer are not particularly concerned to comment on institutional Christianity, but they regularly apply religious language to cultural forging. For them, coming out is a rite or ritual process that became available only with liberation in the late 1960s.[20] Though they share with Savin-Williams a sense of generational break, they locate it not in the rejection of identity, but in a ritual for its achievement. The ritual has "sufficient power and sacred durability" to overcome social resistance.[21] Like other rituals, the "ineffable and sacred" practice of coming out aims to change "the *whole conception of the nature and being of the desires of the youth.*"[22] It is a rite of life crisis, healing, and passage. So far as coming out enacts an answer to a fundamental moral question, it is "the most radical form of *unlearning* anti-gay prejudice and bigotry ever invented."[23] It makes a new self in right relation to a renewed world. The space of Horizons is an alternate sacred space, full of secrets, rites, transmutations, and pilgrimages.

Bodies are unmade and remade in magical transformations. Sexes and desires can be turned upside down or inside out, multiplied and combined, in ritual time and space. So while Herdt and Boxer are concerned with the production of identity, they are much less interested in its normalization or ordinariness than Savin-Williams is. The space of Horizons encourages and protects any number of dissenting gender blends. To normalize them would be to discipline them. A bright future in which the absolutely ordinary "new gay teen" fits contentedly within existing social structures is a future without strange hybrids of gender and desire. It is a future with little room for adolescents who refuse the dichotomies of development. That vision of the future mistakes the depth of gender in our present constructions of permissible desire. Or perhaps it is willing to sacrifice "girlyboys" for the sake of full acceptance.[24] In our present, if not in that future, gayness disconcerts gender conventions. Two men having sex with each other, no matter how butch they are or pretend to be, do not perform normative masculinity. They may make a new masculinity—wishing for one, invoking one. Or they may parody masculinity in its very excess, divorced from procreation and any pairing with femininity. But they are not normal "men"—and cannot become normal without profound change in the cultural construction of gender. The Religious Right is perfectly comfortable with same-sex attractions. They have ways of dealing with them. They can even count them as predictable temptations in their models of godly teen development. It's girlyboys they can't stand.

Girlyboys and other fantastic hybrids are shaped in ritual—at places like Horizons, but also in many other LGBT sites. When the tired metaphor of "LGBT community" retains any meaning, it refers not to marketplaces, political movements, or patches of gentrified real estate, but to ritual spaces for the creation of new selves, with their mythologies and their rites. For some LGBT people, these rites include fierce ceremonies at the dance club, dyke bar, bathhouse, or music festival; the intimate exchange of support groups; the loud proclamation of the rally or the protest action. The ritual calendar centers on the Pride march, often loosely tied to the date of Stonewall, but there are other festivals: Halloween, of course, and New Year's Eve, or now Valentine's Day and National Coming Out Day. Gay men may celebrate the great feasts that mark off summer and its danced pleasures: Memorial Day, July 4th, Labor Day. Beyond them, for those of strict liturgical observance, the year is punctuated by circuit parties. Radical Faeries observe Samhain and Beltane. The Saturday before many Pride parades is Dyke March.

These celebrations should not be denigrated as somehow unreal.[25] The effort and expense of a trip to the annual Pride parade, the buoyant healing it provides, the rhythm it gives to a year's ordinary times—I cannot distinguish these from the pilgrimages I observed as a boy living next to a major Marian shrine in Mexico. I am neither surprised nor offended, then, by the tendency to describe the large gay dance clubs in religious terms. The DJs, leaders of these "rites," hope to be "worshipped." "Divas" sing Gospel lines that pierce heaven. ("Diva" entered gay slang with the opera queens, who knew that it meant divine.) Then, at the liturgically appropriate time, bodies of the gym "gods" materialize on the floor to be adored. When the dance falls on a great day of the liturgical calendar—say, Pride weekend—it will take a special name (like "Mass") and require smaller parties as processional and recessional.

Is it offensive to use religious language in these cases? Or would it be more offensive not to do so? Worry about the power of alternate rites would be better spent on discovering what they have that so many Christian liturgies lack. When Herdt and Boxer transfer religious language to the rituals of liberated gay youth, they are of course writing as anthropologists. They also raise a question about the transfer of strong ritual outside of churches—especially when it comes to sex and gender.

ACCEPTING IDENTITIES IN CHURCH

Christian religious education covers the spectrum of typical views about homosexuality found in the churches, from condemnation to tolerance, but in a refracted way. Conservative churches can speak quite graphically about homosexuality in public debates, but their Sunday school lessons are more restrained, chiefly in view of parental sensitivities over sex education. Even many "liberal" churches treat homosexuality with strained silence or tepid generalization when teaching. In both cases, the identity (or pseudoidentity) is received from outside. It is not something the church has made—or encouraged. Neither conservatives nor liberals want to talk much about why protoqueer girls or boys might be especially attracted to church—why so many altar servers, choir members, and youth group leaders end up, ten or fifteen years on, as dwellers in gay or lesbian enclaves. Very few Christian organizations have developed curricula to teach queer piety to adolescents.

I take as my single example the most sexually explicit of the existing religious education curricula in America: Our Whole Lives (OWL).[26] Produced during the 1990s jointly by representatives of the Unitarian Universalist Association and the United Church of Christ, the curriculum is comprehensive: in its original form, it runs from kindergarten through the twelfth grade, and it has since been extended into adult education.[27] It is also flexible: the material can be presented in a variety of formats and schedules, and much of it consists of instructions for conducting open-ended conversations. Special training is required for those who would teach it, and the complete curriculum, including videos, is only sold to congregations that have a certain number of certified trainers. The workbooks emphasize the importance of enlisting parental and congregational support, especially for the more controversial elements.

There is much to admire in the seriousness with which OWL was drafted and implemented, but it reflects odd choices in regard to the underlying identities. Because the curriculum had to be shared between two denominations with distinct theological views and customs for worship, the common core of sex education is separated from any religious interpretation. This implies that the facts about gender construction and sexual orientation, say, are a neutral, self-contained unit that can be comprehended entirely apart from religious views. At crucial points, the scientific sex education is richly detailed, while the religious framing is meager. In actual teaching, this might be overcome by intercutting the two, rather than adding the religious as prelude or postlude to the main content of the workshop. But that blending would sharpen questions about the implications of endowing received psychological or sexological theories with religious authority.

Consider three workshops on gender role and sexual orientation from OWL's high school curriculum. The workshops are not exercises in self-definition, much less rituals for coming out. They aim to help participants clarify their ideas in relation to scientific accounts and social conceptions. Each workshop uses a different device. The first asks participants to narrate their daily life in a different gender. The second presents them with "mini-lectures" on biological sex, gender identity, gender roles, and sexual orientation, which are wrapped around a contemporary parable. The third workshop features a panel of LGBT-identified speakers who reflect briefly on their own adolescent experiences and then take questions.

What are the participants supposed to learn from these workshops? The objectives of the first are to raise awareness about gender restrictions and misconceptions while building "empathy for people of other genders" and cultivating "an understanding of the similarities between females and males."[28] The second workshop wants to teach participants to "differentiate between biological sex, gender identity, gender roles, and sexual orientation."[29] In explaining these differences, the "mini-lecture" defines "transgender identity" in terms of feelings of being in the "wrong body."[30] It defines sexual orientation in terms of "the gender of the people to whom one is romantically and/or sexually attracted." Acknowledging controversy over its causes, the lecture teaches that "sexual orientation is determined early in a person's life and cannot be changed." Goals of the final workshop, devoted to sexual orientation, include understanding that "sexual orientation is not a choice" and "is not just about with whom we have sex but also about with whom we become friends and with whom we identify."[31] The last word is key. The teacher's guide adopts the language of identity not only to describe the outcomes for participants, but the selection of speakers for the panel. If a panel of speakers cannot be arranged, the curriculum provides stories about coming out.

The curriculum presents clearly one common way of speaking about biological sex, gender identity, gender roles, and sexual orientation. What it does not do is to suggest how controversial some of its claims are among advocates of all political and theoretical stripes—or how fundamentally confused some of the differentiations are. The instability of the distinction between sex and gender has been an axiom of queer theory. The "wrong body" model is hotly contested within trans circles. The claim that sexual orientation is unchangeable would be denied not only by ex-gay ministries, but by antiessentialist queer activists. The notion that orientation is defined by attraction to gender rather than sex is interesting, but certainly in need of an argument. The specimen stories it offers are precisely the sort that Savin-Williams criticizes as unrepresentative and harmful. In short, the curriculum teaches as clear and settled what is unsettled and perhaps incoherent—and teaches it not in a college seminar, but in a church school.

That location is at once the remarkable thing and the risky thing. On the one hand, who cannot be astonished that less than fifty years after the most progressive church thinkers first urged decriminalizing adult homosexuality because it was a pathology, adolescents in church schools are being taught about its intrinsic goodness. On the other hand, what those adolescents are being taught remains, as in the 1950s, an imported product. The explanation of the basic characters for human sexuality—their very naming—has passed from church discourse into the hands of external experts. The characters have no intrinsic connection to Christian scripture, reflection, or worship.

Christian discourses at every level appropriate scientific theories that circulate in the culture. They typically offset the risk of appropriation by subordinating them to perennial religious truths. For these three workshops, the denominational supplements add little to the basic curriculum.[32] The Unitarian Universalist version recommends opening and closing rituals of affirmation. It cites the denomination's historic testimony on behalf of gender equality, and it suggests considering issues of gender and orientation in the context of the local congregation. The United Church of Christ supplement provides more detailed directions for opening and closing rituals, including litanies and a benediction. It mentions four biblical figures who stretch gender expectations, juxtaposes Genesis 1:27 with Galatians 3:28, and then points to scholarship by William Countryman and James Nelson that criticizes prevailing interpretations of scriptural verses. There is no sense in either section that religion might contest or alter the basic categories of the scientific account.

Let me repeat that I find much in OWL that is admirable. Still, I worry that the curriculum simply accepts as true categories for analyzing human sexual experience that are already giving way under criticism. More importantly, more strikingly, it receives identity as something that is constructed and instilled apart from the church. This acceptance not only endows identity with false clarity, it surrenders whatever power there might be in religious community—in religious imagery, code, ritual—to make alternate characters for sexuality. So far as OWL is a serious effort to welcome the voices of the nonheterosexual young into the church, it is praiseworthy. But what does it offer them when they arrive beyond acceptance of what they already are?

There has been in the last twenty years an upsurge in efforts to give voice to LGBT youth in some progressive churches. Publications register their speech. Curricula address them. Youth organizations invite them into leadership. All of this is certainly better than the increasingly explicit proscription offered by churches that condemn homosexuality. But the theology, the worship, and the curricula of the most progressive churches fail to provide a Christian poetics of queer desire. They have yet to deploy religious powers for making alternate characters around sexuality. Is condemnation the only strong rhetoric that churches have for shaping homoerotic desire? Is there no happier narrative for churches to offer through ritual?

CONCLUSION
How Not to Talk about Sex in Church

In my limited archive, we have followed an astonishing succession of characters for same-sex desire within church discourses. Across the relatively short span of fifty years, churches have talked about inverts (as opposed to homosexuals), homophiles, homosexuals (as equivalent to inverts), gays, gays and lesbians, and persons subsumed by one or another letter in an ever-expanding acronym: LGBTIQ-and-so-on. The span of time looks especially short when compared to the sixteen or so centuries during which churches were preoccupied with sodomites.

The scientifically charged term "homosexuality," the individual elements of the expanding acronym, the person afflicted by "same-sex attractions" because of development—these are all characters as much as the sodomite. They are not transparent registers of facts. They are not pieces of a full scientific truth that will arrive next week—or the week after. They are characters with familiar features, attached to pasts and futures, ready for a host of rhetorical deployments. They are characters in part—and especially in church speech—because they all come after the character of the sodomite.

There is a story to be told about *why* churches forsook the sodomite in favor of these other characters. It would describe churches' changing relations to modern regimes of state control over sexuality, to evolving forms of scientifically instructed civic power over bodies that reproduce. It would consider how far groups of churches capitulated to new scientific and legal categories for sex in order to retain any power over it at all. The shift from the sodomite to the homosexual is a striking exhibit for any analysis of Christianity's struggles to continue speaking about sexed bodies as states came increasingly to dictate the terms under which they would be managed. But I have not been telling this story.

I have sorted archival records to show *how* churches abandoned the sodomite after centuries—by what stages, with what consequences. How could the old character, the work of centuries, be abandoned in such short order without anyone much noticing—or without anyone fretting over how ephemeral basic moral categories can be? We have watched a parade of new characters decade after decade in church controversies. Still we do not notice it. We are held back by a variety of inhibitions, no doubt, but I want to emphasize only one: we are surprisingly bad hearers of slow rhetoric.

For a nation of spin doctors and bloggers, Americans are remarkably naive about the deeper forces in language, especially religious language. We pride ourselves on our cynicism about manipulative speech even as we credit it with magical potencies. We laugh at those gullible enough to be deceived, but too rarely ask how exactly they fall under the spell of their deceivers—unless we are interested in producing similar effects ourselves. While we suspect rhetoric everywhere, we look for it in the wrong places. Our notions about rhetorical strategies are confined to the crudest manipulations, those that try to produce immediate and measurable effects. We are connoisseurs of obvious insult, outrageous slander, teary sentiment, and the moralizing of melodramas. Such connoisseurship may be counted the very mark of media savvy, but it is more like rhetorical forgetfulness. We remember at best the simpler side in an ancient debate about the meaning of the word "rhetoric." We now use the word only to deplore crass manipulation (which we also envy). We think that persuasion is changing opinions by moving passions—when it is not supplying slogans for whatever people already wanted to do. We forget that persuasion makes people. Beyond manipulation, "rhetoric" also means—has for twenty-five centuries also meant—a kind of persuasion that slowly produces characters.

The old debate distinguished two kinds of persuasive speech. One was a technology of immediate gratification—false gratification for the listener, slightly more real gratification for the speaker. By offering instant pleasures with mass appeal, a speaker could count on swaying a majority of listeners temporarily. After a while, of course, their mood would wane as pleasure played out, but by then the speaker would have taken the profit and gone in search of other rubes. Teachers of this first rhetoric, which was sometimes called sophistry, promised to make students savvy enough to reap measurable advantages. By contrast, the other rhetoric was a prolonged and indefinite art: long in learning, slow and uncertain in its consequences. It promised no immediate gratification for speaker or hearer and no predictable advantage in present political exchanges. If it sometimes spoke of rewards later on, perhaps in a next life, it mostly assured its students that the reliable pleasures were those of endless seeking.

The opinions that fast rhetoric manipulates depend on the imaginative possibilities that slow rhetoric creates. The purchases, the assured votes, the freeze-dried pleasures in which sophistry traffics are the actions of characters that slow rhetoric elicits and renders viable. Every rhetoric requires a poetics—to repeat the old Greek terms. Every persuasion requires the making of a drama, the staging of characters. So opponents of sophistry anciently argued that slow rhetoric is really the more powerful rhetoric—not just in heaven, but here below; not in some hazy future, but in the present—if not quite the palpable, palpitating *now* of the twenty-second spot. Of course, this claim cannot be proved by the measures of sophistry. An ear accustomed to sophistry has a hard time even hearing the real rhetoric.

The myths in much modern Christian rhetoric about sex focus on adolescence as the decisive period. It is the time between puberty and wedding, between the onset of sexual maturity and its safe assignment to a marriage that will contain it. Queerness threatens to disrupt the smooth passage, to distend adolescence, so that it can never be brought to the safe harbor of wedded . . . bliss. Adolescence is more than a topic for slow church rhetoric. It is the special season for forming character. It is slow rhetoric's own time. The tediums of adolescence—the wasted years of high school, the doldrums of religious education—are the drowsy surface under which slow rhetoric moves. Youth is subject and object of slow rhetoric, its special study and its grand occasion.

There is a whole church repertoire for shaping the pliable adolescent tempted toward queerness. The genres aim not to produce conclusions, but to instill a way of conceiving and performing lived possibilities. They are used in the service of love that slow rhetoric allots or withholds. Slow church rhetoric encourages hearers to embrace certain characters by inviting them into a community built around them. "Be this sort of character so that you can be with us. Be *that* sort of character, and you will be shunned." Slow rhetoric is not about opinions. It is about embrace and abandonment.

The boundaries traced by slow church rhetoric are enforced in many ways, but they are created and sustained by ritual acts. For Christian churches, liturgy is the most powerful slow rhetoric. It reiterates scripture in allotted public readings and applies the pieces, Sunday after Sunday, in preaching. It bestows membership through a rite or sacrament, then regulates it by another. It incorporates the cycles of a single life into the slow spiral of liturgical time—of the repetitive transit from Jesus's departure to his return. Or liturgy tries to do these things. Often it fails, because of ineptness or distraction or lack of preparation. Sometimes it succeeds in unwanted ways.

For some teenagers who come to understand themselves as other than straight, Christian churches have long provided both the space and the material for fashioning an alternate self. Churches have done so regardless of their explicit teaching on sexual sins or their public legislation about church officers and church rites. The most homophobic churches can offer the gaudiest material for the construction of counterselves right in the pulpit, just next to the altar. They offer material for that curious queer mimicry known as camp, but they also and inevitably trouble tidy schemes for regulating loves.

However much it chases after the ideology of the modern state, Christianity remains a repository for archaic, transgressive characters of desire and gender. They are inscribed into its scriptures, especially in the person of its founder. They are written across its history, from virgin martyrs through same-sex communities of celibates to Anita Bryant herself, the prophetess God raised up to do what men wouldn't. The transgressive characters are regularly brought to life in Christian worship, in its liturgy and sacraments. Many churches labor to enforce a dominant moralism, but they inevitably perform a Gospel with a surplus of other possibilities—other characters.

I have recalled from the archives a number of reformers who recognized the power of Christian ritual to make new selves: George Hyde, Chuck Rowland, Troy Perry, the founders of Dignity. I have reread appropriations of Christian ritual through camping or disruptive reversal: the playful rites of the Sisters of Perpetual Indulgence; the angry refusal of ACT UP to respect the line that keeps "politics" from "church"—that keeps infected queers back from the Eucharistic body. I have recited descriptions of rites yet to come: the spiritual cathedral in *Better Angel*; the benediction of the French Quarter in *City of Night*; the healing rituals of *Wanderground*; even the empurpled Eden in *Song of the Loon*. I now claim all of these rituals for queer religion—and even for queer Christianity. Or I want to.

Can we still imagine a Christian community that could form erotic characters in opposition to the state? That community would have to recall the extraordinary power of an englobing rhetoric that can begin in childhood and continue, through every stage of life, into promises for life beyond. It would then need to remember that its rituals are more than the belated ratification or affirmation of civic identities. The basic Christian rites, baptism and Eucharist, actualize strange possibilities for gendered desire, as they establish unusual relations with the bodies and "identities" of Jesus Christ. But the imagined community would have to acknowledge first of all that churches have not yet learned to talk about sexuality. They have relied for more than a century on hasty borrowings and nervous negations. They have mostly ceded their old power for forming characters around sex and gender. They have reduced the theology of gendered desire to a belated pidgin.

The only interesting future for church debates over homosexuality will come with the ritual invention, the poetic projection of a Christian character for same-sex love—I mean, for burning desire beyond the binary of sex and gender.

We need to bring this already blessed sodomite to the baptismal font.

ACKNOWLEDGMENTS

Writing that spans a decade must depend on the kindness of strangers—and even more of friends.

My research was supported in part by the Center for the Study of Law and Religion at Emory University, through a much larger project funded by the Pew Charitable Trusts. The Center's director, John Witte, Jr., has proved a steadfast colleague and a generous friend through many books now. It should go without saying that my heterodox views must not be imputed to him, the Center, or the Pew Trusts.

While teaching at Emory, I had the help of a number of gifted and patient research assistants, including Wesley Barker, Andy Buechel, and Lucas Johnson. I also learned from many cohorts of students, some of whom—like Ben Anthony—remain faithful interlocutors.

I presented an earlier version of the chapter on Anita Bryant at Dartmouth College, where I benefited from the lively commentary of Michael Bronski, Marie Griffith, and Christine Gudorf. Ron Green presided over the occasion as *genius loci*.

My footnotes will show how much I owe to the staff and the collections of the GLBT Historical Society in San Francisco. I thank Mike, John, and Rocky at my other archive—Bolerium Books. Gerard Koskovich, a ravishingly learned bibliophile, tutored me on several occasions.

A living relation to San Francisco's queer religious history came through MCC San Francisco. Penny Nixon, then the church's pastor, not only let me propose interviews to her congregation, she invited me to lead public discussions on queer theology. My heartfelt thanks to all who participated in the Tuesday night sessions and in the interviews.

I could not have spent so much time in San Francisco except for the hospitality of Marci Riseman and Evan Sagerman, designers and builders of the world's most perfect cottage for writing. They are writers themselves—and compassionate parents of children who have the exceptional chance to fashion their own selves, in their own time.

Earlier versions of the whole book were read by a few hearty souls, including Kent Brintnall and Ann Pellegrini. Later readers owe them many thanks. I don't suppose that I would have finished the book at all except for an ancient obligation to Doug Mitchell, who is more Muse than any editor should have to be.

My partner, Bill Holden, lived with the project from start to finish. No small feat. He lent his expertise as archivist to many hunts and his stamina to many long walks through night's cities.

NOTES

INTRODUCTION

1   I first read about Zach in Bagby, "Tennessee Teen Blogs." For an early wire story, Gouras, "DCS Opens Investigation"; for a summary news account, Williams, "Gay Teenager Stirs a Storm." I read the remarks by Zach's father in Brody, "Memphis Group under Fire." A documentary film project has created an online archive of some of the news reports and related sites at http://thisiswhatloveinactionlookslike.blogspot. com. The official website for the ministry is www.loveinaction.org, but note that both its self-description and its program offerings have changed significantly since the summer of 2005, partly in response to the controversy. A copy of what purports to be the 2005 rules for the Refuge program is online at www.boxturtlebulletin.com/Articles/000,022 .htm; another version appears in "Scared Straight," *Harper's* (August 2005).

2   Lucas, letter of April 7, 1964, on the letterhead of the Mattachine Society. The response of the sixteen-year-old is in Lucas, survey material. I return to this survey in chapter 5.

3   See, for example, White, "Proclaiming Liberation," which is a promissory note on a larger institutional history that will do much to restore the missing history of religion in liberation.

4   See the project's website at www.lgbtran.org. Among other resources, the website offers both a dictionary of biographical or autobiographical entries and special "exhib- its" on particular groups or events.

5   Foucault, "La vie des hommes infâmes," 238.

6   Foucault, *L'archéologie du savoir*, especially 169–73.

7   Her readers may suspect that I think here of Taylor, *The Archive and the Repertoire*, and of her notion that repertoire is "a nonarchival system of transfer" (e.g., xvii).

8   I gesture toward a complicated debate that I cannot enter. Perhaps it will be enough to say that I share the worries in McWhorter, *Racism and Sexual Oppression*, 15, even as I acknowledge admirable motives behind the metaphor.

9   Some readers will instantly suspect that I have borrowed this model of writing from Foucault. I have in part, but my confessing as much only raises the old questions about what kind of histories Foucault thought he was writing—because they were evidently

not histories recognizable to most professional historians. It would be equally accurate to confess that I borrowed my ideas about rhetorical tableaux from two American thinkers—the sociologist Erving Goffman and the logologist Kenneth Burke.

CHAPTER ONE

1   Hall, *Life and Confessions*, 378, 360, respectively.

2   Hall, *Life*, 400.

3   For the childhood fear of hell, Hall, *Life*, 88, 377; for apprehension about the end of the world, 377; for fear of nocturnal death after revival sermons, 137; for the conversation with God, 96; for the skates, 114; for the allegory, 126–27.

4   Hall, *Life*, 363 (conceptions of God) and 249 (temple).

5   Hall, *Adolescence*, 2:292, special note 1.

6   Hall, *Adolescence*, 2:346.

7   Hall, *Adolescence*, 1:xiii.

8   Hall, *Adolescence*, 1:xviii.

9   Hall, *Adolescence*, 1:413.

10   Hall, *Adolescence*, 1:xv.

11   Hall, *Adolescence*, 2:347.

12   For some of Hall's other uses, see his "Function of Music," 124 (where patheticism is a morbid chilling of joys and zest); *Educational Problems*, 1:171 (an effect of exaggerating the sufferings of the poor); *Jesus, the Christ*, 1:19 (in depictions of the Virgin Mary); *Morale*, 318 (as consequence of self-pity); *Recreations*, 111 (associated with feminist hysteria and anorexia); *Senescence*, 368 (as a cultural danger).

13   Hall, *Adolescence*, 1:428.

14   Hall, *Adolescence*, 2:349.

15   Hall, *Adolescence*, 1:xiv.

16   Hall, *Adolescence*, 1:432 (quotation), 1:435 (prevalence). I stress that I am here reading only how Hall represents masturbation in *Adolescence*. For an account of his views elsewhere and in connection with other authors, see Romesburg, "The Tightrope of Normalcy."

17   Hall, *Adolescence*, 1:434.

18   Hall, *Adolescence*, 1:431.

19   Hall, *Adolescence*, 1:439.

20   Hall, *Adolescence*, 1:452.

21   Hall, *Adolescence*, 1:453.

22   Hall, *Adolescence*, 1:451 (with note 1) and 1:278–79, respectively.

23   Ellis and Symonds, *Sexual Inversion*, 1, note 1. The etymological complaint is repeated decades later by Legman, who notes that the Greek prefix "homo-" (same) is regularly confused with the Latin noun "homo" (man), so that "homosexuality" is taken as referring only to men. Yet Legman notes the durability of the etymologically confusing word against its many rivals up to around 1940. See his "Language of Homosexuality," 1149.

24   For the letter's occasion, see Féray and Herzer, "Homosexual Studies," 28–29. For a facsimile and transcription, see Herzer, "Ein Brief von Kertbeny." For an English

version of the letter, with discussion of its contexts, see Lombardi-Nash, *Sodomites and Urnings*, 79–85.

25 Féray and Herzer, "Homosexual Studies," 37–38.

26 Kertbeny, *§143 des Preussischen Strafgesetzbuches*, 27, 38, 39 ("homosexualen" as adjective); 38, 41, 47, 57 ("Homosexualen" as noun); 41, 60, 64 ("Homosexualismus"); 37, 47, 54, 55, 61 ("Homosexualisten" or "Homosexualistinen" as noun).

27 Ellis and Symonds, *Sexual Inversion*, 1.

28 Ellis and Symonds, *Sexual Inversion*, 27, though it is worth rereading the whole historical summary, 25–35.

29 Lombroso makes the translation explicit and refers to Krafft-Ebing: "sessualità invertita (*conträre Sexualemfindung*)." See his *L'uomo delinquente*, 2:359.

30 Westphal, "Die conträre Sexualempfindung," with a translation in Lombardi-Nash, *Sodomites and Urnings*, 87–120. Here and elsewhere the translations quoted are my own. It is worth noting that Hall listened to Westphal's lectures while in Germany and at least occasionally put questions to him. See Miles and Miles, "Eight Letters," 329 and 331.

31 Westphal, "Die conträre Sexualempfindung," 107, note *.

32 Westphal, "Die conträre Sexualempfindung," 102 (on the generalized condition); 78, 85 (on melancholy); 79, 107 (on moral insanity).

33 Westphal, "Die conträre Sexualempfindung," 79, 96 (on metal narrowness); 79, 104, and throughout (on imbecility).

34 For a study of these, see Seitler, "Queer Physiognomies," perhaps especially 82–84, 87–92.

35 Foucault, *Histoire de la sexualité*, 1:59.

36 Foucault, *Les anormaux*, 18. Hear "author" with its Foucauldian ironies: "author of the act" may sound like a pure, autonomous agent, but it is in fact an abstract function that ascribes unity in order to impute legal responsibility.

37 Foucault, *Les anormaux*, 22.

38 Ellis and Symonds, *Sexual Inversion*, 1.

39 For these historical cases, Ellis and Symonds, *Sexual Inversion*, 13, 15–17, 21.

40 Ellis and Symonds, *Sexual Inversion*, 39, 144.

41 Ellis and Symonds, *Sexual Inversion*, 110.

42 Ellis and Symonds, *Sexual Inversion*, 45, case 5.

43 Ellis and Symonds, *Sexual Inversion*, 65, case 20.

44 Ellis and Symonds, *Sexual Inversion*, 157.

45 Northcote, *Christianity and Sex Problems*, first edition, 187–93, with exemplary references to Ellis on 187 (including note 1 on terminology), 191, 192. For the correspondence with Ellis, v; for the circumstances of the book's being published in America, second edition, viii, note 7.

46 Anomaly, *The Invert*, xiii, 126 (author's age and religion); vii (practical advice for popular audience). In a justly famous essay, George Chauncey stresses the importance of the distinction between a model of sexual inversion and a model of object choice. See Chauncey, "From Sexual Inversion to Homosexuality." The distinction is indeed important, but it marks an idealized binary rather than a rapid change in the archived texts. It is important to remember, for example, that the invert is still a character in

English translations of the early Freud. For church discourse, moreover, the invert and the homosexual persist, sometimes overlapping, sometimes competing, well into the 1950s—as we will see.

47   Anomaly, *The Invert*, 82–83 (his basic moral principles); 1, 31, 52, 76, 85, 130, 133 (ignorance and prejudice in religion or clergy); 12, 63, 84, 93, 98, 103, and so on (principle of parallelism). I am following these terms in English and chiefly through Ellis, but parallel transmissions are happening in the other languages. By the time Anomaly published, for example, Catholic moral theologians could read, in Scholastic Latin, about Westphal's naming of an "inversio sexualis instinctus" or "sexualis inversio" and its relation to "homo-sexualitas," as distinguished both from "sodomia" and "paederastia" (two of the traditional terms). See Gemelli, *Non moechaberis*, particularly 263, 267, 271, 273.

48   Ted Rolfs, interview by Evans, 3–4. Rolfs was born around 1907.

49   Jordan Lee, interview by Gabriel and Hong, 5–6, 11. Lee was born in 1926.

50   Bill Houston, interview by Duggins, 29. Houston was born in 1925.

51   Hall, *Adolescence*, 2:293–95.

52   Hall, *Adolescence*, 1:464, with the italics added in the second quotation.

53   Ellis and Symonds, *Sexual Inversion*, xiv.

54   Ellis and Symonds, *Sexual Inversion*, 14, for the generalization.

55   Ellis and Symonds, *Sexual Inversion*, 63, case 19.

56   Ellis and Symonds, *Sexual Inversion*, 89, case 29.

57   Ellis and Symonds, *Sexual Inversion*, 5.

58   Ellis and Symonds, *Sexual Inversion*, 147.

59   Wilde, *The Picture of Dorian Gray*, 207.

60   The story has since been attributed to the editor, John Francis Bloxam. It is reprinted in many places, including Mitchell and Leavitt, *Pages Passed from Hand to Hand*, 263–74. I quote the priest's confession from 270–71.

61   Hall, *Adolescence*, 2:420.

62   Hall, *Jesus, the Christ*, 3 (bodily representations) and 166 (Jesus above sex).

63   Conant, *The Virility of Christ*, which is identified as the "second edition of *The Manly Christ* revised and enlarged." The reference is to his *The Manly Christ: A New View*.

64   Conant, *Virility of Christ*, 14, italics in original.

65   Conant, *Virility of Christ*, 96.

66   Conant, *Virility of Christ*, 63.

67   Conant, *Virility of Christ*, 158.

68   Conant, *Virility of Christ*, 153, 156.

69   Conant, *Virility of Christ*, 245.

70   Barton, *A Young Man's Jesus*, 169–70.

71   Barton, *A Young Man's Jesus*, 140.

72   Barton, *A Young Man's Jesus*, 233.

73   Barton, *A Young Man's Jesus*, 115 and 78–79.

74   Hall, *Life*, 394.

75   Hall, *Life*, 144.

76   Hall, *Life*, 216.

77   Hall, *Life*, 5.

78 Hall, *Life*, 221.
79 Hall, *Life*, 11.
80 Hall, *Life*, 407.
81 Hall, *Life*, 407.
82 Hall, *Life*, 131–34.
83 Hall, *Life*, 219.
84 The original edition is Meeker [Brown], *Better Angel* (1933). I follow the more accessible edition with revised introduction by Hubert Kennedy and an epilogue by Brown in his own name (1995). The text also appeared during the 1950s as an undated pulp paperback under the title *Torment*.
85 Meeker, *Better Angel*, 12.
86 Meeker, *Better Angel*, 27.
87 Meeker, *Better Angel*, 30.
88 Meeker, *Better Angel*, 32.
89 Meeker, *Better Angel*, 40, for both quotations.
90 Meeker, *Better Angel*, 62.
91 Meeker, *Better Angel*, 68.
92 Meeker, *Better Angel*, 90.
93 Meeker, *Better Angel*, 112.
94 Meeker, *Better Angel*, 168.

CHAPTER TWO

1 Gore Vidal's "Introduction" to his *The City and the Pillar* (2003), xv.
2 Kinsey, Pomeroy, and Martin, *Sexual Behavior in the Human Male*, 617.
3 Kinsey, Pomeroy, and Martin, *Human Male*, 623.
4 Kinsey, Pomeroy, and Martin, *Human Male*, 610.
5 Kinsey, Pomeroy, and Martin, *Human Male*, 638, fig. 161.
6 Kinsey, Pomeroy, and Martin, *Human Male*, 222.
7 Kinsey, Pomeroy, and Martin, *Human Male*, 666.
8 Kinsey, Pomeroy, and Martin, *Human Male*, 221.
9 Kinsey, Pomeroy, and Martin, *Human Male*, 629.
10 Kinsey, Pomeroy, and Martin, *Human Male*, 663.
11 Kinsey, Pomeroy, and Martin, *Human Male*, 615.
12 Kinsey, Pomeroy, and Martin, *Human Male*, 483. "The differences are not always great, but lie constantly in the same direction" (631). The one striking statistical anomaly is the "phenomenally low" rate of homosexual behavior reported among Orthodox Jews (483).
13 Kinsey, Pomeroy, and Martin, *Human Male*, 483.
14 For a summary of reactions mainly from 1948 and 1949, see Palmore, "Published Reactions."
15 Hiltner, "Kinsey and the Church," 625.
16 For example, Deutsch, *Sex Habits of American Men*, with contributions by Seward Hiltner for Protestantism, Charles G. Wilber for Catholicism, and Louis I. Newman for

Judaism. The volume was reviewed by Joseph Francis Fletcher in the *Journal of Pastoral Care*. Fletcher would gain notoriety a decade later for his views on "situation ethics," especially in regard to sexual matters.

17   Burkhart, "The Church Can Answer."

18   Oates, "A Critique of the Kinsey Report."

19   Robert G. Lee, pastor of an immense Baptist congregation in Memphis, in the introduction to Daniels, *I Accuse*, viii.

20   The two quotations are from Daniels, *I Accuse*, 16 and 15, respectively.

21   Daniels, *I Accuse*, 22, 25, 29.

22   Daniels, *I Accuse*, 82.

23   Graham, "The Bible and Dr. Kinsey," in Daniels, *I Accuse*, 103–12. Daniels identifies the text only as a "message" broadcast by Graham on the ABC radio network. For the details of the broadcast, see the archives of the Billy Graham Center, Wheaton College, collection 191, entry for tape T192f, for September 13, 1953. The archival record suggests that the broadcast was also published by the Billy Graham Evangelical Association.

24   One index of the changed tone is the difference between the two anthologies edited by Geddes, *About the Kinsey Report* and *An Analysis of the Kinsey Reports*.

25   Niebuhr, "Sex and Religion," which was quickly reprinted in *Union Seminary Quarterly Review*. A different version appeared in Geddes, *An Analysis of the Kinsey Reports*, 63-70. I follow the original publication.

26   Niebuhr, "Sex and Religion," 138–39 for all these quotations.

27   Niebuhr, "Sex and Religion," 139–40 for the three quotations.

28   Niebuhr, "Sex and Religion," 140–41 for the quotations.

29   Niebuhr, "Sex and Religion," 138–39 for the quoted phrases.

30   Niebuhr, "More on Kinsey."

31   I follow the version in Menninger, "Kinsey's Study," here at 44.

32   Bergler had earlier collaborated with William S. Kroger to produce *Kinsey's Myth of Female Sexuality*. Bergler is also quoted extensively by Daniels, who touts another of his books; see Daniels, *I Accuse*, 59–62. For sample reviews of Bergler in religious journals, see Wise, Greer, Lussheimer, and Maves. I stress here again that I am describing a generation of American analysts and their particular or peculiar claims on Freud's authority. I am not offering a reading a Freud.

33   Bergler, *Homosexuality*, 8, italics in original.

34   Bergler, *Homosexuality*, 51.

35   Bergler, *Homosexuality*, 67–69.

36   Bergler, *Homosexuality*, 8; see also 89–108.

37   Bergler, *Homosexuality*, 16–29.

38   Bergler, *Homosexuality*, 11.

39   Bergler, *Homosexuality*, 293.

40   Bergler, *Homosexuality*, 296, note 1.

41   Vidal, "Introduction" to his *The City and the Pillar*, xv.

42   Vidal, *City and the Pillar* (1948), 236. The following quotation is from 267. I read this first edition. Vidal rewrote the novel to his later taste for a 1965 edition. He recalls wanting the original to have a "flat gray prose reminiscent of one of James T. Farrell's social documents" ("Introduction" [2003], xv). His rewriting makes the novel shorter and more arch.

43   Vidal, *City and the Pillar*, 308.

44   There are reports that Vidal was forced to add this violent end by his publishers. He denies it ("Introduction" [2003], xvi). The ending, he claims, was exactly what he intended. When Vidal revised the novel in 1965, he changed it: Jim rapes Bob.

45   Vidal, *City and the Pillar*, 314.

46   Vidal, *City and the Pillar*, 229.

47   Vidal, *City and the Pillar*, 131. The following characterization of Rolly refers to 243–44, 265–66.

48   The quoted phrases are from Vidal, *City and the Pillar*, 162, 163, 165.

49   Vidal, *City and the Pillar*, 174.

50   Vidal, *City and the Pillar*, 246.

51   Vidal, *City and the Pillar*, 125.

52   Vidal, *City and the Pillar*, 194.

53   Vidal, *City and the Pillar*, 245.

54   Vidal, *City and the Pillar*, 171.

55   Cory [Sagarin], *The Homosexual in America*, xvi.

56   In what follows, I describe the voice of the narrator in Cory's book. I do not try to describe Cory/Sagarin himself. For an effort at psychobiography, see Duberman, *Left Out*, 59–94.

57   Cory, *Homosexual in America*, 81.

58   Cory, *Homosexual in America*, 85–86 for the quoted phrases.

59   Cory, *Homosexual in America*, 91.

60   Cory, *Homosexual in America*, 72–73.

61   Cory, *Homosexual in America*, 97, for all three quotations. On Jewish notions of homosexuality, 17.

62   Cory, *Homosexual in America*, 170. For other remarks on Vidal, see 136, 172, 174, 176, and 200.

63   Perry, *The Lord Is My Shepherd*, 78.

64   Foucault, *Histoire de la sexualité*, 1:134.

65   Bill W. Jones, interview by Terrence Kissack, 2–4, with the quotation from 4. Jones was born in 1928. He would have been nineteen or twenty when the novel was first published,

CHAPTER THREE

1   Church of England, Lambeth Conference (1930), *Encyclical Letter*, 43–44.

2   Smith, "Contraception and Natural Law," 185.

3   Fagley, *The Population Explosion*, 195–96.

4   Dowell, "The Church and Homosexuals," 28.

5   For some of what follows, I rely on an unpublished typescript of Bailey's memoirs, graciously provided to me by members of the family.

6 See especially Bailey, "Love and Marriage."

7 Bailey, *Thomas Becon*, 111.

8 Bailey, "The Problem of Sexual Inversion," 48.

9 Bailey, "Problem of Sexual Inversion," 49.

10 Bailey, "Problem of Sexual Inversion," 51.

11 See, for example, Northcote, *Christianity and Sexual Problems*, second edition, 294–95.

12 Bailey, "Problem of Sexual Inversion," 50.

13 Warner, "Homosexuality Laws." Defending the church from charges of inaction, the Bishop of London referred to it as a committee of "real experts, not only clergy, but lawyers and doctors." See the newspaper report, "Church Inquiry into Vice."

14 Church of England, Moral Welfare Council, *The Problem of Homosexuality*, 4, in the foreword by Michael, Bishop of St. Albans.

15 "The Problem of Homosexuality: Report by Clergy and Doctors," *Times*, February 26, 1954, 5. The news report places the pamphlet's arguments in public by summarizing them. They were also rebuked at some length in parliamentary debate. See, for example, the remarks of Winterton in "Peers Endorse Inquiry into Homosexuality: Power of Public Opinion," *Times*, May 20, 1954, 4.

16 In Anomaly's *The Invert*, the bisexual serves as the contrast-character for the invert. There the bisexual is the character for whom same-sex desire or activity is voluntary and so more culpable. In the report, that contrast is carried by the pervert. The bisexual is mentioned early on, but then largely forgotten.

17 Church of England, Moral Welfare Council, *Problem of Homosexuality*, 7.

18 Church of England, Moral Welfare Council, *Problem of Homosexuality*, 11, italics in original.

19 Church of England, Moral Welfare Council, *Problem of Homosexuality*, 23.

20 For these three quotations, Church of England, Moral Welfare Council, *Problem of Homosexuality*, 15, 16, and 13, respectively.

21 Church of England, Moral Welfare Council, *Problem of Homosexuality*, 14, italicized in original. Both the analogy to unmarried women and the value of altruistic sublimation are significant topics in Anomaly's *The Invert*.

22 For an Anglo-Catholic attempt to speak "inversion" while rejecting Ellis's narrative of its causality, see Ross, *Letter to a Homosexual*, 4, 9. Ross writes immediately after the appointment of the departmental committee (10).

23 Bailey is struck by the difference between theological, legal, and cultural reactions to male-male acts and those to lesbianism (*Homosexuality and the Western Christian Tradition*, 159–65). He insists both on the relative rarity of mentions of lesbianism in Christian tradition and the much lighter persecution of lesbian acts. He attributes this to psychological and cultural factors, including the logic of "patrist" society, which we would now call patriarchy.

24 Bailey, *Homosexuality and the Western Christian Tradition*, 173.

25 Bailey, *Homosexuality and the Western Christian Tradition*, 169.

26 Bailey's larger authorship—to say nothing of his private views—is of course more complicated. See Carey, "D. S. Bailey."

27   Bailey, *Homosexuality and the Western Christian Tradition*, 167, 176.

28   Bailey, *Homosexuality and the Western Christian Tradition*, 168.

29   Bailey, *Homosexuality and the Western Christian Tradition*, 166.

30   For example, most authoritatively, Gunkel, *Handkommentar zum Alten Testament: Genesis*, 183.

31   Bailey, *Sexual Offenders*. In treating homosexuality, the final report reproduces much of the language of the earlier pamphlet. It adds to it, of course, an extended consideration of prostitution.

32   See especially Duvert, *Good Sex Illustrated*.

33   Moran, *Teaching Sex*, 138–47.

34   Kelly, *Modern Youth*, 4.

35   Kelly, *Modern Youth*, 73.

36   Kelly, *Modern Youth*, 84.

37   Kelly, *Modern Youth*, 72 and 73, respectively, for the last two quotations.

38   Kelly, *Modern Youth*, 87.

39   Duvall, *Facts of Life*, xvi.

40   Duvall, *Facts of Life*, 88.

41   Duvall, *Facts of Life*, 90, italics added.

42   Duvall, *Facts of Life*, 89.

43   Duvall, *Facts of Life*, 90.

44   Duvall, *Facts of Life*, 271.

45   Randy Alfred, interview by Schembari, 3–4, 7, 11. Alfred was born in 1945.

46   Bill Houston, interview by Duggins, 29–30. Houston was born in 1925.

47   Genné and Genné, *Foundations*, vii.

48   Genné and Genné, *Foundations*, vii.

49   Genné and Genné, *Foundations*, 25.

50   Genné and Genné, *Foundations*, 11.

51   Genné and Genné, *Foundations*, 19.

52   Duvall and Duvall, *Sex Ways*, 4.

53   Genné and Genné, *Foundations*, 35.

54   Genné and Genné, *Foundations*, 38.

55   The paper was published, at the urging of the journal's editors, as Hooker, "Adjustment of the Male Overt Homosexual."

56   Hooker, "Adjustment," 23.

57   Hooker, "Adjustment," 30.

58   Hooker, "Homosexuality—Summary of Studies."

59   Genné and Genné, *Foundations*, 166.

60   Genné and Genné, *Foundations*, 170.

61   Genné and Genné, *Foundations*, 173, for both quotations.

62   Genné and Genné, *Foundations*, 172.

63   Genné and Genné, *Foundations*, 180.

64   Genné and Genné, *Foundations*, 187.

65   Genné and Genné, *Foundations*, 256.

66   Genné and Genné, *Foundations*, 253.

67   The Wolfenden report endorsed the same separation from the legal side—and so earned a famous rebuke for trying to separate the law, morals, and religion. See Devlin, *The Enforcement of Morals.*

68   Pedersen [Kepner], "*Homosexuality and the Western Christian Tradition*," and Norton, "Sex, Religion & Myth." See the earlier summary of the Anglican pamphlet in the unsigned note, "A Bold Study by the Church of England."

69   Pedersen, "*Homosexuality and the Western Christian Tradition*," 21.

70   Burns, "The Homosexual Faces a Challenge," 47.

CHAPTER FOUR

1   Heimsoth, *Hetero- und Homophilie*, perhaps especially 14. For Hay's recollections of the term's origin, Timmons, *The Trouble with Harry Hay*, 149. The OED's earliest instance of the world is from 1960 and refers to European models.

2   See Timmons, *Trouble with Harry Hay*, 136, on Hay's first draft of this theory in 1948. Hay was obviously not the first to think of inverts, homosexuals, or homophiles as a minority. We have seen the term already in the widely spaced texts of Anomaly, Bergler, and Cory. There are other examples in related texts, including a 1952 speech by Cory [Sagarin], "Address to the International Committee," 33–34. But Hay understood better than most the cultural and political implications of claming minority status. For the relation to socialist theory, see Cobb, *God Hates Fags*, 82–85, with abundant reference to Will Roscoe.

3   Sodomites have long been likened to an accursed race, people, or tribe, and these comparisons were knowingly retrieved into nineteenth-century reinterpretations of race and nationality. A famous example is Marcel Proust's preface to *Sodome et Gomorrhe*, 3–33. Proust is near enough to the coining of "*homosexualité*" to mark its strangeness. He is exquisitely aware of the term's scientific pretensions, which he doubles and mocks through an extended analogy between the mechanics of male-male mating and the models of modern botany. The narrator favors two other images, an "Oriental city" and a "cursed race." These might also seem ironic variations on nineteenth-century dogmas, on racial theories and "Orientalism." But the images belong in fact to authoritative theological interpretations of the destruction of Sodom in Genesis 19. We see this at once in Proust's section title: "First Appearance of Men-Women, Descendants of those Inhabitants of Sodom Who Were Spared by the Heavenly Fire." The Oriental city is the city of Sodom; the cursed race, those who survived its destruction.

4   I mentioned above the passage in Meeker [Forman], *Better Angel*, 90, on the French "*spirituel*." In Anomaly, *The Invert*, the spiritual is not so much opposed to the religious as extended from it into a general denigration of the merely physical. Compare this generality to the breadth of the term in W. E. B. DuBois—say, in the opening chapter of *Souls of Black Folk*, which is called "Of Our Spiritual Strivings."

5   For a close reading of the use of communion in this way by Anne Lister, see Bray, *The Friend*, 241–42, in the context of the whole chapter.

6   John Boswell has made famous a passage in Montaigne that he takes as a report of a Latin version of a Byzantine rite of *adelphopoiêsis*. See Boswell, *Same-Sex Unions in Premodern Europe*, 264–65. I take it rather as an appropriation of Roman Catholic marriage rites for same-sex purposes. The report, from 1578, is found in Montaigne, *Journal de Voyage*, 231.

7   The "seminary" was the American motherhouse for the Vincentians: St. Mary's of the Barrens, in Perryville, Missouri. For Hyde's story, I combine the extensive interview conducted by Melton with a letter Hyde wrote almost thirty years earlier, but still two decades after the events (letter of February 12, 1977). None of the autobiographical sources is contemporary.

8   Hyde, letter of February 12, 1977, 5. Hyde tells Melton roughly the same story: "I cut loose and told them that they were hypocrites . . . and that they were traumatizing innocent people. That our job as religious was to help to draw people *into* the body of Christ, not to chase them out. And they were building closets in every corner of the church, shutting people away from the altar." Hyde, interview by Melton, 2–3. It would be interesting if Hyde actually used the metaphor of the closet in 1945.

9   Hyde, interview by Melton, 6.

10   Hyde, interview by Melton, 5.

11   There is an account of service by Pappas, "Happy Birthday, Jesus!" The account seems to be based on Hyde's recollections, though it differs in a number of details from his later tellings.

12   Hyde later wrote a history of this church, "Genesis of the Orthodox-Catholic Church of America." For a larger view of the tangled jurisdictional history of the so-called Vilatte succession and its relation to other episcopal lineages, see Anson, *Bishops at Large*, especially 91–129.

13   Hyde, interview by Melton, 18. Compare the account given by Robert Clement in an interview by Melton.

14   See the excerpt "Sodom," *SAGA Newsletter*, 12.

15   For a detailed narrative, see Timmons, *Trouble with Harry Hay*, 143–45 (on the very first meeting) and following; Loughery, *The Other Side of Silence*, 220–24, 226–28.

16   Charles Rowland, letter of December 9, 1990, 2–3, 17–18, 19–20.

17   Jim Kepner, "I Remember Chuck . . ."; Loughery, *Other Side*, 227–28. Rowland's views on culture were also worked out in a published exchange with Jeff Winters [Dale Jennings]. See White, *Pre-Gay L.A.*, 39–40.

18   Loughery, *Other Side*, 229; Sears, *Behind the Mask*, 180–84.

19   The first issue appeared in January of 1953. For a summary of the magazine's early history, including the famous "post office case," see Loughery, *Other Side*, 234–35.

20   According to an account in *ONE*, October 1958.

21   Rowland only joined the corporation in January 1955, but he was active in it much earlier than that. See *ONE Confidential* 1, no. 1 (March 1956): 21: "Charles Rowland, member of the Corporation since January, 1955, and active in various capacities from time to time earlier is now devoting his energies to furthering a newly founded religious movement and not connected with ONE in any way."

22   Reid [Wolf] as chairman, board of directors, letter to Rowland, February 21, 1956. Following Kepner, White describes Rowland's project as a "mission or home for wayward homosexuals" (*Pre-Gay L.A.*, 71). He seems to miss the religious motivation and the fight about it.

23   Rowland, letter to Harry Hay, January 23, 1977, 1–2.

24   Timmons, *Trouble with Harry Hay*, 177.

25   Kepner, "I Remember Chuck . . . ," 5–6. Kepner says that the ordinations were performed by "Dr. Badger" of the "Christian Spiritualist Church" in Los Angeles.

26   In a letter to William Lambert dated March 28, 1956, Rowland writes that he is "immensely optimistic about the Church; it's bigger by far than even I had imagined. As of last Sunday we had 43 members."

27   [Rowland,] "Possible Courses of Action: Advantages and Disadvantages" [n.d.], 1. The document is unsigned, but I attribute it to Rowland because of its advocacy, its style, and some of its apparently pointless details. Most telling is the casual choice of "Methodist" as the example for a Christian service.

28   Pedersen [Kepner], "Smorgasbord," 24. The charge of dishonesty was rebutted in a letter by "M. B." to the editors of *ONE*. In retrospect, Kepner softens his views. See Kepner, "Why Can't We All Get Together," 708.

29   Reid [Wolf], letter to Rowland, April 10, 1956.

30   Rowland, letter to Hay, January 23, 1977.

31   Here I disagree with Loughery, *Other Side*, 236, who seems to follow the view of Rowland held by other members of the corporation rather than the accounts Rowland tries to give of himself.

32   [Rowland], "Possible Courses of Action," 1.

33   Pedersen, "Smorgasbord," 23. In what follows, I rely on this account.

34   "A Bold Study," 17.

35   Pedersen, "Thorn in the Spirit."

36   Garde, "Homosexuals *DO* have a Place in the Church."

37   Dorian Book Service, "Supplement A-1960," 25.

38   Wood, *Christ and the Homosexual*, 203.

39   Wood, *Christ and the Homosexual*, 202; see also 206–8.

40   Wood, *Christ and the Homosexual*, 181.

41   I follow the description in Wood, *Christ and the Homosexual*, 33–35.

42   Wood, *Christ and the Homosexual*, 82.

43   Wood, *Christ and the Homosexual*, 203.

44   This is a complicated story, but one piece of it can be found in the efforts of John Ford both on the papal commission and at Vatican Council II. See, for example, Tentler, *Catholics and Contraception*, 227–28, 238, 248–56; Genilo, *John Cuthbert Ford, SJ*, 58, 68.

45   Wood, *Christ and the Homosexual*, 169–70.

46   Kinsey, Pomeroy, and Martin, *Human Male*, 666.

47   Wood, *Christ and the Homosexual*, 129.

48   Wood, *Christ and the Homosexual*, 93.

49   Wood, *Christ and the Homosexual*, 112, 159.

50   Wood, *Christ and the Homosexual*, 12.

51   Wood, *Christ and the Homosexual*, 189.

52   Wood, *Christ and the Homosexual*, 91.

53   Wood, *Christ and the Homosexual*, 208.

54   Wood, *Christ and the Homosexual*, 80.

55   Wood, *Christ and the Homosexual*, 29.

56   Wood, *Christ and the Homosexual*, 211.

57   Hooker, "Homosexuality—Summary of Studies," 183, item 45.

58   Wood, "Homosexuality and the Church." It is interesting that Wood's 1964 talk was still of interest on the eve of Stonewall—and after so many other developments.

59   Castillo, *Outlaw*, 123–24.

60   Giles, "An Interview with John Rechy," 25.

61   Giles, "Interview," 22.

62   Rechy, *City of Night*, 410, italics in original.

63   Rechy, *City of Night*, 17.

64   Rechy, *City of Night*, 22.

65   Rechy, *City of Night*, 28.

66   Rechy, *City of Night*, 72, 76, 78.

67   Rechy, *City of Night*, 126.

68   Sontag, "Notes on Camp," 287, #36. Rechy's novel appeared a year before Sontag's (in)famous manifesto. He embraces what Sontag so deliberately steps around: the evident affinity of camp taste for churches—for objects and liturgies, but also asceticisms and theologies.

69   With "gutter-baroque," I am playing off of Perlongher's untranslatable Spanish pun, "neo-barroso." See, for example, his *Prosa plebeya*, 99, 101, 115–16. I return to the connection between neobaroque and camp below, when reading through *Song of the Loon*.

70   Rechy, *City of Night*, 397–98.

71   For this paragraph, I read Rechy, *City of Night*, 400, 401, 404 (with italics in the original), 406, 407.

72   Rechy, *City of Night*, 59.

73   Rechy, *City of Night*, 82.

74   Rechy, *City of Night*, 55. For the quoted phrase in the next sentence, 62.

75   Rechy, "Mardi Gras," 60. The cover shows Dean leaning pensively against a manikin, who cradles his head. The lead piece announced on the cover is Edgar Morin, "The Case of James Dean."

CHAPTER FIVE

1   So the recollection of Joanne Chadwick, interviewed by Gabriel, 124.

2   "Homosexual—or Homophile," quoting *Pursuit* [Los Angeles], no. 2. The editor of *Concern*, James Kepner, was also the editor of *Pursuit*. The quotation is a self-citation.

3   Sweet, *Political and Social Action*, 1, quoting Schur, *Crimes without Victims*, 96.

4   See the unsigned notice, "Robert W. Wood Dares to Write *Christ and the Homosexual*."

5   For both contacts with the Daughters, see Martin, "History of the Homophile Movement," 15–19.

6   Pedersen [Kepner] reported regularly on events and publications in England, typically including extensive quotations. See, for example, his survey of recent British sex scandals, "England and the Vice of Sodom"; his review of Bailey's *Homosexuality and the Western Christian Tradition*; and his review of Bailey's edition of the final parliamentary

submission, "On Homosexuality." For other early mentions of Bailey, Legg, review of Buckley, 20; and Daniel, review of *ONE Institute Quarterly*, 8. For another review of Bailey's monograph, see the unsigned notice, "Religious Viewpoint Defined."

7   Keith Wedmore, interview by Galen McNemar Hamann. This account may be corroborated in the text itself, which says that the group was led to the question by a young student "faced with homosexual difficulties." See Heron, *Towards a Quaker View of Sex*, 5.

8   Heron, *Towards a Quaker View*, 5.

9   Heron, *Towards a Quaker View*, 9.

10   Heron, *Towards a Quaker View*, 15.

11   Heron, *Towards a Quaker View*, 13.

12   Heron, *Towards a Quaker View*, 21, italics in original.

13   Heron, *Towards a Quaker View*, 21.

14   Heron, *Towards a Quaker View*, 23.

15   Heron, *Towards a Quaker View*, 24.

16   Heron, *Towards a Quaker View*, 24.

17   Heron, *Towards a Quaker View*, 24.

18   Heron, *Towards a Quaker View*, 36.

19   Heron, *Towards a Quaker View*, 40, italics in original.

20   Heron, *Towards a Quaker View*, 36.

21   See, for one version of this story, the interview with McIlvenna at www.lgbtran.org/Exhibits/CRH/Room.aspx?RID=1&CID=4.

22   See, for example, Mowry, *The Church and the New Generation*, 137–38. Textual juxtaposition suggests that the story Mowry tells on 136–37 about homophile ministry comes from McIlvenna. See also Mowry's mention of homophile rights as part of the "civil rights movement" among the young (16–17).

23   This is the official count from the published attendance list. But reports in the homophile press very quickly made the number fifteen and fifteen.

24   For an account told with a few years retrospect, and after the break with CRH, see Martin and Lyon, *Lesbian/Woman*, 239–42.

25   Quoted from the presentation by "Billie Talmij" in Kuhn, *The Church and the Homosexual*, 13.

26   Sweet, *Political and Social Action*, 104–5.

27   Donovan Bess, "Angry Ministers Rip Police," *San Francisco Chronicle*, September 25, 1965, 1, 4.

28   Kuhn, *Church and the Homosexual*, 2. An abbreviated version appears as "The Church and the Homosexual" in Gearhart and Johnson, *Loving Women/Loving Men*, 3–20.

29   Sweet, *Political and Social Action*, 119.

30   It seems to have been the thinnest of pseudonyms if her legal name was in fact Billye Talmadge. See Gallo, *Different Daughters*, ix, xv, 9, 16.

31   There is a copyedited version of Talmij's talk in Kuhn, *Church and the Homosexual*, 11–18, here at 13. I follow the orthography and punctuation in the typescript, Talmij, "Talk," 2.

32   Talmij in Kuhn, *Church and the Homosexual*, 18, nos. 42–43; compare Talmij typescript, "Fuses," nos. 68–69.

33 Talmij in Kuhn, *Church and the Homosexual*, 12; compare Talmij typescript, "Talk," 1.

34 Talmij in Kuhn, *Church and the Homosexual*, 16, no. 31; compare Talmij typescript, "Fuses," no. 55.

35 Talmij in Kuhn, *Church and the Homosexual*, 17, nos. 33, 34, 36; compare Talmij typescript, "Fuses," nos. 57, 58, 60. For masks and roles in the strategy of the first Mattachine members, see Meeker, *Contacts Desired*, especially 33, 37–39.

36 Martin, "The Church and the Homosexual: A New Rapport," 12.

37 Sweet, *Political and Social Action*, 85–86, 90–91.

38 Donald S. Lucas, interview by Paul Gabriel, 2:4.

39 Donald S. Lucas, letter of April 7, 1964.

40 Lucas's own religious situation was more complicated than might appear. In 1964, he held (ordination?) "certificates" from the First Temple of Spiritualism in Oakland. He writes to its head that he is "proud and grateful" to be a Spiritualist. But he also asks for a year's leave of absence in order to work fulltime with the new CRH. Letter of Lucas to Monroe, January 7, 1965. It should be remembered that Rowland and his associates were ordained by a Spiritualist in Los Angeles.

41 Lucas, *The Homosexual and the Church*. I have silently corrected obvious mistakes in spelling, though not in punctuation. In the case of respondent 2 (below), I follow the original, handwritten text, which is somewhat more vivid than Lucas's version.

42 Lucas, *The Homosexual and the Church*, 20–23.

43 Lucas, *The Homosexual and the Church*, respondent no. 6, Episcopalian.

44 Lucas, *The Homosexual and the Church*, respondent no. 11.

45 Lucas, *The Homosexual and the Church*, respondent no. 4; see also nos. 1–2.

46 Lucas, *The Homosexual and the Church*, respondent no. 14.

47 Lucas, *The Homosexual and the Church*, respondent no. 30; see also no. 11.

48 Lucas, *The Homosexual and the Church*, respondent no. 31; see also nos. 14, 26.

49 Lucas, *The Homosexual and the Church*, respondent no. 1; see also nos. 2, 4, 6, 11, 32, 35.

50 Lucas, *The Homosexual and the Church*, respondent no. 10.

51 Lucas, *The Homosexual and the Church*, respondent no. 7, Episcopalian; see also nos. 22, 28, 30.

52 Lucas, *The Homosexual and the Church*, respondent no. 20.

53 Lucas, *The Homosexual and the Church*, respondent no. 3.

54 For others, see Lucas, *The Homosexual and the Church*, respondent nos. 6, 25, 29.

55 For numerous illustrations of the importance of the illusion of timelessness in debates about homosexuality, see Moon, *God, Sex, and Politics*.

56 The discussion was conducted by "Billie Talmij." The three other members were Cleo Glenn, Phyllis Lyon, and Del Martin. A typescript exists of the questions prepared for the discussion, entitled "Gab 'n' Java: August 28, 1964."

57 For a summary account, see D'Emilio, *Sexual Politics, Sexual Communities*, 192–95; Loughery, *Other Side of Silence*, 285–87; and Boyd, *Wide Open Town*, 233–35, but beware her conclusion that the event shifted the council's concern "from theology to police harassment and abuse" (235). Board minutes for that spring and summer are obviously preoccupied with the event and its sequel, but over a longer period the CRH continued to be much concerned with theology—as I show below.

58   Lewis Durham, interview by Paul Gabriel, 48.

59   Memories vary, of course, about who was arrested and in which sequence. For one first-person account, see the remarks by Pat Lyon, Phyllis's sister, in Gallo, *Different Daughters*, 107.

60   The active involvement of some Daughters of Bilitis with the CRH became an issue within the organization. For some of the correspondence, see Gallo, *Different Daughters*, 110–11.

61   Council on Religion and the Homosexual, *Churchmen Speak Out*, 1, 5–6.

62   Unsigned typescript, "Consultation on Theology and the Homosexual, August 22–24, 1966."

63   Rick Stokes, interview by Paul Gabriel, 5.

64   Herb Donaldson, interview by Paul Gabriel, 9–10.

65   Joanne Chadwick, interview by Paul Gabriel, 104.

66   Don Lucas, interview by Paul Gabriel, 1:299–303, 2:3.

67   Robert Cromey, interview by Paul Gabriel, 22–23.

68   "The Touchstone: Rev. Hansen Leaves," 3.

69   This is the main historical correction in Carter, *Stonewall*.

CHAPTER SIX

1   SIR Board of Directors Resolutions, #16, March 1, 1965. For drafts and minutes related to the committee on religion, see items from April and June 1965.

2   See for example the broadside by Cromey, "Ministry to the Homosexual."

3   See the unsigned report, "Radicals Invade S.I.R. Center at National Gay Conference."

4   This was not, of course, the first time she had voiced disappointment or disagreement with the homophile groups, their policies, and publications. See, for example, *Vector* 6, no. 9 (September 1970): 39.

5   Martin, "Columnist Resigns, Blasts Male Chauvinism."

6   Mendenhall, "The Editor Comments: Women & Nudity," 6.

7   Compare *Vector* 7, no. 4 (April 1971), interview with Tullah Hanley (11), and the box ad (19).

8   For some articles on religion, see the unsigned report, "Grand Opening!" and Roberts, "The Biblical Put Down on Homosexuality."

9   Gigl, "The *Vector* Reader," 12.

10   Although he is not identified, Itkin is the collared speaker at the lectern in the photograph from the NACHO conference, *Vector* 6, no. 10 (October 1970): 14. For his role and that of Troy Perry, 41.

11   Gunnison, letter to the editor of *Vector*, 9.

12   Editor's reply to the letter by Spiegelhofer, 9.

13   Martin, "Columnist Resigns," 37.

14   Red Butterfly, *Gay Liberation*. In most histories, Red Butterfly is described as a Marxist faction that broke off from the Gay Liberation Front. In this pamphlet, it claims Stonewall and the founding of GLF as part of its own authorizing narrative.

15   Red Butterfly, *Gay Liberation*, 3.

16 Red Butterfly, *Gay Liberation*, [14].

17 Red Butterfly, *Gay Liberation*, 2 (slander), 4 (ideology), [14] (radical critique).

18 Red Butterfly, *Gay Liberation*, 3.

19 Earlier Wittman was visible as president of the Swarthmore Political Action Club. He passed from organizing integration actions in Chester, Pennsylvania, to the National Committee of the SDS and its Economic and Action Research Project. In 1967, Wittman moved to San Francisco, where he continued antiwar activity. See Lekus, "Queer and Present Dangers," especially 41–43, 77–84, 93–101.

20 See Wittman's brief items in the newsletter of San Francisco's Committee for Homosexual Freedom.

21 On the protest action, see Teal, *The Gay Militants*, 29–32.

22 Teal, *Gay Militants*, 95 and note 51.

23 See Teal, *Gay Militants*, 86, 95. It should be noted that some passages of the Red Butterfly pamphlet I've already discussed echo Wittman (especially the analysis of forms of oppression), but his manifesto is not mentioned in the footnotes, perhaps because news of its publication had not yet reached New York. Teal himself wrote in 1971 that the "Manifesto" "has become, in effect, the bible of gay liberation" (95). Allen Young describes his first reading of it in Greenwich Village almost as emphatically: "A very important piece for me personally. . . . I was very moved by it." See Young, "Reminiscences," 333.

24 The "Manifesto" is listed among pamphlets available from Berkeley's Committee of Concern for Homosexuals in its newsletter, *Agape and Action*, no.1 (June 5, 1970), no. 2 (June 23, 1970). The "Manifesto" was dropped from the list ten months later in order to make more room for women's material; see *Agape and Action*, no. 7 (February 1971), 3.

25 Wittman, *Refugees from America*. The "Author's Preface: 4 Months Later" is dated "3/70" (iv).

26 Here I follow the first publication: Wittman, "Refugees from Amerika," at 3, column a, and 4, column c.

27 Wittman, "Refugees from Amerika," 4, column c, and 5, column a.

28 Lekus, "Queer and Present Danger," 54, 98, both quoting from an entry in Wittman's journals dated September 17, 1968.

29 Wittman, *Refugees from America*, iii.

30 Henry Abelove insists that the New York liberationists, at least those in Gay Liberation Front, were not committed "to a supposititiously stable or definite identity. [Their movement] was rather predicated on a commitment to a worldwide struggle for decolonization and its potential human benefits" (*Deep Gossip*, 88). Certainly it is true that Wittman does not claim to depict a "stable or definite identity." But it is equally true that Wittman and his readers in New York want to herald and hasten the arrival of another sort of character—a character as distinct from the compromised homophile as the ghettoized present is from the unbounded future.

31 Wittman, "Refugees from Amerika," 5, column a.

32 On Wittman's departure from the Bay Area, see Mungello, "A Spirit of the 60's," 21–22. For a less personalized analysis of the significance of *RFD*, Herring, "Out of the Closets, Into the Woods," 341–72.

33   Marcus, "Love and Life after the Fall," 2. For the attribution of the photograph, see the cover page.

34   Amory, *Song of the Loon*. My copy contains no further information on the copyright page, such as a printing number.

35   Amory, *Song of the Loon*, 88, 188.

36   Amory, *Song of the Loon*, 12, italics added.

37   Amory, *Song of the Loon*, title page, verso.

38   Dirk Vanden [Fullmer], interview by Robert Prager, 6–7.

39   Gearhart and Johnson, *Loving Women*, 69–71 for Johnson's ordination.

40   Gearhart and Johnson, *Loving Women*, x. See, for example, the text of her remarks from the February 1972 pastors' conference at the Pacific School of Religion, "The Lesbian and God-the-Father." The paragraph following is taken from the individual introductory comments, *Loving Women*, xii and 1.

41   Gearhart and Johnson, "The Gay Movement in the Church," in Gearhart and Johnson, *Loving Women*, 61–88, here at 63, 86–87.

42   Gearhart and Johnson, *Loving Women*, 64.

43   Gearhart and Johnson, *Loving Women*, 65–66 (MCC), 67 (Dignity), 69–71 (Johnson ordination).

44   Johnson, "The Good News of Liberation," in Gearhart and Johnson, *Loving Women*, 91–117, here at 91.

45   Johnson, "Good News," 99–101 (discipleship), 101–4 (Pauline passages), 104–7 (countering homophobic condemnations), 107–11 (Christ's models for human relationship).

46   Gearhart, "The Miracle of Lesbianism," in Gearhart and Johnson, *Loving Women*, 119–52, here at 119 and throughout.

47   Gearhart, "The Miracle of Lesbianism," 139 (irreconcilable with feminism), 145 (church dehumanizes), 142 (absolute denial), 149 (daily option of leaving).

48   Gearhart, "The Miracle of Lesbianism," 150–51.

49   Gearheart, *Wanderground*, 2, 148, 168, 172.

50   Gearheart, *Wanderground*, 152.

51   Gearheart, *Wanderground*, 111, 200, 185, respectively.

52   Gearheart, *Wanderground*, 157, 160, respectively.

53   Gearhart and Johnson, "The Gay Movement," in *Loving Women*, 65.

54   The first worship service was held in October 1968. Perry describes writing the book in 1971. I follow the book's first edition, which appeared in August 1972: Perry (with Lucas), *The Lord Is My Shepherd*.

55   Perry, *The Lord*, 78.

56   Perry, *The Lord*, 10.

57   Perry, *The Lord*, 9–11. Compare 22 on boy's semen: "some form of what I had been, and what we all have been."

58   Perry, *The Lord*, 80.

59   I follow the description in Perry, *The Lord*, 120–25.

60   Corman, "MCC/S.I.R. Co-Existence?"

61   Itkin, letter to Broshears, October 12, 1975.

62   Hansen, *The Troublemaker*, 142. The quotation following is from 147.

63 Walker, "Gay Sheep."

64 I follow the chronology in Roche, *Dignity/USA 25*, especially 1–13. I have supplemented that chronology with the recollections of some of the first members of the LA chapter, compiled by Avila and Kyger.

65 See the opening summary in Baum, "Catholic Homosexuals," 7, and the personal recollections in McNeill, *Both Feet*, 80–85.

66 The complete statement can be found inside the front covers of Gramick, Nugent, and Oddo, *Homosexual Catholics: A Primer for Discussion*. For the current version, http://www.dignityusa.org/purpose.

67 "Dignity Speaks to Bishops," in Kathleen Leopold and Thomas Orians, *Theological Pastoral Resources*, 55.

68 McNaught, "The Sad Dilemma," 76–77.

69 The three articles appeared as a short series: McNeill, "The Christian Male Homosexual." At the time, McNeill was an associate professor of philosophy at Le Moyne College. The topic was not one on which he would have been expected to write.

70 Here, as with other authors, I follow the original edition: McNeill, *The Church and the Homosexual*. See ix–xii on the book's origins and slow progress toward publication.

71 For the last three points, see McNeill, *Church*, 41, 103, 105–7, respectively.

72 McNeill, *Church*, 2.

73 McNeill, *Church*, 66.

74 McNeill, *Church*, 42: see also 55–56.

75 McNeill, *Church*, 23.

76 See, for example, McClory, "Gay Theology Pioneer Trusts 'God's Shrewdness.'"

77 Congregation for the Doctrine of the Faith, *Persona humana*, no. 4.

78 *Persona humana*, nos. 3–4.

79 *Persona humana*, no. 5.

80 *Persona humana*, no. 8.

81 *Persona humana*, no. 8.

82 *Persona humana*, no. 1.

83 *Persona humana*, no. 9.

84 For mentions of the category, see the historical review in Tobin, *Homosexuality and Marriage*, 102, 105 (*vitium homosexualitatis*), 106. Tobin tends to impose his own use of "homosexuality" across earlier decisions, which in fact speak of sodomy, sexual inversion, or pederasty. For the principle of incapacity, see Vernay, "L'homosexualité dans la jurisprudence rotale," 30–39; and Grelon, "Homosexualité et pratique judiciaire de l'Église," 12–13.

85 I mentioned in connection with Ellis the early appearance of a full range of sexological terms in the pastoral psychology of Gemelli. The term "homosexuality" occurs in English-language essays in Catholic pastoral theology at least from the 1940s on. See, for example, Moore, "The Pathogenesis and Treatment of Homosexual Disorders," and Harvey, "Homosexuality as a Pastoral Problem." Harvey's authorities include both Anomaly's *The Invert* and Cory's *Homosexual in America*. Moore has a much larger range of reference, but his tastes are decidedly medical and psychoanalytic. He argues consistently against any clear distinction between innate and circumstantial same-sex desire and denies any rational ground for decriminalization.

86 Mank, "General Conference '76."

87 See Boswell, "The Church and the Homosexual: An Historical Perspective, 1979."

88 Congregation for the Doctrine of the Faith, *Homosexualitatis problema*, no. 3.

89 *Homosexualitatis problema*, nos. 10, 17.

90 Lauritsen, "*Culpa ecclesiae*: Boswell's Dilemma," 16. This edition reprints the pages of the first edition from 1981 and then appends a bibliography of reviews (23–34). The original edition was based on papers by Warren Johansson, Wayne Dynes, and Lauritsen presented at a forum held September 14, 1980. For the more general critique of Christianity, see Lauritsen, *Religious Roots of the Taboo on Homosexuality*.

91 Evans, *Witchcraft*, 2.

CHAPTER SEVEN

1 For a sustained version of this argument, drawn primarily from the history of media representations, see Fejes, *Gay Rights and Moral Panic*, 1–2, 7, 71, 218–19.

2 For the earlier performances, see Bryant, *Mine Eyes Have Seen the Glory*, 113.

3 For the testimony, mingled increasingly with advice on how to run a family, *Mine Eyes Have Seen the Glory* (Revell, 1970), *Amazing Grace* (Revell, 1971), and *Bless This House* (Revell, 1972), which includes "a special section of family photos" by husband Bob Green. Then, with Bob as listed coauthor: *Fishers of Men* (Revell, 1973), *Light My Candle* (Revell, 1974), *Raising God's Children* (Revell, 1977). For physical fitness: *Running the Good Race* (Revell, 1976). Revell had started by publishing the sermons of Dwight L. Moody, but by the 1960s the firm was eager to secure the work of Christian celebrities. For the recipes: *Bless This Food: The Anita Bryant Family Cookbook* (Doubleday, 1975).

4 Anita Bryant, *Mine Eyes*, 24.

5 Bryant, *Mine Eyes*, 31.

6 Bryant, *Mine Eyes*, 12.

7 Bryant, *Mine Eyes*, 26, 33.

8 Bryant, *Mine Eyes*, 39.

9 Bryant, *Mine Eyes*, 43–44 for the whole scene.

10 Bryant, *Mine Eyes*, 24.

11 Bryant, *Mine Eyes*, 40.

12 Bryant, *Mine Eyes*, 59 (smoking), 65 (values), and 66 (future wife).

13 Bryant, *Mine Eyes*, 67–69.

14 Bryant, *Mine Eyes*, 115.

15 Bryant, *Mine Eyes*, 128. The events I condense here are told in detail on 118–39. By way of comparison, note that the same allotment of pages at the beginning of the book takes Anita all the way from her birth and family history to the middle of high school.

16 Bryant, *Mine Eyes*, 128–30.

17 Bryant, *Mine Eyes*, 141.

18 Fenton Johnson describes one version of this in the voiceover narration for Rosenblatt's short film, *I Just Wanted to Be Somebody*.

19 For the campaign, I use the archive of contemporary newspaper and television reports, together with the historical narratives in Fejes, *Gay Rights*, 69–151, and Clendinen and Nagourney, *Out for Good*, 291–311.

20 Television news report by Hall broadcast May 30, 1977.

21 For the later history of the national campaign, Fejes, *Gay Rights*, 153–212.

22 For a partly quantitative study of changes in the movement's rhetoric after the Bryant campaign, see Fetner, *How the Religious Right*, especially 23–43.

23 Bryant, *The Anita Bryant Story*. According to a television news report broadcast August 1, 1977, the title was originally announced as *Save Our Children: One Woman's Fight against the Sin of Homosexuality*. But the international relief organization, Save the Children, secured a preliminary injunction requiring that Anita's campaign change its name from Save Our Children to avoid confusion. The injunction applied as well to the book title.

24 Bryant, *Anita Bryant Story*, 13, 22, 34–35, 52.

25 Bryant, *Anita Bryant Story*, 32, 108; compare 18, 30.

26 Bryant, *Anita Bryant Story*, 53.

27 Bryant, *Anita Bryant Story*, 93.

28 Bryant, *Anita Bryant Story*, 95–96.

29 Bryant, *Anita Bryant Story*, 13. For other uses of the image of the "stand," 21, 24, 135.

30 Bryant, *Anita Bryant Story*, 13, 15 (truths); 22 (cries); 14–16, 55 (knowledge); 57 (groans); 16, 29, 53, 58–59, 132–33 (tears); 53–54 (agony, repulsion); 67 (filth); 53 (woman's pain).

31 Bryant, *Anita Bryant Story*, 133.

32 Bryant, *Anita Bryant Story*, 14, 16, 70.

33 The event happened on October 14, 1977, at a press conference in advance of a concert—though the line between Anita Bryant's concerts and rallies had by that time blurred. Video from the conference is widely available online, though usually in truncated form. For the basic story and an early publication of a still photograph, see the unsigned "Notes on People," *New York Times* (October 15, 1977), 16.

34 Bryant, *Anita Bryant Story*, 27, 42, 45, 67, 97.

35 Bryant, *Anita Bryant Story*, 15, 21, 22, 37, 42, 43, 47, 99.

36 War images in *Anita Bryant Story* include "battle for Miami" (21, title), battle lines (21), and Christian foot soldiers (21, 126). They are interwoven with images of social or moral crisis (e.g., 24, 26, 27, 28, 32). Anita sings the "Hymn" for Ronald Reagan and the Florida conservatives, at the Kiwanis Club debate, at rallies.

37 Bryant, *Anita Bryant Story*, 15, 55, 59 (abnormal); 26 (aberrant); 38 (deviant); 43 (abominable); 38, 51 (perverted); 52 (unnatural and ungodly); 42 (epidemic); 37 (selfish); 33, 97 (filth, disease); 25 (condemned by God across history).

38 Bryant, *Anita Bryant Story*, 35, 37, 74, 103, 124.

39 Bryant, *Anita Bryant Story*, 50, 73, 86, 103, 132, 133.

40 Television news report broadcast May 22, 1977, Wolfson Archive WC 07101, clip #13.

41 Bryant, *Anita Bryant Story*, 33, 68–69, 87.

42 For one reading, see Jordan, *Invention of Sodomy*, 45–66.

43 Bryant, *Anita Bryant Story*, 31, 33, 55, 70.

44 Bryant, *Anita Bryant Story*, 69, 73 (choice); 55 (urban enclaves); 72 (ex-gays).

45 Bryant, *Anita Bryant Story*, 114, 118; "an act of homosexuality," 67.

46 Bryant, *Anita Bryant Story*, 55, 96–97.

47 Bryant, *Anita Bryant Story*, 70.

48 Anita elsewhere refers to the MCC and to a conference at the Kirkridge center entitled "Gay and Christian" (103), but only to lump them in with non-Christian attacks on her campaign.

49 Bryant, *Anita Bryant Story*, 108, 113.

50 Bryant, *Anita Bryant Story*, 5 (dedication to Catholic archbishop), 22–24 (range of religious speakers), 44–45 (Catholic), 93 (all denominations), 121 (Mormons), 128 ("blatantly anti-God statements").

51 For Anita's description of the pamphlet, see *Anita Bryant Story*, 89–90. The boxed quotations in the pamphlet are taken from the National Gay Platform adopted at the first meeting of a "National Coalition of Gay Organizations" in Chicago during February 1972. The NGCO was a small, short-lived, and notoriously ineffective lobbying effort. It is now best known just because Save Our Children quoted its demands to smear all homosexuals—and so endowed the "agenda" with an authority it has enjoyed ever since among antihomosexual writers.

52 Television news report by Hall, broadcast June 1, 1977.

53 Television news report broadcast May 23, 1977.

54 The thirty-second television spot entitled "The Parade," released June 18, 1977, embedded in a television news report broadcast May 25, 1977.

55 Bryant, *Anita Bryant Story*, 27.

56 "Gay Rights Showdown in Miami"; compare Fejes, *Gay Rights*, 122.

57 Bryant, *Anita Bryant Story*, 69 (hunting for boys); 47, 118–19 (rape or slavery).

58 Bryant, *Anita Bryant Story*, 47, 62.

59 Fejes, *Gay Rights*, 118, quoting Geto.

60 Bryant, *Anita Bryant Story*, 17, 62 (confused and impressionable); 55 (danger of parade); 59 (influence of teacher); 114–15 (public approval, on the authority of Socarides).

61 Bryant, *Anita Bryant Story*, 118–20 (quoting an authority on lack of fixity); 35 (rebellion)

62 Bryant, *Anita Bryant Story*, 67.

63 Bryant, *Anita Bryant Story*, 93, 122; compare 15, 37, 94. Marie Griffith reminds me that this is also an allusion to a nineteenth-century hymn, with words by John H. Sammis and music by Daniel B. Towner. Something like the phrase is supposed to have been spoken by a new convert at an evangelistic crusade.

64 For these and other slogans from the 1977 Christopher Stree Parade, see O'Neal, Ginsberg, Burroughs, and Miller, *Gay Day*, 48, 49, 58, 60, 68–69, 72.

65 In one lecture series, Foucault calls this kind of power, at once laughable and lethal, "Ubu-esque," after Jarry's satiric tales of "King Ubu." See Foucault, *Les anormaux*, 7, 12.

66 "Gay Rights Showdown in Miami"; Clendinen and Nagourney, *Out for Good*, 312–16.

CHAPTER EIGHT

1   For a news report, Roeder, "Anita's Helping Hand"; for scholarly summary, Fejes, *Gay Rights*, 223, and Erzen, *Straight to Jesus*, 179–80.

2   For the history, Erzen, *Straight to Jesus*, 31–33.

3   See, for example, Ménard, *De Sodome à la Éxode*, especially 226–29.

4   See, for example, the recollections by Sylvia Pennington of her first evangelization in San Francisco's Tenderloin, *But Lord, They're Gay*.

5   The obvious case is Ralph Blair and the founding of Evangelicals Concerned. See Erzen, *Straight to Jesus*, 79–80, noting that the correct date of founding is 1975. For Blair's reaction to the first writings from Worthen's ministry, see http://www.ecinc.org/Reviews/rvwntr_1977.htm.

6   Philpott, "Interview with Brother Frank," in his *The Gay Theology*, 20–37. The anniversary account appears under at least two titles, "Born Anew to a Living Hope" and "From Being Different to Making a Difference." I follow the first text.

7   Erzen, *Straight to Jesus*, 22–23. On the celebration of his eightieth birthday in February 2009, http://www.gracerivers.com/tag/frank-worthen/.

8   Philpott, "Interview," 21; Worthen, "Born Anew," para. 2.

9   Worthen, "Born Anew," para. 1.

10   Worthen, "Born Anew," paras. 5–6.

11   Erzen, *Straight to Jesus*, 23.

12   Philpott, "Interview," 23.

13   Erzen, *Straight to Jesus*, 22.

14   Philpott, "Interview," 24.

15   Worthen, "Born Anew," paras. 7–9. Erzen records the young man's name as Matt (*Straight to Jesus*, 22).

16   Worthen, "Born Anew," paras. 10–12.

17   Philpott, "Interview," 26.

18   Philpott, "Interview," 29.

19   Philpott, "Interview," 32, 34.

20   Worthen, "Born Anew," paras. 9, 11.

21   Worthen, "Born Anew," para. 27.

22   Worthen, "Born Anew," para. 13; Erzen, *Straight to Jesus*, 23.

23   See Erzen, *Straight to Jesus*, 23. Frank paraphrases the ad in different ways. In the 1994 testimony, for example, he says: "The ad read 'Do you want out of homosexuality? Send for a Brother Frank tape on a Christ-centered way out of homosexuality'" ("Born Anew," para. 13). In 2002, he recalled that it read "Do you want out of homosexuality? . . . Send for a free tape." He claims that the "gay community" then forced the newspaper to decline any further ads. See Furges, "A Conversation with Frank Worthen."

24   On the messy circumstances of the refounding or renaming, see Erzen, *Straight to Jesus*, 39–40. The 1973 date is claimed as the founding date by the moved and reorganized Love in Action. See http://www.loveinaction.org/aboutus.

25 See Philpott, *Third Sex?* ix–x on the origins of the counseling; Philpott, *Gay Theology*, 143–94, for the newsletters. In the earlier book, Philpott thanks Frank for his "encouragement and suggestions" (v) and credits two of his tapes as sources for his remarks on counseling (182). A Love in Action newsletter from February 1976 reports that "we have a good tape on this subject by Brother Frank" (*Gay Theology*, 152).

26 Philpott, *Gay Theology*, 36.

27 Worthen, *Steps Out*, 23. For his summary of the steps, which are sometimes obscured in the book, see 136–40.

28 Remember the "Washingtonians," founded in Baltimore in 1840. They emphasized peer accountability to reinforce sudden change, and their genre was the ex-drunkard's testimony, given in public meetings devoted to the telling of these experiences. They sound very much like "New Hope Night" at Open Door church. See, for example, Arthur, "The Experience Meeting."

29 Worthen, *Steps Out*, 33.

30 Worthen, *Steps Out*, 11–14, 17, 20.

31 Worthen, *Steps Out*, 22–23, 32–33.

32 Worthen, *Steps Out*, 4, with reference to SIECUS. See also the reference to Masters and Johnson, 3.

33 For Moberly's influence on the ex-gay movement, see Erzen, *Straight to Jesus*, 145–48. Biographical data, including her academic specialties and research experience, are hard to come by.

34 Worthen, *Steps Out*, 38, quoting Moberly, *Psychogenesis*, 31, with changes in punctuation.

35 Worthen, *Steps Out*, 5.

36 Moberly, *Psychogenesis*, vii.

37 Worthen, *Steps Out*, 150–51.

38 Worthen, *Steps Out*, 2–3.

39 Davies and Rentzel, *Coming Out of Homosexuality*, 5 and 29.

40 Davies and Rentzel, *Coming Out of Homosexuality*, 17. For a later retrospect on his life, Davies, "Looking Back and Looking Forward"; for an interview explaining his retirement, LeBlanc, "Ex-Gay Sheds the Mocking Quote Marks." Bob Davies is not to be confused with the Bob interviewed by Philpott who started the LIA newsletter in 1975. For this confusion, Erzen, *Straight to Jesus*, 36.

41 Davies and Rentzel, *Coming Out*, 15.

42 Davies and Rentzel, *Coming Out*, 22.

43 Davies and Rentzel, *Coming Out*, 15.

44 For example, Davies and Rentzel, *Coming Out*, 84–85, with regard to the repression of fantasies.

45 Davies and Rentzel, *Coming Out*, 96–97.

46 Davies and Rentzel, *Coming Out*, 15 and 27.

47 Davies and Rentzel, *Coming Out*, 159.

48 Davies and Rentzel, *Coming Out*, 27.

49 Davies and Rentzel, *Coming Out*, 29.

50 Davies and Rentzel, *Coming Out*, 102, 63, respectively.

51   Davies and Rentzel, *Coming Out*, 58.

52   Davies and Rentzel, *Coming Out*, 36.

53   Davies and Rentzel, *Coming Out*, 18, 101 (on passivity); 30–34 (on surrender, yielding, submission).

54   Davies and Rentzel, *Coming Out*, 35.

55   Davies and Rentzel, *Coming Out*, 68.

56   Davies and Rentzel, *Coming Out*, 157 (Christian sex manual), 101 (sports page).

57   Davies and Rentzel, *Coming Out*, 161.

58   For a single, but telling example, Davies and Rentzel, *Coming Out*, 105.

59   Erzen, *Straight to Jesus*, 205–15.

60   LaHaye, *The Unhappy Gays*, 7–8.

61   For "Dr. C. A. Tripp" and his *Homosexual Matrix*, LaHaye, *The Unhappy Gays*, 63, 80, 82, 90, and so on, with footnotes. There is no sign that LaHaye understood the points of Tripp's argument.

62   LaHaye, *The Unhappy Gays*, 66 (Hippocrates), 71 (Bieber), 75 (Bieber acclaimed).

63   LaHaye, *The Unhappy Gays*, 121.

64   LaHaye, *The Unhappy Gays*, 34, 72, 77, and especially 140–41.

65   LaHaye, *The Unhappy Gays*, 97.

66   LaHaye, *The Unhappy Gays*, 74–75.

67   LaHaye, *The Unhappy Gays*, 117.

68   On the need to get out of an ex-gay group as quickly as possible, LaHaye, *The Unhappy Gays*, 134–35. Note, however, that he then urges ex-gays to give their testimony of healing only to other ex-gays (140).

69   LaHaye, *The Unhappy Gays*, 194. Although he implies that these headlines come from "my files," a number of the items are exactly those cited by Bryant and reproduced in the Save Our Children pamphlet. LaHaye also adopts Bryant's image of recruitment, elaborating it in detail, 93–94.

70   LaHaye, *The Unhappy Gays*, 152.

71   LaHaye, *The Unhappy Gays*, 128.

72   LaHaye, *The Unhappy Gays*, 204. Here LaHaye calls his exegesis of Daniel 11:37 "highly speculative." (It is also a gross misreading of a faulty English translation, but that is rather beside the point in dealing with LaHaye.) By the time LaHaye gets to the Left Behind series, the anti-Christ, Nicolae Carpathia, is produced by artificial insemination using the DNA of two male lovers, Sorin Carpathia and Baduna Marius. We will have to wait until the end times before deciding whether that is also "highly speculative."

73   LaHaye, *The Unhappy Gays*, 206.

CHAPTER NINE

1   Shilts, *And the Band Played On*, 171. I recognize the melodramatic staging of Shilts's account and the many historical objections that have been raised against it. I use it as the reminder of an influential chronology.

2   Shilts, *And the Band Played On*, 171.

3   Center for Disease Control, "Current Trends."

4 The notion of the jeremiad figures regularly in analyses of the Religious Right. See, for example, Harding, *The Book of Jerry Falwell*, 153–82, especially 161–62. With Harding, I like to keep in mind the precise Christian origins. But I also like to watch the dissemination of the religious genre outside of what we conceive as churches.

5 Kramer, "1,112 and Counting," 33. I follow the pagination in *Reports from the Holocaust*.

6 Kramer, "1,112 and Counting," 42.

7 Kramer, "1,112 and Counting," 46.

8 Falwell, *Listen, America!* 181, italics added.

9 Falwell, *Listen, America!* 182–83.

10 Falwell, *Listen, America!* 185.

11 Falwell, *Listen, America!* 183 (sin-sick),186 (love/hate).

12 Gross, "Falwell Says Government Must Control Homosexuals," and Gross, "Falwell Wants Attack on 'Gay Plague.'"

13 Ziegler, "Falwell Urges Action on AIDS."

14 Shilts, *And the Band Played On*, 347–48.

15 Jerry Falwell, "AIDS: The Judgment of God," as quoted in Mills, "Fear and Passion," 169. This and the other papers in the volume were originally read in 1988 at the national meeting of the American Academy of Religion.

16 Harding, *The Book of Jerry Falwell*, 160.

17 Kramer, "1,112 and Counting," 40. The references to lepers are on 35 and 38.

18 Kramer, "1,112 and Counting," 46.

19 Unsigned wire story, "Lincoln Rejects Gay Rights Measure." Cameron's claim about a bathroom assault on a four-year-old boy was contradicted by local newspapers within a few days. It drew an editorial rebuke from one of them. See the summary in Brown and Cole, letter to the editor, 413.

20 Bognar, "Media Promotes Bigoted Psych."

21 Flanery, "Lincoln Man: Poll Will Help Oppose Gays."

22 Cameron, Proctor, Coburn, and Forde, "Sexual Orientation and Sexually Transmitted Disease."

23 According to the program posted on PR Newswire, July 9, 1984.

24 Daniel, "The Sideshow at a Conservatives' Convention."

25 Cameron presents his numerical claims in many different formats, supplementing his own 1983 survey with other sources. I follow the version printed as an appendix in Cameron, *Exposing the AIDS Scandal*, 148–60. The quotations that follow are from 149, 150 (three times), 151 (three times) respectively. Most of the claims I quote are not referenced to any study, but those that are go back to Cameron's original publication of his 1983 survey findings.

26 Cameron, *Exposing*, 154.

27 Cameron, *Exposing*, 156, 159–60.

28 Cameron, *Exposing*, 132, 136, 142–43, respectively.

29 Brown and Cole, letter to the editor.

30 The *Scofield Reference Bible*, principally edited by Cyrus I. Scofield, was first published by Oxford University Press in 1909. There are innumerable editions, some with lavish illustrations and fanciful covers. My experience in the college classroom is that readers frequently confuse the biblical texts with Scofield's annotations. I suspect that this is a habit carried from church or home.

31   Noebel, Lutton, and Cameron, *Special Report: AIDS*. The self-description is given on the inside of the back cover. An order form in the book lists many of Cameron's other titles, including several versions of his survey results. He is also quoted as an authority throughout the *Special Report*.

32   Cameron, *Exposing*, 12.

33   Cameron, *Exposing*, 146–47.

34   For a collection of statements, see Melton, *The Church Speaks—on AIDS*. For a survey both of statements and of denominational attitudes, see National Research Council, *The Social Impact of AIDS*, 129–57.

35   See, for example, Mark R. Kowalewski, "Religious Constructions of the AIDS Crisis," *Sociological Analysis* 51, no. 1 (1990): 91–96. Kowalewski wrote with much more detail about Catholic responses in his *All Things to All People*.

36   Congregation for the Doctrine of the Faith, *Homosexualitatis problema*, no. 9, where gay advocates remain heedless even though "the practice of homosexuality may threaten the lives and well-being of a large number of people." Other, less authoritative Catholic groups and agencies issued from early on much more compassionate and helpful statements. See, for example, Melton, *The Church Speaks*, 2–8.

37   Southern Baptist Convention, "Resolution on AIDS"; compare Melton, *The Church Speaks*, 129–30. Melton comments that the statement avoids endorsing the notion of divine condemnation. To my eyes, it certainly implies it.

38   "AIDS and the Healing Ministry of the Church," in Melton, *The Church Speaks*, 148–51, here at 148 and 149.

39   With slight changes, this is still the current language of the Social Principles, sect. 161F, as in the *Book of Discipline of the United Methodist Church*, 103–4.

40   "Resolution on Acquired Immune Deficiency Syndrome," as in Melton, *The Church Speaks*, 139–40, here at 139, italics added.

41   "A Pronouncement: Health and Wholeness in the Midst of a Pandemic," as in Melton, *The Church Speaks*, 140–45, here at 142.

42   Melton, *The Church Speaks*, 143–44.

43   Excerpted in Melton, *The Church Speaks*, 82–86.

44   Melton, *The Church Speaks*, 83.

45   For example, LaHaye, *The Unhappy Gays*, 23–25.

46   This was noticed by some of the earliest religious writers on AIDS. See Kowalewski, "The AIDS Crisis," 147.

47   Amos, *When AIDS*, 28, 48–49.

48   Amos, *When AIDS*, 71–74.

49   Fortunato, *AIDS*, 69–71.

50   Russell, *The Church with AIDS*, 7–9.

51   Ingram-Ward, "Space," 69–71.

52   Ingram-Ward, "Space," 75, 78.

53   Parts of the Russell volume document the lives of those struggling with AIDS (Russell-Coons, "John," Clarkson) or models and resources for pastoral response

244 NOTES TO PAGES 182-187

(Kittredge and Mitulski, Clarkson). The exegetical and constructive essays by Davies, Suchoki, Schreiter, and Russell show clearly the reversed perspective.

54 John, "A Journey toward Freedom," 64.

55 For a printed description, Ruskin, *The Quilt*, 137–44.

56 For printed versions of the history, see the essays by Sr. Dana Van Iquity and Sr. Missionary P. DeLight in Leyland, *Out in the Castro,* 213–18 and 201–9, respectively. For the online version at the official website, www.thesisters.org/sistory.html. I also rely on conversations with Sr. SOAMI, formerly Sr. Missionary P. Delight, one of the founding members.

57 Einstein, "Thousands Turn Out Coast to Coast."

58 Cover photograph, *Newsweek*, August 8, 1983.

59 The single, accordion-folded sheet produced in 1982 is substantially different from the version available online at http://thesisters.org/playfair.html. I follow the original: *Play Fair!* (San Francisco: Sisters of Perpetual Indulgence, 1982), one glossy sheet folded into six panels, recto and verso.

60 Crimp and Rolston, *AIDS Demographics*, 14–15.

61 Crimp and Rolston, *AIDS*, 34–35. For one recollection of its impact, see the interview with Wolfe by Sommella, "This Is about People Dying," 412–14.

62 On appropriations of the triangle in America during the 1970s, see Jensen, "The Pink Triangle," 328–30.

63 There are many other resonances in this slogan. For some of them, see Patton, *Inventing AIDS*, 126–31.

64 Crimp and Rolston, *AIDS*, 30, with the caption on 31. The poster puts "Center" in the singular.

65 For descriptions of the installation and its origin, Crimp, "AIDS: Cultural Analysis/Cultural Activism," 32–37; Deitcher, "Gran Fury," 221-22, 231; Meyer, *Outlaw Representation*, 224–26.

66 U.S. Catholic Conference, "The Many Faces of AIDS: A Gospel Response," published December 7, 1987, as in Melton, *The Church Speaks*, 21–33, here at 27. There is also an online version at http://www.usccb.org/sdwp/international/mfa87.shtml.

67 John O'Connor, "Response to 'The Many Faces of Aids: A Gospel Response,'" as in Melton, *The Church Speaks*, 33.

68 Joseph Ratzinger, letter of May 29, 1988, to Pio Laghi, pro-nuncio to the United States, but released to the head of the National Conference of Catholic Bishops, as in Melton, *The Church Speaks*, 34–35.

69 For a brief summary, Smith, *AIDS, Gays, and the American Catholic Church*, 1–4.

70 David Wojnarowicz, "Post Cards from America," 7. A slightly different version is republished by Wojnarowicz in his *Close to the Knives*, 111–23. Wojnarowicz repeats the images in the block of black text that overlays a collage of screened, grayish photographs taken of the corpse of his friend Peter Hujar, "Untitled (Hujar Dead)," 1988–89, in *Fever*, nos. 51, 60. This text is also incorporated into the 1990 lectures entitled "Do Not Doubt the Dangerousness of the 12-Inch-Tall Politician," in Wojnarowicz, *Close to the Knives*, 138–62, here at 160–62.

71 Honan, "Arts Endowment Withdraws Grant for AIDS Show." For the action and some reactions, Meyer, *Outlaw Representation*, 244–47.

72 Crimp and Rolston, *AIDS*, 132, with the caption on 133.

73 Crimp and Rolston, *AIDS*, 135, with the caption on 134.

74 They appear, among other places, in Hilferty's film *Stop the Church*. Some of them, but by no means all, are archived at the New York Public Library's digital image site, http://digitalgallery.nypl.org/nypldigital/.

75 I follow the account in Crimp and Rolston, *AIDS*, 136–40. Both of them participated in the action.

76 See the interview of Vincent Gagliostro by Schulman, 51–58.

77 "The Storming of St. Pat's," *New York Times*, December 12, 1989, A24.

78 I should make clear, if it is not clear in what I write, that I do believe that consecrated bread and wine are "really" the body and blood of Jesus. To that extent, I share the faith of the offended worshipers. But I do not believe that the elements circumscribe Jesus or that Jesus meant them to be more important than the bodies for which he handed himself over.

79 Wojnarowicz in *Witnesses*, 11.

80 Footage of some of the funerals is archived online at http://www.actupny.org/nypl/wentzy.html and http://www.actupny.org/divatv/netcasts/index.html.

81 Wojnarowicz in *Witnesses*, 11.

82 White and Cunningham, *Ryan White*, 16, 38.

83 White and Cunningham, *Ryan White*, 70. Compare 79, 172, 177 (regular, just like everyone else), 178, 186 (ordinary), 193 (fitting in somewhere), 193, 194 (looking normal).

84 White and Cunningham, *Ryan White*, 76.

85 White and Cunningham, *Ryan White*, 104–5, 125.

86 White and Cunningham, *Ryan White*, 211.

87 White and Cunningham, *Ryan White*, 139.

88 White and Cunningham, *Ryan White*, 142.

89 White and Cunningham, *Ryan White*, 92.

90 White and Cunningham, *Ryan White*, 116.

91 White and Cunningham, *Ryan White*, 4. Compare the letters addressed to the "Boy with AIDS," 159.

92 White and Cunningham, *Ryan White*, 173.

93 White and Cunningham, *Ryan White*, 213.

CHAPTER TEN

1 Two passages in which there might be reference to young men in homoerotic situations are sometimes mentioned in longer discussions. The first is the story in Matthew 8:5–13 of the centurion and his *pais* (servant or male lover), the other is the "naked young man" of Mark 14:50–52, which is sometimes linked to the controversy about an alternate version of that Gospel, Morton Smith's "Secret Gospel of Mark." For recent commentary on these pages, see, for example, Jennings, *The Man Jesus Loved*, 109–25

(for Mark) and 132–37, 141–44 (for Matthew). But since these passages are not used in support of condemnation, they do not figure in most debates.

2   Exodus International, *Do I Have To Be . . . ?* 10.

3   The clearest example is Gagnon, *The Bible and Homosexual Practice*, where the exegesis is subordinated to a view of "homosexual practice" derived from "scientific studies" promoted by the Religious Right, "psychological claims" about gay men as "sissies," and the conclusions of ex-gay ministries (respectively and as examples, 396n83, 408n113, 423n139). The principal scientific authority is Joseph Satinover (see especially 471–73).

4   Exodus International, *Do I Have to Be . . . ?* 4–5.

5   For example, Haley, *101 Frequently Asked Questions*, which mixes Bible verses and quotations from prominent evangelists with repeated references to the authoritative work of Joseph Nicolosi and other friendly psychotherapists.

6   See, again, Northcote, *Christianity and Sex Problems*, second edition, 294–95.

7   Hanckel and Cunningham, *A Way of Love*, 15-16.

8   For example, Hanckel and Cunningham, *A Way of Love*, 60 (photograph of two MCC ministers in liturgical garb), 183 (address for information about religious groups).

9   See, for early examples, Heron, *One Teenager in Ten*, especially 29–32, 42–48, 77–78, but compare (for more positive representations) 17, 65–66, 95; Fairchild and Hayward, *Now That You Know*, chapter 7.

10   *Tales of the Closet*, no. 2, page 12.

11   Roesler and Deisher, "Youthful Male Homosexuality" (1972). Savin-Williams singles this out as the "first empirical study of gay adolescence." That claim becomes plausible only with a contentious understanding of "empirical," about which more in a moment. See Savin-Williams, *The New Gay Teenager*, 53.

12   For the first version, Cass, "Homosexual Identity Formation."

13   Brady and Busse, "The Gay Identity Questionnaire."

14   Smith with Denton, *Soul-Searching*, especially 223–24. It is striking that the index contains no entries for homosexuality, gay, and lesbian. That omission is borne out in the rest of the book, where every specific mention of sexual activity that I can find is heterosexual.

15   Kulkin, Chauvin, and Percle, "Suicide among Gay and Lesbian Adolescents and Young Adults," 10.

16   Waldner-Haugrud and Magruder, "Homosexuality Identity Expression among Lesbian and Gay Adolescents," at 318. The quotations following are from 318 and 321, respectively.

17   See, for one example, the "Ex-Gay Declaration of Independence" at the site of Parents and Friends of ExGays and Gays, www.pfox.org/Ex-Gay_Declaration_of_Independence.html.

18   The exact numbers are 202 interviews, 147 male, 55 female, between the ages of fourteen and twenty. See Herdt and Boxer, *Children of Horizons*, xiii–xiv. For the early history of the youth group, 76–80.

19   Herdt and Boxer, *Children of Horizons*, xvi, xiv.

20   Herdt and Boxer, *Children of Horizons*, 4, 9, passim.

21   Herdt and Boxer, *Children of Horizons*, 13. Compare 102 ("sacred symbols—myth and ritual"), 108–9 ("sacred zone"), 109–12 (ritual and magical thinking), 112 ("sacred inner world"), and so on.

22   Herdt and Boxer, *Children of Horizons*, 14, italics in original.

23   Herdt and Boxer, *Children of Horizons*, 21.

24   See, for example, Corbett, "Homosexual Boyhood," 109–10, and, most famously, Eve Kosofsky Sedgwick, "How to Bring Your Kid Up Gay: The War on Effeminate Boys," in *Tendencies*, 154–64.

25   I here reprise, but also develop notions from Jordan, *Blessing Same-Sex Unions*, 151–55.

26   I follow common usage in applying this title to the whole curriculum, including both the components for sex education and for religious formation. Technically, OWL applies only to the former, which was published separately from the religious curriculum for reasons that will become clear.

27   A first committee surveyed denominational needs for such a curriculum from 1991 through 1993. Then the Sexuality Education Task Force Core Committee produced the curriculum from 1994 through 2000. There are a number of other educational or outreach projects by the UAA that would have to be included in any complete history, which this is not. See, for example, "A Welcoming Religious Education Library," on the national website at www.uua.org/obgltc/resource/wrebibc.html.

28   Goldfarb, Casparian, and Frediani, *Our Whole Lives*, 95.

29   Goldfarb, Casparian, and Frediani, *Our Whole Lives*, 99.

30   Goldfarb, Casparian, and Frediani, *Our Whole Lives*, 100–102, for these and the following quotations from the "mini-lecture."

31   Goldfarb, Casparian, and Frediani, *Our Whole Lives* , 109, for this and the following quotation.

32   Morriss, Agate, Gibb, Bassham, and Svoboda, with Frediani, *Sexuality and Our Faith*, 51–55 (UUA) and 147–54 (UCC).

WORKS CITED

The following abbreviations are used for some archival material. "GLBTHS" is the GLBT Historical Society, San Francisco; "OHP" refers to the transcriptions in its Oral History Project. "ONE Archives" is the ONE National Gay and Lesbian Archives, Los Angeles. "Wolfson" is the Lynn and Louis Wolfson II Florida Moving Image Archive, Miami-Dade Public Library, Miami.

Abelove, Henry. *Deep Gossip*. Minneapolis: University of Minnesota Press, 2003.
"A Bold Study by the Church of England." *ONE: The Homosexual Magazine* 2, no. 6 (June 1954): 17–18.
Alfred, Randy. Interview by Roland Schembari. July and November 1998. GLBTHS OHP #98-031.
Amory, Richard. *Song of the Loon: A Gay Pastoral in Five Books and an Interlude*. San Diego: Greenleaf Classics, 1966.
Amos, Jr., William E. *When AIDS Comes to Church*. Philadelphia: Westminster Press, 1988.
Anomaly. *The Invert and His Social Adjustment*. London: Baillière, Tindall, and Cox, 1927. Reprinted Baltimore: Williams and Wilkins, 1929.
Anson, Peter F. *Bishops at Large*. London: Faber and Faber, 1964.
Arthur, T. S. "The Experience Meeting." In *Drunkard's Progress: Narratives of Addiction, Despair, and Recovery*, edited by John W. Crowley, 30–58. Baltimore; Johns Hopkins University Press, 1999.
Avila, Armand, and Jim Kyger. Personal letter of February 22, 1999, with a draft of reflections on the early history of Dignity compiled in 1998.
Bagby, Dyana. "Tennessee Teen Blogs about Forced Trip to Ex-Gay Camp." *Southern Voice*, June 17, 2005.
Bailey, Derrick Sherwin. *Homosexuality and the Western Christian Tradition*. London: Longmans, Green, 1955.
———. "Love and Marriage." *Theology* 44, no. 262 (April 1942): 202–10; and *Theology* 44, no. 263 (May 1942): 275–82.
———. "The Problem of Sexual Inversion." *Theology* 55, no. 380 (February 1952): 47–52.

————, ed. *Sexual Offenders and Social Punishment*. Westminster: Church Information Board, 1956.

————. *Thomas Becon and the Reformation of the Church in England*. Edinburgh: Oliver and Boyd, 1952.

Barton, Bruce. *A Young Man's Jesus*. Boston: Pilgrim Press, 1914.

Baum, Gregory. "Catholic Homosexuals." *Commonweal* 99, no. 19 (1974): 479–82. Reprinted in *Theological Pastoral Resources*, edited by Leopold and Orians, 7–10.

Bergler, Edmund. *Homosexuality: Disease or Way of Life?* New York: Hill and Wang, 1956.

Bergler, Edmund, and William S. Kroger. *Kinsey's Myth of Female Sexuality: The Medical Facts*. New York: Grune and Stratton, 1954.

Bess, Donovan. "Angry Ministers Rip Police." *San Francisco Chronicle*, September 25, 1965, 1, 4.

Bognar, Carl. "Media Promotes Bigoted Psych." *Body Politic*, no. 47 (October 1978): 13.

Boswell, John E. "The Church and the Homosexual: An Historical Perspective, 1979." http://www.dignitysd.org/Archives/Speeches/john_boswell.htm.

————. *Same-Sex Unions in Premodern Europe*. New York: Villard Books, 1994.

Boyd, Nan Alamilla. *Wide Open Town: A History of Queer San Francisco to 1965*. Berkeley: University of California Press, 2003.

Brady, Stephen, and Wilma J. Busse. "The Gay Identity Questionnaire: A Brief Measure of Homosexual Identity Formation." *Journal of Homosexuality* 26 (1994): 1–22.

Bray, Alan. *The Friend*. Chicago: University of Chicago Press, 2003.

Brody, David. "Memphis Group under Fire for Trying to Transform Gays." Originally posted July 13, 2005, at http://www.cbn.com/cbnnews/news/050713aspx, but no longer available on the CBN News website. An archived version is available at www.archive.org.

Brown, Forman. *Better Angel*. Introduction by Hubert Kennedy, epilogue by Brown. Rev. ed., Boston: Alyson, 1995.

Brown, Robert D., and James K. Cole. Letter to the editor, dated September 27, 1985. *Nebraska Medical Journal* 70 (1985): 410–14.

Bryant, Anita. *The Anita Bryant Story: The Survival of Our Nation's Families and the Threat of Militant Homosexuality*. Old Tappan, NJ: Fleming H. Revell, 1977.

————. *Mine Eyes Have Seen the Glory*. Old Tappan, NJ: Fleming H. Revell, 1970.

Burkhart, Roy A. "The Church Can Answer the Kinsey Report." *Christian Century* 65 (September 15, 1948): 942–43.

Burns, Ken. "The Homosexual Faces a Challenge." In Ridinger, *Speaking for Our Lives*, 45–51.

Cameron, Paul. *Exposing the AIDS Scandal*. Lafayette, LA: Huntington House, 1988.

Cameron, Paul, Kay Proctor, William Coburn, Jr., and Nels Forde. "Sexual Orientation and Sexually Transmitted Disease." *Nebraska Medical Journal* 70 (August 1985): 292–99.

Carey, Jonathan Sinclair. "D. S. Bailey and 'the Name Forbidden among Christians.'" *Anglican Theological Review* 70 (April 1988): 152–73.

Carpenter, Edward. *The Intermediate Sex: A Study of Some Transitional Types of Men and Women*. London: S. Sonnenschein, 1908. A first American edition was published in New York in 1912.

———. *Love's Coming of Age: A Series of Papers on the Relations of the Sexes*. Manchester: Labour Press, 1896. The first American editions were published in Chicago shortly after 1900.

Carter, David. *Stonewall: The Riots That Sparked the Gay Revolution*. New York: St. Martin's, 2004.

Cass, Vivienne. "Homosexual Identity Formation: A Theoretical Model." *Journal of Homosexuality* 4 (1979): 219–35.

Castillo, Charles. *Outlaw: The Lives and Careers of John Rechy*. Los Angeles: Advocate Books, 2002.

Center for Disease Control. "Current Trends Prevention of Acquired Immune Deficiency Syndrome (AIDS): Report of Inter-Agency Recommendations." *Morbidity and Mortality Weekly Review* 32, no. 8 (March 4, 1983): 101–3.

Chadwick, Joanne. Interview by Paul Gabriel. April 6, 1998. GLBTHS OHP.

Chauncey, George. "From Sexual Inversion to Homosexuality: Medicine and the Changing Conception of Female Deviance." *Salmagundi* 58–59 (Fall 1982/Winter 1983): 114–46. Reprinted with a postscript in *Passion and Power: Sexuality in History*, edited by Kathy Peiss and Christina Simmons, with Robert A. Padgug, 87–117. Philadelphia: Temple University Press, 1989.

"Church Inquiry into Vice: 'Committee of Experts.'" *Times*, November 17, 1953, 5.

Church of England, Lambeth Conference. *Encyclical Letter from the Bishops with Resolutions and Reports*. London: SPCK, and New York: Macmillan, 1930.

Church of England, Moral Welfare Council. *The Problem of Homosexuality: An Interim Report*. London: Church Information Board, 1954.

Clement, Robert. Interview by J. Gordon Melton. August 18, 2007. Archived online at www.LGBTRAN.org.

Clendinen, Dudley, and Adam Nagourney. *Out for Good: The Struggle to Build a Gay Rights Movement in America*. New York: Simon and Schuster, 1999.

Cobb, Michael. *God Hates Fags: The Rhetorics of Religious Violence*. New York: NYU, 2006.

Conant, Robert Warren. *The Manly Christ: A New View*. Chicago: self-published, 1904.

———. *The Virility of Christ: A New View: A Book for Men*. Chicago: self-published, 1915.

Congregation for the Doctrine of the Faith. *Homosexualitatis problema* [Letter on the Pastoral Care of Homosexual Persons, October 1, 1986]. *Acta Apostolicae Sedis* 79 (1987): 543–54.

———. *Persona humana* [Declaration on Certain Questions Pertaining to Sexual Ethics, December 29, 1975]. *Acta Apostolicae Sedis* 68 (1976): 77–96.

"Consultation on Theology and the Homosexual, August 22–24, 1966." GLBTHS #93-13, Lyon-Martin papers, box 17, folder 11.

Corbett, Ken. "Homosexual Boyhood: Notes on Girlyboys." In *Sissies and Tomboys: Gender Nonconformity and Homosexual Childhood*, edited by Matthew Rottneck, 107–39. New York: NYU Press, 1999.

Corman, Julian. "MCC/S.I.R. Co-Existence?" *Vector* 7, no. 4 (April 1971): 34.

Cory, Donald Webster [Edward Sagarin]. "Address to the International Committee for Sexual Equality." In Ridinger, *Speaking for Our Lives*, 31–40.

———. *The Homosexual in America: A Subjective Approach*. New York: Greenberg, 1951.

Council on Religion and the Homosexual. *Churchmen Speak Out on Homosexual Law Reform*. San Francisco: CRH, 1967.

Crimp, Douglas. "AIDS: Cultural Analysis/Cultural Activism." *October*, no. 43 (Winter 1987): 3–16. I follow the "slightly adapted version" published in Crimp, *Melancholia and Moralism: Essays on AIDS and Queer Politics* (Cambridge, MA: MIT Press, 2002), 27–41.

Crimp, Douglas, and Adam Rolston. *AIDS Demographics*. Seattle: Bay Press, 1990.

Cromey, Robert. Interview by Paul Gabriel. August 7, 1997. GLBTHS OHP #97-027.

———. "Ministry to the Homosexual." Reprinted as an undated single sheet by Society for Individual Rights (San Francisco) from *Living Church* (January 8, 1967).

Daniel, Leon. "The Sideshow at a Conservatives' Convention." United Press International, March 1, 1985.

Daniel, Marc. Review of *ONE Institute Quarterly: Homophile Studies*. *ONE: The Homosexual Magazine* 8, no. 5 (May 1960): 5–11. Translated by T. M. Merritt from *Arcadie* (January 1960).

Daniels, E. J. *I Accuse Kinsey*. Orlando: Christ for the World, 1954.

Davies, Bob. "Looking Back and Looking Forward." http://exodus.to/content/view/558/149/.

Davies, Bob, and Lori Rentzel. *Coming Out of Homosexuality: New Freedom for Men and Women*. Downers Grove, IL: Intervarsity Press, 1993.

D'Emilio, John. *Sexual Politics, Sexual Communities: The Making of a Homosexual Minority in the United States, 1940–1970*. Chicago: University of Chicago Press, 1983.

Deitcher, David. "Gran Fury: An Interview." In *AIDS Riot: Collectifs d'artistes face au Sida / Activist Collectives against AIDS, New York, 1987-1994*, edited by the 12ᵉ Session de l'École du Magasin, 221-231. Grenoble: Magasin, 2003.

Deutsch, Albert, ed. *Sex Habits of American Men*. New York: Prentice-Hall, 1948.

Devlin, Patrick. *The Enforcement of Morals*. Maccabaean Lecture in Jurisprudence. London: Oxford University Press/British Academy, 1959.

"Dignity Speaks to Bishops." In Leopold and Orians, *Theological Pastoral Resources*, 55.

Donaldson, Herb. Interview by Paul Gabriel. September 2, 1996. GLBTHS OHP #02-167.

Dorian Book Service. "Supplement A-1960 to 1960 Catalog." *Dorian Book Quarterly*, no. 2 (1960): 25.

Dowell, Graham. "The Church and Homosexuals." *Theology* 55, no. 379 (January 1952): 28–29.

Duberman, Martin. *Left Out: The Politics of Exclusion, Essays, 1964–1999*. New York: Basic Books, 1999.

Durham, Lewis. Interview by Paul Gabriel. July 18, 1998. GLBTHS OHP.

Duvall, Evelyn Millis. *Facts of Life and Love for Teenagers*. With sketches by Ruth Belew. New York: Association Press, 1950.

Duvall, Evelyn Millis, and Sylvanus M. Duvall, eds. *Sex Ways—in Fact and Faith: Bases for Christian Family Policy*. New York: Association Press, 1961.

Duvert, Tony. *Good Sex Illustrated*. Translated by Bruce Benderson. Los Angeles: Semiotext(e), 2007.

Einstein, David. "Thousands Turn Out Coast to Coast." Associated Press, June 28, 1981.

Ellis, Havelock, and John Addington Symonds. *Studies in the Psychology of Sex.* Vol. 2, *Sexual Inversion.* London: Wilson and MacMillan, 1897.

Erzen, Tanya. *Straight to Jesus: Sexual and Christian Conversions in the Ex-Gay Movement.* Berkeley: University of California Press, 2006.

Evans, Arthur. *Witchcraft and the Gay Counterculture.* Boston: Fag Rag Books, 1978.

Exodus International. *Do I Have To Be . . . ? The Truth about God, Sexuality, and Change.* Orlando: Exodus International, n.d.

Fagley, Richard M. *The Population Explosion and Christian Responsibility.* New York: Oxford University Press, 1960.

Fairchild, Betty, and Nancy Hayward. *Now That You Know: What Every Parent Should Know about Homosexuality.* New York: Harcourt, Brace, Jovanovich, 1979.

Falwell, Jerry. *Listen, America!* Garden City, NY: Doubleday, 1980.

Fejes, Fred. *Gay Rights and Moral Panic: The Origins of America's Debate on Homosexuality.* New York: Palgrave/Macmillan, 2008.

Féray, Jean-Claude, and Manfred Herzer. "Homosexual Studies and Politics in the 19th Century: Karl Maria Kertbeny." Translated by Glen W. Peppel. *Journal of Homosexuality* 19 (1990): 23–47.

Fetner, Tina. *How the Religious Right Shaped Lesbian and Gay Activism.* Minneapolis: University of Minnesota Press, 2008.

Flanery, James Allen. "Lincoln Man: Poll Will Help Oppose Gays." *Omaha World-Herald,* May 23, 1983.

Fletcher, Joseph Francis. Review of Deutsch, *Sex Habits of American Men. Journal of Pastoral Care* 2, no. 1 (Spring 1948): 47.

Focus on the Family. Third Family Forum. Program posted on PR Newswire, July 9, 1984.

Fortunato, John E. *AIDS: The Spiritual Dilemma.* San Francisco: Harper & Row, 1987.

Foucault, Michel. *Les anormaux: Cours au Collège de France (1974–1975).* Edited by Valerio Marchetti and Antonella Salomoni under the direction of François Ewald and Alessandro Fontana. Paris: Seuil/Gallimard, 1999.

———. *L'archéologie du savoir.* Paris: NRF/Gallimard, 1969.

———. *Histoire de la sexualité.* Vol. 1, *La volonté de savoir.* Paris: NRF/Gallimard, 1976.

———. "La vie des hommes infâmes." In *Dits et écrits, 1954–1988,* vol. 3: *1976–1978,* edited by Daniel Defert and François Ewald, with Jacques Lagrange, 237–53. Paris: NRF/Gallimard, 1994.

Furges, Bradley. "A Conversation with Frank Worthen" (dated October 1, 2002). http://www.purelifeministries.org/index.cfm?pageid=162&articleid=196.

"Gab 'n' Java: August 28, 1964" [notes to guide public discussion]. GLBTHS #93-13, Lyon-Martin papers, box 17, folder 14.

Gagliostro, Vincent. Interview by Sarah Schulman. July 8, 2005. ACT UP Oral History Project, Interview #064. http://www.actuporalhistory.org/interviews/interviews_11.html#gagliostro.

Gagnon, Robert A. *The Bible and Homosexual Practice: Texts and Hermeneutics.* Nashville: Abingdon Press, 2001.

Gallo, Marcia M. *Different Daughters: A History of the Daughters of Bilitis and the Rise of the Lesbian Rights Movement.* New York: Carroll & Graf, 2006.

Garde, Noel I. "Homosexuals *DO* have a Place in the Church." *Dorian Book Quarterly*, no. 2 (1960): 6–7.

"Gay Rights Showdown in Miami." *Time*, June 13, 1977.

Gearhart, Sally Miller. "The Lesbian and God-the-Father: All the Church Needs Is a Good Lay—on Its Side." http://lgbtran.org/Exhibits/Sampler/View.aspx?ID=LAG&Page=1.

———. *Wanderground: Stories of the Hill Women.* Watertown, MA: Persephone Press, 1978. Reprinted Denver: Spinsters Ink Books, 2002.

Gearhart, Sally Miller, and William R. Johnson. *Loving Women/Loving Men.* San Francisco: Glide, 1974.

Geddes, Donald Porter. *About the Kinsey Report: Observations by Eleven Experts on "Sexual Behavior in the Human Male."* New York: New American Library, 1948.

———. *An Analysis of the Kinsey Reports on Sexual Behavior in the Human Male and Female.* New York: Dutton, 1954.

Gemelli, Augustino. *Non moechaberis: Disquisitiones medicae in usum confessariorum.* 6th ed. Translated from Italian by Giuseppe Biagioli. Milan: Società Editrice "Vita e pensiero," 1923.

Genilo, Eric Marcelo. *John Cuthbert Ford, SJ: Moral Theologian at the End of the Manualist Era.* Washington, DC: Georgetown University Press, 2007.

Genné, Elizabeth Steel, and William Henry Genné, eds. *Foundations for Christian Family Policy: The Proceedings of the North American Conference on Church and Family (April 30–May 5, 1961).* New York: Department of Family Life, National Council of the Churches of Christ in the U.S.A., 1961.

Gigl, John. "The *Vector* Reader." *Vector* 7, no. 4 (April 1971): 12–13, 36–37.

Giles, James R. "An Interview with John Rechy." *Chicago Review* 25, no. 1 (Summer 1973): 19–31.

Goldfarb, Eva S., and Elizabeth M. Casparian, with Judith A. Frediani. *Our Whole Lives: Sexuality Education for Grades 10–12.* Boston: Unitarian Universalist Association and United Church Board for Homeland Ministries, 2000.

Gouras, Matt. "DCS Opens Investigation into Group Working with Gay Teens." Associated Press, June 23, 2005.

Gramick, Jeannine, Robert Nugent, and Thomas Oddo, eds. *Homosexual Catholics: A Primer for Discussion.* Dignity, 1974.

"Grand Opening! Troy's Church/1,000 Celebrants." *Vector* 7, no. 4 (April 1971): 28, 33.

Greer, I. Review of Bergler. *Journal of Pastoral Care* 4, no. 1–2 (1950): 66–67.

Grelon, Jean. "Homosexualité et pratique judiciaire de l'Église: Vers un nouveau regard des tribunaux ecclésiastiques?" In Schlick and Zimmermann, *L'homosexuel(le) dans les sociétés*, 9–14.

Gross, Sue. "Falwell Says Government Must Control Homosexuals to Stop AIDS." Associated Press, July 4, 1983.

———. "Falwell Wants Attack on 'Gay Plague.'" Associated Press, July 5, 1983.

Gunkel, Hermann. *Handkommentar zum Alten Testament: Genesis.* 2d ed. Gottingen: Vandenhoeck und Ruprecht, 1902.

Gunnison, Foster. Letter to the editor. *Vector* 6, no. 11 (November 1970): 9, 42.

Haley, Mike. *101 Frequently Asked Questions about Homosexuality.* Eugene, OR: Harvest House, 2004.

Hall, G. Stanley. *Adolescence: Its Psychology and Its Relations to Physiology, Anthropology, Sociology, Sex, Crime, Religion, and Education.* New York: D. Appleton and Company, 1904.

———. *Educational Problems.* New York: D. Appleton, 1911.

———. "The Function of Music in the College Curriculum." *Pedagogical Seminary* 15 (1908): 117–26.

———. *Jesus, the Christ, in the Light of Psychology.* New York: Doubleday, 1917. The work, in two volumes, is paginated continuously.

———. *Life and Confessions of a Psychologist.* New York: D. Appleton, 1923.

———. *Morale: The Supreme Standard of Life and Conduct.* New York: D. Appleton, 1920.

———. *Recreations of a Psychologist.* New York: D. Appleton, 1920.

———. *Senescence: The Last Half of Life.* New York: D. Appleton, 1922.

Hall, Joan. Television news report on WTVJ Miami. Broadcast May 30, 1977. Wolfson WC07101 T1, clip #18.

———. Television news report on WTVJ Miami. Broadcast June 1, 1977. Wolfson WC07101 T1, clip #21.

Hanckel, Frances, and John Cunningham. *A Way of Love, A Way of Life: A Young Person's Introduction to What It Means to Be Gay.* New York: Lathrop, Lee, and Shepard, 1979.

Hansen, Joseph. *The Troublemaker.* New York: Harper and Row, 1975.

Harding, Susan Friend. *The Book of Jerry Falwell.* Princeton: Princeton University Press, 2001.

Harvey, John F. "Homosexuality as a Pastoral Problem." *Theological Studies* 16, no. 1 (March 1955): 86–108.

Heimsoth, Karl-Günther. *Hetero- und Homophilie: Eine neuorientierende An- und Einordnung der Erscheinungsbilder der "Homosexualität" und der "inversion" in Berücksichtigung der sogennanten "normalen Freundschaft" auf Grund der zwei verschiedenen erotischen Anziehungsgesetze und der bisexuellen Grundeinstellung der Mannes.* Inaugural-Dissertation zur Erlangung der Doktorwürde der medizinischen Fakultät der Universität zu Rostock. Dortmund: Schmidt & Andernach, 1924.

Henry, George W. *All the Sexes: A Study of Masculinity and Femininity.* Toronto: Rinehart, 1955.

Herdt, Gilbert, and Andrew Boxer. *Children of Horizons: How Gay and Lesbian Teens Are Leading a New Way Out of the Closet.* Boston: Beacon Press, 1996.

Heron, Alastair, ed. *Towards a Quaker View of Sex: An Essay by a Group of Friends.* London: Friends Home Service Committee, 1963.

Heron, Ann, ed. *One Teenager in Ten.* Boston: Alyson, 1983.

Herring, Scott. "Out of the Closets, Into the Woods: *RFD, Country Women,* and the Post-Stonewall Emergence of Queer Anti-Urbanism." *American Quarterly* 59, no. 2 (June 2007): 341–72.

Herzer, Manfred. "Ein Brief von Kertbeny in Hannover an Ulrichs in Würzburg." *Capri* [Berlin] 1 (1987): 25–35.

Herzfeld, John, director. *The Ryan White Story*. Released January 16, 1989.

Hilferty, Robert, director. *Stop the Church*. VHS. 24 minutes. 1991.

Hiltner, Seward. "Kinsey and the Church—Then and Now." *Christian Century* 90 (May 30, 1973): 624–29.

"Homosexual—or Homophile." *Concern: Newsletter of the Southern California Council on Religion and the Homophile*, no. 1 (July 1966): 5.

Honan, William H. "Arts Endowment Withdraws Grant for AIDS Show." *New York Times*, November 9, 1989, A1, C28.

Hooker, Evelyn. "The Adjustment of the Male Overt Homosexual." *Journal of Projective Techniques* 21 (1957): 18–31.

———. "Homosexuality—Summary of Studies." In Duvall and Duvall, *Sex Ways*, 166–83.

Houston, Bill. Interview by Jim Duggins. December 17, 1994. GLBTHS OHP #95-034.

Hyde, George A. "Genesis of the Orthodox-Catholic Church of America." Edited by Gordon Fisher. http://www.orthodoxcatholicchurch.org/history.html.

———. Interview by J. Gordon Melton. July 6, 2005. http://www.lgbtran.org/Exhibits/OralHistory/Hyde/GHyde.pdf.

———. Letter to Raymond Broshears, February 12, 1977. GLBT HS, Broshears papers, carton 4, Hyde folder.

Ingram-Ward, Beryl. "Space for Hospitality and Hope." In Russell, *The Church with AIDS*, 69–78.

Itkin, Michael. Letter to Raymond Broshears, October 12, 1975. GLBTHS #1996-03, Broshears papers, carton 4, Itkin folder.

Jennings, Theodore W., Jr. *The Man Jesus Loved: Homoerotic Narratives from the New Testament*. Cleveland: Pilgrim Press, 2003.

Jensen, Erik N. "The Pink Triangle and Political Consciousness: Gay, Lesbians, and the Memory of Nazi Persecution." *Journal of the History of Sexuality* 11, no. 1–2 (January–April 2002): 319–49.

John. "A Journey toward Freedom." In Russell, *The Church with AIDS*, 53–65.

Jones, Bill W. Interview by Terrence Kissack. April 2001. GLBTHS OHP #02-149.

Jordan, Mark D. *Blessing Same-Sex Unions: The Perils of Queer Romance and the Confusions of Christian Marriage*. Chicago: University of Chicago Press, 2005.

———. *The Invention of Sodomy in Christian Theology*. Chicago: University of Chicago Press, 1997.

Kelly, Gerald. *Modern Youth and Chastity*. St. Louis: The Queen's Work, 1943. Reprinted 1949. This text substantially reproduces the "planograph" version circulated beginning in 1941 under the title *Chastity and Catholic Youth*.

Kepner, James. "I Remember Chuck . . ." February 2, 1991(?). ONE Archives, "Chuck (Charles) Rowland" subject file.

———. "Why Can't We All Get Together, and What Do We Have in Common?" In Ridinger, *Speaking for Our Lives*, 700–720.

Kertbeny, Karl Maria. *§143 des Preussischen Strafgesetzbuches vom 14. April 1851 und seine Aufrechterhalthung als §152 im Entwurfe eines Strafgesetzbuches für den Nordeutschen Bund.* Published as supplement to *Jahrbuch für sexuellen Zwischenstufen mit besonderer Berücksichtigung der Homosexualität* 7. Leipzig: Max Spohr, 1905.

Kinsey, Alfred C., Wardell B. Pomeroy, and Clyde E. Martin. *Sexual Behavior in the Human Male.* Philadelphia: W. B. Saunders Co., 1948.

Kowalewski, Mark R. "The AIDS Crisis: Legitimation of Homophobia or Catalyst for Change?" In Stemmeler and Clark, *Homophobia and the Judaeo-Christian Tradition,* 147–63.

———. *All Things to All People: The Catholic Church Confronts the AIDS Crisis.* Albany: SUNY Press, 1994.

———. "Religions Constructions of the AIDS Crisis." *Sociological Analysis* 51, no. 1 (1990): 91–96.

Kramer, Larry. "1,112 and Counting." *New York Native,* no. 59 (March 14–27, 1983). Reprinted in Kramer, *Reports from the Holocaust: The Story of an AIDS Activist* (London: Cassell, 1995), 33–51.

Kuhn, Donald. *The Church and the Homosexual: A Report on a Consultation.* San Francisco: Glide Urban Center, [1964]. There is a typescript of the text in GLBTHS #93-13, Lyon-Martin papers, box 17, folder 14.

Kulkin, Heidi S., Elizabeth A. Chauvin, and Gretchen A. Percle. "Suicide among Gay and Lesbian Adolescents and Young Adults: A Review of the Literature." *Journal of Homosexuality* 40 (2000): 1–29.

LaHaye, Tim. *The Unhappy Gays: What Everyone Should Know about Homosexuality.* Wheaton IL: Tyndale House, 1978.

Lauritsen, John. "*Culpa ecclesiae:* Boswell's Dilemma." In *Homosexuality, Intolerance and Christianity: A Critical Examination of John Boswell's Work,* Gai Saber Monograph 1, 16–22. 2d enlarged ed., New York: Scholarship Committee, Gay Academic Union/New York City, 1985.

———. *Religious Roots of the Taboo on Homosexuality: A Materialist View.* New York: Come! Unity Press, 1974.

LeBlanc, Douglas. "Ex-Gay Sheds the Mocking Quote Marks." *Christianity Today,* January 7, 2002, 52–55.

Lee, Jordan. Interview with Paul Gabriel and Philip Hong. August 10, 1995. GLBTHS OHP #95-63.

Legg, W. Dorr [William Lambert]. Review of Michael J. Buckley, *Morality and the Homosexual. ONE: The Homosexual Magazine* 8, no. 8 (August 1960): 19–20.

Legman, Gershon. "The Language of Homosexuality: An American Glossary." In *Sex Variants: A Study of Homosexual Patterns,* edited by George W. Henry, 2:1149–79. New York: Paul B. Hoeber/Harper & Brothers, 1941.

Lekus, Ian K. "Queer and Present Dangers: Homosexuality and American Antiwar Activism during the Vietnam Era." Ph.D. diss., Duke University, 2003.

Leopold, Kathleen, and Thomas Orians, eds. *Theological Pastoral Resources: A Collection of Articles on Homosexuality from a Pastoral Perspective.* 6th ed. Washington, DC: Dignity, 1981.

Leyland, Winston. *Out in the Castro: Desire, Promise, Activism*. San Francisco: Leyland Publications, 2001.

"Lincoln Rejects Gay Rights Measure." Associated Press, May 12, 1982.

Lombardi-Nash, Michael A., ed. *Sodomites and Urnings: Homosexual Representations in Classic German Journals*. Binghamton, NY: Harrington Park Press, 2006.

Lombroso, Cesare. *L'uomo delinquente in rapporto all'antropologia, alla giurisprudenza ed alle discipline carcerarie*. 5th ed. Turin: Fratelli Bocca, 1896.

Loughery, John. *The Other Side of Silence: Men's Lives and Gay Identities: A Twentieth-Century History*. New York: Henry Holt, 1998.

Lucas, Donald S. *The Homosexual and the Church*. San Francisco: Mattachine Society, 1966.

———. Interview by Paul Gabriel. March 7, 1998. GLBTHS OHP #97-032.

———. Letter of April 7, 1964. GLBTHS #1997-25, Lucas papers, box 7, folder 1.

———. Letter of January 7, 1965, to Reverend Monroe. GLBTHS #1997-25, Lucas papers, box 17, folder 1.

———. Survey material, April–May 1964. GLBTHS #1997-25, Lucas papers, box 17, folders 1–2.

Lussheimer, Paul. Review of Bergler. *Pastoral Psychology* 3, no. 24 (1952): 63–64.

M. B. Letter to the editors of *ONE*. April 1956. ONE Archives, "Chuck (Charles) Rowland" subject file.

Mank, Herm. "General Conference '76." *Christian Circle* [MCC San Francisco] 2, no. 8 (September 1976): 11.

Marcus. "Love and Life after the Fall." *San Francisco Free Press*, December 22, 1969–January 7, 1970.

Martin, Del. "The Church and the Homosexual: A New Rapport." http://lgbtran.org/Exhibits/Sampler/View.aspx?ID=CAH&Page=1.

———. "Columnist Resigns, Blasts Male Chauvinism." *Vector* 6, no. 10 (October 1970): 35–37, 53.

———. "History of the Homophile Movement." In *Essays on Religion and the Homosexual*, 1:15–19. San Francisco: Council on Religion and the Homosexual, [1966?].

Martin, Del, and Phyllis Lyon. *Lesbian/Woman*. San Francisco: Glide, 1972.

Maves, P. B. Review of Bergler. *Pastoral Psychology* 8, no. 75 (June 1957): 60–63.

McClory, Robert J. "Gay Theology Pioneer Trusts 'God's Shrewdness.'" *National Catholic Reporter*, November 11, 2005.

McIlvenna, Ted. Interview by LGBTRAN. http://www.lgbtran.org/Exhibits/CRH/Room.aspx?RID=1&CID=4.

McNaught, Brian. "The Sad Dilemma of the Gay Catholic." *U.S. Catholic*, August 1975, 6–11. Reprinted in Leopold and Orians, *Theological Pastoral Resources*, 73–77.

McNeill, John J. *Both Feet Firmly Planted in Midair: My Spiritual Journey*. Louisville: Westminster John Knox, 1998.

———. "The Christian Male Homosexual." *Homiletic and Pastoral Review* 70, no. 9 (June 1970): 667; *Homiletic and Pastoral Review* 70, no. 10 (July 1970): 747–58; *Homiletic and Pastoral Review* 70, no. 11 (August 1970): 828–36.

————. *The Church and the Homosexual.* Kansas City: Sheed, Andrews, & McMeel, 1976.

McWhorter, Ladelle. *Racism and Sexual Oppression in Anglo-America: A Genealogy.* Bloomington: Indiana University Press, 2009.

Meeker, Martin. *Contacts Desired: Gay and Lesbian Communications and Community, 1940s–1970s.* Chicago: University of Chicago Press, 2006.

Meeker, Richard [Forman Brown]. *Better Angel.* New York: Greenberg, 1933.

Melton, J. Gordon. *The Church Speaks—on AIDS.* Detroit: Gale Research, 1989.

Ménard, Guy. *De Sodome à l'Éxode: Jalons pour une théologie de la libération gaie.* Montreal: l'Aurore, 1980.

Mendenhall, George. "The Editor Comments: Women & Nudity." *Vector* 6, no. 10 (October 1970): 6, 17.

Menninger, Karl. "Kinsey's Study of the Sexual Behavior in the Human Male and Female." *Pastoral Psychology* 5 (1954): 43–48.

Meyer, Richard. *Outlaw Representation: Censorship and Homosexuality in Twentieth-Century American Art.* New York: Oxford University Press, 2002.

Miles, W. R., and C. C. Miles. "Eight Letters from G. Stanley Hall to H. P. Bowditch, with Introduction and Notes." *American Journal of Psychology* 41, no. 2 (April 1929): 326–36.

Mills, Bruce L. "Fear and Passion: A Psychological Reflection on the Construction of Homophobia in the Context of AIDS." In Stemmeler and Clark, *Homophobia and the Judaeo-Christian Tradition*, 165–87.

Mitchell, Mark, and David Leavitt, eds. *Pages Passed from Hand to Hand: The Hidden Tradition of Homosexual Literature in English from 1748 to 1914.* Boston: Houghton Mifflin, 1994.

Moberly, Elizabeth R. *Psychogenesis: The Early Development of Gender Identity.* London: Routledge & Kegan Paul, 1983.

Montaigne, Michel de. *Journal de Voyage en Italie par la Suisse et l'Allemagne en 1580 and 1581.* Edited by Charles Dédéyan. Paris: Société de Belles Lettres, 1946.

Moon, Dawne. *God, Sex, and Politics: Homosexuality and Everyday Theologies.* Chicago: University of Chicago Press, 2004.

Moore, Thomas V. "The Pathogenesis and Treatment of Homosexual Disorders: A Digest of Some Pertinent Evidence." *Journal of Personality* 14 (September 1945): 47–83.

Moran, Jeffrey P. *Teaching Sex: The Shaping of Adolescence in the 20th Century.* Cambridge, MA: Harvard University Press, 2000.

Morriss, Makanah Elizabeth, Jory Agate, Sarah Gibb, Lizann Bassham, and Gordon J. Svoboda II, with Judith A. Frediani. *Sexuality and Our Faith: A Companion to Our Whole Lives Grades 10–12.* Boston: Unitarian Universalist Association and United Church Board for Homeland Ministries, 2000.

Mowry, Charles E. *The Church and the New Generation.* Nashville: Abingdon Press, 1969.

Mungello, D. E. "A Spirit of the 60's." *Gay and Lesbian Review Worldwide* 15, no. 3 (May 2008): 21–22.

National Research Council, Panel on Monitoring the Social Impact of the AIDS Epidemic. *The Social Impact of AIDS in the United States*. Washington, DC: National Academy Press, 1993.

Niebuhr, Reinhold. "More on Kinsey." *Christianity and Crisis* 13, no. 23 (January 11, 1954): 182–83.

———. "Sex and Religion in the Kinsey report." *Christianity and Crisis*, 13, no. 18 (November 2, 1953): 138–41.

Noebel, David A., Wayne C. Lutton, and Paul Cameron. *Special Report: AIDS, Acquired Immune Deficiency Syndrome*. Manitou Springs, CO: Summit Ministries, 1986.

Northcote, Hugh. *Christianity and Sex Problems*. Philadelphia: F. A. Davis, 1906. 2d ed., Philadelphia: F. A. Davis, 1916.

Norton, Donald. "Sex, Religion & Myth: A Book Review in Dialogue Form." *Mattachine Review* 1, no. 6 (November/December 1955): 10–12.

Note on Rowland. *ONE Confidential* 1, no. 1 (March 1956), 21.

"Notes on People." *New York Times* (October 15, 1977), 16.

Oates, Wayne E. "A Critique of the Kinsey Report." *Review and Expositor* 46 (July 1949): 348–62.

O'Neal, Hank, Allen Ginsberg, William S. Burroughs, and Neil Miller. *Gay Day: The Golden Age of the Christopher Street Parade*. New York: Abrams Image, 2006.

Palmore, Erdman. "Published Reactions to the Kinsey Report." *Social Forces* 31, no. 2 (December 1952): 165–72.

Pappas, Helen. "Happy Birthday, Jesus! Happy Anniversary, Beloved Church!" *SAGA Newsletter* (December 1976): 8–11. SAGA is identified as the publication of the "National Alliance of Christian Homosexuals . . . an extra-diocesan ministry of the Orthodox Catholic Church of America."

Parents and Friends of Ex-Gays and Gays. "Ex-Gay Declaration of Independence." http://www.pfox.org/Ex-Gay_Declaration_of_Independence.html.

Patton, Cindy. *Inventing AIDS*. New York: Routledge, 1991.

Pedersen, Lyn [James Kepner]. "England and the Vice of Sodom." *ONE: The Homosexual Magazine* 2, no. 5 (May 1954): 4–17.

———. "*Homosexuality and the Western Christian Tradition*" [review of Bailey]. *ONE: The Homosexual Magazine* 3, no. 11 (November 1955): 19–21.

———. "On Homosexuality" [review of Bailey, *Sexual Offenders and Social Punishment*]. *ONE: The Homosexual Magazine* 4, no. 5 (June–July 1956): 8–11.

———. "Smorgasbord." *ONE Confidential* 1, no. 1 (March 1956): 23–26.

———. "Thorn in the Spirit: The Homosexual on the Horns of a Christian Dilemma." *ONE: The Homosexual Magazine* 2, no. 6 (June 1954): 21–24.

"Peers Endorse Inquiry into Homosexuality: Power of Public Opinion." *The Times* (London), May 20, 1954, 4.

Pennington, Sylvia. *But Lord, They're Gay: A Spiritual Pilgrimage*. Hawthorne, CA: Lambda Christian Fellowship, 1982.

Perlongher, Néstor. *Prosa plebeya: Ensayos 1980–1992*. Edited by Christian Ferrer and Osvaldo Baigorria. Buenos Aires: Ediciones Colihue, 1997.

Perry, Troy, with Charles L. Lucas. *The Lord Is My Shepherd and He Knows I'm Gay.* Los Angeles: Nash Publishing, 1972.

Philpott, Kent. *The Gay Theology.* Plainfield, NJ: Logos International, 1977.

———. *The Third Sex? Six Homosexuals Tell Their Stories.* Plainfield, NJ: Logos International, and London: Good Reading, 1975.

"The Problem of Homosexuality: Report by Clergy and Doctors." *The Times* (London), February 26, 1954, 5.

Proust, Marcel. *Sodome et Gomorrhe = À la recherche du temps perdu* 4. Edited by Antoine Compagnon. Paris: Gallimard, 1989.

"Radicals Invade S.I.R. Center at National Gay Conference." *Vector* (October 1970): 14–15, 41.

Rechy, John. *City of Night.* New York: Grove Press, 1963.

———. "Mardi Gras." *Evergreen Review,* no. 5 (Summer 1958): 60–70.

Red Butterfly. *Gay Liberation.* New York: Red Butterfly, February 13, 1970.

Reid, Ann Carll [Irma "Corky" Wolf]. Letter to Rowland, February 21, 1956. ONE Archives, "Chuck (Charles) Rowland" subject file.

———. Letter to Rowland, April 10, 1956. ONE Archives, "Chuck (Charles) Rowland" subject file.

"Religious Viewpoint Defined." *Mattachine Review* 2, no. 2 (April 1956): 43–44.

Ridinger, Robert B., ed. *Speaking for Our Lives: Historic Speeches and Rhetoric for Gay and Lesbian Rights (1892–2000).* New York: Harrington Park Press/Haworth Press, 2004.

Roberts, Paul. "The Biblical Put Down on Homosexuality." *Vector* 7, no. 4 (April 1971): 35.

"Robert W. Wood Dares to Write *Christ and the Homosexual.*" *Dorian Book Quarterly,* no. 2 (1960): 5.

Roche, Pat, compiler. *Dignity/USA 25: A Chronology, 1969–1994.* Washington, DC: Dignity/USA, 1995.

Roeder, Bill. "Anita's Helping Hand." *Newsweek,* May 8, 1978, 27.

Roesler, T., and R. W. Deisher. "Youthful Male Homosexuality: Homosexual Experience and the Process of Developing Homosexual Identity in Males Aged 16 to 22 Years." *Journal of the American Medical Association* 219, no. 8 (February 21, 1972): 1018–23.

Rolfs, Ted. Interview by Len Evans. Ca. 1983. GLBTHS OHP.

Romesburg, Don. "The Tightrope of Normalcy: Homosexuality, Developmental Citizenship, and American Adolescence, 1890–1940." *Journal of Historical Sociology* 21, no.4 (December 2008): 417–42.

Rosenblatt, Jay, director. *I Just Wanted To Be Somebody.* VHS. 10 minutes. 2007.

Rowland, Charles. Letter of March 28, 1956, to William Lambert. ONE Archives, "Chuck (Charles) Rowland" subject file.

———. Letter of January 23, 1977, to Harry Hay. ONE Archives, "Chuck (Charles) Rowland" subject file.

———. Letter of December 9, 1990, to his sister, Mildred. ONE Archives, "Chuck (Charles) Rowland" subject file.

———— [attributed]. "Possible Courses of Action: Advantages and Disadvantages," n.d., 1. ONE Archives, "Chuck (Charles) Rowland" subject file.

Ross, Kenneth N. *Letter to a Homosexual*. London: SPCK, 1955.

Ruskin, Cindy. *The Quilt: Stories from the NAMES Project*. New York: Pocket Books, 1988.

Russell, Letty M., ed. *The Church with AIDS: Renewal in the Midst of Crisis*. Louisville: Westminster/John Knox, 1990.

Savin-Williams, Ritch C. *The New Gay Teenager*. Cambridge, MA: Harvard University Press, 2005.

"Scared Straight." *Harper's Magazine* (August 2005): 19–21.

Schlick, Jean, and Marie Zimmermann, eds. *L'homosexuel(le) dans les sociétés civiles et religieuses*. Strasbourg: CERDIC, 1985.

Schur, Edwin M. *Crimes without Victims: Deviant Behavior and Public Policy*. Englewood Cliffs, NJ: Prentice-Hall, 1965.

Sears, James T. *Behind the Mask of the Mattachine: The Hal Call Chronicles and the Early Movement for Homosexual Emancipation*. New York: Harrington Park Press/Haworth Press, 2006.

Sedgwick, Eve Kosofsky. *Tendencies*. Durham: Duke University Press, 1993.

Seitler, Dana. "Queer Physiognomies; or, How Many Ways Can We Do the History of Sexuality?" *Criticism* 46, no. 1 (2004): 71–102.

Shilts, Randy. *And the Band Played On: Politics, People, and the AIDS Epidemic*. Twentieth-anniversary edition, New York: St. Martin's Griffin, 2007.

SIR (San Francisco), Board of Directors. Resolutions of March 1, 1965, #16. GLBTHS #1997-25, Lucas papers, box 11, folder 1.

Sisters of Perpetual Indulgence (San Francisco). *Play Fair!* San Francisco: Sisters of Perpetual Indulgence, 1982.

Smith, Christian, with Melinda Lundquist Denton. *Soul-Searching: The Religious and Spiritual Lives of American Teenagers*. New York: Oxford University Press, 2005.

Smith, Harmon L. "Contraception and Natural Law: A Half-Century of Anglican Moral Reflection." In *The Anglican Moral Choice*, edited by Paul Elmen, 181–200. Wilton, CT: Morehouse-Barlow, 1983.

Smith, Richard L. *AIDS, Gays, and the American Catholic Church*. Cleveland: Pilgrim Press, 1994.

"Sodom." *SAGA Newsletter* (December 1976): 12. Reprinted from "VIA—Newsletter of the Church of the Holy Eucharist" (1947).

Sontag, Susan. "Notes on Camp." *Partisan Review* 31, no. 4 (Fall 1964): 515–30. I follow the corrected version in her *Against Interpretation and Other Essays* (New York: Farrar, Straus, Giroux, 1966), 275–92.

Southern Baptist Convention. "Resolution on AIDS" (June 1987). http://www.sbc.net/resolutions/amResolution.asp?ID=40.

Spiegelhofer, Sebastian Dion. Letter to the editor. *Vector* 6, no. 11 (November 1970): 9, 42.

Stemmeler, Michael L., and J. Michael Clark, eds. *Homophobia and the Judaeo-Christian Tradition*. Dallas: Monument Press, 1990.

Stokes, Rick. Interview by Paul Gabriel. September 9, 1996. GLBTHS OHP #02-176.

"The Storming of St. Pat's" (editorial). *New York Times*, December 12, 1989, A24.

Sweet, Roxanna Thayer. *Political and Social Action in Homophile Organizations*. New York: Arno Press, 1975. This reproduces the typescript of her 1968 doctoral dissertation in criminology at the University of California, Berkeley.

Tales of the Closet, no. 2, *Family*. "Words and pictures" by Ivan Veloz, Jr. New York: Hetrick-Martin Institute, Fall 1987.

Talmij, Billie [Billye Talmadge]. "Talk" [at 1964 Consultation]. http://lgbtran.org/Exhibits/CRH/Room.aspx?RID=1&CID=5&AID=15 (accessed August 25, 2008).

Taylor, Diana. *The Archive and the Repertoire: Performing Cultural Memory in the Americas*. Durham: Duke University Press, 2003.

Teal, Donn. *The Gay Militants*. New York: Stein and Day, 1971. Rev. ed., New York: St. Martin's Press, 1994.

Tentler, Leslie Woodstock. *Catholics and Contraception: An American History*. Ithaca: Cornell University Press, 2004.

Timmons, Stuart. *The Trouble with Harry Hay: Founder of the Modern Gay Movement*. Boston: Alyson, 1990.

Tobin, William J. *Homosexuality and Marriage: A Canonical Evaluation of the Relationship of Homosexuality to the Validity of Marriage in the Light of Recent Rotal Jurisprudence*. Rome: Catholic Book Agency, 1964.

"The Touchstone: Rev. Hansen Leaves." *Vanguard* [San Francisco] 1, no. 1 (August 1966): 3.

United Methodist Church. *Book of Discipline of the United Methodist Church*. Nashville: United Methodist Publishing House, 2008.

Vanden, Dirk [Fullmer]. Interview by Robert Prager. May 15, 2001. GLBTHS OHP #01-01.

Vernay, Jacques. "L'homosexualité dans la jurisprudence rotale." In Schlick and Zimmermann, *L'homosexuel(le) dans les sociétés*, 25–40.

Vidal, Gore. *The City and the Pillar*. New York: Dutton, 1948. Rev. ed., New York: Vintage/Random House, 2003.

Waldner-Haugrud, Lisa K., and Brian Magruder. "Homosexuality Identity Expression among Lesbian and Gay Adolescents: An Analysis of Perceived Structural Associations." *Youth and Society* 27 (1996): 313–33.

Walker, Merv. "Gay Sheep" [review of Perry]. *Body Politic*, no. 9 (June 1, 1973): 10.

Warner, Hugh C. "Homosexuality Laws" (letter to the editor). *Times* (London), December 1, 1952, 5.

Wedmore, Keith. Interview by Galen McNemar Hamann. February 27, 2009.

Westphal, C. "Die conträre Sexualempfindung, Symptom eines neuropathischen (psychopathischen) Zustandes." *Archiv für Psychiatrie und Nervenkrankheiten* 2, no. 1 (1869): 73–108.

White, C. Todd. *Pre-Gay L.A.: A Social History of the Movement for Homosexual Rights*. Urbana: University of Illinois Press, 2009.

White, Heather Rachelle. "Proclaiming Liberation: The Historical Roots of LGBT Religious Organizing, 1946–1976." *Nova Religio* 11, no. 4 (2008): 102–19.

White, Ryan, and Ann Marie Cunningham. *Ryan White: My Own Story*. New York: Signet, 1992.

Wilde, Oscar. *The Picture of Dorian Gray*. New York: Ward Lock, 1891.

Williams, Alex. "Gay Teenager Stirs a Storm." *New York Times*, July 15, 2005.

Wise, Carroll A. Review of Bergler. *Pastoral Psychology* 1, no. 1 (1950): 63–64.

Wittman, Carl. Untitled items in newsletter of San Francisco's Committee for Homosexual Freedom, April 22 and 29, 1969.

———. *Refugees from America: A Gay Manifesto* (with a new preface). San Francisco: Council on Religion and the Homosexual, May 1970.

———. "Refugees from Amerika: A Gay Manifesto." *San Francisco Free Press*, December 22, 1969–January 7, 1970, 3–5.

Wojnarowicz, David. *Close to the Knives: A Memoir of Disintegration*. New York: Vintage/Random House, 1991.

———. *Fever: The Art of David Wojnarowicz*. Edited by Amy Scholder. New York: Rizzoli, 1998.

———. "Post Cards from America: X-Rays from Hell." In *Witnesses: Against Our Vanishing: November 16, 1989, to January 6, 1990*, edited by Nan Goldin, 6–11. New York: Artists Space, 1989.

Wolfe, Maxine, and Laraine Sommella. "This Is about People Dying: The Tactics of Early ACT UP and the Lesbian Avengers in New York City." In *Queers in Space: Communities, Public Places, Sites of Resistance*, edited by Gordon Brent Ingram, Anne-Maire Bouthillette, and Yolanda Retter, 407–37. Seattle: Bay Press, 1997.

Wood, Robert W. *Christ and the Homosexual (Some Observations)*. New York: Vantage Press, 1960.

———. "Homosexuality and the Church." *Ladder* 13 (1968–69): 4–13.

Worthen, Frank. "Born Anew to a Living Hope." http://www.newhope123.org/frank_testimony.htm.

———. "From Being Different to Making a Difference." http://www.anotherway.com/pages/frank_w.html.

———. *Steps Out of Homosexuality*. San Rafael, CA: Love in Action, 1984.

WTVJ Miami. Broadcast of May 22, 1977. Wolfson WC07101 T1, clip #13.

WTVJ Miami. Broadcast of May 23, 1977. Wolfson WC07101 T1, clip #15.

WTVJ Miami. Broadcast of May 25, 1977. Wolfson WC07101 T1, clip #14.

WTVJ Miami. Broadcast of August 1, 1977. Wolfson WC07101 T1, clip #37.

Young, "Reminiscences of Pre-Stonewall Greenwich Village." In *Queer Representation: Reading Lives, Reading Cultures*, edited by Martin Duberman, 331–39. New York: New York University Press, 1997.

Ziegler, Jan. "Falwell Urges Action on AIDS." United Press International, July 12, 1983.

INDEX

indefinite prolongation of adolescence, 155; scientific authority to disprove genetic basis for homosexuality, 159; *Steps Out of Homosexuality* (book), 158–59; *Steps Out of Homosexuality* (tape), 157, 239n23, 240n25;

testimonies, 151–57; testimony as rhetorical performance, 151–52; therapy for gender disorders, 160

Young, Allen, 233n23